DAY BY DAY
IN JEWISH
HISTORY

DAY BY DAY
IN JEWISH
HISTORY

A Chronology and Calendar of Historic Events

by

ABRAHAM P. BLOCH

KTAV PUBLISHING HOUSE, INC.
NEW YORK

Library of Congress Cataloging in Publication Data

Bloch, Abraham P.
    Day by day in Jewish history.

    Bibliography: p.
    Includes index.
    1. Jews—History—Miscellanea. 2. Jews—
Biography—Anniversaries, etc. I. Title
DS114.B55   909'.04924   82-7769
ISBN 0-87068-736-0   AACR2

MANUFACTURED IN THE UNITED STATES OF AMERICA

This book is affectionately dedicated to
My wife, Belle
My children,
A. Zachary and Liebe M. Apfel
Raphael S. and Dorothy Bloch
My grandchildren,
Stuart and Sari, Mark, Howard and Bruce Apfel
David and Joel Bloch.

Contents

Names of Hebrew Months

Tishri	Nisan
Ḥeshvan	Iyar
Kislev	Sivan
Tevet	Tammuz
Shevat	Av
Adar	Elul

Bibliographical Abbreviations

AJHSP	American Jewish Historical Society Publications
ATGY	Anziklopedia leToledot Gedolei Yisrael
DDD	Dor Dor veDorshav
DYY	Devar Yom beYomo
EJUD	Encyclopaedia Judaica
HY	Hakhmei Yisrael
JE	Jewish Encyclopedia
OY	Ozar Yisrael
TP	Toledot haPosekim
UJE	Universal Jewish Encyclopedia
ZYO	Zikhronot Yemot Olam

Foreword

During the thousands of years of Jewish existence, a vast body of history and lore has been accumulated. Both are represented in this book, since a knowledge of both is essential for a full understanding of the Jewish national character. All the entries based upon biblical sources, as well as those dealing with events in the periods after the era treated by the Bible, should be regarded as factual. The entries culled from Jewish folklore, on the other hand, may be deemed legendary.

The anniversary of a historical event should be commemorated on the appropriate day whenever the correct date is known, but it is permissible to fix an approximate date when the correct date cannot be determined. Jewish tradition, in fact, sanctions this practice, and as a result I have occasionally included dates in this book that are open to question. The primary sources were not reliable in these cases, and there was no other chronological information available.

A cross-reference to civil dates is provided for those who prefer to observe anniversaries according to the civil calendar. Most of the corresponding civil dates are based on the calendrical tables in Eduard Mahler's *Handbuch der Jüdischen Chronologie*. A table of years has also been included for those who wish to mark round-figure anniversaries.

A day-by-day chronology of events provides a telescopic view of history. The confluence on certain days of related events from different periods, amply commented on in the notes, clearly reveals the strange phenomenon of the coincidence. While coincidences may have no historical significance, they provide much material of human interest and therefore are still of value to the reader.

I have given space in this book mainly to personalities and events that were directly involved in Jewish life, making an exception only in the case of "firsts," since these have a significance all their own. I have not indicated my sources where the topic is covered in readily available standard reference books. Where research would be necessary to locate further information, however, I have supplied my sources. My notes, in addition, occasionally amplify the entries.

The topics discussed or mentioned in the pages that follow vary in importance. Some possess more historical significance than others. Each of them, however, has educational value, and many could provide the basis for timely and relevant discussions.

Regretfully, Jewish history has often received scant attention, even in periods when the majority of the Jewish people was conversant with the Bible and Talmud and with other branches of our sacred literature. This neglect of history is especially apparent today, when most Jews are grievously ignorant of their heritage. To counteract this dangerous trend, congregational pulpits, traditionally forums for biblical exegesis, should also be used for instruction in history. As a practicing rabbi, I customarily use the occasion of blessing the New Moon as an opportunity to discuss the historical highlights of the coming Hebrew month. Rabbis who wish to adopt the same practice will find this book helpful.

Many individuals have been helpful to me in the course of my preparation of this work. I am particularly indebted to the late Professor Sidney B. Hoenig for his evaluation of the manuscript and many useful suggestions and to the late Isaac Barrow for his encouragement and support.

Abraham P. Bloch

Chronological Entries

TISHRI 1

1. First day of Rosh Ha-Shanah (Lev. 23:24).
2. Creation of Adam and Eve (*Sanhedrin* 38b).
3. Adam and Eve were expelled from the Garden of Eden (ibid.).
4. Birth of Cain (ibid.) and Abel (*Bereshit Rabbah* 22).
    See Kislev 25:2.
5. Noah dispatched the dove and removed the cover of the ark (Gen. 8:5, 8:13, Rashi).

    Dates of the successive stages of the biblical flood are based on Rashi's interpretation of Rabbi Eliezer's opinion in the Talmud (*Rosh Ha-Shanah* 11b). Ibn Ezra disagrees with Rashi (Gen. 8:5, 8:10).
6. Falasha holiday named "The Commemoration of Abraham" or "The Festival of the Light Has Appeared" (Leslau, *Falasha Anthology*).

    Falasha interpretation of the Bible is in substantial agreement with the views of other nonrabbinic sects, such as the Samaritans, Sadducees, and Karaites. They did not accept the traditional view of Rosh Ha-Shanah as the New Year and the Day of Judgment. Since it is the only holiday in the Bible described as a "memorial" day (Lev. 23:24), the Falashas apparently linked this "memorial" with an ancient tradition, preserved in the Talmud, that Abraham was born and died in the month of Tishri (*Rosh Ha-Shanah* 10b). Their alternate name for this holiday, "The Festival of the Light Has Appeared," reflects a legendary account of the light which filled the cave when Abraham was born (*Sotah* 12a). According to the Falasha epic *Teezaza Sanbat*, Abraham was born on Tishri 8.
7. Sarah, Rachel, and Hannah prayed for offspring. According to the Talmud, their prayers were granted on Rosh Ha-Shanah (*Yevamot* 64b). The Midrash says that the prayers of Rebecca and Leah were also granted on this day (*Tanḥuma, Vayera*).

1

The biblical account of Sarah's and Hannah's conceptions is read in the synagogue on the first day of Rosh Ha-Shanah.

8. Joseph was released from prison (*Rosh Ha-Shanah* 10b).

9. Pharaoh freed the Jews from slavery (ibid. 11a).

10. Beginning of the biblical plague of *arov* (*Zihron Yemot Olam*).

11. Elisha prophesied the birth of a son to the Shunamite (2 Kings 4:16; *Zohar, Be-Shallah*).

12. Satan was granted permission to test Job's character, according to an ancient Palestinian tradition (*Targum Jerus.*, Job 1:6).

13. Zerubbabel brought the first offering on the new altar in Jerusalem, 538 B.C.E. (Neh. 8:2).

14. Ezra read the Torah to the assembled Jews at the water-gate in Jerusalem, 444 B.C.E. (Neh. 8:2).

15. Yahrzeit of Rabbi Amnon, author of the liturgical poem *U-Netanneh Tokef* (*Zikhron Yemot Olam*).

16. Services were conducted for the first time on September 22, 1267, in the new synagogue opened by Nahmanides for the reorganized Jewish community of Jerusalem.

17. Copies of the Talmud confiscated in Crete and Rome were burned by the Inquisition on September 9, 1553.
    See Elul 2:3.

18. Beth Jacob, the first synagogue in Amsterdam, Holland, was dedicated on September 13, 1597.

19. Rioters attacked Jews of Mogilev, Russia, during Tashlikh services on September 21, 1645.

20. The first Jewish congregational service in Manhattan was held on September 12, 1654 (*AJHSP*, no. 44, p. 93).

21. Rabbi Dov Baer b. Nathan Nata, author of *Nitei Sha'ashuim*, died on September 11, 1760.

22. Rabbi Judah Ayash, author of *Lehem Yehudah*, commentary on Maimonides, died on September 11, 1760.

23. Rabbi Isaac Abbele Ha-Kohen, author of responsa *Keter Kehunnah*, died on September 22, 1808.

24. The first Jewish congregational service was held in St. Louis, Mo., on September 12, 1836.

25. Rabbi Meir Loeb Malbim, Bible exegete, author of *Ha-Torah ve-ha-Miz-vah* and other works, died on September 18, 1879.

26. Rabbi Jacob b. David of Slutsk, author of *Ridbaz*, commentary on the Jerusalem Talmud, died on September 9, 1915.

27. The *Daf Yomi*, a daily selection of a talmudic portion studied by Jews in many countries, was initiated by Rabbi Meir Shapira of Lublin on September 11, 1923.

28. The first organized attack upon Jews by Nazi storm troopers took place in Berlin on September 12, 1931.
29. The ghetto of Uman, Russia, was liquidated by the Nazis on September 22, 1941.

TISHRI 2

1. Second day of Rosh Ha-Shanah.
    The story of the *Akedah*, the 'binding' of Isaac (Gen. 22), is the subject of the Torah portion on the second day of Rosh Ha-Shanah. The association is derived from the rabbinic interpretation of the shofar as a symbolic reminder of the ram which was substituted for Isaac (*Rosh Ha-Shanah* 16a). The *Zohar* explains the association by the coincidence of this holiday with Isaac's birthday. This contradicts a talmudic source which alleges that he was born on Nisan 15 (*Rosh Ha-Shanah* 10b; *Tanḥuma, Vayera*).
2. On Tishri 2 "God blessed the seventh day and sanctified it because on it he had rested from all his work . . ." (Gen. 2:3; *Sanhedrin* 38b).
3. The letters engraved upon the Tablets of the Law were created in the "dusk of the eve of the first Sabbath" (*Pirkei de-Rabbi Eliezer* 19).
4. Rabbi Eliezer b. Joseph of Chinon, French talmudist, was martyred on September 25, 1321 (JE).
5. Tobias Bacharach of Ruzhany, Russia, founder of a famous scholarly family, was beheaded on September 19, 1659, in Rushoni, Russia, on a charge of ritual murder.
6. Glueckel of Hameln, author of a historical diary, died on September 19, 1724.
7. British troops occupied New York on September 15, 1776. The occupation disrupted the life of the Jewish community, whose leaders were forced to flee.
    See Ḥeshvan 30:3.
8. New privileges granted to Sweden's Jews were revoked by the Swedish government on September 21, 1838.
9. The Vichy government of France published, on October 4, 1940, the "Statut des Juifs," which deprived refugee Jews of civil rights.
10. Experimental executions by gassing began at Auschwitz on September 23, 1941. See Tammuz 5:10
11. Forty rabbis of the ghetto of Lodz were executed by the Nazis on September 13, 1942.

TISHRI 3

1. Gedaliah b. Ahikam, governor of Judea after the destruction of the First Temple, was assassinated on Tishri 3 (2 Kings 25:25). A fast-day was decreed to commemorate his murder and the dispersal of the remnants of Judea's population (Zech. 7:5; *Megillat Taanit* chap.7; *Rosh Ha-Shanah* 18b).

    The Karaites observe the Fast of Gedaliah on Tishri 24. The Bene Israel of India call the fast of Tishri 3 "Navuyacha Roja," New Year's Fast. See Neh. 9:1.
2. The victorious Jewish insurgents decreed in 65, the discontinuance of references to the Roman emperor in dates of Jewish documents. The anniversary of this decree was designated a holiday (*Megillat Taanit* chap. 7).
3. Gedaliah ibn Yahya b. David, author of *Shivah Enayim*, a book of philosophy and astrology, died on September 20, 1487 (JE).
4. Jews of Mogilev, Russia, were massacred on October 4, 1655.
5. Rabbi Jacob b. Joseph Abendana, author of *Leket Shikhah* and translator of Judah Halevi's *Kuzari* into Spanish, died on September 12, 1695 (JE).
6. Rabbi Zevi Hirsch Harif of Halberstadt, author of *Ateret Zevi*, died on September 7, 1747.
7. The foundation stone of Ararat, a planned city of refuge for displaced Jews on Grand Island in the Niagara River, was laid by Mordecai M. Noah in Buffalo, N.Y., on September 15, 1825.
8. Rabbi Israel Lipschutz, author of *Tiferet Yisrael*, a popular commentary on the Mishnah, died on September 19, 1860.
9. Nazis raided Jewish homes in Denmark on October 2, 1943, and seized 472 Jews for deportation to Theresienstadt.

    About 94 percent of all Danish Jews were secretly smuggled into Sweden by the underground. Of the deportees, 51 died in Theresienstadt and the balance were returned to Sweden before the end of the war.

TISHRI 4

1. Bene Israel of India celebrate a holiday called "Kiricha San" (Pudding Festival).
2. "Di Gildene Rojsze," famous for her many virtues and piety, died on September 23, 1637 (See EJUD-LVOV and NACHMANOVICH).
3. Expulsion of all Jews from French possessions in America was ordered by King Louis XIV on September 24, 1683.

4. Rabbi Joel b. Isaac Halpern Ba'al Shem, widely reputed to be a miracle worker, died on September 24, 1713.
5. The first Jewish congregation in Stockholm, Sweden, was founded on September 28, 1775.
6. Rabbi Abraham b. Jehiel Danzig, author of the popular code, *Hayyei Adam*, died on September 12, 1820.

   The *Hayyei Adam* attained great popularity soon after its publication. Its simple style and concise phraseology made it a handy reference book for laymen. Societies named *Hevrat Hayyei Adam* were organized in most East European congregations for the study of this code. Similar societies were eventually established in many American Orthodox synagogues.
7. Blood-libel charges in Galatz (Galati), Rumania, sparked riots on October 3, 1867, in which 90 Jews were wounded and four synagogues destroyed.
8. The Hebrew Union College, an American seminary for the training of Reform rabbis, opened on October 3, 1875.

TISHRI 5

1. Traditional birthday of Jacob's son Naphtali (*Yalkut Shimoni*).
2. Roman authorities imprisoned Rabbi Akiva (*Megillat Ta'anit* 19a).

   This entry is based on a text in *Megillat Ta'anit* which reads: "And Rabbi Akiva was imprisoned and he died." The concluding phrase merely implies that he died a prisoner, but does not indicate a date of death. An account in the Talmud (*Berakhot* 61b) mentions his imprisonment without any reference to his death. Since Rabbi Akiva was a political prisoner, the Romans must have put him on trial which would require considerable time. The Talmud also indicates that Rabbi Akiva's students contrived to get instruction from him after his imprisonment. A midrashic source states that he was executed on Tishri 9 (*Pesahim* 62a; Jer. *Yevamot* 12). According to Maharam Rothenburg, Rabbi Akiva was imprisoned on Sivan 27 (*Minhagim*).
3. Jews of Klausenburg, Hungary (now Cluj, Rumania), were massacred on September 13, 1600.
4. Rabbi Naphtali ha-Kohen of Lublin, son-in-law of the Maharal of Prague, was martyred on September 21, 1648.
5. The second trial of Alfred Dreyfus ended in his conviction on September 9, 1899.
6. Nazis removed 1,000 Jews from the ghetto of Kovno (Kaunas), Lithuania, and executed them on September 26, 1941. It was the first mass execution of residents of that ghetto.

TISHRI 6

1. The Spanish Inquisitor Pedro de Arbués was attacked and mortally wounded on September 15, 1485.
2. The Jewish community of Berlin, Germany, was organized on September 10, 1671.
3. Rabbi Aryeh Leib of Shpola, Hasidic leader known as "Der Shpoler Zeide," died on October 4, 1810.
4. Israel Jacobson, father of the German Jewish Reform movement, died on September 14, 1828.
5. Grace Aguilar, novelist and writer, died on September 16, 1847.
6. German forces occupied Lukow, Poland, on September 19, 1939 and killed many Jews.
7. Egypt opened a large-scale offensive in the Negev on October 9, 1948.

TISHRI 7

1. Traditional birthday of Jacob's son Zebulun (*Midrash Tadshei*).
2. Birthday of Dinah, twin of Zebulun (*Book of Jubilees*).
3. Death of the worshippers of the golden calf (*Megillat Ta'anit; Kol Bo*).
4. Rabbi David b. Abraham Oppenheim, author of *Mo'ed David* and owner of a large collection of rare books and manuscripts, died on September 12, 1736.
5. Rabbi Hayyim Volozhiner issued a proclamation, on October 3, 1802, in which he urged the establishment of a yeshivah. This school became the leading Torah institution of Europe for more than a century.
6. 34,000 Jews of Kiev, Russia, lost their lives in a two-day massacre which began on September 28, 1941.
7. The second truce between Israel and the Arabs in the War of Independence came to an end on October 10, 1948.
8. A new U.S. immigration law, which eliminated national origin as the basis for quota allocations, was signed on October 3, 1965.

TISHRI 8

1. Birthday of Abraham in the Falasha tradition (Leslau, *Falasha Anthology; Teezaza Sanbat*).
    The Falasha tradition is in accord with the view of Rabbi Eliezer in the Talmud that the birth and death of Abraham occurred in the

month of Tishri (*Rosh Ha-Shanah* 10b). This comes close to some rabbinic sources which place Abraham's birthday on Tishri 10. See Elul 18:3.
2. Commencement of the seven-day Feast of Dedication of Solomon's Temple (2 Chron. 7:10, Rashi).
3. Maimonides authorized Samuel ibn Tibbon, on September 30, 1199, to translate the *Guide of the Perplexed* from Arabic into Hebrew.
4. Reinhard Heydrich met with his aides in Berlin, on September 21, 1939, to discuss the "Final Solution of the Jewish problem."
5. Menachem Ribalow, founder of the American Hebrew weekly *Ha-doar*, died on September 17, 1953.
6. Saul Raskin, artist and writer, died on September 22, 1966.

TISHRI 9

1. Rabbi Akiva was executed in Caesaria (*Semaḥot* 8). According to rabbinic tradition, he was buried on the following day by the prophet Elijah, ca. 135 C.E. (*Ma'aseh Asarah Harugei Malkhut*, second version).

   The author of *Seder ha-Dorot* states that Rabbi Akiva was executed on Yom Kippur. This is contradicted by the text of *Midrash Eleh Ezkerah*, which mentions Elijah's encounter with Rabbi Akiva's disciples on the eve of Yom Kippur and his disclosure that the rabbi was dead.
2. Traditional birthday of Rabbi Judah ha-Nasi, editor of the Mishnah, ca. 135 C.E. (*Seder ha-Dorot*).

   Seder ha-Dorot adopts a literal interpretation of the talmudic statement: "When Rabbi Akiva died, Rabbi Judah ha-Nasi was born" (*Kiddushin* 72b). However, it was most likely a figurative expression of a belief in the uninterrupted continuity of Jewish scholarship.
3. Emperor Hadrian proscribed the rite of circumcision, ca. 135 C.E. (Tosafot, Amar Lei, *Avodah Zarah* 10b).
4. Rabbi Eleazar b. Simeon, supposed co-author of the *Zohar*, was buried near his father's tomb in Meron (*Bava Mezia* 84b).
5. Rabbi Abraham b. Jacob Saba, author of *Zeror ha-Mor*, popular commentary on the Bible, died aboard ship (approximately 1508).
6. The first Jewish congregational service on the South African subcontinent was held in Cape Town on September 24, 1841.
7. Anti-Jewish riots broke out in Storodov, Russia, on October 2, 1881.
8. The Jewish Institute of Religion, a seminary for the training of rabbis, was established in New York on October 1, 1922.
9. The disappearance of Barbara Griffith of Massena, N.Y., on Septem-

ber 23, 1928, led to the first blood-ritual inquiry by a law official in the
United States.

10. The Jewish community of Zagare, Lithuania, headed by its rabbi,
    Israel Reif, was liquidated by the Nazis on September 30, 1941.

11. On September 30, 1941, Nazis buried 3,721 Jewish men, women, and
    children, many of them still alive, in the Babi Yar ravine, on the
    outskirts of Kiev, Russia.

TISHRI 10

1. Yom Kippur.
   There is a rabbinic tradition which links the date of Moses' descent
   from Mt. Sinai, carrying the second Tablets of the Law, with the date
   of Yom Kippur (*Seder Olam Rabbah* 6; Tishri 10:8). The new tablets were
   a token of God's forgiveness in answer to Moses' plea after the golden
   calf incident: "And pardon our iniquity and our sin" (Exod. 34:9).
   This date was therefore set aside as a day of forgiveness for all time.
   The Book of Jubilees alleges that on Tishri 10 Jacob mourned and
   wept upon receiving a false report of Joseph's death. That date was
   for that reason designated a day of fasting and weeping.
   Bene Israel of India call Yom Kippur "Darfalnicha San," the Festival
   of the Closing of the Doors. No one leaves his home on this day. This
   custom may be related to the injunction to the Jews in Egypt to stay
   indoors when the angel of death appears (Exod. 12:22). On Yom
   Kippur, too, life and death are decreed.

2. Traditional birthday of Abraham and Ishmael (Gen. 17:26, Rashi).

3. Abraham was circumcised and admitted into the covenant (*Pirkei
   de-Rabbi Eliezer* 29).
   There are two dates mentioned for the day of Abraham's circumcision, Nisan 13 (*Bereshit Rabbah* 50) and Tishri 10. According to Rashi,
   Abraham was circumcised on his birthday (Gen 17:26). It would
   therefore follow that Abraham was born either on Tishri 10 or Nisan
   13. See Nahmanides on Exod. 17:27; *Daat Zekenim miBaalei Tosafot,*
   Gen 17:26.

4. Abraham placed Isaac on the altar on Mt. Moriah (*Pirkei de-Rabbi
   Eliezer; Akedat Yizhak, Asarah Maamarot* 3).
   See note on Tishri 2:1.

5. Traditional birthday of Rebecca (*Bereshit Rabbah* 57; *Seder ha-Dorot*
   2088).

6. Jacob's sons reported Joseph's death to their father (Book of Jubilees).
   After the restoration of the tablets, Moses ordered an obligatory

contribution of half a shekel per person for the construction of the sanctuary. A midrash (*Tanhuma, Ki Tissa* 10) views this tax as an atonement for the golden calf, for which many Jews had contributed half a shekel each, and for the sale of Joseph, for whom the brothers had each received a coin. For an explanation of this interpretation, see note on Tishri 10:1

7. Death of Jacob's wife Bilhah (ibid.).
8. Moses brought down from Mt. Sinai the second Tablets of the Law (Exod. 34:29–30, Rashi). He recited part of the Torah to the Jewish people (*Seder Olam Zuta*).
9. Consecration festivities of Solomon's Temple were continued on Yom Kippur (*Mo'ed Katan* 9a).
10. Zechariah b. Jehoiada, high priest and prophet, was killed in the Temple (2 Chron. 24:21; *Eikhah Rabbah* 4:14).
11. Ezekiel saw in a vision the new sanctuary which was to replace Solomon's Temple. 573 B.C.E. (Ezek. 40).
12. Rabbi Eleazar b. Shammua, one of the Ten Martyrs, was executed by the Romans (*Asarah Harugei Malkhut*, first version).
13. Rav Aḥai b. Avuha, a *savora*, died on September 19, 511.
14. Alexander Susskind, who gave his whole fortune in payment for permission to remove the body of Rabbi Meir of Rothenburg from the fortress of Ensisheim, died on September 7, 1307.
    See Iyar 4:13.
15. The Jewish quarter of Paris was plundered on September 17, 1394. King Charles VI ordered the expulsion of Jews from France.
16. Jews of Perpignan, France, were expelled by a royal decree issued on September 21, 1493.
17. The first Jewish public worship in Amsterdam, Holland, was held on October 2, 1596, in the home of Don Samuel Polack, ambassador of the Moroccan emperor.
    See Tishri 1:18.
18. Shabbetai Ẓevi, the pseudomessiah whose activities led to internal Jewish upheavals in the 17th and 18th centuries, died on September 30, 1676.
19. Jews of Baden, Germany, were granted equality on October 4, 1862.
20. Jews of Tunis and Tripoli were massacred on October 10, 1864.
21. Samuel David Luzzatto, Hebrew poet and scholar, died on September 30, 1865.
22. Abraham Mapu, father of Hebrew novelists, died on October 9, 1867.
23. Joseph Opatoshu, Yiddish novelist, died on October 7, 1954.
24. Egyptian and Syrian forces opened the Yom Kippur War on October 6, 1973, with invasions of Sinai and the Golan Heights.

25. The Israeli navy destroyed three Syrian missile-boats, a mine-sweeper, and a torpedo boat off the port of Latakia on October 6, 1973.

TISHRI 11

1. Moses expounded the laws of the Sabbath (Exod. 35:1, Rashi). He opened the first judicial session with the help of Jethro (ibid. 18:13–23, Rashi).
   See note on Nisan 24:1.
2. Moses appealed for contributions of material and metal for the building of the Tabernacle (Exod. 31:18, Rashi).
3. Bene Israel of India celebrate Shila San, post-holiday. Gifts are sent to the poor and friends exchange visits.
4. Rav Tavyomi, popularly known as Mar Bar Rav Ashi, one of the last editors of the Babylonian Talmud, died at the end of Yom Kippur, October 6, 466 (*Iggeret Rav Sherira Ga'on*).
5. Rabbi Abraham Abish of Frankfort, author of *Birkhot Avraham*, died on September 22, 1768.
6. Judah Shershevsky, Hebraist, author of *Kur le-Zahav*, died on September 20, 1866.
7. David L. Yulee, Florida's first senator and the first Jew elected to the U.S. Senate, died on October 10, 1886 (*AJHSP*, no. 25, p. 29).
   Yulee was seated in the Senate on December 1, 1845.
   The first Jewish law-enforcement officers in America were sworn in on October 15, 1718 (Tishri 19:3). Isaac Miranda, the first Jewish judge in America, was appointed on June 10, 1727 (Sivan 21:3). David Emanuel, the first Jewish governor in the U.S., was sworn in on March 3, 1801 (Adar 18:4). Mordecai Manuel Noah became, in 1813, the first American Jew to hold a diplomatic post. Oscar Straus was the first American Jew to serve in the cabinet (1906).
8. Six Paris synagogues were bombed on October 2, 1941.
9. Large-scale fighting was resumed between Israel and Egypt on October 14, 1948.

TISHRI 12

1. Angels informed Abraham that Sarah would bear a son.
   See note on Tishri 13:1.
2. Jews continued to bring materials for the building of the Tabernacle, in response to the appeal of Moses (Exod. 35:21; *Exodus Rabbah* 5).
3. On September 16, 1747, Jewish converts to Christianity were prohibited by Pope Benedict XIV from granting their wives religious divorces.
4. Rabbi Abraham b. Dov Baer of Mezhirech, author of *Hesed le-Avraham*, popularly known as the Malakh, died on September 25, 1776.
5. On October 4, 1786, Aaron Levy registered plans with the state of Pennsylvania for the site of a new village in Penn Valley, to be named Aaronsburg.
6. On October 7, 1938, Germany decreed that Jewish passports must be stamped with the letter J.
7. The Grand Council of the Fascist Party of Italy issued a series of anti-Jewish decrees on October 7, 1938.
8. Menahem Ussishkin, president of the Jewish National Fund and the first Jew to deliver an address in Hebrew before an international assembly (Paris Peace Conference), died on October 3, 1941.
9. Britain informed the U.N. on September 26, 1947, of its intention to surrender the mandate and leave Palestine.
10. The New York Fair Sabbath Law, permitting New York City Sabbath-observing business owners to trade on Sunday, went into effect on September 30, 1963.
    See Tammuz 20:10.

TISHRI 13

1. Destruction of Sodom and Gomorrah.
   Abraham was circumcised on Tishri 10 and visited by the angels on Tishri 12 (Bava Mezia 86b). Sodom was destroyed one day later, Tishri 13. According to a second rabbinic tradition, Abraham was circumcised on Nisan 13. It would therefore follow that Sodom was destroyed on Nisan 16.
   See note on Tishri 10:3.
2. Cestius, commander of the Roman forces in Palestine, camped at Bet-Horon to prepare for an assault on Jerusalem, 66 C.E.
3. Emperor Alexander I of Russia appointed a commission, on October 9, 1802, to draft plans for improving the condition of Russian Jewry.

4. Rabbi Akiva Eger of Poznan, outstanding talmudic authority and author, died on October 12, 1837.
5. Religious liberty was granted to the Jews of Morocco on September 18, 1880.
6. Jacob Henry Schiff, American philanthropist and patron of scholarship, died on September 25, 1920.
7. 15,000 Jews were removed from the "Little Ghetto" of Kovno and executed by the Nazis on October 4, 1941.
8. A demonstration by Moscow Jews on October 16, 1948, at the main synagogue, in honor of the Israeli Ambassador, Golda Meir, touched off a wave of Soviet anti-Jewish measures.
9. Operation Magic Carpet, which transferred the entire Jewish community of Yemen to Israel, was completed on September 24, 1950.

   Yemenite Jews, given to mysticism and Kabbalah, were emotionally receptive to messianic movements to speed the return to Zion. They eagerly grasped at the reports of the pseudomessiah Shabbetai Zevi and hastened to make preparations for mass emigration to Palestine. The Yemenite government suppressed the movement with harsh severity. It was not until 1882 that the first group of Yemenite Jews secretly left for Palestine. The process was completed 68 years later, in 1950.
10. Israel announced, on October 9, 1973, the loss of the Bar Lev defense line on the Suez Canal.

TISHRI 14

1. The dedication ceremony of Solomon's Temple was completed (2 Chron. 7:9).
2. Emperor Caius Caligula's decree to place his statue in the Temple reached Jerusalem on Tishri 14 in the year 39 (*Megillat Ta'anit* 11). See Shevat 22:1.
3. On October 2, 1392, Jews of Aragon were invited by King Juan I to reestablish the Jewish community of Barcelona, which had been destroyed on August 5, 1391. The Jews declined the invitation.
4. Columbus' second expedition to the New World, financed with money confiscated from the Jews expelled in 1492, set out on September 24, 1493.
5. All the Hebrew books in the synagogue of Frankfort, Germany, were seized on September 28, 1509 in accordance with the order of King Maximilian.
6. Jews of Lublin were massacred on October 15, 1655.

7. The Hebrew German Society, Rodeph Shalom, parent of the earliest German Jewish congregation in America, was founded in Philadelphia on October 10, 1802. (*AJHSP*, no. 9, p. 125).

   The first Jewish arrivals in New Amsterdam in 1654 (Elul 25:3) included Sephardim and Ashkenazim. Their first congregation, Shearith Israel, adopted the Sephardic ritual, reflecting a membership which was preponderately Sephardic. The establishment in 1802 of Rodeph Shalom signalled the arrival of substantial numbers of German Jews. The founding of a Russian Jewish congregation in 1852 (Sivan 17:5) was a harbinger of the new wave of East European immigrants.

8. Rabbi Israel Hapstein, known as the Maggid of Kozienice (Koznitz), died on October 18, 1815.

9. About 30 Jewish merchants of San Francisco announced in the *San Francisco Hebrew* of October 4, 1865, that their places of business would henceforth be closed on the Sabbath.

10. The establishment of a Jewish ghetto in Warsaw was decreed by the Nazis on October 16, 1940.

11. Louis Dembitz Brandeis, justice of the Supreme Court of the U.S., Zionist pioneer and communal leader, died on October 5, 1941.

12. The ghetto of Berdichev, Russia, was liquidated by the Nazis on October 5, 1941.

TISHRI 15

1. First day of Sukkot (Lev. 23:34).
2. Abraham's servant, Eliezer, left for Nahor to find a wife for Isaac (ZYO).
3. Birth of Jacob and Esau (ibid.).

   The date of Jacob's birth was erroneously based on the tradition that men of outstanding virtue die on their birthdays (*Kiddushin* 38a). However, Tishri 15, mentioned in *Seder ha-Dorot* (no. 4), refers to Jacob's burial, not his death.

   The assumption that Jacob was buried in the fall is corroborated by a reference in the Bible to the "threshing-floor of Atad" (Gen. 50:10). It was there that the children of Israel paused for seven days to mourn Jacob prior to his burial. The choice of that site leads us to believe that it was in the fall season when large crowds assemble to thresh their harvest.

   Atad is described as being *b'ever ha-Yarden* ("across the Jordan"). But was it on the western or eastern side of the Jordan? To Abraham, who came from the east, *b'ever ha-Yarden* designated the western bank. Moses retained this patriarchal connotation (Deut. 3:20). Whenever he mentioned the eastern bank, he clarified it with a specific reference (Deut. 1:1, 4:41, 47, 45:5). After the conquest of Palestine, *b'ever ha-Yarden* came to mean the eastern bank (1 Sam. 31:7; Isa. 8:23). Joshua reflected the ambivalence of the phrase in the transitionary period (Josh. 12:1, 7). As a rule, whenever he quoted Moses he retained the Mosaic usage of the term (Josh. 1:15, 22:4). When he spoke for himself, he referred to the eastern bank (Josh. 7:7, 24:8). We may conclude that the Mosaic identification of Atad refers to a location on the western bank, close to Hebron.

4. Burial of Jacob (*Seder ha-Dorot* 2255). Esau was killed and buried (*Sotah* 13a).
5. The construction of the Tabernacle was begun in the desert. The "Clouds of Glory," which had disappeared at the time of the golden calf, reappeared.
6. On September 19, 1622, Isaac Jeshurun of Ragusa was imprisoned on blood-ritual charges. He was released after surviving cruel torture.
7. Jews of Dubno were massacred by Chmielnicki's forces on October 1, 1648.
8. Joseph Solomon Delmedigo (Yashar of Candia), author of a philosophical work, *Ya'ar Levanon*, died on October 16, 1655.
9. Emperor Paul I of Russia introduced censorship of Jewish books on October 17, 1796.
10. Anti-Jewish riots broke out in Pressburg, Hungary (now Bratislava, Czechoslovakia), on September 28, 1882.
11. Captain Alfred Dreyfus, first Jewish officer assigned to the general staff of the French army, was arrested on October 15, 1894, and charged with espionage against France. The arrest set off a chain of events which rocked the French Republic.
    See Tishri 16;10.
12. Close to 7,000 Jews were expelled from the province of Kiev, Russia, on October 1, 1898.
13. Hungary set up a *numerus clausus* for the admission of Jewish students in universities, on September 27, 1920.
14. Jewish ritual slaughtering was prohibited in Italy, on October 10, 1938.
15. Saul Tchernichowsky, Hebrew poet, died on October 14, 1943.
16. Hundreds of Jewish prisoners escaped from the Sobibor extermination camp during an uprising on October 14, 1943.
17. Operation Ten Plagues was opened by Israel against the Egyptian army in the Negev on October 18, 1948.

TISHRI 16

1. Second day of Sukkot.
2. Simḥat Beit ha-Shoevah, the ritual of the libation of the altar, was performed on the second day of Sukkot, according to the statement of Rabbi Judah b. Bathyra in the Talmud (*Ta'anit* 3a).

   According to the prevailing talmudic view, the ritual of libation began on the first day of Sukkot and was performed on each successive day of the festival (*Sukkah* 42b).
3. Cyrus, king of Persia, captured Babylon in 539 B.C.E.
4. Jews of Krems, Germany, were massacred in the Black Death riots on September 29, 1349.
5. On October 3, 1430, the city council of Eger (Cheb), Bohemia, was given royal permission to expel the Jewish population.
6. Rabbi Moses Zacuto (Remez), kabbalist, author of *Kol ha-Remez*, died on October 1, 1697.
7. Rabbi Isaac ha-Kohen, kabbalist, author of *Berit Kehunat Olam*, died on October 15, 1780.
8. Simon M. Levy, member of the first graduating class of the Military Academy at West Point, received his commission on October 12, 1802.

   The enrollment of that class numbered only two students.
9. Rabbi Seligmann Baer Bamberger, leader of German Orthodox Jewry and author of *Moreh la-Zovehim*, died on October 13, 1878.
10. Alfred Dreyfus was released from imprisonment on Devil's Island on September 20, 1899.

    See Tishri 15:11.
11. The American warship *North Carolina* arrived in Jaffa, on October 16, 1914, after clearing the British blockade. It delivered to the beleaguered Jewish community financial assistance contributed by American Jews.
12. Germany occupied Warsaw on September 29, 1939, and trapped its Jewish population, estimated at 340,000.
13. Rabbi Moses Rosen, author of *Nezer ha-Kodesh,* monumental commentary on the talmudic order of *Kodashim,* died on October 11, 1957.

TISHRI 17

1. Third day of Sukkot.
2. Antonia Jose de Silva, Brazilian Marrano poet and dramatist, was burned at the stake in Lisbon, Portugal, on October 19, 1739.

3. Blood-ritual charges triggered anti-Jewish riots in Galatz (Galati), Rumania, on October 3, 1868.
4. David Ben-Gurion, founding father and first prime minister of Israel, was born on October 16, 1886.
5. Reuben Asher Braudes, Hebrew novelist, died on October 18, 1902.
6. The first transport of Jews from Rome to extermination camps left on October 16, 1943.
7. Jordan entered the Yom Kippur War on October 13, 1973.

TISHRI 18

1. Fourth day of Sukkot.
2. Death of Jacob (Lowenstein, *Dor Dor ve-Dorshav*). See note on Tishri 15:3.
3. Rabbi Meshullam Phoebus b. Israel Samuel, head of Yeshivah of Brest Litovsk and author of *Shemot Gittin*, died on October 17, 1617.
4. Jews of Barbados were forbidden, on October 23, 1668, to engage in retail trade.
5. Rabbi Nahman b. Simhah of Bratslav, Hasidic philosopher, author of *Likkutei Moharan*, died on October 6, 1811.
6. The first Reform temple in Germany was opened in Hamburg on September 28, 1817.
7. The first Reform temple in Berlin was dedicated on October 18, 1818.
8. Italy granted equality to Jews and abolished the Roman ghetto on October 13, 1870.
9. Israel Abrahams, scholar and historian, died on October 6, 1925.
10. On October 14, 1927, the Polish government decreed the formation of a single religious organization to include all Polish Jews.
11. Beersheba was occupied by Israel on October 21, 1948.
    Israel occupied Beersheba, the hometown of Jacob, on his traditional yahrzeit (no. 2)
12. The Vatican II ecumenical council gave its final approval to the Schema on the Jews on October 14, 1965.

TISHRI 19

1. Fifth day of Sukkot.
2. The first auto-da-fé in Lisbon, Portugal, was held on September 20, 1540.
3. Nathan Samson and Samuel Levy, the first Jews in America to be-

come law-enforcement officers, were sworn in on October 15, 1718.

4. Rabbi Elijah b. Solomon Zalman, known as the Gaon of Vilna, the outstanding talmudic personality of the 18th century, died on October 9, 1797.
5. Rabbi Isaac Raphael Finzi of Ferrara, first Italian rabbi to preach in Italian, author of responsa *Peri Zaddik*, died on September 25, 1812.
6. The first organizational meeting of the Order of B'nai B'rith was held at Sinsheimer's Cafe, 60 Essex Street, New York City, on October 13, 1843.
7. Solomon Judah Leib Rapoport (Shir), historian and poet, died on October 18, 1867.
8. Charles (Yizhak) Netter, founder of Mikveh Israel, first agricultural school in Palestine, died on October 2, 1882.
9. Rabbi Aaron Freedman, hasidic leader, author of *Kedushat Aharon*, died on September 30, 1912.
10. The British mandate in Palestine came into force on September 29, 1923.
11. A Nazi plan for the establishment of ghettos for Jews in all big cities was announced for the first time by Hermann Goering on October 14, 1938.
12. The Egyptian flagship *King Farouk* was sunk by Israeli forces on October 22, 1948.

TISHRI 20

1. Sixth day of Sukkot.
2. Oholei Shem Association, organized to foster the study of the Hebrew language, literature, and history, was founded in New York on October 8, 1895.
3. 6,300 Jews of the Baden area were deported by the Nazis on October 22, 1940.
4. Jewish Sonderkommando in Birkenau staged an uprising on October 7, 1944.
5. Syrian troops withdrew from the Jordan region on October 13, 1949, in compliance with the terms of the truce.
6. The crossing of Israeli forces to the western side of the Suez Canal on October 16, 1973, marked a turning point in the Yom Kippur War.

TISHRI 21

1. Hoshana Rabbah.
2. Birth of Joseph (*Midrash Tadshei*).
    According to the *Book of Jubilees*, Joseph was born on Tammuz 1. This statement seems to support the rabbinic tradition that Rachel's prayer for a child was answered on Rosh Ha-Shanah (Tishri 1:7) as the first of Tammuz is nine months after Rosh Ha-Shanah.
3. In 520 B.C.E., the Prophet Haggai exhorted Zerubbabel to proceed with the construction of the Temple (Hag. 2:1).
    The following is a timetable of events from the declaration of Cyrus to the rebuilding of the Temple:
    The declaration, 538 B.C.E. (Ezra 1:1–4).
    The laying of the first foundation of the Second Temple, Iyar 1, 537 B.C.E.
    Haggai's exhortation to begin the construction work, Tishri 21, 520 B.C.E.
    The laying of the second foundation of the Temple, Kislev 24, 520 B.C.E.
    Zechariah's call for resumption of work, Shevat 24, 519 B.C.E.
    Completion of the Temple, Adar 3, 515 B.C.E.
    Dedication of the Temple, Adar 23, 515 B.C.E.
4. Columbus discovered America on October 12, 1492.
5. On October 23, 1625, Jews of Rome were prohibited from erecting tombstones on their cemetery.
6. Rabbi Mordecai ha-Kohen of Berzon, author of *Zon Kedoshim*, died on September 27, 1630.
7. Rabbi Jacob Joseph of Polonnoye, a disciple of Israel Baal Shem Tov, died on October 17, 1783. (ATGY and TP).
8. Rabbi Dov Baer of Zagor (Zagare), author of *Revid ha-Zahav*, died on October 7, 1803.
9. An invitation to the Jews of France to send delegates to a session for the purpose of founding a "Sanhedrin" was announced by Napoleon on October 3, 1806.
10. On October 13, 1881, Eliezer Ben-Yehuda and his friends agreed to use Hebrew exclusively in their daily conversations and transactions. This marked the modest beginning of the revival of Hebrew as a living tongue (*Zikhronot Erez Yisrael*, vol. 1, p. 337).
11. 3,400 Jews of Kolomyya, Galicia, were executed by the Nazis on October 12, 1941.
12. The U.N. War Crimes Commission was set up in Moscow on October 20, 1943.
13. Ten major Nazi war criminals, sentenced to death in the Nuremberg

war trial, were hanged on October 16, 1946. Hermann Goering, Reichsmarshal of Germany, committed suicide on the same day.

The execution of the major Nazi war criminals took place on the third anniversary of the setting up of the War Crimes Commission.

TISHRI 22

1. Shemini Azeret (combined with Simhat Torah in Israel).
2. God informed Moses: "Behold, thy days approach that thou must die" (Deut. 31:14, *Midrash Petirat Moshe Rabbenu*). Moses prayed to be spared.

A midrashic source, which dates from the 11th century, alleges that Moses was forewarned of his death 10 times during the period from Tishri 22 to Shevat 1. We must therefore assume that the first biblical quotation in the Midrash (Deut. 31:14) was uttered on Tishri 22. Despite the allegation of ten warnings, in fact the text cites only six quotations, all from Deuteronomy: 4:22; 31:14, 29; 32:6; 34:5, 7.

An analysis of the six quotations reveals three categories: (1) forewarning of death, (2) Moses' acknowledgment of the warning, (3) his death. There are two quotations for each category.

An examination of the biblical sources reveals that there are indeed ten references to the death of Moses in the Bible: Num. 27:13; Deut. 4:22; 31:14, 16, 27, 29; 32:50; 33:1; 34:5, 7. In addition to these, there are also ten references to the decree barring Moses from Palestine: Num. 20:12; 27:13; Deut. 1:37; 3:27; 4:21, 22; 31:2, 23; 32:52; 34:4. The midrash apparently addresses itself to a tradition that Moses did not believe that the decree was irrevocable until it was repeated 10 times.

A previous passage in the same midrash alleges that Moses prayed 515 times for remission of the decree. This is based on the numerical value of *Va-ethannan*. It is possible that the author of the dates in the second passage used the same method of calculation. The phrase *va-ethannan-El* consists of eight letters. The last four have a numerical value of 131, the total number of days devoted by Moses to prayer and instruction. This is inclusive of the 36 days spent on composing Deuteronomy, from Shevat 1 to Adar 7 (Deut. 1:3). The period of prayer therefore began 95 days earlier on Tishri 22. The first four letters of the phrase have a numerical value of 415, corresponding to the number of Moses' prayers. Three daily prayers for a period of 131 days equal 393 prayers. One additional prayer on each of the 19 Sabbaths of that period brings us to a total of 412 prayers. Add three more prayers on the day of his death and we arrive at the number 415.

The current version of the midrash is garbled and full of errors.

Tishri 22 might have been the date of Moses' first prayer but surely not of the warning mentioned in Deut. 31:14. *Seder ha-Dorot* correctly states that that warning was uttered on Adar 6.

3. King Solomon dismissed the people at the end of the dedicatory festivities of the Temple (1 Kings 8:66).
4. Hundreds of Jews of Cracow were killed in the synagogue during *Hakafot* services on October 7, 1555.
5. Rabbi Marcus Jastrow, scholar and communal leader, author of *Dictionary of the Targumim*, died on October 13, 1903.
6. Anshel Bondi, "Fighter for Freedom," right-hand man of John Brown, died on September 30, 1907.
7. Bar-Giora, a pioneer watchmen's organization of Palestinian Jewry, was founded on September 30, 1907.
8. The Israeli army opened a new road to Sodom on October 25, 1948.

TISHRI 23

1. Simḥat Torah (outside Israel).
2. Traditional yahrzeit of Rebecca's nurse, Deborah (*Book of Jubilees*).
3. Moses waged war on Og (*Tanḥuma, Ḥukkat* 24).
4. A Roman force captured Gamala, a fort in Transjordanian Galilee, and killed all its inhabitants, 67 C.E. (Josephus, *Jewish Wars* 4:1).
5. Rabbi Ḥanokh b. Moses, one of the four emissaries sent by the Babylonian academies to Africa and Europe, died on September 30, 1013.
6. Juan de San Martin and Miguel de Morillo, first heads of the Spanish Inquisition, were appointed on September 27, 1480.
7. Herzliah, Palestine's first Hebrew gymnasium (secondary school), was established in Jaffa on October 22, 1905.
8. Naphtali Herz Imber, Hebrew poet, author of "Ha-Tikvah," died on October 8, 1909.
9. On October 6, 1939, Hitler announced that "an experiment will be made with organizing and regulating the Jewish problem," foreshadowing the doom of Jewry.

TISHRI 24

1. Ezra and Nehemiah convened the Jewish community in Jerusalem to purge its heathen elements and to renew the ancient covenant, 444 B.C.E. (Neh. 9:1).
2. Leon Pinsker's pamphlet *Autoemancipation,* a major contribution to the emergence of Russian Zionism, was published on October 7, 1882.
3. The first mass deportation of German Jews to East European ghettos began on October 15, 1941 (Poliakov, *Harvest of Hate,* p. 146).
4. Jews caught outside the walls of Polish ghettos were made subject to the death penalty by a Nazi decree published on October 15, 1941 (ibid., p. 40).
5. 5,000 Jews of Dubno, Russia, were massacred on October 5, 1942.
6. Nizzanim, a settlement in the Negev, was recaptured by Israel on October 27, 1948.
7. In a speech delivered on October 10, 1974, General George S. Brown, chairman of the Joint Chiefs of Staff, deplored Jewish influence in America.

   This speech was the first anti-Semitic attack by an active American military officer since General Sherman of the Civil War.

TISHRI 25

1. On September 21, 1451, Jews of Arnhem, Holland, were ordered by Cardinal Nicholas of Cusa to wear the Jew-badge.
2. The hasidic sect was excommunicated in Cracow on September 29, 1785.
3. Rabbi Benjamin b. Aaron of Zalozce, famous itinerant preacher, author of *Ahavat Dodim,* died on October 1, 1793.
4. Rabbi Levi Isaac of Berdichev, popular hasidic leader, author of *Kedushat Levi,* died on October 5, 1809.
5. Rabbi Moses Sofer, leading talmudist and founder of the yeshivah of Pressburg (Bratislava), author of *Hatam Sofer,* died on October 3, 1839.
6. *Ha-Meliz,* early Russian Hebrew periodical, was published for the first time on October 11, 1860.
7. The first Jewish self-defense organization in Russia was founded in Homel on October 16, 1903.
8. Asefat ha-Nivharim, the representative assembly elected by the Yishuv in Palestine, opened its first session on October 7, 1920.

9. A pogrom against the Jews of Lodz, Poland, was instigated by Nazis on October 8, 1939.
10. A ban on ritual slaughtering, Belgium's first anti-Jewish law, was published on October 27, 1940.
11. Rumanian legionnaires entered Odessa, Russia, on October 16, 1941, and immediately instituted an extermination program which accounted for the death of 150,000 Jews.
12. S.S. Obergruppenführer (Lieut. Gen.) Kurt Daluege, head of the Nazi Ordnungspolizei, was hanged in Prague on October 20, 1946.
13. Menahem Brahinsky (Mani Leib), Yiddish writer, died on October 4, 1953.
14. The Israeli navy acquired its first submarine on October 9, 1958.

TISHRI 26

1. Simon Bar Giora inflicted heavy losses upon the Roman forces at Bet Horon, 66 C.E.
2. Religious freedom in the colonies of the West Indies was granted to Jews by the Dutch West India Company in a charter published on October 13, 1629 (*AJHSP*, no. 42, p. 217).
3. The political rights of the Jews of the Duchy of Warsaw were suspended by Duke Frederick Augustus on October 17, 1808.
4. Rabbi Aaron of Zhitomir, kabbalist, author of *Toledot Aharon*, died on October 22, 1821.
5. Maimonides College, the first American Jewish institution for advanced learning, was opened in Philadelphia on October 25, 1867.
6. Israeli forces captured Meron and Gush-Halav on October 29, 1948.
7. On October 22, 1973, a cease-fire resolution was passed by the U.N. Security Council to halt the Yom Kippur War. Israel and Egypt announced their acceptance.

TISHRI 27

1. Rabbi Abraham b. Avigdor, author of a commentary on the *Tur* code, died on October 27, 1542.
2. The influential and wealthy Jewish community of Venice was sacked and impoverished on September 26, 1570.
3. Rabbi Aryeh Leib Heller, author of the popular *Kezot ha-Hoshen*, novellae on the code, died on October 3, 1812.

4. The rabbinical seminary of Budapest, Hungary, was founded on October 4, 1877.
5. The town of Netanyah, Israel, named for the philanthropist Nathan Straus of New York, was founded on October 23, 1927 (Bein, *The Return to the Soil*, 567).
6. The practice of raiding the Kovno ghetto to fill the quota of Jews for transportation to extermination camps was started by the Nazis on October 26, 1943.
7. Operation Ḥiram was successfully completed by Israeli forces on October 30, 1948.

   The end of the operation gave Israel effective control of the Galilee. The battle was waged against the Arab Liberation Army, headed by Fawzi al-Kaukji, whose symbol was a crooked dagger dripping blood, piercing a shield of David.
8. Fighting was resumed in the Yom Kippur War on October 23, 1973. Egypt, Syria, and Israel announced their acceptance of a second cease-fire passed by the Security Council.

   Fighting continued until October 26. The estimated losses up to February 12, 1974 were: Israel—2,522 killed, 1,578 wounded, 107 planes, 840 tanks, 1 ship; Egypt—7,500 casualties, 242 planes, 895 tanks, 20 ships; Syria—7,300 casualties, 179 planes, 880 tanks, 9 ships.

   In the War of Independence (1948–49) 6,200 Israelis died, among them 1,700 civilians. The total wounded was put at 12,500. In the 1956 Suez campaign, 190 were killed. In the war of 1967, the death toll was 806, including 26 civilians; 3,006 were wounded, including 195 civilians.

TISHRI 28

1. Rabban Gamaliel VI, last patriarch (*nasi*) of Palestine, was removed from office by a joint decree of Emperors Honorius and Theodosius II on October 17, 415.

   With the removal of Rabban Gamaliel VI, the last vestiges of Jewish autonomy in Palestine disappeared. The publication of the British White Paper (see below, no. 5), 1,515 years later, sought to accomplish the same ends.
2. Sultan Saladin captured Jerusalem from the Crusaders on October 2, 1187. Jews were permitted to return to the city after an absence of 88 years.
3. Bernadino da Feltre, an Italian Franciscan friar who had advocated physical extermination of Jews, died on September 28, 1494.

4. Rabbi Ephraim Solomon Schor, author of *Tevu'ot Schor*, a popular commentary on the code, died on October 24, 1633 (JE).
5. The British White Paper, which restricted Jewish immigration into Palestine and the right to purchase land from Arabs, was published on October 20, 1930.
6. Temple Anshei Emet of Atlanta, Ga., was extensively damaged by a bomb on October 12, 1958. The bombing pointed up a resurgent anti-Semitism which emerged in the wake of desegregation in the South.

TISHRI 29

1. Traditional yahrzeit of Simeon the Just, high priest and member of the Knesset ha-Gedolah (*Yoma* 39b).
    See L. Ginzberg, *Legends of the Jews*, 6:447; J. Klausner, *Historiah shel Bayit Sheni*, 2:38; S. Hoenig, *The Great Sanhedrin*, p. 31.
2. Jews of Lower Bavaria were expelled by Ludwig IX on October 5, 1450.
3. Don Isaac Abrabanel, leader of Spanish Jewry and Bible exegete, died on September 22, 1508.
4. Isaac Adolphe Crémieux, Franco-Jewish statesman and minister of justice, granted emancipation to the Jews of Algeria on October 24, 1870.
5. The first Jewish deportees from Vienna and Bohemia left for Nisko, Poland, on October 12, 1939.
6. The deadline for Warsaw Jews to move into the ghetto was October 31, 1940.
7. The first decree of deportation of Jews from the Reich to Lodz was published on October 20, 1941.
8. The last transport of 1,300 Austrian Jews left for Theresienstadt on October 10, 1942.

TISHRI 30

1. A Roman legion under the command of Cestius entered the suburbs of Jerusalem, forcing the Jewish defenders to retreat behind the walls of the inner town, 66 C.E.
    The foundation stone of the Knesset in Jerusalem (no. 5) was laid on the anniversary of this attack, which eventually led to the loss of Jewish independence.

2. Rabbi Zevi Hirsch Chajes, talmudist and historian, author of *Ateret Zevi*, died on October 12, 1855.

3. *Hadoar*, the first Hebrew daily newspaper in America, appeared on November 1, 1921.

   Hadoar was converted into a weekly on July 7, 1922. Publication was briefly suspended after the appearance of the issue of October 19, 1923, and resumed on December 9, 1923.

4. He-Halutz, an organization for the training of American youth for farming in Palestine, was founded on October 30, 1932.

5. The foundation stone of Israel's Knesset was laid in Jerusalem on October 14, 1958.

6. Israeli forces reached the city of Suez on October 26, 1973, and trapped the Egyptian 3rd Army on the eastern side of the Suez.

ḤESHVAN 1

1. The beginning of the biblical plague of *dever* (ZYO).
2. The opening of the sowing season in Palestine (Rabbi Simeon, *Bava Meẓia* 106b).
3. The seventh and last of the Christian Crusades was brought to an end by a treaty concluded by King Louis IX of France and the Berbers of North Africa on October 18, 1270.
4. Rabbi Isaac Karo's exegesis on the Bible, *Toledot Yiẓḥak,* was printed in Mantua, Italy, on October 13, 1558.
5. Rabbi Judah Ḥasid and Ḥayyim Molcho arrived in Jerusalem with 400 of their followers on October 14, 1700.

   Rabbi Judah Ḥasid died three days after his arrival in Jerusalem. A house of worship was subsequently built on land which he had procured for that purpose, and was named the Synagogue of Rabbi Judah Ḥasid. The Arabs set it on fire on November 9, 1720, when the Jews were unable to meet an installment due on a communal debt. The ruin was thereafter known as Ḥurvat Rabbi Judah he-Ḥasid. It was rebuilt and dedicated on January 7, 1837, but was totally wrecked by the Arabs in 1948.
6. W. D. Robinson, an American citizen, published a pamphlet in London on October 20, 1819, calling upon European Jews to come to America to "establish a Jewish settlement in the United States" (Schappes, *Documentary History of the Jews in the United States,* p. 141).
7. The Rabbinical Seminary for Orthodox Judaism, founded in Berlin by Rabbi Azriel Hildesheimer, was dedicated on October 22, 1873.
8. *Ha-Devorah,* first American Hebrew periodical devoted to humor and satire, was published on October 23, 1911.
9. Anti-Jewish riots in Memel, Lithuania, on October 26, 1938, resulted in many injuries.

ḤESHVAN 2

1. Purim Mo'ed Katan was annually celebrated by the Jews of Shiraz, Persia, in commemoration of their escape from forced conversion upon the sudden death of the apostate Jew, Abu Al Hasan, on Ḥeshvan 2.
2. Rabbi Samuel b. Moses di Medina (Rashdam), talmudist, author of responsa *Piskei Rashdam*, died on October 12, 1589.
3. Emperor Joseph II abolished distinctive Jewish dress and other restrictions on October 21, 1781.
4. A pogrom in Odessa, Russia, on October 31, 1905, took a toll of 300 Jewish lives.
5. The Yeshivah of Mir, a leading academy for 124 years, was forced to close its doors on October 15, 1939.
6. Nazis executed 260 Jews of Chernigov, Russia, on October 23, 1941.
7. Nazis executed 10,000 Jews of the Vilna ghetto in three days, beginning on October 23, 1941.
8. Pope Paul VI promulgated the Declaration on Jews with a decree dated October 28, 1965.
9. The ancient Jewish settlement of Aden came to an end with the arrival of its last Jew in Israel on November 5, 1967.

ḤESHVAN 3

1. King Cyrus of Persia formally occupied the city of Babylon in 539 B.C.E. The Babylonian empire, which had crushed Judea in 586 B.C.E. came to an end 47 years later.
2. The last of the 16,000 English Jews expelled by King Edward I left England on October 9, 1290.
   See Av 9:9.
3. 27 Jews were burned in Mecklenburg, Germany, on October 24, 1492.
4. Rabbi Aryeh Leib of Poznan and three other Jews, imprisoned on blood-ritual charges, were tortured and martyred on October 19, 1735.
5. On October 31, 1753, Rabbi Jonathan Eybeschuetz was cleared, by a rabbinical council at Yaroslav, of charges of Shabbatean heresy.
6. Rabbi Israel of Ruzhin, ḥasidic leader, died on October 9, 1850.
7. Rabbi Joseph Sundel Salant, a founder of the Musar movement, died on October 23, 1865.
   The Musar movement, which stressed piety and ethics in addition to scholarship, gained many adherents among Lithuanian Jews. Like

Ḥasidism, it was intended to stem the tide of secularism and assimilation, which had followed in the wake of emancipation. Unlike Ḥasidism, the Musar movement appealed primarily to scholars and yeshivah students but lacked popular support.

8. Jews of Polish origin were rounded up in Germany on October 28,
   1938, and deported in sealed cars to the Polish border.
9. Germany occupied Kharkov, Russia, on October 24, 1941; 20,000
   Jews fell into Nazi hands.
10. Israel freed the settlement of Yad Mordecai from Egyptian occupation
    on November 5, 1948.

ḤESHVAN 4

1. Maimonides reached Jerusalem on October 12, 1165, six months after
   his arrival in Palestine. In commemoration of this event, he set aside
   Ḥeshvan 4 as a private holiday for himself and his family.
   See Iyar 4:2.
2. The fanatical Tomás de Torquemada was appointed inquisitor-gen-
   eral of Spain on October 17, 1483.
3. Purim Edom was annually celebrated by Jews of Algeria in commemoration of their escape from capture by a Spanish army on October 25,
   1541.
4. The oldest existing tombstone in New York stands in the Spanish and
   Portuguese cemetery on the Bowery at the grave of Benjamin Bueno
   de Mesquita, who died on October 24, 1683 (AJHSP, no. 1, p. 91).
5. Rabbi Judah Ḥasid, leader of a large Ashkenazic aliyah, died in
   Jerusalem on October 17, 1700, three days after his arrival.
   See Ḥeshvan 1:5.
6. A decree forbidding Jews of Austria to adopt first names of Christian
   saints was published on November 6, 1834.
7. Rumanian soldiers massacred 26,000 Jews of Odessa, Russia, in a
   three-day pogrom which ended on October 25, 1941.
8. The Nazis liquidated the Riga ghetto on November 2, 1943.
9. David Ben-Gurion, prime minister of Israel, and four cabinet members were wounded on October 29, 1957, by a bomb thrown in the
   Knesset.

ḤESHVAN 5

1. On October 21, 1468, Jews of Landau, Germany, were ordered to wear a yellow badge.
2. On November 5, 1655, Jacob Barsimson and Asser Levy of New Amsterdam petitioned for the right to stand guard and be relieved of the special tax imposed on Jews in lieu of guard duty.

    The imposition of special taxes upon Jews was one facet of the complex and oppressive restrictions to which they had been subjected in the diaspora. The earliest example of this onerous tax was the Fiscus Judaicus instituted by Emperor Vespasian in the year 70. The medieval yellow badge which Jews were compelled to wear was exploited by some rulers as a means for extorting additional revenues. Exemptions from wearing the badge were obtainable in some French and German cities in 1405, in return for a payment of a Dress Tax.
3. Rabbi Abraham Rice, influential Orthodox leader of Baltimore, Md., and founder, in 1845, of one of the earliest Hebrew schools in the United States, died on October 29, 1862.
4. Rabbi Abraham Sutro, author and leader of Orthodox Jewry in Germany, died on October 10, 1869.
5. Rabbi Zevi Hirsch Kalischer, moving spirit of Ḥibbat Zion, author of *Derishat Ziyyon*, died on October 16, 1874.
6. Rabbi David Tevele Ephrati, author of *Toledot Anshei Shem*, died on October 24, 1884.
7. The British government of Palestine announced, on October 17, 1920, that Hebrew would become one of the official languages in the courts of the land.
8. An alliance between Germany and Italy (Axis) was concluded on October 21, 1936.

    See Iyar 15:11.
9. Baruch Naḥman Charney (B. Vladeck), Yiddish writer, died on October 30, 1938.
10. Msgr. Bernard Lichtenberg of the St. Hedwig Cathedral of Berlin, outspoken critic of Nazi persecution of Jews, died on November 3, 1943, on the way to the Dachau concentration camp.
11. Israel signed the Sinai disengagement pact with Egypt on October 10, 1975.

ḤESHVAN 6

1. Decoration of the exterior of synagogues was forbidden by order of King Frederick III of Sicily on October 12, 1366.
2. The first printed edition of the Former Prophets with Kimhi's commentary was published in Soncino, Italy, on October 15, 1485.
3. Solomon Molcho, kabbalist, author of *Shemen Mishhat Kodesh*, died in Jerusalem on October 28, 1786.
4. Rabbi Samuel Ḥayyim of Constantinople, author of *Shemen ha-Mishhah*, died on October 10, 1842.
5. Rabbi Joseph Leib Bloch, dean of the Yeshivah of Telz, died on November 9, 1929.

   The Yeshivah of Telz was one of the outstanding talmudical academies of Eastern Europe. Its official existence came to an end in 1940, when the Russians closed it. Some of its leaders, who happened to be on a tour of the United States at that time, were fortunately able to found a new Telz Yeshivah in Cleveland, Ohio, and thus assure the perpetuation of the Telz academic program.

   Rabbi Joseph Leib Bloch, dean of the yeshivah, died on Ḥeshvan 6. Rabbi Ḥayyim Rabinowitz, a successor, died on Ḥeshvan 8 (no. 8). Rabbi Simon Shkop, a former dean of the school, died on Ḥeshvan 9 (no. 6). The American Telz Yeshivah was founded on Ḥeshvan 7 (no. 3).
6. Lippa Kestin, Yiddish journalist and author, was executed by the Nazis in Lukewe, Poland, on October 19, 1939.
7. 100 Jews of Florence, Italy, were rounded up on November 4, 1943, and deported to extermination camps.
8. The first census taken by the government of Israel on November 8, 1948, listed 712,000 Jews and 68,000 Arabs.

ḤESHVAN 7

1. On November 3, 1878, the first settlers arrived at the site of Petaḥ Tikvah to prepare the ground for a new colony.
2. Rabbi Meir Shapira, founder of Yeshivat Ḥakhmei Lublin and organizer of Daf Yomi, a worldwide society for the study of a designated daily portion of the Talmud, died on October 27, 1933.
3. The Telz Yeshivah was founded in Cleveland, Ohio, on October 28, 1941.

   See note on Ḥeshvan 6:5.
4. 10,000 Jews were removed by the Nazis from the Kovno ghetto on October 28, 1941, and executed on the following day.

5. Jewish children under the age of 12 were removed from the ghetto of Shavl (Siauliai), Lithuania, and executed on November 5, 1943.
6. The Arab siege of Negbah, Israel, was lifted on November 9, 1948.
7. Professor Simḥa Assaf, member of Israel's Supreme Court, scholar, and author, died on October 16, 1953.

ḤESHVAN 8

1. Jewish insurgents returned to Jerusalem from their victorious pursuit of the defeated Roman forces under Cestius, 66 C.E. (Josephus, *Jewish Wars*, 2, 19).
2. Rabbi Meir b. Simeon ha-Kohen of Narbonne, France, author of *Sefer ha-Me'orot,* died on October 13, 1263.
3. Rabbi Jonah b. Abraham Gerondi, of Spain, talmudist and moralist, author of *Sha'arei Teshuvah,* died on October 13, 1263

   Rabbi Jonah was one of the most revered scholars of his generation. In his pious zeal, he violently opposed the rationalist philosophy of Maimonides which led to the burning of the latter's books by the Franciscan and Dominican friars of Paris.

   Rabbi Jonah soon realized the calamity which the internal Jewish feud was inviting. His worst fears came to plague the Jewish people when the Talmud was burned in 1242, in the same place where the works of Maimonides had previously been burned (Tammuz 6:3). Overcome with remorse, he is reputed to have written his famous book on ethics, *Sha'arei Teshuvah,* as an act of penance.
4. Congregation Beracha VeShalom of Surinam, one of the oldest congregations in America, was dedicated on November 5, 1685.
5. The Rabbi Judah Ḥasid Synagogue of Jerusalem was set afire on November 9, 1720. The Ashkenazic community dispersed to escape imprisonment as hostages for the payment of a communal debt.
6. David Sassoon, founder of David Sassoon & Co. and celebrated Indian Jewish philanthropist, died on November 7, 1864.
7. The Federation of Hungarian Jews in America was organized on November 1, 1919.
8. Rabbi Ḥayyim Rabinowitz, dean of the Yeshivah of Telz, died on October 30, 1930.
9. Rabbi Mordecai Krimer of Kovno was martyred by the Nazis on October 29, 1941. Mass executions the same day took a toll of 10,000 lives.
10. The House of Bishops of the Protestant Episcopal Church issued a proclamation in St. Louis, Mo., on October 14, 1964, clearing Jews of the charge of deicide.

ḤESHVAN 9

1. Maimonides left Jerusalem for Hebron and Egypt on October 17, 1165.
2. Rabbi Asher b. Jehiel (Rosh), outstanding talmudist and codifier, died in Toledo, Spain, on October 25, 1327.

   The controversy aroused by the philosophical works of Maimonides continued to agitate the Jewish world in the 14th century. Like his predecessor, Rabbi Jonah Gerondi, rabbi of Toledo in the 13th century, Rabbi Asher banned the study of Maimonides' *Guide for the Perplexed*. Rabbi Jonah died on Ḥeshvan 8 (no. 3). Rabbi Asher died on Ḥeshvan 9. See Av 4:2.
3. King Casimir III of Poland, on October 9, 1334, renewed Jewish privileges granted by his predecessors.

   Unlike the Jews of Western Europe, who were decimated by the Crusaders and Black Death rioters, the Jews of Poland and Lithuania enjoyed comparative peace and freedom until the 16th century. Casimir III granted important privileges to the Jews of his realm.
4. An earthquake caused the death of several hundred Safed Jews on October 31, 1759.
5. Jews of the region of Widdin on the Danube commemorated their escape from destruction, on November 10, 1807, with an annual celebration, known as the Purim of the Poisoned Sword.
6. Rabbi Simon Shkop, head of the Yeshivahs of Telz and Grodno, author of *Shaarei Yashar*, died on October 22, 1939.

   See note on Ḥeshvan 6:5.

ḤESHVAN 10

1. Birthday of Jacob's son Gad *(Midrash Tadshei)*.
2. Jews of England were imprisoned on November 17, 1278, on charges of circulating counterfeit money. Many of them suffered martyrdom.
3. Asser Levy was granted a butcher's license on October 15, 1660. The supply of kosher meat in New Amsterdam was thus assured.
4. Rabbi Jehiel Michel Teimer, author of *Seder Gittin*, died on November 11, 1720.
5. A firman (decree) against ritual charges was issued by the sultan of Turkey on November 6, 1840.
6. The right to acquire real estate in rural areas of Sweden was granted to Jews on October 26, 1860.
7. The *Jewish Spectator*, the first Jewish weekly in the South, was founded in Memphis, Tenn., on October 19, 1885.

8. Theodor Herzl arrived in Jaffa on his only visit to the Holy Land, on October 26, 1898.
9. The Weizmann Institute of Science was dedicated in Reḥovot, Israel, on November 2, 1949.

ḤESHVAN 11

1. Yahrzeit of Methuselah (*Yalkut Shimoni* 56).
2. Birthday of Jacob's son Benjamin (*Midrash Tadshei*).
3. Yahrzeit of Rachel.
   Rachel is the only biblical woman whose yahrzeit is commemorated by posterity. See note on Ḥeshvan 15:2.
4. 180 Jews were killed in Munich, Germany, on October 11, 1285.
5. Rabbi Menahem Nahum of Chernobyl, disciple of the Baal Shem and author of *Ma'or Einayim*, died on October 31, 1797.
6. Osip Rabinovich, founder and editor of *Razsvet*, the first Jewish journal published in Russia, died on October 16, 1869.
7. The moshav Balfouriyyah was founded in Palestine on November 2, 1922, the anniversary of the Balfour Declaration.
8. Abraham Liessin, Yiddish poet, died on November 5, 1938.
9. A distinctive Jewish badge was ordered for the first time by the Nazis in Wloclawek, Poland, on October 24, 1939.
10. The Nazi war-criminals trial opened at Nuremberg on October 18, 1945.
11. Abraham D. Beame, the first Jewish mayor of New York City, was elected on November 6, 1973.

ḤESHVAN 12

1. A requirement of corroboration of Jewish witnesses in all blood-ritual accusations was published in a papal decree on October 8, 1272.
2. 200 Jews of Heilbronn, Germany, lost their lives in the Rindfleisch massacres on October 19, 1298.
3. Rabbi Isaac Abrabanel began to write his exegesis of the Bible on October 13, 1483.
4. Giulio Bartolocci, Christian publisher of *Bibliotheca Magna Rabbinica*, an early bibliography in Latin of Hebrew literature, died on October 19, 1687.
5. Rabbi Israel b. Aaron Jaffe of Shklov, kabbalist, author of *Or Yisrael*, died on November 7, 1707.
6. Jews' College, the rabbinical seminary of London, was opened on November 10, 1856.

The Jewish communities of America and England are of approximately the same age. The first theological seminary of British Jewry was established 200 years after the resettlement of Jews in England. It similarly took a little over two centuries of development of the American Jewish community for the establishment of the first institution of advanced Jewish learning (Tishri 26:5).

7. Rabbi Abraham Geiger, scholar and author, died on October 23, 1874.
8. Rabbi Abraham Isaac Weinberger, author of *Pnei Yizḥak,* died on October 31, 1884.
9. The U.N. Social, Humanitarian, and Political Committee passed a resolution, on October 17, 1975, calling on the Assembly to determine "that Zionism is a form of racism and racial discrimination."

ḤESHVAN 13

1. Jews of England were imprisoned by order of King John on November 1, 1210.
2. Volumes of the Talmud were burned in Venice on October 21, 1553.
3. The first Jewish prayerbook printed in America was published on October 23, 1760.
4. Sir Moses Montefiore, Anglo-Jewish philanthropist and social leader, was born on October 28, 1784.
5. The Nazi governor of Poland prohibited Jewish ritual slaughtering of animals, on October 26, 1939.

   Agitation against ritual slaughtering of animals, allegedly on humane grounds, received its most ardent support from anti-Semitic circles. The hypocrisy of the anti-*kashrut* campaign was brazenly demonstrated by the Nazi governor of Poland, who prohibited kosher slaughtering even as he proceeded to exterminate millions of Jews, calling to mind the bitterly sarcastic outcry of the prophet Hosea: "They that sacrifice men kiss the calves" (13:3).
6. Jews of Poland were subjected to forced labor by a decree issued on October 26, 1939.
7. Anne Frank, the young author whose diary stirred worldwide interest, was deported, on October 30, 1944, from Auschwitz to Belsen, where she died five months later.
8. The last transport for the Auschwitz extermination camp arrived at Birkenau on October 30, 1944.
9. Joseph Klausner, popular historian, died on October 27, 1958.

ḤESHVAN 14

1. Jews of Prague miraculously escaped destruction, on October 22, 1619, when the city was attacked during the Thirty Years War.
2. Rabbi Baruch Kassov, author of *Amud ha-Avodah,* died on November 12, 1886.
3. Jehiel Brill, publisher and editor of the Hebrew periodical *Ha-Levanon,* died on November 12, 1886.
4. The moshav Gederah was attacked by Arabs on October 19, 1888.
5. Russia declared war on Turkey on November 3, 1914.
6. The British government gave its final approval to the Balfour Declaration on October 30, 1917.

   The Balfour Declaration, according to some historians, derived from several factors.

   1. The top-secret Sykes-Picot agreement, negotiated by Britain with France and Russia, provided for the partition of the Ottoman Empire. As soon as the agreement was signed, however, Britain sought to invalidate its terms by keeping the French out of the Middle East, particularly out of Palestine. The British felt that their espousal of Zionism would lead to a demand by world Jewry that Britain alone should protect Jewish interests in Palestine. This would provide the pretext for a repudiation of the secret agreement with France. Exclusive British sovereignty over Palestine would assure the security of the Suez Canal.

   2. There was hope in some British circles that the Balfour Declaration would draw the Russian Jewish intellectuals away from the leftist parties and win their support for Russia's continued participation in the war on the side of the allies.

   3. The segment of the British people which drew its inspiration from the Bible saw in the restoration of a Jewish state in Palestine the fulfillment of biblical prophecy. To them, the geographical demarcation, "From Dan to Beersheba," was still a relevant phrase.

   The Balfour Declaration, dated November 2, was released on November 9. By that time the British Foreign Office had lost interest in the document. The British Army had entered Gaza and the Bolshevik Revolution had broken out in Russia. It has been justly concluded that if the declaration had not been approved by October 30, it never would have been approved at a later date.
7. Jewish males were rounded up by the Nazis in Norway and deported to Auschwitz on October 25, 1942.

ḤESHVAN 15

1. Mattathias b. Yohanan, head of the Hasmonean family, died in 166 B.C.E. (DDD).
2. Annual pilgrimage day of Jerusalem's Jews to the tomb of Rachel.
   Jews of Jerusalem used to commemorate Rachel's yahrzeit by going on a pilgrimage to her tomb on Ḥeshvan 15. However, according to the implication of the biblical text (Gen. 35:17), Rachel died while giving birth to Benjamin. We must, therefore, assume that her yahrzeit actually coincides with the traditional birthday of Benjamin, Ḥeshvan 11.
3. Rabbi Avtalyon b. Solomon, author of *Mikveh Yisrael*, died on October 26, 1616.
4. Rabbi Eleazar Kallir of Kolin, Czechoslovakia, author of *Or Ḥadash*, died on October 22, 1801.
5. Beersheba was occupied by the British on October 31, 1917.
6. The Yeshivah of Slobodka opened a branch in Hebron, Palestine, on November 12, 1924.
7. Rabbi Mendes H. Pereira, author and communal leader, died on October 20, 1937.
8. A huge Nazi pogrom, which later became known as Kristallnacht (the Night of the Broken Glass), took place throughout Germany and Austria on the night of November 9–10, 1938.
   Officially sparked by the murder by a Jew of a German embassy official in Paris, Kristallnacht was thinly disguised as a "spontaneous" act of retaliation by the "Aryan" population. Hundreds of Jewish businesses and homes, as well as nearly three hundred synagogues, were destroyed. Among the ruins was the famous Rashi Chapel of Worms. The Rashi chair was hidden in 1938 in the museum of Worms and thus escaped destruction. See Kislev 26:11.
9. The Judenrat of Warsaw completed its census of the Jewish population of the city on October 28, 1939. It listed 359,827 Jews.
10. All entrances to the Warsaw ghetto were closed by the Nazis on November 16, 1940.
11. Rabbi Avraham Yeshayahu Karelitz, noted talmudic scholar and leader of Orthodox Jewry, author of *Hazon Ish*, died on October 24, 1953.

ḤESHVAN 16

1. King Casimir III of Poland, a benefactor of the Jews, died on November 5, 1370.
2. General Ulysses S. Grant, on November 9, 1862, issued the first in a series of orders barring Jews from entering the military department under his command (*AJHSP*, no. 17, p. 71).
3. Rabbi David Einhorn, leading American Reform rabbi, died on November 2, 1879.
4. Britain declared war on Turkey on November 5, 1914.

   One day after the declaration of war, Lord Herbert Samuel, president of the Local Government Board, met with Prime Minister Asquith to urge the establishment of a Jewish state in Palestine. See note on Heshvan 14:6.
5. *The Day*, a daily Jewish newspaper, began publication in New York on November 5, 1914.
6. 500 Jews of the Moka section of Kolomyya, Galicia, were executed by the Nazis on November 6, 1941.
7. 15,000 Jews were massacred in Rowno, Poland, on November 6, 1941.
8. An order to suspend extermination and dismantle the crematoria was sent to Auschwitz from Berlin on November 2, 1944.
9. The "Magic Carpet" aliyah of Yemenite Jews to Israel began on November 8, 1949.
10. In a face-to-face session, on the western side of the Suez Canal, Israel and Egypt signed a six-point cease-fire agreement on November 11, 1973.
11. Yizhak Navon arrived in Cairo on October 16, 1980. It was the first visit of an Israeli head of state to Egypt.

ḤESHVAN 17

1. Beginning of the biblical flood (Gen. 7:11; Rabbi Eliezer, *Rosh Ha-Shanah* 11b).

   According to Rabbi Joshua, the flood began on Iyar 17 (ibid.)
2. King Saul's seven sons were removed from the gallows (*Midrash Rabbah, Naso* 8).
3. A three-day fast was to be declared in the land of Israel if no rain fell by Heshvan 17.
4. Chmielnicki's forces massacred 12,000 Jews of Narol, Podolia, on

November 2, 1648. The anniversary of this date was proclaimed a commemorative fast-day (Hanover, *Yeven Mezulah*, chap. 13).

5. *Urim ve-Tummim* by Rabbi Aaron Hart, the first Hebrew book printed in London after the resettlement of Jews in England, was published on October 25, 1706.

6. Rabbi Sabato Morais, one of the founders of the Jewish Theological Seminary of America and its first president, died on November 12, 1897.

7. Theodor Herzl arrived in Jerusalem on November 2, 1898.

    On his arrival, Herzl was granted an audience with Kaiser Wilhelm of Germany, who was touring Palestine at the time. Herzl pleaded for German support of a Jewish state in Palestine. His plea, rejected by the kaiser, was partially fulfilled 19 years later, on November 2, 1917, by the Balfour Declaration when the British were engaged in an all-our war with the same kaiser.

8. The Balfour Declaration, calling for the establishment of a Jewish homeland in Palestine, was issued on November 2, 1917.

9. Micha Josef Berdyczewski, Hebrew writer, died on November 18, 1921.

10. Vidkun Quisling, the Nazi head of Norway, who was responsible for the death of many Jews, was executed on October 24, 1945.

ḤESHVAN 18

1. Rabbi Abraham Menahem Rapoport, author of *Minhah Belulah*, died on November 6, 1593 (HY).

2. Hovevei Zion, the pioneer Russian Zionist movement, was founded on November 6, 1884, at the first international Zionist convention, in Kattowitz (Katowice), Poland.

    Hovevei Zion was the first to link the nationalist movement with the term Zion. Ninety-one years after the adoption of "Zion" as the emblem of Jewish nationalism, the U.N. condemned Zionism by equating it with racism (Heshvan 12:9).

3. Leo Motzkin, Zionist leader and fighter for Jewish civil rights in the Diaspora, died on November 7, 1933.

4. Consideration of Madagascar as a home for European Jewry was announced by Hermann Goering on November 12, 1938.

5. 16,000 Jews were killed in Pinsk, Russia, on October 29, 1942.

ḤESHVAN 19

1. Rabbi Naphtali Isaac Siegel, author of *Naftali Sva Razon*, died on October 4, 1555.
2. The earliest known Yiddish letter from America was written by Barnard Gratz of Philadelphia to his brother Michael in London on November 20, 1785 (*AJHSP*, no. 34, p. 79).

   The widespread use of Yiddish by American Jews began in the 1880s when large masses of Yiddish-speaking immigrants came to the United States in the wake of Russian pogroms. According to the U.S. census of 1940, 1,750,000 Jews spoke Yiddish at home.
3. Heinrich Friedrich Gesenius, Christian Hebraist, author of a Hebrew and Aramaic thesaurus and a Hebrew grammar, died on October 23, 1842.
4. The first B'nai B'rith lodge was organized on November 12, 1843 in New York.
5. A seminary for the training of modern rabbis and teachers was established by government decree in Vilna and opened on October 29, 1847.
6. The territory of Birobidzhan was proclaimed a national Jewish administrative unit by the Soviet government on October 30, 1931.
7. Rabbi Abraham Zevi Kamai, head of the Yeshivah of Mir, was among the 1,500 Jews of Mir who were killed by the Nazis on November 9, 1941.

ḤESHVAN 20

1. In 407 B.C.E., Jedoniah, head of an ancient Jewish colony in Egypt, petitioned the Persian governor of Judea for permission to rebuild the destroyed Jewish temple at the fortress of Yeb (Kobler, *Letters of Jews Through the Ages*, Vol. I, p. 23).
2. The rights of Jews in Carinthia and Styria, Austria, were restricted in a charter issued on October 23, 1396.
3. Rabbi Elijah b. Jacob Ragoler of Kalisz, author of *Yad Eliyahu*, died on November 5, 1849.
4. Rabbi Joel Manuel, writer and scholar, died on November 3, 1890.
5. Israel Giladi, one of the founders of Ha-Shomer, early Palestinian self-defense organization, died on October 26, 1918.
6. Abraham Baer Birnbaum, composer of liturgical music, died on November 11, 1922.

7. Hannah Szenes, Palestinian poetess who volunteered to parachute behind Nazi lines, was executed in Budapest on November 6, 1944.
8. On November 5, 1974, Richard Stone was elected U.S. senator from Florida. He was the first Jewish senator from a southern state since the Civil War.
See Tishri 11:7.

HESHVAN 21

1. Rabbi David b. Solomon ibn Abi Zimra (Radbaz), kabbalist and talmudic scholar, author of responsa, died on November 9, 1571 (HY).
2. Rabbi Abraham b. Mordecai Azulai, author of *Or ha-Hamah*, died on November 3, 1643 (HY).
3. Warder Cresson (Michael Boaz Israel), first American consul in Jerusalem and a convert to Judaism, died on November 6, 1860.
4. Jewish students were barred from German schools on November 15, 1938.
5. Chaim Weizmann, the father of the State of Israel and its first president, died on November 9, 1952.
6. Yizhak Lamdan, Hebrew poet, died on November 17, 1954.

HESHVAN 22

1. Jewish physicians were barred from treating Christians by an order issued by the council of Piazza, Sicily, on October 20, 1296.
2. Rabbi Yom Tov Lipmann Heller completed his monumental work, *Tosefot Yom Tov*, a commentary on the Mishnah, on October 13, 1616.
3. Rabbi Moses b. Isaac Judah Levy, author of *Helkat Mehokek*, a commentary on the code, died on November 9, 1656.
4. Purim de los Ladrones (Purim of the bandits) was annually celebrated by the Jewish community of Gumeldjina, Turkey, on Heshvan 22 in commemoration of their rescue on November 13, 1786.
5. Rabbi David Solomon Eibenschutz, author of *Levushei Serad*, died in Safed on November 1, 1809.
6. A petition written by Lewis Way, an English missionary, requesting the restoration of an independent Jewish nation in the land of Israel, was submitted by Czar Alexander I of Russia to the Congress of Aix-la-Chapelle on November 21, 1818.
Napoleon was the first modern head of government to propose the renewal of a Jewish state in Palestine (Nisan 15:21). The proposal was

made during his campaign in the Near East and was intended to rally Jewish support. After the failure of the campaign, Napoleon lost interest in Palestinian Jewry. His promise had never received any publicity in Europe. It is ironic that the Congress of Aix-la-Chapelle, which met to pick up the pieces of Napoleon's collapsed empire, placed on the agenda the question of restoring a Jewish state in Palestine. Czar Alexander was allegedly sympathetic to the petition but nothing is known of the attitude of the other leaders and nothing came of the petition.

7. Hannah Adams, early American author of a book on Jewish history, died on November 15, 1832.
8. Leopold Hilsner was found guilty of the ritual murder of Agnes Hruza of Polna, Bohemia, on November 14, 1900.
9. Judah Behak, Hebrew writer and the last of the Maskilim, died on November 14, 1900.
    See Shevat 20:4.
10. The British captured Gaza, Palestine, from the Turkish army on November 7, 1917.
11. On November 4, 1939, Jews of Warsaw were notified that plans for the setting up of a ghetto had been drawn up by the Nazi administration.
12. Deportation of Budapest Jews began on November 8, 1944.

HESHVAN 23

1. The stones of the altar, which had been defiled by the Greeks, were removed from the Temple (ca. 164 B.C.E.). The anniversary of this day was designated a holiday (*Megillat Ta'anit* 8).
2. *Mishlei Shu'alim*, a book of fables and parables by Berechiah ha-Nakdan, was printed for the first time in Mantua, Italy, on October 15, 1557.
3. Rabbi Isaac b. Samuel Lampronti, author of an early talmudic encyclopedia, died on November 16, 1756.
    Rabbi Lampronti's monumental work, *Pahad Yizhak*, was the product of a lifetime of scholarly creativity. Only two volumes were printed in his lifetime; 127 years elapsed between the printing of the first and the last (14th) volume of the encyclopedia.
4. Rabbi Aaron Katzenellenbogen of Brisk, author of *Minhat Aharon*, died on November 23, 1777.
5. Saul Berlin, moving spirit of Progressive Judaism, author of *Mizpeh Yokte'el*, died on November 16, 1794.

6. Judah b. Mordecai Halevi Hurwitz, physician and author of *Sefer Amudei Bet Yehudah*, a work on moral philosophy, died on November 12, 1797.
7. Rabbi Joseph Raphael Hazzan (Yerach), author of *Hikrei Lev*, died on November 11, 1819.
8. Abraham Dov Levenson (Adam ha-Kohen), Hebrew poet, died on November 19, 1878.
9. The American Jewish Committee was organized on November 11, 1906.

   The objectives of the American Jewish Committee were "to prevent the infraction of the civil and religious rights of Jews . . . to alleviate the consequences of persecution . . . and to afford relief from calamities affecting Jews."

   Defense of civil rights and welfare were the major causes which stimulated American Jewish communal activities in the 19th century. The Board of Delegates of American Israelites, the first Jewish communal public-relations body, was organized in 1859 for the purpose of defending Jewish civil rights throughout the world. The Russian pogroms of 1903–1905 led to the formation of the American Jewish Committee. World War I led to the formation of the Joint Distribution Committee and the American Jewish Congress.
10. An Italian anti-Semitic code, patterned after the Nuremberg Laws, was published on November 17, 1938, affecting also the Italian possessions of Libya and the Aegean Islands.
11. The town of Karmi'el was founded in Galilee, Israel, on October 29, 1964.

    The founding of Karmi'el initiated an effort to populate the Galilee with large numbers of Jewish settlers.

HESHVAN 24

1. Rabbi Uri Shraga b. Elijah ha-Kohen was martyred in Cracow on October 20, 1677.
2. Rabbi Hayyim ben Benjamin Asael of Salonika, author of *Sam Hayyai*, died on November 1, 1706.
3. Jews of Nikolayev and Sevastopol, Russia, were expelled on November 20, 1829.
4. Kehillath Anshe Ma'arav (K.A.M.), the first Jewish congregation in Chicago, was established on November 3, 1847.

   The membership of K.A.M. was of German Jewish extraction. Twenty years later, Congregation Bet Hamedrash Hagadol U'bnai

Jacob was founded by East European Jews. In the East, the first German Jewish congregation had been founded in 1802 (Tishri 14:7) and the first Russian Jewish congregation in 1852 (Sivan 17:5).
5. Baron Edmond de Rothschild, famous philanthropist and patron of the *Yishuv* in Palestine, died on November 2, 1934.
6. On November 25, 1940, the *Patria*, a steamer carrying illegal immigrants, sank in the port of Haifa with the loss of 200 people.
7. Israeli forces crossed into Egyptian territory in the Sinai Peninsula on October 29, 1956, and occupied El-Kuntilla.

HESHVAN 25

1. King John Hyrcanus reduced Samaria, the capital of the Samaritans, in the year 109 B.C.E. The anniversary of this victory was designated a holiday.
   The Samaritans, an ancient sect which has survived to the present day, had posed a serious threat to the political and religious integrity of the Jewish community in the land of Israel for more than eight centuries. The Hasmonean conquest of Samaria put an end to this internal threat.
2. Riotous mobs attacked the Jewish community of Cracow on October 26, 1407.
3. Rabbi Mordecai Gimpel Jaffe, writer and Zionist pioneer, died on November 26, 1891.
4. On October 30, 1956, Israel captured the Egyptian military post at El-Thamad, a supply base near Nakhl and the fortified road junction of Kusseima. Parachutists landed at the Parker Memorial near the eastern mouth of the Mitla Pass, 180 miles from the Israeli border.

HESHVAN 26

1. The first printed edition of Immanuel of Rome's *Mahbarot* was published on October 30, 1491.
2. Rabbi Raphael Yekutiel Zalman, author of *Torat Yekutiel*, died on November 11, 1803 (DYY).
3. Rabbi Meir Menahem Bouk, author of *Hukkat ha-Pesah*, died on October 30, 1842 (DYY).
4. The first Jewish wedding in Buenos Aires, Argentina, was performed on November 11, 1860 (*Jewish Year Book*, Buenos Aires, 5714).
   Spain had barred Jews from Argentina. Seven years after the Span-

ish regime was overthrown in 1853, all anti-Jewish restrictions were removed. The first synagogue was founded there in 1862.
See Av 17:5.
5. Nahum Meyer Shaikevich (Shomer), Yiddish novelist and playwright, died on November 24, 1905.
6. The moshav Herzlia was founded in Palestine on November 23, 1924.
7. The first anti-Semitic attack over a radio network in the U.S. was broadcast by Father Coughlin on November 20, 1938.
8. Nazis executed 12,000 Jews of the ghetto of Minsk, Russia, on November 6, 1942.
9. Moses Kleinman, editor of the Hebrew periodical *Ha-Olam*, died on November 28, 1948.
10. Israel captured the Egyptian destroyer *Ibrahim el-Awal* in a naval battle during the Sinai Campaign, on October 31, 1956.
11. Israel captured the Daika Pass and Abu Aweigila on October 31, 1956.
12. The first freighter arrived in the new Israeli port of Ashdod on November 21, 1965.

ḤESHVAN 27

1. Noah left the ark a little over a year after the beginning of the flood (Gen. 8:14).
    The Talmud and Midrash occasionally refer to the 12 months' duration of the flood (*Edduyot* 2:10; *Bereshit Rabbah* 28:9), which appears to be in conflict with the biblical account of the flood ending on the eleventh day after the first anniversary of its inception (Gen. 7:11, 8:14). However, the 11 additional days following the lunar year make up a complete solar year, or 12 solar months. It is likely that the rabbis were referring to 12 solar months inasmuch as the Bible links the solar seasons to the flood.
2. Rabbi Raphael Ashkenazi, author of *Mareh Einayim*, died on November 8, 1825.
3. Rabbi Meir Benjamin Danon, author of *Be'er ba-Sadeh*, died on November 23, 1848.
4. The United States agreed not to protest against Swiss discrimination against American Jews. A commercial treaty permitting such discrimination was ratified on November 8, 1855 (*Jewish Frontier*, September 1956, "U.S. Policy Changes").
5. Simon Aaron Eibeschuetz, Danish Jewish philanthropist, died on November 25, 1856.
6. Israel captured the fedayeen base at Rafa and the Mitla Pass and reached the coastal road on the Gulf of Suez on November 1, 1956.

ḤESHVAN 28

1. Anti-Jewish riots in Bucharest, Rumania, took the lives of many Jews on November 23, 1593.
2. Rabbi Zev Wolf, author of *Nahlat Binyamin*, died on November 15, 1686 (DYY).
3. Rabbi David Lida, author of *Be'er Mayim Hayyim*, died on November 16, 1694 (HY).
4. The *Jewish Chronicle*, oldest Anglo-Jewish newspaper, was published for the first time in London on November 12, 1841.
5. Jews' College, a seminary in London, England, for the training of rabbis and Hebrew teachers, was founded by Rabbi Nathan Adler on November 9, 1855.
6. Senior Sachs, Hebrew scholar, died on November 18, 1892.
7. The Jewish population of Israel reached one million on November 20, 1949.
8. Israel captured Sheham, the base at El-Arish, and the city of Gaza on November 2, 1956. On the same day, an armored brigade reached the Suez Canal opposite Ismailia, ending all operations in the central sector of the Sinai Peninsula.

   Gaza, one of five major Philistine cities, was always considered part of the territory of Israel. It was allotted to the tribe of Judah (Josh. 15:47), which later took possession of it (Judg. 1:18). The repatriates from Babylonia did not resettle the Gaza area, but it was reconquered by the Hasmoneans. There were Jewish settlements in Gaza throughout the Middle Ages, except for the period of the Crusaders. Religious laws relating to the duration of holidays in the land of Israel applied also to Gaza.

   The Council for Immigrant Aid, founded in 1882, investigated conditions in Gaza with a view toward future colonization there by Jews. The committee was impressed with the potentialities of the area and handed in a favorable report (*Zikhronot Erez Yisrael*, vol. 1, p. 404). However, there were no Jews living in the area during the British rule and it remained outside the borders of the new Jewish state.

ḤESHVAN 29

1. Jews were permitted to continue to reside in Alexandria by the treaty of November 8, 641, which sealed the Arab conquest of Egypt.

   Jews settled in Alexandria at the time of its founding in 332 B.C.E.
2. Rabbi Moses Ḥefeẓ (Gentili), author of *Melekhet Maḥashevet*, died on November 11, 1711.

3. Rabbi Hayyim Rapoport of Ostrowiec, author of *Mayim Hayyim*, died on November 6, 1839.
4. The Philadelphia Conference of Reform Rabbis, the first Reform rabbinical convention in the U.S., opened on November 3, 1869. It rejected any movement for the restoration of a Jewish homeland.
5. Israel Bak, founder of the first Hebrew printing press in Jerusalem, and the first modern Jew to engage in farming in the land of Israel, died on November 9, 1874 (*Zikhronot Erez Yisrael*, vol. 1, p. 144).
6. Israel captured Khan Yunis on November 3, 1956. This concluded the occupation of the Gaza Strip.
   See note on Heshvan 28:8; Iyar 27:10.

HESHVAN 30

1. Rabbi Joseph Samuel of Frankfort, author of *Mesorat ha-Shas*, comprehensive talmudic index, died on November 8, 1703.
2. Rabbi Joseph b. Mordecai Ginzburg, author of *Leket Yosef*, died on November 26, 1715 (DYY).
3. American forces marched into New York on November 25, 1783. The Jewish residents, who had fled the city in 1776 because of their revolutionary sympathies, were able to return soon after the retreat of the British.
   See Tishri 2:7.
4. On November 12, 1939, Jews of Lodz, Poland, were ordered by the Nazis to attach yellow armbands to their sleeves.
   See Kislev 2:6; 11:6.
5. Israeli forces, on November 4, 1956, captured the Egyptian military fortifications at Ras Natsrani and the naval batteries commanding the Straits of Tiran.

KISLEV 1

1. The beginning of winter in Israel (Rabbi Judah, *Bava Meẓia* 106b).
2. Egypt was smitten with the plague of boils (ZYO).
3. Emperor Flavius Claudius Julianus (Julian the Apostate), who favored the return of the holy city of Jerusalem to the Jews, was born on November 17, 331.
4. Rabbi Shalom Shakhna b. Joseph, leading Polish talmudist and founder of the first yeshivah in Poland, died on November 12, 1558.
    The mass immigration of Jews from Asia to the European continent brought about a shift of Jewish cultural centers from the Orient to Europe. The first yeshivah on the European continent was established in Spain (Cordova) in the first half of the 10th century. The spread of yeshivot in other countries continued: Germany (Mayence), in the second half of the 10th century; France (Troyes), in the 11th century; and England (London), in the 12th century. Rabbi Shakhna and his teacher, Rabbi Jacob Polak (Sivan 23:3), are considered the founders of the first yeshivot in Eastern Europe. They introduced the new method of *pilpul* (legal dialectics) which became popular in most East European academies.
5. Joseph Siegel (Ish Lito) published, on November 7, 1611, *Givat ha-Moreh*, the first critical discussion of Maimonides' philosophy written in Lithuania.
6. Talmudic volumes were burned in Kamenets-Podolski, Russia, on November 13, 1757, at the instigation of the anti-talmudic followers of Jacob Frank.
7. The first Jewish social and civic club in America was founded in Newport, R.I., on November 25, 1761.
8. The British occupied Tel Aviv and Jaffa on November 16, 1917.
9. Hitler informed his military leaders, at a secret meeting held on November 5, 1937, of his decision to go to war.
10. Israel captured Sharm-el-Sheikh, Egyptian strongpoint at the entrance to the Gulf of Aqaba, on November 5, 1956. The gulf was opened to Israeli shipping.
11. Jacob Cohen, Hebrew poet and writer, died on November 20, 1960.
12. Jacob Glatstein, Yiddish poet and essayist, died on November 19, 1971.

KISLEV 2

1. Kislev 2 was proclaimed a day of fast and prayer in ancient Palestine if no rain had fallen by that date.
2. Isaac (Balthazar) Orobio de Castro, Marrano philosopher and poet, died on November 7, 1687.
3. The General Assembly of New York, on November 15, 1727, passed an act permitting Jews to omit the phrase "upon the faith of a Christian" from the oath of abjuration.
4. Rabbi Moses Mordecai Epstein, head of the Yeshivah of Slobodka, author of *Levush Mordecai*, novellae on the Talmud, died on November 20, 1933.
5. Rabbi Bernard Revel, head of the Rabbi Isaac Elchanan Theological Seminary, founder and president of Yeshiva College (later Yeshiva University), the first college under Jewish auspices in the diaspora, died on December 2, 1940.
6. Jews in the Free Zone of France were ordered, on November 11, 1942, to attach to their clothes a yellow Star of David with the word *Juif*.
7. The Prague Trial of Jewish communists, which opened on November 20, 1952, highlighted Soviet anti-Semitism.
8. Rabbi Aaron Kotler, talmudist, Orthodox leader, founder of Bet Midrash Govoha of Lakewood, N.J., died on November 29, 1962.

KISLEV 3

1. Roman ensigns and images were removed from the Temple court by order of Pontius Pilate when the Jews threatened a war unto death (Zeitlin, *Megillat Ta'anit*, chap. 9).
2. The first printed edition of *Seder Olam Rabbah*, attributed to the tanna Yose bar Halafta, a chronology of Jewish history from Creation to the time of Emperor Hadrian, was published in Constantinople on October 29, 1516.

A major portion of the Bible is devoted to the history of the Jewish people. Postbiblical literature, on the other hand, failed to give much space to historical records. It was undoubtedly felt that a chronicle of oppression would serve no useful purpose. There were periods, however, when the need for a written chronology was strongly felt. A major catastrophe could conceivably obliterate all oral tradition and sever the sense of continuity. Ancient victories had to be perpetuated for the sake of morale. Martyrdom, too, had to be immortalized as an epitaph to an era. The Books of the Maccabees were written when

Rome threatened Judean independence. *Megillat Ta'anit*, a chronology of feasts celebrated in the period of the Second Commonwealth, was edited, according to the Talmud, shortly before the destruction of the Temple. The close of the era of the Talmud, precipitated by waves of persecution, produced *Seder Olam Rabbah*.

3. The first auto-da-fé in the Americas, in which a number of Jewish martyrs were burned, was held at Lima, Peru, on October 29, 1581.
4. 36 Jews were killed in an explosion in Lemberg (Lwow), Poland, on November 23, 1702. The anniversary of this tragedy was observed as a communal fast day.
5. Rabbi Joseph David of Salonika, author of responsa *Bet David*, died on November 7, 1736 (DYY).
6. Purim of Amtchislav (Mstislavl, Belorussian S.S.R.) was annually observed by that community in commemoration of a happy event on November 13, 1844.
7. Emma Lazarus, Jewish American poetess, died on November 19, 1887.
8. Israel Fine, Hebrew poet, died on November 23, 1930.
9. The first Nazi mass murder of Warsaw Jews took place on November 15, 1939.
10. 1,538 Jews of Poltava, Russia, were executed by the Nazis on November 23, 1941.
11. Israel occupied Shu'ut, Sheikh Nieran, and Khirbat Main on December 5, 1948, consolidating its hold on the Negev.

KISLEV 4

1. A delegation of Babylonian Jews arrived in Jerusalem in 518 B.C.E., to inquire from the prophet Zechariah whether the fast of Av should be discontinued (Zech. 7:1).

    It took five years to construct the Second Temple, from 520 to 516 B.C.E. The Babylonian delegation arrived in 518 B.C.E., two years after the construction had begun. Their inquiry mentioned only the fast of Av, which was the principal post-exilic fast day. The discontinuation of this fast would, ipso facto, have led to the elimination of the other three fast days.
2. Jews of Pressburg, Hungary (now Bratislava, Czechoslovakia), were expelled on November 9, 1526, by decree of Maria of Hapsburg.

    Queens were dominated and influenced by fanatical clergy to a greater degree than kings, and they often proved more heartless than their male counterparts. Such was the case with Isabella of Spain and her daughter, Isabella of Portugal, who instigated the tragic expulsions from Spain and Portugal (Kislev 5:1); with Empress Maria Theresa of Austria, who expelled the Jews from Bohemia (Tevet 13:2); and with Catherine I of Russia, who expelled the Jews from the Ukraine (Iyar 15:9).

3. Rabbi Elijah Kovo of Salonika, author of *Aderet Eliyahu*, died on November 27, 1688.

4. A private Purim was observed by the Jewish community of Tiberias to commemorate the lifting of a siege by Suleiman Pasha of Damascus, on December 1, 1742 (Ya'ari, *Zikhronot Erez Yisrael*, vol. 1, p. 96).

5. Empress Elisabeth, on December 1, 1742, ordered the expulsion of all Jews from Great Russia.

6. The first Reform Prayer House of Berlin was closed by Emperor Frederick William III of Prussia, on December 6, 1815, on the ground that it was detrimental to the established rights of the Jewish "Church."

7. The Anti-Nazi League was incorporated on November 22, 1933, for the purpose of combating racial discrimination.

8. Rabbi Baruch Ber Leibowitz, talmudist, head of the Yeshivah of Kamenetz, died on November 16, 1939.

9. "Life certificates" were distributed to some of the Jewish residents of the Vilna ghetto on November 24, 1941. Those who did not receive the certificates were deported to extermination camps.

10. Louis Ginzberg, talmudist and scholar, author of *The Legends of the Jews*, died on November 11, 1953.

KISLEV 5

1. The period of grace given to the Portuguese Jews in the decree of expulsion of December 5, 1496 (Kislev 29:2) came to an end on October 31, 1497.

2. Rabbi Samuel Eliezer b. Judah ha-Levi Edels (Maharsha), eminent talmudic commentator, author of *Ḥiddushei Maharsha*, died on November 30, 1631.

   Maharsha attained unprecedented popularity among students of the Talmud. The study of his novellae has been a must for all talmudic scholars since 1680, when his work was included in the printed editions of the Talmud.

3. Fast day of the Jewish community of Posen, Poland, in commemoration of assaults by anti-Semitic gangs on their quarters on November 10, 1687. The Jewish quarters were successfully defended by the Jews and the attackers were repulsed (Berenfeld, *Sefer Ha-Dema'ot*, vol. 3).

The fast day of Posen commemorates one of the earliest successful self-defense actions engaged in by a medieval Jewish community. Jews fought heroically to repel Chmielnicki's murderous hordes in the 17th century, but they rarely succeeded in saving their lives. Only in the few exceptional instances when the Polish nobility supported the Jews were they able to escape destruction. In the Posen mob violence of 1687, the Jews fought a battle which lasted for three days and they emerged triumphant.

4. Solomon b. Joshua Maimon, philosopher, died on November 22, 1800.
5. The Hebrew Education Society met in Philadelphia on December 4, 1864, and resolved to establish a Jewish Theological Seminary, the first in America.
6. Rumanian Jews were barred, on December 4, 1864, from the practice of law.
7. Saul Pinchas Rabinowitz (Shefer), writer and historian, died on December 6, 1910.
8. The Nazis set up ghettos in the districts of Radom, Cracow, and Galicia on November 14, 1942.
9. The "Road of Valor," cut through the Hills of Judea to connect besieged Jerusalem with the rest of the Yishuv, was officially opened on December 7, 1948.
10. The settlement of Mishmar David was founded in Israel on December 7, 1948.

Mishmar David, the new settlement bordering on the Road of Valor, was named for David (Mickey) Marcus, the West Pointer who was instrumental in the building of the new road and the lifting of the siege of Jerusalem.
11. Dr. Pinkhos Churgin, Hebrew scholar and author, founder and first president of Bar-Ilan University in Israel, died on November 28, 1957.
12. The Alma oilfields in the Gulf of Suez were surrendered by Israel to Egypt on November 25, 1979.

KISLEV 6

1. Rabbi Isaiah b. Abraham ha-Levi Horowitz (Shelah) arrived on November 19, 1621, in Jerusalem, where he completed his famous book, *Shenei Luhot ha-Berit*.
2. Charles II, on December 3, 1685, barred Jews from settling in Stockholm, Sweden.
3. Rabbi Zevi Hirsch Rosanes, author of *Tesha Shitot*, novellae on the Talmud, died on November 9, 1804.

4. Rabbi Jacob of Karlin, author of *Mishkenot Ya'akov*, died on November 17, 1844.
5. Mordecai Isaac Yast, the first Jewish historian to write a Jewish history in a modern European language, died in Frankfort on November 20, 1860.
6. The first issue of the *American Hebrew*, an Anglo-Jewish periodical, was published on November 21, 1879.
7. Rabbi Jacob Brill, author of *Mavo ha-Mishnah*, died on November 29, 1889.
8. Rabbi Jonathan b. Mordecai, author of *Darkhei Hora'ah*, died on November 20, 1898.
9. Jacob Benjamin Katzenelson (Ben-Yemini), Hebrew and Yiddish writer, died on November 26, 1930.
10. The recapture of Rostov by Russian forces, on November 26, 1941, marked the first major setback suffered by Germany in World War II.
11. Jerusalem's new reservoir was opened on November 18, 1958. The city was assured of an adequate supply of water for the first time in its long history.

    Jerusalem's greatest weakness in time of military siege was its chronic shortage of water. The city's collapse during the Arab siege of 1948 had been avoided by the construction of the Road of Valor (Kislev 5:9). Exactly 10 years after the opening of that road the new reservoir was opened to assure an adequate supply of water for the holy city.
12. David Ben-Gurion, founding father of modern Israel and its first prime minister, died on December 1, 1973.
13. The U.N. Assembly, on November 10, 1975, adopted a resolution defining Zionism as "a form of racism and racial discrimination."

KISLEV 7

1. King Jehoiakim burned the scroll which had been dictated by Jeremiah to Baruch b. Neriah in 603 B.C.E. (Jer. 36:23). This date was proclaimed a fast-day (*Megillat Ta'anit*, concluding chap.).
2. Death of King Herod the Great, 4 B.C.E. The anniversary of this date was proclaimed a holiday (*Megillat Ta'anit* 9).

    According to Josephus, Herod the Great died in the month of Adar. Some historians amended the text of *Megillat Ta'anit* by substituting the name of King Alexander Jannaeus the Hasmonean, who died in the year 76 B.C.E. Professor Zeitlin suggests that the ancient holiday of Kislev 7 commemorated the victory of the Jews over the Roman general Cestius on November 25, 65.

3. Abraham ibn Ezra published a pamphlet, *Iggeret ha-Shabbat*, on October 30, 1158.
4. The first printed edition of the Former Prophets with Kimhi's commentary was published on October 15, 1485.
5. Rabbi Judah Aryeh Leib b. David of Amsterdam, author of *Gur Aryeh*, died on November 10, 1709.
6. Marcus Baer Friedenthal, scholar, author of *Ikkarei Emunah*, died on December 3, 1859.
7. An armistice, marking the end of World War I, was proclaimed on November 11, 1918.
   World War I broke out on Tishah be-Av. It came to an end on Kislev 7, an ancient Jewish holiday.
8. The Genocide Convention was unanimously approved by the U.N. General Assembly on December 9, 1948.
9. Rabbi Jacob Moses Harlap, author of responsa *Bet Zevul*, died on December 6, 1951.

KISLEV 8

1. Solomon Molcho, Marrano kabbalist and mystic, was burned at the stake on November 7, 1532.
2. Rabbi Menahem Seforno, author of *Netivot ha-Hokhmah*, died on November 19, 1643.
3. Rabbi Isaac Navon of Jerusalem, author of *Dayan Emet*, novellae on Maimonides and the *Tur*, died on November 29, 1786.
4. The U.N. General Assembly passed a resolution, on November 22, 1974, approving the right of the Palestinians to a sovereign state at the expense of Israel.

KISLEV 9

1. Jews of Paris and the entire royal domain of France were expelled by Charles VI for the last time on November 3, 1394.
   This expulsion brought to an end the medieval Franco-Jewish community, although the Jews of Lyons continued undisturbed for another 25 years. The last remnants of French Jewry, the Jews of Provence, were expelled in 1493. It is curious that almost exactly a century elapsed between each of the major expulsions of the large West European Jewish communities: English Jewry was expelled in 1290 (Heshvan 3:2), French Jewry in 1394, and Spanish Jewry in 1492 (Av 9:12).

2. Abraham b. Meir, known as "Der Shtehendiger Chosid," died on December 2, 1813.
3. Rabbi Isaac Grosshaber, author of *Makel No'am*, died on November 19, 1825.
4. Rabbi Dov Baer Schneersohn of Lubavich, known as the "Middle Rebbe," author of *Imrei Binah*, died on November 28, 1827.
5. The American Jewish Joint Distribution Committee for the relief of Jewish war sufferers was established on November 27, 1914.

   The Joint was organized on the eve of Sabbath Va-Yeẓei. It is in the portion of the Bible read that week that the classical expression of Jewish voluntary charity was first enunciated: "And of all that thou shalt give me, I will surely give the tenth unto thee" (Gen. 28:22). See note on Ḥeshvan 23:9.
6. Illegal Jewish immigrants who had reached Haifa aboard the *Atlantic* were deported by the British to the island of Mauritius on December 9, 1940.

   See Elul 16:9.
7. The first Israeli train arrived in Gaza on November 13, 1956, after its occupation by Israel.

KISLEV 10

1. Rabbi Simon b. Israel Frankfurter, author of *Sefer ha-Ḥayyim*, died on December 9, 1712.
2. Yechiel Michael Zabludowsky, Hebrew scholar and author, died on November 14, 1869.
3. Moses Joseph Novomisky (M. Olgin), Yiddish writer, died on November 22, 1939.
4. 27,000 Jews were taken out from the Riga ghetto for execution on November 30, 1941.
5. Heinrich Himmler ordered the demolition of the Auschwitz crematoria on November 26, 1944.
6. A U.N. Conciliation Commission was appointed, on December 12, 1948, to mediate the Israeli-Arab conflict.
7. Rabbi Isser Zalman Meltzer, head of the Yeshivah of Slutsk and then of the Eẓ Ḥayyim Yeshivah in Jerusalem, author of *Even ha-Ezel*, novellae on Maimonides, died on November 17, 1953.
8. President Anwar el Sadat of Egypt addressed the Knesset in Jerusalem on November 20, 1977.

KISLEV 11

1. Abraham of Augsburg, a proselyte to Judaism, was martyred on November 21, 1265.
2. Rabbi Moses Mordecai Margolis of Cracow, author of *Hasdei ha-Shem*, died on December 2, 1615.
3. Rabbi Jacob Isaac Halevi of Pressburg, author of *Imrei Ravrevei*, novellae on the Talmud, died on November 27, 1762.
4. Rabbi Raphael b. Yekutiel Suskind, author of *Torat Yekutiel*, died on November 27, 1762 (TP, 597).
5. Rabbi Jehiel b. Aaron Heller of Plungian, Lithuania, author of *Amudei Or*, died on November 14, 1861.
6. Hans Frank, Nazi governor of Poland, issued an order, on November 23, 1939, requiring all Jews to wear a white armband with a blue Star of David embossed on it.
   See Heshvan 30:4; Kislev 2:6.
7. 7,000 Jews of the ghetto of Minsk, Russia, were executed on November 20, 1942.
8. The charter of Yeshiva College was amended by the New York State Board of Regents on November 16, 1945, making it the first American university under Jewish auspices.

   Christian universities were closed to Jewish students throughout the Middle Ages. There were very few exceptions to this rule. The most famous schools were in countries from which Jews had been expelled so that Jewish students had no access to them. Furthermore, universities were primarily ecclesiastical schools, closely linked to the Church, and as a result, Jewish students were inevitably excluded, even in countries where Jews enjoyed the right of residence. The University of Padua, Italy, was a notable exception. From the middle of the 16th century it attracted Jewish students from all over Europe. The University of Leyden, Holland, adopted a similar liberal policy in the 17th century. The earliest known effort to establish a university under Jewish auspices was made in Sicily. King John granted authorization, on January 17, 1466, to open such a school (Tevet 29:2) but the project never materialized. Rabbi Abraham Provençal attempted to found a Jewish university in Italy in the 16th century, but he too failed.

   The first Jewish university was established in Jerusalem. It opened on April 1, 1925 (Nisan 7:6). Yeshiva University was the first Jewish university in America, established in the tradition of the American pluralistic cultural pattern.

KISLEV 12

1. Rabbi Solomon Luria (Maharshal), famous talmudist, author of *Yam shel Shelomoh*, novellae on the Talmud, died on November 7, 1573 (JE).
2. Pasha Muhammad ibn Farukh, tyrannical governor of Jerusalem, was driven from the city on December 1, 1626 (Ya'ari, *Zikhronot Erez Yisrael*, vol. 1, p. 71).
3. Solomon Schechter, discoverer of the Cairo Genizah and founder of the United Synagogue of America, died on November 19, 1915.
4. Alexander Harkavy, Yiddish writer and lexicographer, died on November 24, 1939.
5. Dr. Ben-Zion Mosenson, Hebrew writer and scholar, died on November 21, 1942.
6. Rabbi Abba Hillel Silver, Zionist leader and author, died on November 28, 1963.

KISLEV 13

1. Ravina, co-editor of the Babylonian Talmud, died in 499. His death marked the end of the talmudic period *(Iggeret Rav Sherira Gaon)*.
2. Azariah b. Moses Dei Rossi, author of *Me'or Einayim*, essays on Jewish history, died on November 12, 1578.
3. Rabbi Moses Darshan of Cracow, author of *Darash Mosheh*, died on November 17, 1736.
4. Mass murder of the Jews of Mogilev, Podolia, December 9, 1761.
5. Rabbi Jacob b. Samuel Meyuḥas, talmudist, was martyred on November 23, 1768 (DVY).
6. Rabbi Joseph Samuel Landau, author of *Mishkan Shiloh*, died on November 22, 1836.
7. New Palestinian schools, with Hebrew as the official language of instruction, were opened on December 12, 1913, ending the prolonged "battle of languages."
8. Hillel Zlatopolsky, Zionist leader, founder of Keren Hayesod (Palestine Foundation Fund), was murdered in Paris on December 12, 1932.
9. The first ḥasidic town in the United States, New Square, N.Y., elected its first mayor on November 21, 1961.

    The population of New Square, at the time of its establishment, consisted of 69 families, comprising 530 souls.

KISLEV 14

1. Birth of Reuben, Jacob's first son (*Midrash Tadshe*).
2. Joseph Shalom Gallego, neo-Hebraic poet, died on November 25, 1624.
3. Czar Nicholas I of Russia issued a decree, on November 13, 1844, providing for the establishment of schools for Jewish students and a seminary for the training of rabbis and teachers.
4. Rabbi Solomon Zalman Abel, author of *Bet Shelomoh*, addenda to the code, died on November 25, 1882 (HY).
5. Abraham Michael Sharkansky, Yiddish poet, died on November 20, 1907.
6. David Goldstein, Yiddish poet, died on November 24, 1931.
7. A Nazi ordinance of December 4, 1941, placed the Jews of Poland outside the civil and penal law, and beyond the protection of the courts (Poliakov, *Harvest of Hate*, p. 40).
8. The first plane in Operation Magic Carpet, the transportation of Yemenite Jews to Israel, left Aden on December 16, 1948.
9. The Israeli flag was hoisted atop Mt. Sinai on December 18, 1956.

KISLEV 15

1. An altar dedicated to Zeus Olympius was set up by Athenaeus, the Syrian in charge of public worship, in the Temple of Jerusalem, 167 B.C.E.

    See Kislev 25:4.
2. Rabbi Nathan ben Jehiel of Rome completed his classic talmudic dictionary, *Ha-Arukh*, on November 24, 1105, one year before his death.

    Two classic keys to the Talmud have been the priceless heritage of all talmudic students ever since the 12th century. These keys made the Talmud an open book to all who desire to study it. The first is the commentary of Rashi, the second is Rabbi Nathan's dictionary, *Ha-Arukh*. Both date from the year 1105. Rabbi Nathan completed his dictionary in that year. Rashi's final revision of his commentary came to an abrupt end with his death on July 13, 1105 (Tammuz 29:1).
3. Pulver Purim, a private Purim, was set aside by Rabbi Abraham Danzig, author of *Hayyei Adam*, to be celebrated annually in commemoration of a miraculous escape on November 18, 1804.
4. Rabbi Simhah Bunem Sofer, author of *Shevet Sofer*, a book of responsa, died on December 15, 1902.

KISLEV 16

1. Rabbi Solomon Calahora, famed talmudic scholar, died on November 28, 1566.
2. Rabbi Joshua Isaac Yair Hurwitz of Lemberg, author of *Emmunot ve-De'ot*, died on November 21, 1850.
3. Hermann Ahlwardt, apostle of modern German anti-Semitism, was elected to the Reichstag on December 5, 1892.

   Nazi anti-Semitism was an offshoot of 19th-century modern German racism, of which Ahlwardt was a leading figure. His election to the Reichstag marked the beginning of political anti-Semitism through its involvement in national politics. With singular foresight he linked the success of German anti-Semitism with American sympathy and support. In furtherance of this objective, he undertook, in 1896, a personal lecture tour through the United States in order to spread his gospel of hate. The tour ended in complete failure and brought about his decline.

   See Kislev 20:8
4. The Nazi governor-general of Poland, Hans Frank, on November 28, 1939 ordered the transformation of the Jewish *Kehillah* organization into the Judenrat.

   The Judenrat, unlike the *Kehillah*, could not sponsor Jewish communal activities and enjoyed no autonomous rights. Its function lay primarily in the implementation of Nazi orders.
5. The 22nd World Zionist Congress met in Basle, Switzerland, on December 9, 1946. It approved resistance to British colonial policy in Palestine.
6. The first Japanese ambassador to Israel presented his credentials on December 9, 1957.

KISLEV 17

1. Jews of Augsburg, Germany, were massacred on November 29, 1349.
2. Many Jews lost their lives in anti-Jewish riots which broke out in Paris on November 16, 1380.
3. Luis de Carabajal, first Jewish author in America, and his mother, Francisca Nuñez, were burned in an auto-da-fé in Mexico City on December 8, 1596.
4. Rabbi Isaac Korite, kabbalist, author of *Ma'aseh Rokem*, died on November 20, 1804.

5. Jews of Nassau, Germany, were granted equality on December 12, 1848.
6. Rabbi Solomon Baer, author of *Divrei Shelomoh*, died on December 9, 1868.
7. Anti-Jewish violence broke out in Bucharest, Rumania, on December 12, 1897.
8. Rabbi Joseph Josel Horowitz, founder of the Nowardok (Novogrudok) Yeshivah, which concentrated on a dynamic approach to *musar*, died on November 28, 1920.
9. Abraham Adelson, Hebrew journalist, leader of the Hovevei Zion movement, died on December 7, 1922.
10. The death marches of Hungarian Jews were stopped by order of Heinrich Himmler on December 3, 1944.
11. The U.N. voted in favor of the partition of Palestine on November 29, 1947.
12. The Arab terrorist campaign opened in Palestine on November 30, 1947.

KISLEV 18

1. Rabbi Abraham Maimon ha-Nagid (also known as Abraham Maimuni), son of Moses Maimonides, author of *Milḥamot ha-Shem*, died on December 7, 1237.
2. The first printed edition of *Ḥazut Kashah*, popular book of parables by Rabbi Isaac Arama, was published in Sabionetta, Italy, on November 10, 1551.
3. The directory council on the district of Strasbourg, Alsace-Lorraine, decreed, on November 22, 1793, the prohibition of the rite of circumcision and the wearing of beards. It also ordered the burning of all books written in Hebrew.

   This prohibition is illustrative of the frenzy of the extremists of the French Revolution in their anti-religious campaign. Not since the days of the Roman Emperor Hadrian and the persecutions of Yezdegerd II in the year 456 during the neo-Persian period, were Jews subjected to such legislation. The Nazis banned circumcision in most of the ghettos and concentration camps.
4. Rabbi Moses Zevi Hirsch Meisels (Meizlisch), author of responsa *Ḥemdah Genuzah*, died on December 5, 1800.
5. Professor Chaim Weizmann, first president of Israel, was born on November 27, 1874.

6. Rabbi Mordecai Eliasberg, author of *Shevil ha-Zahav*, leading pioneer of the Ḥovevei Zion movement, died on December 11, 1889.

7. The first kibbutz, Deganyah Alef, was founded in Palestine on December 1, 1909.

   The colony played an important part in the War of Independence. Left defenseless in the face of advancing Syrian forces, since the only trained Israeli forces were withdrawn to aid in the defense of Jerusalem, the Deganyah defenders repulsed the attempt of the enemy to continue its westward advance. The U.N. resolution to internationalize Jerusalem was passed on the anniversary of the founding of Deganyah (Kislev 18:11), but was never implemented.

   See Sivan 20:5.

8. Polish forces attacked the Jewish community of Lemberg (Lwow) on November 22, 1918.

9. Simon Dubnow, eminent historian, was killed by Nazis in Riga, Latvia, on December 8, 1941.

10. Canada recognized Israel on December 20, 1948.

11. The U.N. General Assembly passed a resolution, on December 9, 1949, calling for the internationalization of Jerusalem.

KISLEV 19

1. Ferrara, Italy, was shaken by a violent earthquake on November 18, 1571. The Jewish community miraculously escaped disaster.

2. Rabbi Abraham b. Moses Halperin Ashkenazi, author of *Ahavat Zion*, died on November 5, 1649.

3. Rabbi Dov Baer of Mezhirech, known as the "Maggid of Mezhirech," famous ḥasidic leader, died on November 26, 1771.

   The Maggid of Mezhirech and his disciple, Rabbi Shneur Zalman of Lyady, were the two moving spirits of early Ḥasidism and were equally instrumental in promoting the phenomenally rapid spread of the movement. Kislev 19 is a significant day to many Ḥasidim. It is the yahrzeit of the Maggid and also the day on which Rabbi Shneur Zalman was released from jail. His release legalized the ḥasidic movement in Russia.

4. Rabbi Shneur Zalman, author of *Tanya*, the philosophy of Ḥabad Ḥasidism, and the founder of the Lubavitch ḥasidic movement, was released from the St. Petersburg jail on November 27, 1798.

5. Jews of Saxony, Germany, were granted civil equality on December 3, 1868.

6. Herbert H. Lehman, prominent leader of American Jewry, first Jewish governor of New York, died on December 5, 1963.

KISLEV 20

1. Ezra urged the Jews who had assembled in Jerusalem to purge the Jewish community of all foreign elements and to dissolve all inter-marriages, 456 B.C.E. (Ezra 10:9).
2. The first printed edition of the talmudic tractate *Sanhedrin* was published on November 16, 1497.
3. Arabs attributed a severe shortage of water in 1521 to the use of sacramental wine by the Jews of Jerusalem. On November 20, all wines were dumped and a heavy fine was imposed on the Jewish community.
4. Rabbi Manasseh ben Israel, the famous rabbi of Amsterdam who was responsible for the resettlement of Jews in England, died on November 26, 1657.

   Manasseh ben Israel believed that the restoration of Israel hinged upon the prior total dispersion of Jews throughout the world. This belief motivated his successful efforts to gain the readmission of Jews into England. His eagerness to discover Jews in every part of the world led to his willing acceptance of the theory that the Indians of North America were the descendants of the lost ten tribes.
5. Rabbi Dov Berish of Byala, author of *Divrei Zaddikim*, died on December 18, 1837.
6. Rabbi Isaac Elijah Landau, preacher and communal leader, author of *Ma'aneh Eliyahu*, died on December 6, 1876.
7. Leo Pinsker, author of *Autoemancipation*, died on December 21, 1891.
8. Hermann Ahlwardt, member of the Reichstag and notorious leader of German anti-Semitism, was imprisoned on December 9, 1892, as a result of a libel suit in which he was the defendant.

   See note on Kislev 16:3
9. Rabbi Zevi Perez Chajes of Vienna, writer and scholar, died on December 14, 1927.

KISLEV 21

1. Mt. Gerizim Day, an ancient festival, marked the Jewish victory over the Samaritans in the year 331 B.C.E.(*Megillat Ta'anit* 9).
2. Rabbi Moses of Lublin, author of *Mahadura Batra*, novellae on the Talmud, died on November 25, 1668.
3. Austrian military forces pillaged and killed many Jews in Prague on November 25, 1744.
4. Rabbi Benjamin Rapoport of Berezhany, Galicia, author of *Gevulot Binyamin*, novellae on the Talmud, died on December 8, 1770.

5. Rabbi Jacob Meir Padua of Brisk, talmudist, author of *Mekor Hayyim*, died on December 12, 1854.
6. Leopold Stein, neo-Hebraic poet, died on December 2, 1882.
7. Isaac Levovich Ashkenazi, famous painter of Jewish scenes, died on December 21, 1902.

KISLEV 22

1. Crusaders wounded Rabbi Eleazar b. Judah of Worms, liturgical poet and author of *Sefer ha-Roke'ah*, classical work on customs and ceremonies. His wife and two children were killed on December 4, 1197.
2. Charles IV issued Letters of Protection to the Jews of Strasbourg, Alsace, on November 25, 1357.
   The Letters of Protection proved worthless two years later. An enraged mob, stirred by rumors of well-poisoning, burned 1,000 Jews and forced the remainder into baptism.
3. Rabbi Eliezer b. Elijah Ashkenazi of Cairo, author of *Yosef Lekah*, commentary on the Book of Esther, died on December 13, 1585.
4. King Christian IV of Denmark, on November 26, 1622, invited the Jews of Amsterdam to settle in Norway, guaranteeing them freedom of religion.
5. Rabbi Shalom Margintu, author of *Darkhei Shalom*, died on November 30, 1809.
6. Getzl Zelikovitch, Yiddish writer, died on November 28, 1926.
7. Rabbi Zevi Judah Maisels of Lask, Poland, author of responsa *Hedvat Ya'akov*, died on December 21, 1932.
8. Mordecai b. Hillel ha-Kohen, Hebrew writer, who delivered the first Hebrew speech at the 1st Zionist Congress, died on December 6, 1936.
9. David Yellin, pioneer Hebraist, died on December 12, 1941.
10. The Knesset, on December 13, 1949, voted to transfer Israel's seat of government to Jerusalem.
11. Izhak Ben-Zvi was elected second president of Israel on December 10, 1952.

KISLEV 23

1. An announcement by Rudolph of Oron, bailiff of Lausanne, on November 15, 1348, that some Jews had confessed to the poisoning of wells in the Rhine Valley, started a "year of terror" which swept away most of the Jewish communities of Alsace.
2. Massacre of the Jews of Nuremberg in the Black Death riots on December 5, 1349.
3. An agreement, signed upon the surrender of Muslim Granada to the Castilian Christian forces on November 25, 1491, provided for the peaceful departure of Jews and Moors from the province.
4. A charter for the establishment of Congregation Mikveh Israel of Savannah, Ga., was granted on November 30, 1790.
5. Rabbi David Tevele Schiff, rabbi of the Great Synagogue, London, author of *Leshon Zahav*, died on December 8, 1792.
6. Rabbi Hayyim Trier, kabbalist, author of *Be'er Mayim Hayyim*, popular commentary on the Pentateuch, died on November 27, 1812.
7. David Friedlander, writer and communal leader, first Jew to sit in the Berlin municipal council, died on December 25, 1834.
8. Shalom Jacob Abramovitsch (better known as Mendele Mokher Seforim), father of modern Hebrew and Yiddish literature, died on December 8, 1917.
9. Anti-Jewish riots broke out in the protectorate of Aden on December 6, 1947; 75 Jews lost their lives.
10. Israel captured Bir Tamila and Mushrife, in the Negev, on December 25, 1948.

KISLEV 24

1. The foundation of the Second Temple was completed in 520 B.C.E. (Hag. 2:18).

   The eve of Hanukkah marks three important anniversaries: (1) the completion of the foundation of the Second Temple; (2) the prophecy of Haggai predicting the restoration of Israel; (3) the liberation of Jerusalem by the British.

   See note on Tishri 21:3.
2. The prophet Haggai predicted, in 520 B.C.E., the downfall of the Persian Empire and the salvation of Israel (Hag. 2:20).
3. Numerous Jews were killed in Hanover and Brussels in the Black Death riots of December 6, 1349.

   See Kislev 23:1.

4. The first printed edition of Jedaiah b. Abraham Bedersi's *Behinat Olam* was published on December 12, 1484.
5. The first printed edition of Bahya ibn Paquda's *Hovot ha-Levavot* was published on November 18, 1489.
6. Rabbi David Conforte, kabbalist and historian, author of *Korei ha-Dorot*, died on December 21, 1704.
7. Aaron b. Moses Fuld, scholar, leader of German Orthodox Jewry, died on December 2, 1847.
8. The new Austrian constitution, adopted on December 21, 1867, abolished all civil disabilities based on religious differences.
9. Raphael Nathan Nata Rabbinovicz, talmudic scholar and antiquarian, author of the monumental work *Dikdukei Soferim*, died on November 28, 1888.
10. The British captured Jerusalem from the Turks on December 9, 1917.
11. Rabbi Judah L. Magnes, president of the Hebrew University of Jerusalem, died on December 26, 1948.
12. The desecration of a new synagogue in Cologne, Germany, on Christmas Eve, December 24, 1959, sparked a wave of anti-Jewish incidents throughout Western Europe, the Americas, Australia, and Africa.
13. Franz Stangl, the SS commander of Hitler's Treblinka death camp in Poland, was sentenced on December 22, 1970, to life imprisonment.

    Stangl was arrested in Brazil in 1967. It is estimated that 781,000 persons, more than half of them Jews, died at Treblinka between July 1942 and October 1943.

KISLEV 25

1. First day of Hanukkah.
2. Cain killed Abel *(Bereshit Rabbah* 22).
3. The construction of the Tabernacle was completed by Moses *(Numbers Rabbah* 13).

    Two important Second Temple anniversaries coincide with two anniversaries of the Tabernacle: the dedication of the Second Temple was on Adar 23 (1 Esdras 7), which is also the anniversary of the dedication of the Tabernacle (Adar 23:3), and the Hasmonean reconsecration of the Temple took place on the traditional anniversary of the completion of the construction of the Tabernacle.

    1 and 2 Maccabees as well as Josephus stress the significance of the coincidence between the dates of the profanation of the altar (Kislev 25:4) and its rededication by the Maccabees (Kislev 25:5). There seems

to be a subtle implication that the Maccabees chose Kislev 25 for its historical significance.

4. The first pagan sacrifice was offered on the altar of Zeus Olympius in the Temple in Jerusalem, 168 B.C.E.

5. Judah Maccabee cleansed the Temple and offered the daily sacrifice on the new altar, 165 B.C.E.

6. Rabbi Solomon Zalman, talmudist, father of the Gaon of Vilna, died on December 25, 1758.
   Grandfather and grandson died on the same date, 50 years apart (no.9).

7. Rabbi Moses Israel of Rhodes, author of *Moshe Yedaber*, died on December 12, 1781.

8. Rabbi Jacob Israel of Kremenets, Russia, famed preacher, author of *Shevet me-Yisrael*, died on December 23, 1799.

9. Rabbi Abraham b. Elijah of Vilna, author of *Midrash Aggadat Bereishit*, died on December 14, 1808.

10. Baruch b. Jonah Zeitelis, talmudist and communal worker, author of *Ammudei ha-Shahar*, died on December 18, 1813.

11. Order No. 11 was issued from General Grant's headquarters in Hot Springs, Miss., on December 17, 1862, providing for the expulsion "within 24 hours" of "the Jews, as a class" from the Department of Tennessee.
    See Tevet 16.2.

12. Rabbi Jacob Ettlinger, author of *Bikkurei Ya'akov*, dissertation on the laws of Sukkot, died on December 8, 1871.

13. The moshav Zikhron Ya'akov was founded in Palestine on December 6, 1882.

14. The moshav Menahemiyyah was founded in Palestine on December 25, 1902.

15. Rabbi Hayyim Hezekiah Medini, author of *Sedeh Hemed*, a twenty-volume talmudic encyclopedia, died on December 3, 1904.

16. The General Federation of Labor (Histadrut) was organized in Palestine on December 6, 1920.

17. The department of Jewish studies was founded at the Hebrew University of Jerusalem on December 22, 1924.

18. 53 Jews, comprising the first batch of hostages rounded up by the Nazis in Paris, were executed on December 15, 1941.

19. The strategic base of Auja, in the southwestern Negev, was captured by Israel on December 27, 1948.
    The capture of Auja marked the end of the Egyptian campaign on Israeli soil. Thereafter the Egyptian army concentrated on the defense of Egyptian soil.

20. The first synagogue built in Spain in 600 years was dedicated in Madrid on December 16, 1968.
See note on Tevet 1:17
21. The order of expulsion of the Jews issued by King Ferdinand and Queen Isabella in 1492 was officially voided by the government of Spain on December 16, 1968.
The order of expulsion was, in effect, annulled by the constitution of 1869, which granted religious tolerance to all residents of Spain. The barrier to legal residence of Jews in Spain was thereby removed. But nearly a century was to elapse before an official revocation of the original order was promulgated by the Spanish government.
See Nisan 2:3.

KISLEV 26

1. Second day of Ḥanukkah.
2. *Iggeret Rabban Yoḥanan b. Zakkai*, a letter to the Jewish community of Rome, allegedly written by the famous tanna as a warning against early Christian missionary activities, was dated Kislev 26, 53 C.E.
The letter represents a rare specimen of Jewish polemical literature. Unlike Maimonides' *Iggeret ha-Shemad*, which was addressed to Jews who had been forced to convert to Islam, the *Iggeret Rabban Yoḥanan b. Zakkai* exhorted Jews in Christian countries not to be misled by missionaries into voluntary conversion. Its extensive usage of kabbalistic terminology is conclusive evidence that it was written, at the earliest, in the 13th century. It may have been inspired by Maimonides' letters, which had gained universal fame. Its outspoken criticism of Christian theology leads us to the assumption that it originated in a Muslim country.
3. The First Crusade was proclaimed by the Council of Clermont on November 26, 1095.
4. Rabbi Abraham b. David of Posquieres (Rabad), talmudic scholar, author of critical annotations on the code of Maimonides, died on November 27, 1198.
5. The Touro Synagogue of Newport, R.I., the oldest existing synagogue in the U.S., was dedicated on December 2, 1763.
6. Rabbi David of Novogrudok, author of *Galya Masekhet*, novellae on the Talmud, died on December 5, 1836.
7. Emancipation was granted to the Jews of Hungary on December 23, 1867.

8. Gederah, the first settlement of the Biluim, was founded in Palestine on December 14, 1884.
9. Eliezer Ben Yehuda, leader of the movement for the revival of the Hebrew language in Palestine, died on December 16, 1922.
10. The Israeli army crossed the Egyptian border on December 28, 1948.
11. The rebuilt Rashi Chapel in Worms, Germany, was dedicated on December 4, 1961.

    The synagogue was among those destroyed in the notorious Kristallnacht of November 9, 1938 (see Heshvan 15:8). The original synagogue of Worms was built and destroyed many times in its history, the first time by the Crusaders in 1096. The Rashi Chapel was added to the main building in 1642. (A stone chair allegedly used by Rashi as a student was hidden in the Worms city museum in 1938 and thus escaped destruction.)

    The synagogue was rebuilt by the German government at a cost of about $125,000. The post-war Jewish population of Worms numbered 22 persons, compared with 1,200 before the Nazi era.
12. The World Council of Churches, meeting in New Delhi, India, on December 4, 1961, called upon its 198 member denominations to "resist every form of anti-Semitism."

    The council, representing both Protestant and Orthodox churches, took note of Pope John XXIII's removal of the reference to "perfidious" Jews from the Roman Catholic Good Friday liturgy. The resolution requested that Christian teachings should not be presented in a light which would fasten upon modern Jews "responsibilities which belong to our corporate humanity." The call to "resist every form of anti-Semitism" was issued on the 846th anniversary of the proclamation of the First Crusade (no. 26:3), which let loose a flood of hatred and violence upon the Jewish communities of Western Europe.
13. Leivick Halpern (H. Leivick), famous Yiddish poet and playwright, died on December 23, 1962.
14. 11 persons, 9 of them Jews, were convicted in Leningrad, on December 24, 1970, for the attempted hijacking of a Russian plane. Two of the Jews were sentenced to death.

    The trial, part of an anti-Semitic campaign to discourage Jewish emigration to Israel, aroused worldwide protests by Jews, the Vatican, democratic governments, and Western Communist parties. The death sentences were subsequently commuted by the Soviet Supreme Court.
15. A peace conference between Israel, Egypt, and Jordan opened at

Geneva on December 21, 1973, under the auspices of the U.N., and the joint chairmanship of the United States and the Soviet Union.

KISLEV 27

1. Third day of Ḥanukkah.
2. The biblical flood rains stopped (Gen. 8:3; Rashi, according to Rabbi Eleazar).
3. Emperor Frederick III expelled the Jews of Schlettstadt (Sélestat), Alsace, on December 12, 1479.
4. The first printed edition of *Mikra'ot Gedolot*, the rabbinical Bible, was published in Venice, Italy, on December 11, 1517.
5. Rabbi Raphael Solomon Zeror, author of *Peri Zaddik*, died on December 20, 1737.
6. Jews of Breslau, Silesia, were expelled on December 9, 1738.
7. The synagogue of Congregation Beth Elohim, the fourth oldest in the United States, was dedicated in Charleston, S.C., on December 19, 1794.
8. Judah Leib Levin (Yehalel), Hebrew poet, died on December 14, 1925.
9. Israel captured Abu Aweigila, an important Egyptian junction, on December 29, 1948.
10. Shmuel Yosef Agnon and Nelly Sachs shared the Nobel Prize for literature, awarded on December 10, 1966. It was the first international recognition of a Hebrew writer.
11. Rev. Georges de Nantes, a reactionary priest, was found guilty on December 11, 1974, by a Parisian court of libeling Jacques Isorni, author of *The True Trial of Jesus*, which attributed the crucifixion of Christ entirely to Pontius Pilate.

    Jacques Isorni, an ultra-conservative French lawyer, based his exoneration of Jews of the charge of deicide on biblical and historical research. According to Isorni, Jesus was executed because of his rebellion against the Roman occupation and not due to Jewish pressure.

    The Abbot de Nantes accused Isorni of falsifying the New Testament and of being a Christian renegade and an "unpaid lawyer for the Jewish people."

KISLEV 28

1. Fourth day of Hanukkah.
2. Rabbi Uziel Maisels, author of *Tiferet Zevi*, novellae on the Talmud, died on November 30, 1785.
3. Rabbi Baruch Yuteles of Prague, author of *Ta'am ha-Melekh*, died on December 21, 1813.
4. Rabbi Abraham Dov of Avritz, author of *Bat Ayin*, comments on the Pentateuch, died on December 23, 1840.

    Rabbi Abraham Dov was rabbi of the Ashkenazic community of Safed. He was captured by the Druze and held for ransom. When the money was not forthcoming, they placed a sword at his throat and threatened to use it if there was no immediate payment. The rabbi, calm and courageous, asked to make a last request. His captors were so impressed when, instead of pleading for his life, the rabbi asked for water to wash his hands so he could recite his final prayers, that they thereupon released him from captivity.

KISLEV 29

1. Fifth day of Hanukkah.
2. King Manuel I, on December 5, 1496, ordered the expulsion of all Jews from Portugal.

    See Kislev 5:1; Nisan 15:15.
3. Rabbi Hezekiah b. David daSilva, author of *Peri Hadash*, famous commentary on the code, died on December 6, 1695.
4. The first Yiddish newspaper, the weekly *Direnfurter Privilegirte Zeitung*, was published in Direnfurt, Germany, on December 6, 1771.
5. Rabbi Gedaliah b. Isaac of Lunitz, author of *Teshuvot Hen*, a book of sermons, died on December 12, 1784.
6. Rabbi Abraham b. Samuel Meyuhas, kabbalist, author of *Sedeh ha-Arez*, responsa and sermons, died on December 20, 1767.
7. Rabbi Shneur Zalman of Lyady, author of *Tanya*, was released from imprisonment by the Russian government on December 16, 1800 and permitted to carry on his hasidic work.

    Early Hasidism met with violent opposition from the rabbinic leadership of Lithuanian Jewry. The latter viewed with suspicion the emergence of the new sect, with its leanings to mysticism, which might duplicate the tragic events of the Shabbetai Zevi movement. The authority of the government was occasionally invoked to help suppress dissident groups. Such was the case with the imprisonment

of Rabbi Shneur Zalman, the suppression of the first Reform movement in Berlin (Kislev 4:6), and the decree against changes in the
"divine service" (Tevet 7:4).

8. Rabbi Meshullam Solomon ha-Kohen, author of *Bigdei Kehunah*, died
   on December 17, 1819.
9. Jews of Tel Aviv were expelled by the Turkish authorities and sent to
   Egypt on December 17, 1914.
10. Max Brod, author, dramatist, and musician, died on December 20,
    1968.

KISLEV 30

1. Sixth day of Ḥanukkah.
2. Rabbi Samuel Levin Eger, author of *Atteret Paz*, died on December 3,
   1842.
3. Equality was granted to the Jews of Wurttemberg, Germany, on
   December 3, 1861.
4. A congress of Hungarian Jews which convened on December 14,
   1868, resulted in the splitting of the Jewish community into three
   religious factions.

   The congress, dominated by sympathizers of Reform, organized a
   liberal community, known as the Israelite Chancery. The Orthodox
   followed in 1871 with the establishment of the Orthodox Israelite
   Chancery. In 1929, those communities which had remained independent of either national group, formed their own national organization.

TEVET 1

1. Seventh day of Ḥanukkah.
2. Egypt was smitten by the plague of *barad* (Exod. 9:24; ZYO).
3. King Nebuchadnezzar of Babylonia marched into Jerusalem and sent King Jehoiachin and 10,000 Jews into captivity, 597 B.C.E. (2 Kings 24:11–14; ZYO).
4. Esther was presented to King Ahasuerus (Esther 2:16).

   The marriage of Esther to Ahasuerus is a unique event in Jewish history, reflecting social and political conditions completely devoid of racial and religious discrimination. Even after Esther's disclosure of her origin, her position and influence at the court were in no way prejudiced or undermined. The intermarriage of Esther was viewed by traditionalists as an exceptional event, divinely ordained to effectuate the salvation of Israel. It is ironical to note that Tevet 1, the anniversary of Esther's presentation to the king, is also the anniversary of Ezra's convocation, summoned to undo the threat to Judaism posed by the widespread intermarriages in his period.
5. Ezra opened a convocation on the problem of intermarriage, 456 B.C.E. (Ezra 10:16).
6. The second printed edition of *Kol Bo*, a popular compilation of customs and ceremonies, was published in Constantinople on November 23, 1519.
7. Manuel Fernando de Villareal, Portuguese Jewish statesman, was executed by the Inquisition of Lisbon on December 1, 1652.
8. Rabbi Yair Ḥayyim Bacharach, author of responsa *Ḥavvot Yair*, died on January 1, 1702.
9. A decree, barring Jews from holding leases on land in rural areas, and from keeping inns and taverns in the prohibited areas, went into effect on January 1, 1808, in most provinces of Russia (see Tevet 7:3).
10. Rabbi Solomon Eger, author of *Gilayon Maharsha*, talmudic annotations, died on December 11, 1852 (HY).
11. The Société des Etudes Juives, French society for the study of Jewish history and literature, received official recognition from the government by decree dated December 6, 1896.
12. Ber Borochov, leader of Po'alei Zion, Zionist labor movement, died on December 16, 1917.

71

13. A Nazi Ghetto Decree, passed on December 5, 1937, ordered the eviction of Jews from the fashionable part of Berlin.
14. 13 Haganah members, escorting a convoy to Ben Shemen, Palestine, were ambushed and killed on December 14, 1947.
15. Egypt, on January 2, 1949, agreed to negotiate an armistice with Israel.
16. A public synagogue was dedicated in Madrid, Spain, on January 2, 1949.

    The first synagogue in Madrid since 1492 was established in 1917, during World War I. Its opening followed the signing by King Alfonso XIII of a law passed by the Spanish Cortes, voiding the prohibition of synagogues in Spain. World War II and the Nazi persecution led to a modest influx of Jews into Spain. The second synagogue since 1492 was dedicated on January 2, 1949; it was ultimately relocated and rededicated in 1959. The first newly constructed synagogue in Madrid was dedicated on December 16, 1968 (Kislev 25:20).
17. A national referendum, held on December 14, 1966, approved a new Spanish constitution which included a provision for free exercise of religion to be granted to Jews and Protestants.

    The granting of legal status to Judaism was the culminating step in a series of liberal enactments. The existence of synagogues in Spain had been legalized in 1917 (see note on Tevet 1:16), and the situation was clarified in a Statement of Tolerance adopted in 1945. Jewish communal worship was permitted, but synagogues could not display any symbols or insignia on the exterior walls. In 1965 the government granted legal status to the organized Jewish community of Madrid as the representative of its Jews. The new constitution removed all restrictions on the free exercise of religion and permitted the Jewish community to own a cemetery. The constitution was approved on the anniversary of the dedication of the Madrid synagogue. (See Sivan 18:7).

TEVET 2

1. Eighth day of Ḥanukkah.
2. Rabbi Meir b. Ezekiel ibn Gabbai, prominent kabbalist, completed the manuscript of *Marot Elohim* on December 22, 1530 (ATGY).
3. 300 Jews of Bychow, Russia, were massacred on December 17, 1659.
4. The first Yiddish newspaper in Poland, *Der Beobakhter an der Weykhsel*, was published in Warsaw on December 4, 1823.
5. The first written proposal to introduce Reform Judaism in America

was published in a memorial signed by 47 members of Congregation Beth Elohim of Charleston, S.C., on December 23, 1824.·

The Reform movement gained momentum in the wake of the growing political and economic emancipation of Jews in Europe and America. Unlike the ancient dissident sects of Israel, which introduced new dogmas and, at times, a strict fundamentalism, modern Reform sought merely the liberalization of Orthodox traditions. It reflected to a large extent, a universal trend emanating from the Renaissance which aimed at the lessening of religious discipline and practices. Reform Judaism early evolved into a social rather than a theological creed, providing a modus vivendi for the non–observant Jew in the midst of a non-Jewish society.

6. Rosh Pinnah, first Jewish settlement in the Galilee, was founded on December 12, 1882.
7. Vilna massacres ended on December 22, 1941, having taken a toll of 32,000 Jews.
8. The Arab Legion of Jordan laid siege to Jerusalem and isolated it from the rest of Palestine on December 15, 1947.
9. Yehuda Karni, Hebrew poet, died on January 3, 1949.

TEVET 3

1. The first printed edition of the Siddur of Rabbi David b. Joseph Abudarham was published in Lisbon on November 25, 1489.

The popularity of Abudarham's work is attested by the nine editions which were published in the four centuries following its initial publication. Much of the information included in the Siddur was culled from rare ancient manuscripts which are no longer in existence.
2. Rabbi Noah Mendes, author of *Parparot le-Ḥokhmah*, died on December 22, 1797 (DYY).
3. Anti-Jewish riots broke out in Warsaw on December 25, 1881.

TEVET 4

1. Isaac ha-Levi Satanow, Hebrew scholar and poet, died on December 25, 1805 (JE).
2. Rabbi Moses Zev of Bialystok, author of *Marot ha-Ẓova'ot*, novellae on the code, died on December 30, 1829 (DYY).
3. Solomon Ettinger, Yiddish playwright, died on December 31, 1856.

4. Rabbi Joshua Isaac Shapira of Slonim, known as Reb Eisele Harif, author of *Emek Yehoshua*, novellae on the code, died on January 3, 1873.
5. Israel David Miller, Orthodox writer, militant opponent of Haskalah movement, died on January 2, 1914.

   Miller was one of many spokesmen of Russian Orthodox Jewry who fought the Haskalah (Enlightenment) movement, which was founded in 1863 (Tevet 10:9). Reform Judaism gained no foothold in Russia because of the medieval anti-Jewish repression, widespread poverty, and exclusion of the masses from secular education. The Haskalah leaders sought to introduce Western culture and standards to the backward East European Jews. As a substitute for religion, Haskalah embraced a passionate nationalism. Different conditions prevailed in Western Europe and America, where the combination of freedom and economic prosperity fostered the Reform movement. The early reformers branded Jewish nationalism a reactionary force.
6. Jews were excluded by the Nazis from all employment benefits on December 16, 1939.
7. The Cairo Peace Conference, with the participation of Egypt, Israel, the U.S. and the U.N., opened on December 14, 1977.

TEVET 5

1. News of the destruction of Jerusalem reached the prophet Ezekiel, 586 B.C.E. (Ezek. 33:21).

   The prophet Zechariah mentions four commemorative fast days which were introduced in the post–exilic period: "The fast of the fourth, and the fast of the fifth, and the fast of the seventh, and the fast of the tenth . . . " (Zech. 8:19). According to Rabbi Akiva, the prophet referred to the fast of Tammuz 9 (4th month), Tishah be-Av (5th month), Fast of Gedaliah (7th month), and the fast of Tevet 10 (10th month). They were listed in the order of their sequence in the religious calendar, commencing with Nisan as the first month. Rabbi Simon, however, felt that the fasts were listed by the prophet in their historical order. He therefore interprets the "fast of the tenth" as referring to a fast of Tevet 5, in commemoration of the day when news of the destruction of Jerusalem reached the diaspora (*Rosh ha-Shanah* 18b). Thus it was the last of the four fasts adopted by Babylonian Jewry. Rabbi Simon's opinion did not prevail. Since Zechariah limits the number of post-exilic fast days to four, the inclusion of a fast on Tevet 5 would automatically exclude the fast of Tevet 10. Ezekiel 24:2,

however, makes it quite clear that Tevet 10 was to become a commemorative day.

2. Dutch municipalities were granted home rule on December 12, 1619.
The law gave each locality the right to permit its Jewish residents to
meet in public assembly.

   The granting of home rule in Holland was an important step taken
by the government toward the normalization of freedom of religious
practice by its Jewish population. The concentration of Jews in Amsterdam made the question of freedom of worship an urgent issue.
The first public Jewish service was held in that city in a private home
in 1596 (Tishri 10:17); the first synagogue was dedicated in 1597 (Tishri
1:18). Home rule permitted the gradual spread of religious freedom
throughout the country.

3. The Dutch States General issued a proclamation on December 26,
1634, guaranteeing freedom of religion to Jews and Catholics in Brazil
(UJE).

4. Empress Catherine of Russia issued a ukase, on December 31, 1791,
restricting the right of Jewish residence in Russia, the beginning of
the notorious Pale of Settlement.

5. New York City authorities issued a warning on December 29, 1870
cautioning the Jewish community that incompetent and unscrupu-
lous *mohelim* were causing the death of many Jewish infants (*AJHSP*,
no. 37 p. 43).

6. Mathias Strashun of Vilna, Russia, bibliophile, author of *Reḥovot
Kiryah*, died on December 13, 1885.

TEVET 6

1. A special Jewish badge was introduced for the first time in the Middle
Ages, by a decree of Pope Innocent III on November 30, 1216.

   The badge was not a Christian innovation. It was used by the
Sassanid rulers of Persia in the 3rd century in their persecution of
Christians. Caliph Haroun al-Rashid, in 807, ordered that Jews wear a
yellow badge, Christians a blue badge, and Magians a black badge.
The badge introduced by Pope Innocent III was enforced in most
Catholic countries for five centuries. It had disappeared by the end of
the 18th century but was re-introduced by the Nazis in 1939 (Heshvan
30:4).

2. Rabbi Meir of Emdin, author of *Tevu'ot Shemesh*, died on December 25,
1808.

3. A seminary for the training of traditional rabbis and teachers was

opened by its founder, Dr. Sabato Morais, on January 2, 1887, in New York.

The seminary, a predecessor of the Jewish Theological Seminary, used the facilities of Congregation Shearith Israel. The first class had an enrollment of eight students, among them Joseph H. Hertz, who later became chief rabbi of the British Empire.

4. Israeli forces shot down five British planes flying over the battle front on the Egyptian border on January 7, 1949.
5. David Shimoni, Hebrew poet, died on December 10, 1956.
6. Rabbi Morris B. Tomashov (Mabit), author of *Avnei Shoham* and editor of *Yagdil Torah*, a prominent talmudic journal, died on January 6, 1960.

TEVET 7

1. Rabbenu Ameimar b. Mar Yenuka, Rabbi Mesharsheya b. Pekuda, and Huna bar Mar Zutra, the exilarch of Babylonian Jewry, were arrested by Mazdaite officials of Persia on December 7, 468. The arrests foreshadowed a wave of persecution of the Jews of Babylonia (*Iggeret Rav Sherira Gaon*).
   See Tevet 18:1.
2. Hevrat Doreshei Leshon Ever, a society for the promotion of the study of Hebrew, was founded in Berlin on December 12, 1782.
3. Czar Alexander I of Russia, on December 9, 1804, issued a Statute Concerning the Organization of the Jews.
   The so-called Jewish Constitution of 1804 was presented as a charter of new liberties for Jews by a government moved "by solicitude for the true welfare of the Jews." In reality, it camouflaged an edict of economic ruin for half of Russian Jewry. By the terms of this charter Jews were barred from holding leases on land or from keeping taverns and inns in the provinces of Astrakhan, Caucasia, Little Russia, New Russia, and most other provinces, beginning on January 1, 1808.
   See Tishri 13:3.
4. The Prussian government, on December 9, 1823, decreed that "the divine service of the Jews must be conducted in accordance with the traditional ritual and without the slightest innovation in language, ceremonies, prayers and songs."
   The decree was aimed at the fledgling Reform movement in Germany, which had provoked the fierce opposition of Orthodoxy. Its purpose was twofold, support of traditionalism in all segments of society, and maintenance of law and order. The intervention of the authorities came at the behest of traditionalist Jewish leaders who

failed to perceive the inherent danger of government aid in the suppression of dissident religious views. Unfortunately, historical precedence had established the lesson that intervention by the authorities in internal Jewish affairs is eventually detrimental to the Jewish community.

5. Rabbi Ezekiel Baneth of Neutra, Hungary, talmudic scholar and pietist, died on December 28, 1854.

6. Nahum Slouschz, early Zionist, orientalist, and traveler, died on December 20, 1966.

 He was the son of Rabbi David Solomon Slouschz (Shevat 20:5).

TEVET 8

1. Ancient fast-day, commemorating the completion of the Greek translation of the Pentateuch, known as the Septuagint (*Megillat Ta'anit*).

 The translation of the Bible into Greek was considered a tragic event by the early rabbis. Although its purpose was to meet the needs of Greek-speaking Jews in Alexandria, Syria, Mesopotamia and Asia Minor, it was extensively used by early Christian missionaries. Widespread Jewish proselytizing in the declining period of paganism was not hampered by the lack of a translation of the Bible. Judaism attracted the intellectual elite. Christianity went after the masses, to whom the language barrier would have been insurmountable. The rabbis deplored the need for the Septuagint both as a symptom of the growing Jewish ignorance of the Hebrew text and as a bridge to the outside world which was destined to drain some of the Jewish vitality and strength.

 The Talmud attributed the publication of the Septuagint to the initiative of King Ptolemy (*Ta'anit* 9a).

2. Frei Diogo da Silva was appointed first inquisitior-general of Portugal on December 17, 1531.

3. Lord George Gordon, English convert to Judaism, was born on December 26, 1751 (JE).

4. The National Jewish Hospital for Consumptives was founded on December 10, 1899.

5. Israel's first minister to an Asian country presented his credentials to the emperor of Japan on December 26, 1952.

6. Adolf Eichmann, head of the Jewish Bureau of the SS, was sentenced to death by an Israeli tribunal in Jerusalem, on December 15, 1961, for crimes against the Jewish people and humanity.

TEVET 9

1. Ancient fast day (*Megillat Ta'anit*).
2. Death of Ezra (*Seliḥot of Asarah be-Tevet, Ezkerah Maẓok*).
   Ezra holds a very prominent place in Jewish history generally and in the development of rabbinic Judaism in particular. Tradition ascribes to him many innovations which have become part of the Jewish religious way of life. He was crowned with the title of "Restorer of the Torah" and is regarded as the founder of the Great Assembly, a body in which was vested supreme religious authority to interpret the law. He adopted the square Hebrew script which is still in use today. He instituted the scriptural readings at services on Monday and Thursday mornings and Saturday afternoons. Above all, he is said to have established the synagogue in its all-important central position in Jewish life.
3. Death of Nehemiah (*Kol Bo*).
   Kol Bo's assumption must have been based on the intimate relationship which linked Ezra and Nehemiah in biblical history. There is no historical basis for this assertion, however.
4. Joseph ibn Nagrela, vizier and rabbi of the community of Granada, was crucified at the gates of the city on December 30, 1066; 4,000 Jews lost their lives in the ensuing riots.
5. Rabbi Ezra ha-Navi, tosafist and kabbalist, teacher of Naḥmanides, died on December 20, 1227.
   He is mentioned in Tosafot: *Shavuot* 25a, *Gittin* 88a, and *Bava Batra* 28a.
6. Jews of Speyer, Germany, who returned after their expulsion in 1349, were permitted to open a school and a synagogue on December 24, 1354.
7. Followers of Zechariah of Kiev were burned in Moscow, on December 27, 1503, on charges of Judaizing.
8. Rabbi Abraham Shor of Belz, author of *Ẓon Kadoshim*, died on January 3, 1632.
9. The first room for prayer meetings was opened in Copenhagen, Denmark, on December 16, 1684.
10. All Jewish Kahals in the Russian Empire were abolished by ukase on December 19, 1844.
11. Rabbi Nathan Bratslaver, hasidic scholar, editor of *Likkutei Halakhot*, died on December 19, 1844.
12. Alfred Dreyfus was subjected to military degradation on January 5, 1895.
13. Samuel Charney (S. Niger), Yiddish writer and literary critic, died on December 24, 1955.

TEVET 10

1. Fast of Asarah be-Tevet.
   The fast of Asara be-Tevet is one of four commemorative fast-days mentioned by the prophet Zechariah (8:19): Tevet 10 (siege of Jerusalem); Tammuz 9 (breach of the city walls); Av 9 (destruction of the Temple); Fast of Gedaliah (assassination of the Jewish governor). These fast-days were discontinued after the return from Babylonia and the rebuilding of the Second Temple (Zech. 8:19; *Rosh Ha-Shanah* 18b). Upon the destruction of the Second Temple, the four fast-days were reinstated. The fast of the Tevet 10 and the fast of Gedaliah were reintroduced to commemorate the tragic events before and after the first destruction. Tammuz 9 was replaced by Tammuz 17 to commemorate the breaching of the walls of Jerusalem by the Romans (*Ta'anit* 28b). Av 9 was retained as a commemorative day for the destruction of both Temples.
2. Nebuchadnezzar laid siege to Jerusalem, 588 B.C.E. (2 Kings 25:1).
3. Jeremiah purchased a field and prophesied: "Houses and fields and vineyards shall yet again be bought in this land," 587 B.C.E. (Jer. 32:9–15; *Zikhron Yemot Olam*).
4. Death of the prophet Zechariah b. Berechiah (DDD).
5. Death of the prophet Malachi, the last of the prophets of Israel (DDD).
6. King Herod captured Jerusalem in 37 B.C.E., ushering in his long reign (Josephus, *Antiquities* 14:16; Zeitlin, *Megillat Ta'anit*).
7. Rabbi Judah Leib Eilinburg of Nicholsburg, author of *Minḥat Yehudah*, died on December 26, 1610.
8. Rabbi Jacob Reisher of Prague, author of *Shevut Ya'akov*, died on December 28, 1732.
9. Ḥevrat Mefiẓei ha-Haskalah, a society for the dissemination of modern culture among Russian Jews, was founded on December 20, 1863.
   One of the major achievements of the Haskalah movement was the creation of a modern Hebrew literature. Hayyim Nachman Bialik, who was born on the 10th anniversary of the founding of Mefiẓei ha-Haskalah (no. 10), was one of the greatest contributors to the growth and development of that literature.
10. Hayyim Nachman Bialik, foremost modern Hebrew poet, was born on January 9, 1873.
11. The Decree for the Elimination of Jews from German Economic Life took effect on January 1, 1939.
12. The Nazi district commander of Warsaw decreed, on January 9, 1941, that no Jew was to greet a German in public.

13. 3,000 Jews lost their lives in anti-Jewish riots in Bucharest on January 9, 1941.
14. A wave of massacres came to an end in Simferopol, Crimea, on December 30, 1941, having taken a toll of 10,000 Jewish lives.
15. Memorial Day for the 6 million Jews killed by the Nazis (by proclamation of the Chief Rabbinate of Israel).
16. The first native Jewish child in Spain, since the expulsion in 1492, was born to Mr. and Mrs. Joseph Shuman at Cadiz, on January 2, 1966.

TEVET 11

1. Rav Saadiah Gaon cautioned the Jews of Egypt on December 15, 921, to reject the religious calender adopted by Rabbi Aaron b. Meir, head of the Palestinian yeshivah in Ramleh.

   The religious calendar devised by the talmudic sages is one of the chief instruments linking Jews all over the world into a unified religious community. Early dissidence, threatening the stability of the established calendar, brought swift and stern retributions by Rabban Gamaliel II (*Rosh ha-Shanah* 25a). The unique calendar promulgated by the Book of Jubilees and the calendar of the Qumran sect posed little threat to rabbinic hegemony. The first major challenge to the established calendar was made by the Karaites, who created their own calendar which differed from the traditional calender. The consequent observance of holidays on divergent dates set the Karaites apart from the rest of the Jews and lessened their influence.
2. 100,000 Jews of Sicily were expelled on December 31, 1492.
3. Purim of Lepanto was annually celebrated on Tevet 11 by the Jews of Lepanto (Naupaktos), Greece, to commemorate a miraculous escape from destruction.
4. The Portuguese congregation of Paramaribo, Surinam, appealed on January 9, 1797, to the Ashkenazic congregation to join in the effort of establishing a rabbinical seminary. This is the first record of such a project in the Western Hemisphere.
5. President Abraham Lincoln promised, on December 14, 1861, to press for immediate passage of an amendment to the chaplaincy law, which originally provided for Christian military chaplains only. Soon thereafter Rabbi Arnold Fischel became the first Jewish chaplain.

   This removed the last of the Jewish disabilities in the United States due to creed.
6. Solomon Buber, scholar, editor of midrashic works, died on December 28, 1906.

TEVET 12

1. Ezekiel prophesied the impending downfall of Egypt and the triumph of the Babylonians, 587 B.C.E. (Ezek. 29:1).
2. A violent earthquake rocked Palestine on December 6, 1033. Part of the walls of Jerusalem, the Tower of David, and other structures collapsed (Koblenz, *Treasury of Jewish Letters*, vol. 1, p.131).
   See note on Tevet 24:4.
3. Mordecai and Esther, residents of Medzibezh, saved the Jewish inhabitants from Chmielnicki's army on December 27, 1648. The day was designated "Mordecai Purim."
4. Moses Raphael d'Aguilar, author and book-collector, died in Amsterdam on December 15, 1679.
5. Rabbi Moses b. Simeon Margoliot, author of *Penei Moshe*, popular commentary on the Jerusalem Talmud, died on January 9, 1781.
6. The American Jewish Congress held its first meeting on December 15, 1918, in Philadelphia.
7. The Israel Philharmonic Orchestra was founded on December 26, 1936. Its first concert was played under the direction of Arturo Toscanini.
8. Talks were opened on the island of Rhodes, on January 13, 1949, to discuss an armistice between Israel and the Arabs.

TEVET 13

1. The first work printed by the Hebrew printing press of Amsterdam, a prayerbook, was published on January 1, 1627. The press was founded by Rabbi Manasseh ben Israel.
2. Empress Maria Theresa, on December 18, 1774, issued a decree expelling all Jews from Prague and the rest of Bohemia and Moravia.
   See note on Kislev 4:2.
3. The first Jewish censor was appointed by the Russian government on January 1, 1798, to censor all Hebrew books printed in Russia or imported from other countries.
4. Rabbi Menahem Eliezer of Minsk, author of *Yair Kino*, novellae on the Talmud, died on December 24, 1806.
5. Rumanian Jews were excluded from the medical profession on December 27, 1868.
6. Members of the Baruch family of Alexandria, Egypt, were released from jail on January 4, 1882, and exonerated from ritual murder charges in the Fornaraki affair.

7. Mikhel Gordon, Yiddish poet and Hebrew writer, died on January 5, 1890.

TEVET 14

1. Jews of Laibach, Austria (now Ljubljana, Yugoslovia) were expelled on January 1, 1515.
2. The "Court Jew" Leffmann Behrends, financial agent of the duke of Hanover, died on January 1, 1714.

    The "Court Jew" was an official of considerable importance, attached to the courts of the Austrian emperors and German princes in the 17th and 18th centuries. Court Jews usually served in the capacity of financial agents. Due to their exalted status they enjoyed privileges denied to other Jews. Many Court Jews took advantage of their special position to intercede with the government in behalf of their co-religionists. Leffman Behrends won a well-deserved reputation as a public servant and Jewish leader.
3. Rabbi Moses Sofer, author of *Or Pnei Moshe*, comments on the Pentateuch, died on December 16, 1804 (HY).
4. Window Purim, a private festival of the Sephardic community of Hebron, was observed annually on Tevet 14 in commemoration of the community's delivery from a crushing tax.

    See Av 1:10.
5. The 9th World Zionist Congress met in Hamburg, Germany, on December 26, 1909.

    The political climate of Germany was considered by Jews to be sympathetic to Zionism. Unlike Russia, where Zionist meetings and fund collections were banned on June 24, 1903, the German emperor assured Herzl, on November 2, 1902, of his "good will and interest." Herzl had planned to hold his first congress in Germany in the city of Munich. It was only due to local Jewish opposition that the site was shifted to Basle, Switzerland.
6. The first fund-raising drive of the American Jewish Joint Distribution Committee was launched on December 21, 1915.
7. Pinhas (Piotr) Rutenberg, the industrialist who brought electricity to Palestine, died on December 22, 1942.
8. The population of Israel reached the 3 million mark on January 11, 1971, with the arrival of Mr. & Mrs. Nathan Cherolnikov and their daughter, from Russia.

TEVET 15

1. The first printed edition of *Sefer Mitzvot Gadol*, a popular work by Rabbi Moses b. Jacob of Coucy, was published in Soncino, Italy, on December 9, 1488.
2. Joseph b. Joshua ha-Kohen, historian, author of *Emek ha-Bakha*, an account of Jewish martyrology, was born on December 20, 1496.
3. Simon Ginzburg, Hebrew poet, editor, and scholar, died on January 11, 1944.
4. Solomon Mikhoels, director of the Yiddish Art Theater of Moscow and chairman of the Jewish Anti-Fascist Committee, was murdered in Minsk, Russia, by government agents on January 13, 1952. The murder was the initial move in the drive to liquidate Yiddish culture in Russia.
   See Av 21:11.
5. The first desalinating plant in Israel opened in Eilat on December 31, 1963.
6. Menahem Begin, prime minister of Israel, and Anwar el-Sadat, president of Egypt, met on December 25, 1977, at Ismailia, Egypt, to discuss terms of peace between Israel and the Arabs.

TEVET 16

1. Emperor Joseph II of Austria issued an Edict of Toleration on January 2, 1782, repealing most of the ecclesiastical restrictions of Jews, dating from the time of the Vienna Council.
   The Edict of Toleration failed because its true objective was not emancipation but assimilation. It was therefore opposed by Jews as well as reactionary non-Jews. Napoleon's efforts, a few decades later, to attain the emancipation of Jews, were similarly linked to assimilation. This was equally true of the policies of the Russian government in the 19th century. The history of Jewish emancipation in the Protestant countries of England and Holland took a different course, beginning with the middle of the 17th century, when a large measure of freedom was granted to the Jewish residents. The granting of emancipation stemmed from prevailing liberal policies rather than anti-Jewish prejudices and hopes for their ultimate assimilation and conversion.
2. General-in-Chief Henry W. Halleck instructed General Ulysses S. Grant, on January 7, 1863, to revoke Order No. 11, which had provided for the expulsion of all Jews from the Department of Tennessee.
   See Kislev 25:11.

3. The 5th Zionist Congress met in Basle, Switzerland, on December 26, 1901.
4. Hermann Struck, artist, leader of Mizrachi movement, died on January 12, 1944.
5. The ship *The 29th of November*, carrying illegal Jewish immigrants to Palestine, was driven off the coast by the British on December 29, 1947.

TEVET 17

1. The organization of the Jewish community of Rome was approved by Pope Clement VII on December 12, 1524.
2. Frederick William of Brandenburg, the "Great Elector," issued a decree, on January 3, 1676, safeguarding the privileges of the Jews of Berlin.
3. Rabbi Abraham b. Moses, author of *Zera Avraham*, commentary on the midrash, and a *maggid* (itinerant preacher), died on December 21, 1725.

   The 18th century brought two innovations to the Jewish scene—Hasidism and "Maggidism." The widespread ignorance of rural Jews scattered through the Ukraine and other countries led to lax religious observance. Hasidism stepped into the breach, with a strong appeal to the emotions and enthusiasm of the common people. Like Hasidism, the appeal of the maggid was also directed to the general masses who were outside of the small circle of scholars and students. The immediate impact of the maggidim was strong, but their influence was not enduring. Tevet 17 is the anniversary of two maggidim: Abraham b. Moses, the son of a famous preacher and author, whose homiletical work won great popularity, and the Dubno Maggid, Rabbi Jacob Kranz (no. 6).

4. Congregation Shearith Israel of New York purchased, on December 17, 1728, a lot on Mill Street, lower Manhattan, for the purpose of erecting the first synagogue structure in New York.

   Shearith Israel, organized in 1656, is the oldest congregation in North America. Its first synagogue was dedicated on April 8, 1730 (Nisan 21:10). The six oldest congregations in the United States are: (1) Shearith Israel, New York City; (2) Yeshuat Israel, Newport, R.I., organized in 1677; dedicated its synagogue in 1763; (3) Mikveh Israel, Savannah, Ga., organized in 1733; built its first synagogue in 1820; (4) Mikveh Israel, Philadelphia, Pa., organized in 1745; built its first synagogue in 1782; (5) Beth Elohim, Charleston, S.C., organized in

1749; built its first synagogue in 1794; (6) Beth Shalom, Richmond, Va., organized in 1789.

5. Rabbi Aaron Zelig b. Joel Faivush of Ostrog, Russia, author of *Toledot Aharon*, died on December 31, 1754.
6. Rabbi Jacob Kranz, the Maggid (preacher) of Dubno, author of *Ohel Ya'akov*, a collection of his sermons, died on December 19, 1804. The most famous of the itinerant preachers, he was dubbed the "Jewish Aesop" by Moses Mendelssohn.
7. 40 Jewish workers were killed by Arabs at the Haifa oil refineries on December 30, 1947.
8. Aaron Glanz-Leyeles, Yiddish poet, died on December 30, 1966.

TEVET 18

1. Rabbi Huna Mori bar Mar Zutra, exilarch of Babylonian Jewry, and Mesharshya b. Pekuda were executed in Pumpedita on December 18, 468 (*Iggeret Rav Sherira Gaon*).
   See Tevet 7:1.
2. Pope Martin V issued a bull, on December 23, 1420, banning the conversion of Jewish children under 12 without the consent of their parents.
3. Rabbi Zevi Elimelech Shapira of Dynow, leader in the fight against the Haskalah movement, author of *Benei Yissaskhar*, died on January 11, 1841.
4. The organizational meeting of the National Council of Young Israel, an association of Orthodox synagogues in the U.S., met on December 28, 1912.
5. The first provisional council of Palestinian Jewry was founded on January 12, 1917.
6. The ships *Independence* and *In-Gathering*, carrying illegal immigrants to Palestine, were taken by the British to Cyprus for internment (January 10, 1947).
   Exactly two years later the British announced their decision to release the Jewish internees (no. 7).
7. The British announced on January 19, 1949, their intent of releasing the Cyprus internees.

TEVET 19

1. A petition made by the local Classis (administrative organ of the Church) of Recife, Brazil, on January 5, 1638, led to the closing of both synagogues then in existence in that city.
2. Rabbi Abraham Ashkenazi Halperin, author of *Ahavat Zion*, died on December 30, 1648.
3. Judah Touro, outstanding American Jewish philanthropist, died on January 18, 1854.
4. Rabbi Abraham Samuel Benjamin Sofer, author of the popular *Ketav Sofer*, commentary on the Pentateuch, died on December 31, 1871.
5. Laurence Oliphant, English author, early Christian Zionist, died on December 23, 1888. He envisioned the re-creation of a Jewish nation in Palestine through the acquisition of land, the establishment of Jewish agricultural settlements, and the exploitation of natural resources.
6. Emile Zola published his famous open letter entitled "J'Accuse" on January 13, 1898, forcing a revision of the Dreyfus trial.
7. The Jewish National Fund (Land Redemption Fund) was established at the 5th Zionist World Congress in Basle, Switzerland, on December 29, 1901.

TEVET 20

1. Rabbi Moses b. Maimon (Rambam; also known as Maimonides) outstanding talmudist, codifier, and philosopher, died on December 13, 1204.
2. The first printed edition of the tractate *Berakhot* of the Babylonian Talmud, was published in Soncino, Italy, on December 19, 1483.

   This historic edition included the commentary of Maimonides on the Mishnah. A precedent was thus set for most of the later publications of the Talmud. The tractate was published on Maimonides' 279th yahrzeit (no. 1).
3. An earthquake rocked Ancona, Italy, on December 22, 1690, causing much damage. The Jewish community miraculously escaped unscathed. The event was commemorated by a local fast day.
   See Tevet 21:3.
4. Rabbi Abraham Tiktin of Breslau, author of *Petah ha-Bayit*, novellae on the Talmud, died on January 7, 1820.
5. Adolf Jellinek, Jewish scholar, died on December 29, 1893.
   Jellinek compiled a catalogue of the vast halakhic literature which

had grown up around Maimonides' code. He died on the anniversary of Maimonides' death.

6. Kalman Schulman, Hebrew writer and novelist, died January 2, 1899.
7. The Nazis, on January 1, 1940, prohibited Jews from congregating in synagogues or private homes for prayer.
8. The Nazis prohibited the Jews of occupied Poland from changing their residences, beginning January 1, 1940. This decree foreshadowed the establishment of ghettos.
9. 6,000 Jews lost their lives in Bucharest, Rumania, in the pogroms which broke out on January 19, 1941.
10. Alexander Marx, Jewish historian and bibliographer, died on December 26, 1953.
11. Pope Paul VI visited Christian shrines in Israel on January 5, 1964.
    Sixty years prior to the historic papal pilgrimage to Israel, Theodor Herzl was received in audience by Pope Pius X on January 25, 1904. The pope expressed the opposition of the Church to Jewish control of Jerusalem.

TEVET 21

1. Birth of Simon, son of Jacob (*Midrash Tadshe*).
2. The first printed edition of Albo's *Ikkarim* was published on December 29, 1485.
3. Purim Ancona, celebrated annually on Tevet 21, was instituted in commemoration of the community's miraculous escape from an earthquake on December 22, 1690.
    See Tevet 20:3; Tevet 22:2.
4. Jews of Galicia, Austria, were ordered to adopt fixed and hereditary family names by January 1, 1788.
    The Austrian decree ordering Jews to adopt family names was motivated by the policy of Emperor Joseph II, which aimed at the Westernization of Austrian Jewry. The state officials, however, used this decree to force degrading animal names upon the poor who could not afford to pay the extortionist prices for desirable names.
    See Heshvan 2:3.
5. Rabbi Zevi Hurwitz of Rzeszow, Poland, author of *Ge'on Zevi*, novellae on the Talmud, died on December 29, 1798 (DDD).
6. A Russo-U.S. trade treaty, originally ratified in 1832, was abrogated by President Taft on December 31, 1912, because of Russian discrimination against Jews who were American citizens.

TEVET 22

1. Moses b. Ḥanokh Altschul, the shammash of the Meisel synagogue in Prague, designated Tevet 22 Curtain Purim, in commemoration of the escape of Joseph Thein from the gallows in the year 1622.
2. Anti-Jewish riots broke out in Ancona, Italy, on January 10, 1798.
    The riots broke out on the day following the local Purim, which had been observed by the Ancona Jewish community since 1691 (Tevet 21:3).
3. Roman mobs attempted to set fire to the ghetto of Rome and to sack it on January 10, 1798.
4. A much publicized pro-slavery sermon, delivered by Rabbi Morris J. Raphall of New York on January 4, 1861, evoked a widespread reaction.

TEVET 23

1. A fire broke out on January 14, 1711, in the house of Rabbi Naphtali Katz of Frankfort on the Main. The resulting conflagration practically destroyed the entire Jewish ghetto.
2. Rabbi Jacob Katz, author of *Shev Ya'akov*, died on January 23, 1740.
3. Alexander I of Russia issued an edict on January 13, 1825, ordering the removal of Jews from villages to towns and cities in the governments of Mogilev and Vitebsk.
    See Tevet 1:9.
4. Caucasian Jews who were serfs of Muslim masters were freed on January 13, 1836.
5. Menorah Association, an intercollegiate Jewish students' organization, was founded on January 2, 1913.
6. Nathan Straus, American communal leader and philanthropist, died on January 12, 1931.
7. Dr. Hillel Jaffe, early member of Ḥovevei Zion, fighter against tropical diseases in Palestine, died on January 18, 1936.
8. The Iron Guard revolt in Rumania, on January 22, 1941, led to the first massacre of Jews there in World War II.
9. France extended recognition to Israel on January 24, 1949.
10. Joseph Heftman, Hebrew journalist and editor of *Ha-Boker*, died on January 17, 1955.

TEVET 24

1. The Jews of Tripoli designated Tevet 24 Purim of Sherif in commemoration of a victory in 1745.
2. Haym Salomon, financial agent of Robert Morris, superintendent of finance during the Revolutionary War, died on January 6, 1785.
3. Rabbi Shneur Zalman of Lyady, founder of the Habad hasidic movement and author of *Tanya*, the basic work of Lubavitch Hasidism, died on December 27, 1812.
4. A violent earthquake shook Palestine on January 1, 1837. Over 2,000 Jews were killed in Safed and another 700 Jews lost their lives in Tiberias.
   See Tevet 12:2.
5. Mt. Sinai Hospital of New York, the first hospital in America under Jewish auspices, was founded on January 16, 1852.
6. Jacob b. Moses Bacharach, scholar, author of *Ha-Yahas le-Ketav Ashuri*, died on December 29, 1896.
7. Merhavyah, the first settlement in Israel's Emek Yizre'el, was founded on January 24, 1911.
8. Elections for the first Knesset of the State of Israel were held on January 25, 1949.
9. Israel and Egypt signed an agreement, on January 18, 1974, on the disengagement of their forces in the Suez Canal area.

TEVET 25

1. Anti-Jewish riots broke out in Judenburg and Furstenfeld, Austria, on December 25, 1312.
2. The first critical edition of *Hovot ha-Levavot*, the classical work on Jewish ethics by Rabbi Bahya b. Joseph ibn Paquda, was published in Mantua, Italy, on January 4, 1559.
3. Shalom Jacob Abramowitsch (Mendele Mokher Seforim), founder of modern Hebrew literature, was born on January 2, 1837.
4. Shalom Cohen, poet, editor of *Bikkurei ha-Ittim*, died on January 4, 1845.
5. Salomon Sulzer, famous composer of liturgical music, died on January 17, 1890.
6. Rabbi Moses Levi Ehrenreich, translator of part of the Bible into Italian, died on December 27, 1899.
7. Switzerland extended diplomatic recognition to Israel on January 26, 1949.
   See note on Tevet 28:6.

TEVET 26

1. King Frederick III of Sicily issued a decree, on December 25, 1369, requiring all Jews to wear a special badge.
   See note on Tevet 6:1.
2. Rabbi Naphtali Katz of Frankfort, author of *Semikhat Ḥakhamim*, novellae on the Talmud, died on January 17, 1719. See Tevet 23:1.
3. Rabbi Zevi Hirsh Deutsch of Brody, Galicia, author of *Shulḥan ha-Tahor*, died on January 23, 1781.
4. Rabbi Abraham Ḥayyim of Zloczow, author of *Oraḥ le-Hayyim*, died on December 29, 1812.
5. Maryland's "Jew Bill," which went into effect on January 5, 1826, qualified Jews for public office if they subscribed to a belief in rewards and punishments in the hereafter.
   It was not until 50 years after the establishment of the United States that Maryland permitted its Jewish citizens to hold public office. Ever since the founding of the colony as an asylum for Catholics in 1634, the denial of the validity of Christianity had been a crime punishable by death. Theoretically, every Jew residing in Maryland was liable to legal execution for professing Judaism. The practice of Judaism was legalized in Maryland in 1776 but many civic restrictions had remained in force.
6. Judah Leib Katzenelson (Buki ben Yogli), Hebrew writer, died on January 12, 1915.
7. Dr. Arthur Ruppin, leader of Zionist colonization, died on January 3, 1943.
8. The publication in the Soviet *Pravda*, on January 13, 1953, of a report on "The Arrest of the Group of Doctor-Wreckers," touched off a virulent anti-Semitic campaign throughout Russia.

TEVET 27

1. Rabbi Shabbetai b. Meir ha-Kohen (Shakh) completed the manuscript of his book *Nekudat ha-Kessef* on January 22, 1648.
2. Full civic rights were granted to the Jews of Westphalia by Jerome Bonaparte on January 27, 1808.
3. Rabbi Samuel Austerer of Brody, Galicia, author of *Ketav Yosher*, died on January 2, 1829.
4. Rabbi Samson Raphael Hirsch, theologian and philosopher, dynamic leader of German Orthodox Jewry, died on December 31, 1888.
   Rabbi Hirsch was one of the chief architects of modern Orthodoxy

in Germany. In a country where State and Church were not separated and the Jewish communal representatives controlled the religious life of every Jew, he found it necessary to fight for "separatist Orthodoxy" so that the Orthodox element could survive in the midst of a rapidly assimilating Jewry. The following anecdote is a fitting epitaph to his life. It was his custom to receive three months' salary in advance. When he made out his will he inserted a clause requiring his family to make restitution to the community of part of his salary in the event of his death within the three-month period. His family was spared the effort. He died precisely on the last day of the three-month period.

5. The Federation of Jewish Farmers of America was organized on January 20, 1909.
6. The Jewish National Workers Alliance received its charter on January 6, 1913.
7. Diplomatic recognition was extended to Israel on January 28, 1949, by Australia, Belgium, Chile, Great Britain, Holland, Luxembourg, and New Zealand.

TEVET 28

1. Rabbi Simon b. Shetah reorganized the Sanhedrin by eliminating its Sadducean members. The anniversary of this Pharisaic victory was observed as a holiday (Skolion, *Megillat Ta'anit*, ch. 10).
2. The Sanhedrin met in the year 66 to elect Joseph b. Gorion and the high priest Anan as administrative heads of the government of Judea. The revolt against King Agrippa and Rome made the Jewish state a republic (Zeitlin, *Megillat Ta'anit*).
3. Rabbi Berechiah Berakh b. Isaac Shapiro of Cracow, author of *Zera Beirakh*, a book of sermons, died on January 26, 1664.
4. Rabbi David Nieto, Hakham of the Sephardic community of London, author of *Esh Dat*, died on January 10, 1728.
5. Czar Nicholas I, on January 5, 1837, ordered the discontinuation of all arrangements for the establishment of Jewish settlements in Siberia.
6. Jews of Switzerland were granted civic equality on January 15, 1866.
   The government of Switzerland granted civic rights to Jews after considerable prodding by diplomatic representatives of the United States who had interceded for American Jewish citizens. Just 83 years later, on Tevet 25, 1949, the Swiss government extended diplomatic recognition to Israel, again following the lead of the United States.
7. Micheline Araten, an Austrian Jewish girl, was abducted on Decem-

ber 30, 1899, and taken to a convent. The incident became a cause célèbre.

8. Asher Ginsberg (Aḥad Ha-Am), father of cultural Zionism, died on January 2, 1927.
9. The Arab Liberation Army invaded Palestine on January 10, 1948, and attacked Kefar Szold.

TEVET 29

1. End of winter (Rabbi Judah, *Bava Mezia* 106b).
2. The earliest authorization for the establishment of a university under Jewish auspices, including medical and juridical departments, was granted by King John to Benjamin Romano of Syracuse, Sicily, on January 17, 1466 (Cecil Roth, *Personalities and Events in Jewish History*, p. 110.)

   This authorization is a historical oddity. It reflects the pressing urge for higher education, which was practically barred to Jewish students in Christian Europe. The plans for a university did not materialize, however, since all Jews were expelled from Sicily just 26 years after King John issued his historic grant.

   See note on Kislev 11:8.
3. Recife, Brazil, fell to the Portuguese on January 27, 1654, bringing to an end the legal existence of its prosperous Jewish community.
4. Purim of Tripoli was celebrated annually by the local community to observe the downfall of Burgel Pasha on January 13, 1793.
5. Rabbi Alexander Sander Margolis of Satanov, Russia, author of responsa, *Teshuvot ha-Ram*, died on January 3, 1802.
6. Ezekiel Hart, first Jew to be elected to the Canadian Parliament, was denied his seat on January 29, 1808 because of his refusal to take the customary oath "upon his faith as a Christian."
7. Rabbi Noah Samuel Lipshitz, author of *Zer Zahav*, died on January 2, 1832.
8. Rabbi Nathan Marcus Adler, chief rabbi of the British Empire, author of *Ḥiddushim*, died on January 21, 1890.
9. Rabbi Moses Joshua Leib Diskin, leader of Orthodox Jewry, author of a book of responsa, died in Jerusalem on January 23, 1898.
10. The American Jewish Conference was founded in Pittsburgh on January 6, 1943.

    The American Jewish Conference met for the last time on December 2, 1947. Its dissolution was due to intramural disagreement on the future of Palestine and the refusal of major organizations to submit to the discipline of the Conference (see *Jewish Life*, vol. 32, no. 1, p. 26).

SHEVAT 1

1. The biblical plague of *arbeh* (locusts) *(Zikhron Yemot Olam)*.
2. Moses began to review the Torah; the instructions continued until the day of his death, 36 days later (Deut. 1:3).
3. God commanded Moses to observe the Promised Land from the top of a mountain; he was also instructed to prepare Joshua for the leadership of Israel (Deut. 3:27–28; *Midrash Petirat Moshe Rabbenu).*
    See note on Tishri 22:2.
4. Jews of Genoa, Italy, were expelled on January 8, 1598.
5. The congregational minute-book of Congregation Magen Avraham, Recife, Brazil, one of the two oldest congregations in the Americas, opens with an entry dated January 4, 1649.
    The Jewish community of Recife dated from the conquest of the city by the Dutch in 1631. The number of Jews rapidly grew after the Dutch guaranteed to the Jews in 1634 the free exercise of their religion (Tevet 5:3). The local Calvinist authorities succeeded in closing both congregations in 1638. However, the Jews by that time outnumbered the non-Jews and influenced the national office to compel the reopening of the synagogue in 1642. In the same year they invited Rabbi Isaac Aboab da Fonseca from Amsterdam to head the Jewish community. He was the first rabbi to serve an American Jewish congregation.
6. The first Jewish newspaper, the Judaeo-Spanish *Gazeta de Amsterdam,* was published on January 24, 1678.
7. Rabbi Solomon Lichtenstein of Bialystok, Russia, author of *Hokhmat Shelomo,* died on January 4, 1783.
8. Major David Salisbury Franks, an officer in the American Revolutionary Army, was granted 400 acres of land on January 28, 1789.
9. Rabbi Eliezer b. Joseph of Altona, Germany, author of *Mishnat de-Rabbi Eliezer,* died on January 22, 1814.
10. Rabbi Moses b. Joseph Schick, of Hust, Hungary, author of responsa *Maharam Schick,* died on January 25, 1879.

SHEVAT 2

1. Death of the Hasmonean King Alexander Yannai (Jannaeus), 76 B.C.E. The anniversary of his death was designated a holiday (Megillat Ta'anit).

   King Yannai was a mortal enemy of the Pharisees. During his reign the Sadduceans gained the upper hand and dominated the religious scene. If Yannai's policies had not been reversed upon his death, it is very likely that rabbinic Judaism would have been stifled in the early stages of its development. The anniversary of his death was logically considered to be a happy day by the Pharisees.
2. Rabbi Menahem Mendel b. Abraham Krochmal of Nikolsburg, Moravia, author of responsa Zemah Zedek, died on January 2, 1661 (JE).
3. Rabbi Meshullam Zushya Auerbach of Hanipoli (Annopol), hasidic leader, author of Menorat Zahav, died on January 28, 1800.
4. Samuel Joseph Fin, Hebrew writer, editor of Ha-Karmel, died on January 11, 1891 (OY).
5. The Nazi Gestapo leader, Reinhard Heydrich, on January 20, 1942, met with top representatives of the German police, the SS, and the Nazi Party in the Wannsee section of Berlin to discuss implementation of the "final solution of the Jewish question."

   Hitler was appointed chancellor of Germany on Shevat 3, 1933. On Shevat 10, 1939, he announced in his annual speech that Jews would be exterminated in the event of war (Shevat 10:5). On Shevat 2, 1942, Heydrich outlined the implementation of the final liquidation of the Jewish people. He was appointed head of the Jewish Emigration Office on Shevat 4, 1939.
6. Judah Gur, Hebrew philologist, author of a standard Hebrew dictionary, died on January 20, 1950.

SHEVAT 3

1. Jewish mourners at the funeral of Rabbi Shemariah b. Elhanan (disciple of Rav Sherira Gaon) were attacked in Fostat, Egypt, on January 1, 1012. The anniversary was designated a communal fast-day.
2. Shem Tov b. Isaac ibn Shaprut, physician, philosopher, author of Even Bohan, participated in a public disputation with Cardinal Petro de Luna (later Pope Benedict XIII) on December 26, 1375.
3. Leon b. Joshua completed the manuscript of Sefer ha-Tadir on January 20, 1466. The work included Aramaic and Hebrew texts of the Scroll of Antiochus.

4. The Inquisition was established in Peru on January 9, 1570.
5. Rabbi Joseph Katz, of Cracow, author of *She'arit Yosef,* died on January 28, 1591.
6. Rabbi Joseph Rakover Eibenschitz, author of *Mirkevet ha-Mishnah,* died on January 18, 1706.
7. Mordecai M. Noah, American Jewish diplomat, petitioned the legislature of the state of New York, on January 19, 1820, for the sale of Grand Island in the Niagara River for the purpose of founding there a settlement for Jewish immigrants from Europe.
8. Adolph Hitler was appointed chancellor of Germany on January 30, 1933.
   See note on Shevat 2:5.
9. The Society for Youth Aliyah was established in Berlin on January 30, 1933.
   The society was founded on the day the Nazis came to power in Germany. It transported to Israel over 115,000 children of the ages of 12–16.

SHEVAT 4

1. Meir Bacharach of Pressburg (Bratislava), Hebrew poet, died on January 4, 1729 (JE).
2. Rabbi Moses Leib of Sasov, popular hasidic figure, died on January 13, 1807.
3. Rabbi David b. Mordecai of Brody, Austria, author of *Yefe Einayim,* died on February 3, 1816.
4. Rabbi Asher of Tiktin, author of *Birkat Rosh,* died on January 20, 1866.
5. Hermann Goering appointed Reinhard Heydrich head of the Jewish Emigration Office on January 24, 1939.
6. Yeshivat Kol Ya'akov, a seminary for religious functionaries to provide religious leadership for Russian Jewry, was established in Moscow on January 6, 1957.
   Yeshivat Kol Ya'akov, which was founded in Moscow with the approval of the Soviet authorities, was a token seminary designed to counter charges of Soviet anti-Semitism and suppression of religion. It is of interest to note that the opening of the Moscow yeshivah came close to the 65th anniversary of the dissolution by the Russian government of the Yeshivah of Volozhin (Shevat 5:6), the oldest and most famous of all the yeshivot of Russian Jewry.

SHEVAT 5

1. Charles the Bourbon, king of Naples and Sicily (the Two Sicilies), invited Jews, on February 3, 1740, to return to Sicily.
2. Moses Mendelssohn, famous Jewish philosopher and scholar, died on January 4, 1786.
3. A state of siege was declared in Jerusalem on January 11, 1799, as Napoleon's army approached Gaza and Jaffa.
4. Rabbi Hayyim David Hazzan, of Smyrna, Turkey, talmudist, author of *Torat ha-Zevach*, died on January 17, 1869.
5. Bilu, early Russian Zionist organization, was founded in Kharkov, Russia, on January 25, 1882.

    Several important Palestinian anniversaries fall on the fifth day of Hebrew months. On the positive side of the calendar: Elul 5, 1809—the disciples of the Gaon of Vilna arrived in Safed; Shevat 5, 1882—Bilu was founded, marking the beginning of Zionism; Heshan 5, 1920—Hebrew became one of the official languages of Palestine; Iyar 5, 1948—the State of Israel proclaimed its independence; Kislev 5, 1948—the Road of Valor, which defeated the Arab siege of Jerusalem, was officially opened; Av 5, 1970—a cease-fire went into effect on the Egyptian, Jordanian, and Lebanese fronts. On the negative side: Tevet 5, 586 B.C.E.—the news of the destruction of Jerusalem by the Babylonians reached the Jews of the diaspora; Sivan 5, 68—the Roman general Vespasian left Caesaria to begin his assault on Jerusalem; Tammuz 5, 70—the innermost wall around Jerusalem was captured by the Romans; Nisan 5, 1917—the Jews of Tel Aviv and Jaffa were expelled from Palestine; Adar 5, 1957—Israeli forces completed their withdrawal from the Gaza Strip.
6. The Russian government, on February 3, 1892, ordered the dissolution of the Yeshivah of Volozhin.

    The Yeshivah of Volozhin was closed by the Russian government a few times in the course of its long and illustrious existence. It was closed for the first time in 1879 because the yeshivah leadership would not submit to the modernization decrees of the government. It was subsequently reopened and closed again in 1892 on the pretext that the yeshivah harbored students who were sympathetic to the revolutionaries.

    See note on Shevat 4:6.
7. David Cassel, historian and scholar, died on January 22, 1893.
8. Rabbi Judah Leib Alter, second in succession of the Gerer dynasty, author of *Sefat Emet*, comments on the Pentateuch, died on January 11, 1905.

9. Max Nordau, philosopher, early Zionist leader, died on January 22, 1923.
10. 35 members of Haganah who set out to relieve besieged Gush Ezyon (Ezyon Bloc) were ambushed and killed in the hills of Hebron on January 16, 1948.
11. The genocide pact, ratified by the U.N., went into effect on January 12, 1951.

SHEVAT 6

1. Jews of Majorca were guaranteed protection in an edict issued by the governor on January 21, 1393.
    The edict was issued in order to reassure the Jewish populace after the horrible massacres of August 24, 1391. The Majorca edict, like most medieval protective decrees, was soon forgotten. Ferdinand of Aragon renewed the persecution by a decree issued on March 20, 1413. The Jewish community was destroyed in 1435.
2. Don Alfonso V of Aragon, on December 26, 1424, granted the city of Barcelona the right to exclude Jews for all time.
3. Elijah b. Asher (Baḥur) Levita, grammarian, author of *Bove-Bukh*, the first printed Yiddish book, died on January 5, 1549.
4. Rabbi David b. Joseph of Breslau, talmudist, author of *Shoresh Yosef,* died on January 22, 1752.
5. Kasriel Hersch Sarasohn, journalist, founder of the *Jewish Gazette* and the *Yidisher Tageblat,* died on January 12, 1905.
6. Abraham Goldfaden, composer of the operettas *Bar Kokhba* and *Shulamit,* died on January 9, 1908.
    See Nisan 4:5.

SHEVAT 7

1. A decree requiring compulsory attendance of the Jews of Sicily at conversionist services, was repealed on January 1, 1430.
2. Samuel Cahen, Hebraist, author of an 18-volume translation of the Bible into French, died on January 8, 1862.
    Shevat 7 is the yarhzeit of two famous Bible translators. Samuel Cahen was the first Jew to translate the Bible into French. Yehoash was the author of a literary translation of the Bible into Yiddish (no. 6).
3. Rabbi Isaac Aaron Ettinger of Lemberg, author of *Responsa of Mahari Halevi,* died on January 16, 1891.
4. Isaac Meir Dick, Hebrew and Yiddish writer, died on January 24, 1893.

5. Israel Isidor Elyashev (Baal-Makhshoves), Yiddish essayist, died on January 13, 1924.
6. Yehoash Solomon Bloomgarden (Yehoash), Yiddish poet, author of a classic translation of the Bible into Yiddish, died on January 10, 1927.
7. The 5th Aliyah to Palestine began on February 5, 1930.

SHEVAT 8

1. The period of the Elders, the contemporaries of Joshua, came to an end. The death of the Elders was commemorated by a fast-day (Megillat Ta'anit).
2. Jews of Colmar, Upper Alsace, were arrested on well-poisoning charges on December 28, 1348 and burned on August 24, 1349.
3. Rabbi Elijah b. Moses Israel of Alexandria, author of responsa Kol Eliyahu, died on January 7, 1786.
4. Rabbi Isaac Guetta, author of Sedeh Yizhak, died on February 2, 1857.
5. The first invocation by a rabbi at the opening of a session of the U.S. Congress was delivered by Rabbi Morris J. Raphall on February 1, 1860.
6. Rabbi Isaac Leeser, founder of the Occident and American Jewish Advocate, the leading Anglo-Jewish publication of the United States in its time (1843–69), died on February 1, 1868.
7. The Women's League of the United Synagogue of America was organized on January 21, 1918.
8. Avigdor Shpritzer, author of Yiddish stories and texts for children, died in Buenos Aires, Argentina, on February 4, 1952.
9. The public execution of 9 Jews in Damascus on January 27, 1969, led to worldwide protests.
   The executions were the occasion for the first Vatican protest against Arab racism.
10. Israel and Egypt established normal diplomatic relations on January 26, 1980.

SHEVAT 9

1. Jews of Toulouse, France, who had buried a convert to Christianity who returned to Judaism in the Jewish cemetery, were tried by the Inquisition on January 4, 1278. Rabbi Isaac Males was condemned to the stake (UJE, Inquisition).
   Medieval Christian authorities meted out capital punishment not

only to Christians who had converted to Judaism but also to the Jews who had offered them aid and refuge after their conversion. Rabbi Isaac Males was martyred for permitting the burial of a convert's body on a Jewish cemetery. The severity of the punishment demonstrated the need of a deterrent against those who might feel drawn to Judaism. Among the famous Roman pagans who were attracted to the Jewish faith were Sabina Poppaea, the wife of the Emperor Nero, the Consul Flavius Clemens, nephew of Emperor Vespasian, and his wife, Domitilla Flavia. King Yūsuf Dhu Nuwās, the ruler of Yemen, embraced Judaism in the year 515. The royal court of the Khazars was converted to Judaism in the 8th century.

2. Moses Mordecai Buedinger, educator, author of *Derekh Emunah*, died on January 31, 1841.
3. Rabbi Yehosoph Schwarz, early Palestinian geographer, author of *Tevu'ot ha-Arez*, died on February 5, 1865.
4. Moritz Steinschneider, father of modern Jewish bibliography, died on January 24, 1907.
5. Rabbi Eliezer Silver, leader of American Orthodoxy and dynamic communal worker, author of *Anfei Erez*, talmudic dissertations, died on February 7, 1968.
6. The border between Israel and Egypt was declared open on January 27, 1980.

SHEVAT 10

1. Seven Jews of Bischofsheim on the Baden, Germany, were tortured and burned at the stake on January 1, 1235.
2. The responsa of Rabbi Nissim b. Reuben Gerondi (Ran) were printed for the first time in Rome on January 13, 1546.
3. Dr. Jacob Lumbrozo, first Jewish physician to settle in North America, established himself in Maryland on January 24, 1656 (JE).
4. Rabbi Shalom Sharabi, kabbalist, author of *Emet ve-Shalom*, died on January 25, 1782 (HY).
5. Hitler announced, in his annual speech on January 30, 1939, his intention to exterminate the Jewish race in the event of a war in Europe.
6. Rabbi Joseph Isaac Shneersohn, leader of the Lubavich Habad, died on January 28, 1950.
7. Max Weinreich, a founder of the Yiddish Scientific Institute (YIVO), Yiddish linguist and author of *History of the Yiddish Language*, died on January 29, 1969.

SHEVAT 11

1. A degree ordering the expulsion of Jews from Colmar, Germany, was issued on January 22, 1510.

   The Jews of Colmar, Germany, suffered martyrdom in the 14th century on Shevat 8 (no. 2). Their expulsion was ordered in the 16th century on Shevat 11.
2. Hebrew books and manuscripts which had been confiscated by Church authorities in Rome were burned on January 14, 1601.
3. Baron József Eötvös, Hungarian statesman and emancipator of the Jews, died on February 2, 1871.
4. The English Zionist Federation was founded on January 22, 1899.

   Bilu, the earliest Russian Zionist society, was founded on Shevat 5. The English Zionist Federation was organized on Shevat 11.

SHEVAT 12

1. A decree ordering the expulsion of Jews from Colmar, Germany, was issued on January 22, 1510.

   His father, Rabbi Zevi Hirsch Chajes, was a famous scholar and talmudist. See Tishri 30:2.
2. Nazis provoked the first anti-Jewish riots in Amsterdam, Holland, on February 9, 1941. The attackers were driven off by the Jews.

   The resistance of the Jews of Amsterdam, on Shevat 12, 1941, and the subsequent resistance of the Jews of Warsaw, on Shevat 12, 1943 (no. 3), were successful operations. They failed, however, to attain any lasting results.
3. Jews of the ghetto of Warsaw put up their first resistance to the Nazis' final liquidation efforts on January 18, 1943.

   The early attack in the Warsaw ghetto by a few Jews who were in a column of deportees was merely a prelude to the full-scale uprising which broke out two months later (Nisan 14:13; see also Adar 2:7).
4. Philip Max Raskin, poet and editor, died on February 6, 1944.
5. The Russian army liberated 2,819 survivors of the Auschwitz camps on January 26, 1945.
6. Rabbi Joseph Herman Hertz, chief rabbi of the British Empire, scholar, and author, died on January 14, 1946.

SHEVAT 13

1. Rabbi Israel Samuel Kalihari, author of *Yismah Yisrael*, novellae on the code, died on February 6, 1640.
2. Yuspi Shammash of Worms, author of a historical chronicle of his times, died on February 5, 1678.
3. The French National Assembly, on January 28, 1790, granted full equality and citizenship to the Portuguese and Avignonese Jews. France became the first European country to pass such liberal legislation.

    France pioneered in many phases of Jewish legislation and public relations. It was the first European country to grant full citizenship to Jews. Napoleon was the first modern statesman to promise the restoration of Palestine to Jews (Nisan 15:21). France was also the first European country to grant financial support to the religious institutions of the Jewish community (Shevat 25:3).

    See note on Shevat 23:1.
4. Rabbi Yom Tov Netel, author of *Tehor Ra'ayonim*, died on January 30, 1817.
5. Rabbi Eliezer Landau, author of *Dammesek Eliezer*, died on January 21, 1883 (DDD).
6. Rabbi Kaufmann Kohler, scholar and author, died on January 28, 1926.
7. Benzion Katz, Hebrew scholar and author, died on February 3, 1958.

SHEVAT 14

1. Joseph b. Issachar Suesskind Oppenheimer (Jud Suess), financial expert, was executed in Vienna on February 4, 1738.
    See Shevat 24:4 and note on Tevet 14:2.
2. Rabbi Jacob Joshua Falk, outstanding talmudist, author of *Penei Yehoshu'a*, died on January 16, 1756.
3. The National Federation of Temple Sisterhoods was organized on January 22, 1913.

    American women have played a much greater role in the policy-making and fund-raising activities of American congregations than their sisters in the Old World. The social and economic emancipation of the American woman offered a greater opportunity for participation in synagogue and church affairs. The tendency of many American men to leave all religious and educational problems to their wives left a vacuum which women were quick to fill. The National Federation of Temple Sisterhoods, representing the Reform wing, was organized on January 22, 1913. The Women's League of the United Synagogue of America, representing the Conservative wing, was organized on January 21, 1918 (Shevat 8:7).

SHEVAT 15

1. Hamishah-Asar bi-Shevat (Tu bi-Shevat), the New Year of the Trees (*Rosh Ha-Shanah* 2a).
2. The prophet Elijah ascended to heaven (tradition of Bene Israel of India).
3. The Bene Israel celebrate this anniversary as the holiday of Eliyu Hanabicha Urus—The Fair of Elijah the Prophet.
    The renewal of the soil's life-giving productivity in the spring is symbolic of the resurrection (*Sanhedrin* 90b). Elijah's future role in the resurrection may account for the link in Bene Israel lore of the prophet's ascension with Shevat 15, the New Year of the Trees.
3. Rabbi Nehemiah of Dubrovno, Russia, author of *Divrei Nehemyah*, died on February 7, 1849.
4. The custom of tree-planting on Tu bi-Shevat was initiated by the children of Jerusalem on January 25, 1910.
5. The Haifa Technion was opened on February 9, 1925.
6. The first Siyyum of the Talmud celebrated by Daf Yomi students was held on February 2, 1931.
7. A Nazi decree, published on January 25, 1940, provided for the establishment of a ghetto in Lodz, Poland.
8. The Knesset opened its first session in Jerusalem on February 14, 1949.

SHEVAT 16

1. Rabbi Jonah Navon, author of *Nehpah ba-Kessef*, a book of responsa, died on February 3, 1760.
2. Rabbi Jacob Simon Sofer, of Cracow, author of *Maor Shemesh*, died on January 22, 1837.
3. Markus Edinger, first Jew of Mayence to serve as a juror, died on February 9, 1879.
4. Aaron Bernstein, writer, advocate of religious reform for German Jewry, died on February 12, 1884.
5. Perez Smolenskin, Hebrew novelist, publisher of *Ha-Shahar*, died on February 1, 1885.

Perez Smolenskin, a Russian Jew (Shevat 16:5), and Aaron Bernstein, a German Jew (no. 4), died on the same day, one year apart. Both were distinguished writers and communal workers, and both sought solutions to the Jewish problem. Smolenskin advocated secular nationalism in Palestine, Bernstein advocated Reform Judaism and complete integration with the culture of the country of residence. Russia consistently denied the rights of Jews to national existence in Palestine. Germany ultimately denied the rights of Jews to any kind of existence.
6. Rabbi Shalom Mordecai b. Moses Ha-Kohen Shvadron (Maharsham) of Brezen, Galicia, author of Da'at ha-Torah, died on February 14, 1911.
7. Israel Singer, Yiddish writer, died on February 10, 1944.

SHEVAT 17

1. Purim of Saragossa was celebrated by the Jews of that city in commemoration of their escape from destruction on February 4, 1428.
   Purim of Saragossa was one of many special Purim-type festivals which were instituted in the course of time by individuals or communities in commemoration of happy events. The biblical Purim set the pattern for the manner of celebrating the special holidays. Some communities decreed only the holding of a feast on the anniversary of the event. Others (including Saragossa) prescribed the reading of a scroll in the synagogue and the recitation of psalms as an added feature of the celebration. Most communities also called for the distribution of gifts to the needy and the exchange of presents. There were also a few communities which ordained a fast on the day preceding the festival.
2. The first printed edition of Ibn Gabirol's Mivhar ha-Peninim was published on January 14, 1484.
3. Rabbi Hayyim b. Benjamin Bechner of Cracow, talmudist and grammarian, author of Or Hadash, died on February 2, 1684.
4. Rabbi Hayyim b. Jacob Polani, prolific writer, author of Lev Hayyim, novellae on the code, died on February 10, 1868.
5. The first commencement exercises of the Hebrew University of Jerusalem were held on January 25, 1932.
6. Generalissimo Francisco Franco met with Jewish representatives on January 20, 1965, to discuss the legal status of the Jewish community of Spain. It was the first meeting between Jews and the head of a Spanish government since the expulsion in 1492.

SHEVAT 18

1. King Alfonso V, on February 5, 1428, ordered the attendance of Sicily's Jews at conversive sermons.
   See Shevat 7:1.
2. Francisco Maldonado da Silva Solis, Peruvian Marrano poet, was burned at the stake in Lima, Peru, on January 23, 1639.
3. Abraham Schwab founded a yeshivah in Metz, France, on January 24, 1704. This yeshivah ultimately evolved into the Séminaire Isráelite de France, the French rabbinical seminary.
4. Rabbi Israel Jonah Landau, author of *Ma'ayan ha-Berakhot*, novellae on the tractate *Berakhot*, died on January 18, 1824 (HY).
5. Bnai Israel, the oldest Jewish congregation west of the Allegheny Mountains, was organized in Cincinnati, Ohio, on January 18, 1824.
6. Ze'ev Jawitz, historian, father of the Mizrachi movement, died on January 24, 1924.
7. Chaim Weizmann was elected the first president of Israel on February 17, 1949.
   The official title conferred on Dr. Chaim Weizmann upon his election to the presidency of Israel was "Nasi." The first Jew in postbiblical history to be honored with the title "Nasi" was Hillel (*Pesaḥim* 66a). The title was borne by the heads of the Patriarchate, most of them direct lineal descendants of Hillel, until the year 425, when Emperor Theodosius II abolished the office.
8. The Egyptian parliament voted on February 5, 1980, to end the boycott of Israel.

SHEVAT 19

1. Jews of Basle, Switzerland, were burned alive on January 9, 1349, in a wooden house, erected for that purpose on an island in the Rhine (JE).
   Basle, Switzerland, was a hotbed of anti-Semitism in medieval times. In modern history it became the host city of the 1st Zionist Congress and subsequently extended similar hospitality to many other congresses. The Zionist program formulated at Basle provided a blueprint for the State of Israel. Six hundred years after the horrible massacre of the Jews of Basle the new State of Israel elected its first president (Shevat 18:7).
2. Berthold Auerbach, Jewish German writer and scholar, died on February 8, 1882.

3. The Independent Order of Brith Abraham was established in New York on February 13, 1887.
4. Peter Wiernik, Yiddish journalist and historian, died on February 12, 1936.

SHEVAT 20

1. Birth of Asher, son of the Patriarch Jacob (*Midrash Tadshe*).
2. The first printed edition of *Zeror ha-Mor*, popular commentary on the Pentateuch by Rabbi Abraham Sebag, was published in Venice on February 5, 1523.

    Rabbi Abraham Sebag sought refuge in Portugal upon his expulsion from Spain in 1492. Instead of refuge he met with persecution. His two sons were forcibly baptized and taken away from him. His only remaining treasure, the manuscripts of his exegetical work on the Bible, had to be buried for fear of confiscation and destruction. Among these papers was the manuscript of *Zeror ha-Mor*. He never saw the manuscripts again. When Rabbi Sebag finally reached Africa, after his release from a Portuguese prison, he assumed the laborious task of rewriting some of his works. It was the second manuscript of *Zeror ha-Mor* which was published in Venice in 1523. Its appearance symbolized Jewish perseverance and determination to rise from the ruins.
3. Jewish physicians of Galicia, on February 4, 1782, were granted the right to attend to Christian patients by the Austrian authorities.
4. Isaac Baer Levinsohn, father of the Haskalah movement in Russia, author of *Te'udah be-Yisrael*, died on February 12, 1860.

    See note on Tevet 4:5.
5. Rabbi David Solomon Slouschz, early Zionist and author, died on February 15, 1906.

    See Tevet 7:6.
6. Israeli forces withdrew, on January 22, 1957, from the Sinai Peninsula, with the exception of the Gaza Strip and the approaches to the Gulf of Aqaba.

SHEVAT 21

1. Rabbi Ephraim Alnakwa, kabbalist and physician, author of Sha'ar Kevod ha-Shem, died on February 2, 1442.
2. Rabbi Judah Leib Hanlish, author of *Vayigash Yehudah*, novellae on the *Turim*, died on January 21, 1596.
3. Oliver Cromwell granted the right of residence in England to Luis Carvajal on February 4, 1657. This day became known in Anglo-Jewish history as Resettlement Day.
   The tolerant attitude of the English government toward its Jewish residents was a major factor in the early history of the Jewish settlers in the British colonies in America and other parts of the empire. Cromwell's grant of the right of residence to Carvajal in 1657 was considered by historians to be the earliest official British act of tolerance in favor of the Jews. However, the eminent historian Dr. Cecil Roth made the momentous discovery that the British Council of State, on June 25, 1656, had already granted Rabbi Manasseh ben Israel's petition for the right to practice Judaism in England (see Tammuz 3:4).
4. Rabbi Moses b. Jonathan Galante (Ha-Magen) of Jerusalem, author of *Zevaḥ ha-Shelamim*, novellae on the Talmud, died on February 11, 1689.
5. Rabbi Judah Navon, author of *Kiryat Melekh Rav*, died on January 26, 1761 (HY).
6. Marshal Oscar von Lubomirski on January 22, 1775, demolished the Jewish homes built on the outskirts of Warsaw in the settlement of "New Jerusalem." All Jews were expelled from Warsaw following the demolitions.
7. The *Palestine Post* building in Jerusalem was bombed on February 1, 1948, resulting in a great loss of life.

SHEVAT 22

1. A decree by Caius Caligula, providing for the placing of pagan images in the Temple, was voided upon his death by assassination on January 24, 41. The anniversary was observed as a holiday (*Megillat Ta'anit* 11).
   The anti-religious laws of antiquity decreed by the Seleucids in the early Hasmonean period and later by the Romans Hadrian and Caius Caligula were motivated by a political policy which sought to impose

homogeneity upon the state. The anti-religious laws of the Nazis aimed at the demoralization of the Jewish inmates of the ghettos by depriving them of the comfort which religion has to offer. The inspiring story of Rabbi Shusterman's defiance of the Nazi anti-religious laws (no. 6) forms one of the most heroic chapters in the book of Jewish martyrology. The sainted rabbi proved again that the spirit is often mightier than the sword.

2. Rabbi Jacob b. Benjamin Papiers of Frankfort, author of a book of responsa *Shev Ya'akov,* died on February 19, 1740 (TP).
3. The Jewish community of Livorno (Leghorn), Italy, observed a fast day on Shevat 22 in commemoration of an earthquake on January 27, 1742.
4. Rabbi Menahem Mendel of Kotsk, eminent hasidic rabbi, died on January 27, 1859.
5. Nazis raided the Jewish community of Amsterdam on February 19, 1941, and seized 429 young Jews for deportation.
6. Rabbi Gabriel Shusterman, author of *Ben Moshe Yedaber,* who defied the Nazi anti-religious laws, died on February 16, 1944 (Oshry, *Hurban Litte,* p. 122).

SHEVAT 23

1. The Israelites assembled to wage war on the tribe of Benjamin (Judg. 20:1; *Megillat Ta'anit,* concluding chap.).

   The ancient battle of the Hebrew tribes was practically reenacted by modern French Jewry (no. 5). In their desperate efforts to coax equality out of the reluctant French National Assembly, the Jews of Spanish and Portuguese descent, concentrated in Bordeaux, put forth the claim that they were the only pure-blooded descendants of the tribe of Judah, while the Alsatian Jews, like all German Jews, were descended from the ten lost tribes. The National Assembly happily accepted this legend, and on January 28, 1790, granted equality to the Sephardi Jews only (Shevat 13:3). The Alsatian Jews, however, continued to clamor for their rights. Their efforts were rewarded a year later when the assembly extended equality to them on January 28, 1791.
2. The Synod of Breslau, on February 9, 1267, ordered the Jews of Silesia to wear a special cap in public (JE, Silesia).
3. Rabbi Levi b. Gershom (Ralbag; also known as Gersonides) completed the manuscript of his commentary on the Pentateuch on January 14, 1338.

4. Frumet Meisel, famous for her piety and philanthropy, died on January 31, 1625 (JE).
5. The French National Assembly granted equality to Jews of Alsace on January 28, 1791.
6. Abraham Stern, Hebrew poet and inventor, died on February 3, 1842.
7. The *Jewish Abend-Post*, Yiddish daily newspaper, was founded in New York on February 3, 1899.
8. The Jewish Agricultural Industrial Aid Society was organized on January 23, 1900.
9. The Jewish Legion, officially designated the 38th Battalion, Royal Fusiliers, left England for Palestine on February 5, 1918.
    This Jewish fighting force was the successor to the Zion Mule Corps, which had been disbanded on May 26, 1916. It was committed to battle in Palestine on June 27, 1918.
10. The Nazis, on February 20, 1941, issued an order barring all Polish Jews from using public transportation facilities.
11. The first transport of Jews to concentration camps left Plotsk (Plock), Poland, on February 20, 1941.

SHEVAT 24

1. The prophet Zechariah, in 519 B.C.E., predicted the restoration of Zion and encouraged the resumption of the construction of the Temple building (Zech. 1:7).
    Exactly 2,415 years after the prophecy of Zechariah, Theodor Herzl's *Der Judenstaat* appeared, predicting the third restoration of Zion (Shevat 30:4).
2. The first printed Pentateuch, bound together with the Five Scrolls, was published on January 23, 1492.
3. Rabbi Meir b. Isaac Katzenellenbogen (Maharam of Padua), author of responsa, died on January 26, 1565.
4. The Court Jew Lippold, protege of Elector Joachim II, was executed in Berlin on January 28, 1573.
5. Rabbi Abraham Auerbach of Coesfeld, Germany, instituted an annual fast in commemoration of his expulsion on January 31, 1674 (UJE).
    See note on Shevat 17:1.
6. Rabbi Mordecai of Brisk, author of *Mayim Ammukim*, died on February 15, 1765.
7. Jews who had moved out of the ghetto of Frankfort on the Main were

forced, by a decree issued on February 13, 1776, to return to the ghetto (JE).

8. Duke Karl Eugene, on February 10, 1779, decreed that no Jew should be deprived of the right of residence in Stuttgart, Germany.
9. Rabbi Ezekeiel Feivel b. Ze'ev Wolf, the Maggid of Vilno, author of *Musar Haskel,* died on February 13, 1833.
10. The first synagogue in 425 years was dedicated in Madrid, Spain, on February 16, 1917.
11. Aharon David Gordon, writer and Palestinian labor leader, died on February 22, 1922.
12. Joseph Rumshinsky, composer of many Jewish operettas, died on February 6, 1956.

SHEVAT 25

1. Rabbi Meir Posner of Danzig, author of *Bet Meir,* novellae on the code, died on February 3, 1807.
2. Louis Bonaparte, on February 23, 1808, freed the Jews of Emden, Germany, of all restrictions and granted them the privileges enjoyed by French Jews.
3. The French government, on February 8, 1831, decreed the extension of financial support to Jewish religious institutions on an equal footing with aid to Christian institutions.
    See note on Shevat 13:3.
4. Rabbi Israel b. Ze'ev Wolf Salanter (Lipkin), dynamic leader of the Musar movement, author of *Or Yisrael,* died on February 2, 1883.
    Rabbi Israel Salanter promoted the Musar movement in an effort to check the deep inroads of 19th-century assimilationism into Jewish traditional life. He was aware of the rapid decline of Orthodoxy in Western Europe and the threat it had posed to East European Jewry. Rabbi Salanter developed a sizable and influential following in Eastern Europe, but he met with no response in Western Europe. East European rabbis were not trained for leadership in a free and emancipated Jewish community. The overwhelming majority of them realized this fact and left the battle to the native Orthodox leaders and the rabbis they had produced. See note on Heshvan 3:7.
5. The first ship to break through the British blockade of Palestine landed its illegal immigrants on February 10, 1934.
    The worldwide publicity gained by the heroic efforts of illegal immigrant ships was an important factor in England's ultimate decision to surrender the mandate.

6. The Nazis, on February 22, 1941, issued a decree prohibiting the sale of merchandise to Jews outside the ghetto.
7. Israel and Egypt signed an armistice agreement on February 24, 1949.
8. Zishe Weinper, Yiddish poet, died on January 27, 1957.
9. Joseph Pearlman (Ossip Dymov), playwright, died on February 3, 1959.
10. Oil was pumped for the first time into the newly completed 42-inch Eilat-Ashkelon pipeline on February 1, 1970.

SHEVAT 26

1. Rabbi David b. Samuel Halevi (Taz), popular author of a commentary on the code, died on February 20, 1667.
   Hundreds of commentaries and novellae were written on Caro's code, the *Shulhan Arukh*. Rabbi David's commentary gained immediate and widespread acceptance. Since its publication it has been permanently appended to the text, and it is reprinted in every edition of the code. The second major commentator, whose work gained equal fame, was the Shakh. He was a contemporary of the Taz, and his yahrzeit falls five days later on Adar 1 (no. 9).
2. Russia broke diplomatic relations with Israel on February 11, 1953.
3. Israel exported copper ore, extracted from the copper mines of King Solomon, on February 4, 1959. It was the first such export since the days of the ancient kingdom.

SHEVAT 27

1. Joseph Sanalbo, a convert to Judaism, was burned at the stake in Rome on February 19, 1583.
2. Rabbi Tanhum Ha-Kohen of Cracow, talmudist, died on February 22, 1618.
3. The Jewish community of New Amsterdam was granted a site for burial purposes by an order dated February 22, 1656 (*AJHSP*, no. 3, p. 77).
   The first site for the erection of a synagogue was purchased by the congregation on Tevet 17, 1728 (Tevet 17:4).
4. The Reformed Society of Israelites which had seceded from Congregation Beth Elohim of Charleston, S.C., adopted the first constitution of a Reform congregation in the United States on February 15, 1825 (Friedman, *Pilgrims in a New Land*, p. 157).
   See note on Tevet 2:5.

5. Rabbi Zundel the Preacher, author of *Kenaf Rananim*, died on February 13, 1847.
6. Micha Joseph Levenson (Michal), Hebrew poet, died on February 17, 1852.
7. Isaac Adolphe Crémieux, statesman and leader of French Jewry, died on February 9, 1880.

   19th-century Jewry produced three outstanding communal leaders of international renown: Moses Montefiore (Av 13:5), Adolph Crémieux, and Rabbi Isaac Elchanan Spector (Adar 21:3).
8. Menachem Bareisha, Yiddish poet, died on February 14, 1942.
9. The surrender of the last German army in Stalingrad, Russia, on February 2, 1943, marked the turning of the tide in the long string of Nazi victories in World War II.

SHEVAT 28

1. King Antiochus V lifted the siege of Jerusalem, 163 B.C.E. The anniversary was observed as a holiday (Zeitlin, *Megillat Ta'anit*).
2. Massacre of Jews of Norwich, England, on February 6, 1190.

   The Jews of England were expelled a century later on July 18, 1290 (Av. 9:9).
3. Jews who lived in the vicinity of Strasbourg were granted permission, on February 21, 1792, to enter the city to take an oath of allegiance. See Adar 25:3.
4. Rabbi Joseph David Sinzheim, author of *Yad David*, novellae on the Talmud, head of the Sanhedrin convened by Napoleon, died on February 11, 1812.
5. Jacob Raphael Furstenthal, Hebrew writer and poet, died on February 16, 1855.
6. Louis Lewandowski, famous composer of liturgical music, first Jew to be admitted to the Berlin Academy of Arts, died on February 4, 1894.
7. A Zionist committee set out, on February 25, 1903, to investigate the feasibility of a British proposal to Jews to colonize El-Arish, on the Mediterranean coast of the Sinai Peninsula.

   53 years later during the Sinai Campaign, Israeli forces captured El-Arish (Hesvan 28:7).
8. Mrs. Radcliffe N. Salomon (Nina David), poetess and author, died on February 22, 1925.
9. Rabbi Alexander Goode, one of the four chaplains who surrendered their life-jackets to soldiers, perished with the sinking S.S. *Dorchester* off Greenland on February 3, 1943.

SHEVAT 29

1. King Philip II, on February 7, 1569, established the holy office of the Inquisition in the province of South America (*AJHSP*, no. 12, p. 5). See Shevat 3:4.
2. Rabbi Eliezer b. Samuel Avila, author of *Ozen Shemuel*, homilies and eulogies, died on February 3, 1761.
3. The Jewish Court of Arbitration, the first organized Jewish institution devoted to the settlement of disputes of specifically Jewish character, held its first session on February 18, 1920.
4. Rabbi Nathan Zevi Finkel, founder of the Yeshivah of Slobodka, outstanding Torah academy, author of *Etz Peri*, died on February 1, 1927.
5. The first large ghetto in Poland was established by the Nazis in Lodz, by an order issued on February 8, 1940.

    Lodz had a Jewish population of over 200,000. The setting up of a ghetto in Lodz required considerable time and planning. Little time was wasted in the establishment of ghettos in towns with smaller Jewish communities. The very first Polish ghetto was set up in Piotrkow, which had been occupied by the Nazis on September 5, 1939 (see Elul 21:7).
6. Henrietta Szold, founder of Hadassah and Youth Aliyah, died on February 12, 1945.
7. Evacuation of Israeli forces from the bridgehead on the western bank of Suez, on the African continent, was completed on February 21, 1974.

SHEVAT 30

1. A humiliating medieval practice, to which the Jews of Rome had been annually subjected, came to an end on February 14, 1667, when they ran the foot-races at the Roman carnival for the last time.

    The Monday on which the Roman carnivals usually opened was known to the Jews of Rome as the Black Monday. Beginning with the 14th century Jews were compelled to contribute heavily to the expense of the carnival. In the 15th century a note of indignity was added by the authorities. Jewish runners were forced to open the foot-races. Eight scantily clad Jews had to run the entire course of 400 yards amid shouts and blows. The exertion not infrequently proved fatal to Jewish runners. Following the initial race, the rabbis and leading Jews had to walk the length of the course on foot to submit to the insults and derision of the howling mob.

2. Rabbi Reuben Horowitz, hasidic leader, author of *Dudaim ba-Sadeh*, commentary on the Pentateuch, died on February 4, 1810.

3. Salomon Munk, orientalist, publisher of an Arabic edition of Maimonides' *Moreh Nevukhim* with a modern translation and annotations, died on February 5, 1867.

4. *Der Judenstaat* by Theodor Herzl was published on February 14, 1896.

5. Abraham Kaplan, Hebrew writer, died on February 2, 1897.

6. Rabbi Isaac Jeroham Diskin, prominent Orthodox leader, died on February 24, 1925.

ADAR 1

1. The beginning of the ninth biblical plague—darkness (*Zikhron Yemot Olam*).
2. Abraham ibn Ezra, Bible exegete, poet, and philosopher, died on January 27, 1164.
3. The first printed edition of Nahmanides' *Sha'ar ha-Gemul* was published on January 23, 1490.
4. The first printed edition of Kimhi's *Shorashim* was published on February 11, 1491.
5. King Sigismund I appointed Michael Yosefovich "senior" of all Lithuanian Jews on February 27, 1514 [AdarII] (Dubnow, *Hist. of the Jews in Russia and Poland*, I, p. 72).
6. Jews of Tyrnau, Hungary (now Trnava, Czechoslovakia), were expelled on February 19, 1539.
7. Rabbi Yom Tov Lipmann Heller designated Adar 1, the day of his installation as rabbi of Cracow (February 20, 1643), a private Purim to mark the end of his many troubles.

    See note on Shevat 17:1.
8. Rabbi Azariah Figo (Picho), author of the popular work *Giddulei ha-Terumah*, died on February 6, 1647 (TP).

    Even though Rabbi Figo and the Shakh were contemporaries, the latter respected the authoritativeness of his senior colleague and liberally quoted him in his works. Both share a common yarhrzeit (no. 9).
9. Rabbi Shabbetai b. Meir Ha-Kohen (Shakh), author of the popular commentary, *Shiftei Kohen* on the code, liturgical poet, died on February 20, 1662.
10. Rabbi Gabriel b. Judah Loew Eskeles of Nikolsburg, Moravia, leading talmudist of his age, died on February 2, 1718.
11. Lord Harrington, member of the British government, instructed the British ambassador to Vienna, Austria, on March 5, 1745, to protest an impending expulsion of Jews from Bohemia. (*AJHSP*, no. 35, p. 215).
12. A scroll dated II Adar 1, 5543 (March 5, 1783) was published in

commemoration of the right of residence which was granted to the Jews of Kovno by King Stanislaus Augustus Poniatowski of Poland.

13. The French Sanhedrin convened by Napoleon opened its sessions on February 9, 1807.

14. The Common Council of New York City passed an ordinance, on February 1, 1813, restricting the right to sell kosher meat to butchers licensed by Congregation Shearith Israel.

The colonial Jewish community depended upon gentile butchers to supply it with kosher meats. The discovery of fraud led to a Jewish request for the legislation passed by the Common Council. The ordinance was repealed one week after its adoption due to a split which had developed among the members of Shearith Israel.

15. Rabbi Menahem Mendel of Shklov, leader of the aliyah of the disciples of the Gaon of Vilna to Palestine, died on February 28, 1827.

16. The disappearance of Father Thomas of Damascus, on February 5, 1840, led to the infamous Damascus ritual affair. Thirteen Jews were arrested and tortured. Four died of their injuries.

17. The Jewish Reform movement in Germany was publicly announced on March 10, 1845 (Adar II).

18. *Ha-Levanon*, the first Hebrew periodical in Palestine, was published on February 20, 1863.

19. The Baron de Hirsch Fund was established on February 9, 1891, to subsidize Jewish agricultural and trade instruction.

20. The British commander-in-chief in Palestine, on March 11, 1921, (Adar II), quashed all military proceedings against Vladimir Jabotinsky and 19 of his collaborators for participating in the Jewish self-defense measures during the Arab riots in Jerusalem.

21. Prime Minister Ben-Gurion of Israel, on March 4, 1957, ordered the withdrawal of Israel's forces from the Gaza Strip and other occupied territory, in compliance with the U.N. resolution.

22. Israel opened an embassy in Cairo, Egypt, on February 18, 1980.

ADAR 2

1. Emperor Justinian of the Byzantine Empire issued an order, on February 13, 553, providing for the public reading of a Greek translation of the biblical portion read in the synagogue on Sabbath mornings. The same order prohibited rabbis from giving aggadic interpretations of the Bible.

2. Jews of Speyer, Bavaria, threatened by mob violence, retired to their

homes, set fire to them, and perished in the flames on January 22, 1349.

3. Anti-Jewish riots were staged by students in Cracow on March 13, 1682 (Adar II).
4. The Elector Clemens August decreed on February 3, 1718, that all Jews of Paderborn, Prussia, desiring to enter into marriage must obtain prior permission of the sovereign.
5. Moses Leib Lilienblum (Malal), Hebrew writer and leading member of Hovevi Zion, died on February 11, 1910.
6. Nazis confiscated, on February 19, 1942, all books and Torah scrolls found in the ghetto of Kovno.
7. The first armed struggle between Jews and Nazis on the streets of the Warsaw ghetto took place on February 7, 1943.
8. The first transport of Greek Jews from Salonika left for Nazi extermination camps on March 9, 1943 (Adar II).
   The port of Salonika was virtually in Jewish hands. Its stevedores, mainly Jews, were called *amali*, the Hebrew term for workers. Of the 50,000 Salonika Jews at the time of the invasion, only 1,200 survived.
9. An earthquake razed Agadir, Morocco, on February 29, 1960, killing about 5,000 people. Hundreds of Jews, including some students of the local Lubavich Yeshivah, were among the victims.
10. The Knesset passed a bill, on March 10, 1970 (Adar II), defining a Jew as one born to a Jewish mother or a convert to the Jewish faith.
    The legal definition of a Jew adopted by the Knesset is in accord with halakhic interpretation. It rejects the secular contention that the Jewish religion and nationality are divisible. By implication of this definition, conversion to another faith results in the loss of Jewish nationality.

ADAR 3

1. The building of the second Temple of Jerusalem was completed in 515 B.C.E. (Ezra 6:15).
   See note on Tishri 21:3.
2. Rabbi Mordecai b. Abraham Jaffe, author of *Levushim*, a set of codes, died on March 7, 1612 (Adar II).
3. Jews of Lubeck, Germany, were expelled on March 4, 1699 (Adar II).
   See note on Adar 6:8.
4. Rabbi Noah Hayyim Zevi Berlin, author of *Azei Arazim*, novellae on the code, died on March 7, 1802 (Adar II).

5. A poll-tax levied on Russo-Polish Jews entering Austrian Galicia on business, was abolished on March 7, 1851 (Adar II).
6. Rabbi Elijah David Rabinowitz of Jerusalem, talmudist, died on February 8, 1905.
7. Mordecai Rabinowitz (Ben-Ammi), Yiddish writer, died on February 10, 1932.
8. The Security Council of the U.N. recommended, on March 4, 1949, the admission of Israel into the United Nations.
9. The first permanent government of Israel, headed by David Ben-Gurion, assumed office on March 4, 1949.
   Israel's first permanent government assumed office on the day when the Security Council recommended its admission to the U.N. (no. 8).
10. Itzik Manger, Yiddish poet and playwright, died on February 21, 1969.

ADAR 4

1. Vespasian occupied the city of Gadara, 68 C.E.
   The interplay in the histories of Rome and Judea is illustrated by entries 1 and 6.
2. Rav Aḥai b. Rav Ḥuna, early member of the Saboraim (post-talmudic sages), died on March 3, 506.
3. The body of Rabbi Meir b. Baruch (Maharam of Rothenburg) was released for burial on February 7, 1307, 14 years after his death.
   See Tishri 10:14.
4. A religious disputation between representatives of Jews and the apostate Solomon Levi Burgos started on February 6, 1413, by order of Benedict XIII.
5. Rabbi Aryeh Leib Sarahs, disciple of Rabbi Dov Baer of Mezhirech, prominent communal worker, died on March 10, 1791 (Adar II).
6. Jews of Rome were declared free citizens by the French Army under General Berthier on February 20, 1798.
7. Rumania passed a law, on February 28, 1887, excluding Jews from public service and from the tobacco trade.
8. Rabbi Eliezer Gordon, founder of the Yeshivah of Telz, Lithuania, died on February 13, 1910.
   See note on Ḥeshvan 6:5.
9. The Youth Aliyah from Germany started on February 19, 1934.

ADAR 5

1. Sara Coppio Sullam, Jewish poetess, died on February 14, 1641. (Kobler, *A Treasury of Jewish Letters*, p. 436).
   Sara Coppio Sullam was not the first Jewish woman to write Italian poetry. Deborah Ascarelli, a Roman Jewish woman, had her work of Italian verse published in Venice as early as 1602. Her book consisted mainly of translations into Italian of ancient Hebrew liturgical poems for use in the synagogue. Rachel Akerman of Vienna, Austria (1522–44), was the first Jewish woman to write poetry in the German language.
2. Rabbi Israel Muschkat, author of *Harei Besamim*, died on February 28, 1868 (HY).
3. The Federation of Rumanian Jews in America was organized on March 8, 1908.
4. Menahem Mendel Dolitzky, poet and novelist, died on February 22, 1931.
5. Israeli forces completed their withdrawal from the Gaza Strip and the Sharm-el-Sheikh area on the Gulf of Aqaba on March 8, 1957 (Adar II).

ADAR 6

1. Moses completed his review of the Torah, which began 36 days earlier on Shevat 1 (*Seder Olam* 8).
   The anniversary of the completion of Moses' instruction of the Torah appropriately coincides with the anniversary of the first printing of a comprehensive edition of the Pentateuch (no. 4). Rashi's commentary on the Pentateuch was the first dated printed Hebrew work (Adar 11:2). The book reflected the indispensability of Rashi to the Bible student. It was unsatisfactory, however, because the publishers failed to include the text of the Pentateuch in the same work. This glaring fault was corrected by the Bologna edition, which became the standard form for most subsequent Pentateuchal editions everywhere, for centuries to come. It fully met the traditional requirements, relating to the reading of the weekly portion of the Torah. By the use of this book one was able to read, understand, and chant the scriptural text as well as read the Targum which was ritually required
2. Moses was informed that the day of his death was approaching (Deut. 31:14; *Seder ha-Dorot*).
   See note on Tishri 22:1.

3. Rabbi Samuel b. Natronai, a tosafist, was broken on the wheel and martyred on January 27, 1197 (JE).
4. The first printed edition of the complete Pentateuch, with vowel signs, accents, Targum Onkelos (an Aramaic translation), and Rashi, was published in Bologna, on January 26, 1482.
5. The first printed edition of tractate *Bezah* of the Babylonian Talmud was published in Soncino, Italy, on February 2, 1484.
6. The first printed edition of tractate *Gittin* of the Babylonian Talmud was published in Soncino, Italy, on February 18, 1488.
7. The Society of the Friends of the Constitution, founded at Strasbourg, admitted the first Jew to membership on February 20, 1790.
8. The Senate of the Free City of Lubeck, Germany, ordered the expulsion of all Jews on March 6, 1816.

   Jews of the Free City of Lubeck were expelled on Adar 3, 1699 (no. 3) and again on Adar 6, 1816.
9. Yehiel Michael Pines, Hebrew writer and pioneer of the Hovevei Zion movement, died on February 13, 1913.
10. The Cracow ghetto was liquidated by the Nazis on March 13, 1943 (Adar II).
11. Count Folke Bernadotte, vice-president of the Swedish Red Cross, met with Heinrich Himmler, chief of the Nazi Gestapo, on February 19, 1945, to discuss prisoner-of-war problems and also the Jewish question.

    Count Bernadotte's negotiations with Himmler brought him a universal reputation and prominence which led to his appointment as mediator in the Arab-Israel war. The first Arab military battle (no. 12) erupted on the third anniversary of Bernadotte's meeting with Himmler.

    See Elul 13:8.
12. The first organized Arab military battle in Palestine, the attack on Tirat Zevi by the Arab Liberation Army, ended in defeat on February 16, 1948.
13. The Jewish Sea Service, forerunner of Israeli Navy, was organized on March 17, 1948 (Adar II).
14. An Israeli unit established a base at 'Ayn Husb, at the junction of the Beersheba-Sodom and Sodom-Eilat tracks, on March 7, 1949.

ADAR 7

1. Birth of Moses (*Sotah* 12b).

   The birthday and yahrzeit of Moses were fixed by the Talmud and universally accepted by tradition. *Midrash Ge'ulat Esther* offers a dissenting opinion: Moses was born in the month of Nisan and died on Adar 1.
2. Moses recited the "Shirah" to the people of Israel (Abraham ibn Ezra, Deut. 32:48).
3. Moses offered his farewell benediction (Deut. 33:1, Rashi).
4. Death of Moses (*Kiddushin* 38a).
5. The fall of manna came to an end (ibid.).
6. All copies of the Talmud in the possession of the Jews of France were seized on the Sabbath, March 3, 1240 (Adar II), and held for ultimate disposition by the Church.

   The confiscated copies of the Talmud were ultimately burned in 1242. This tragedy led to the decline of rabbinic scholarship in France.
7. The first auto-da-fé instituted by the Spanish Inquisition was held at Seville on February 6, 1481 (Roth, *A Hist. of the Marranos*, p. 43).
8. Rabbi Ephraim Solomon b. Aaron of Luntshits, author of *Keli Yakar*, popular commentary on the Pentateuch, died on February 21, 1619 (Adar II).
9. Leopold I, on February 27, 1670, ordered the expulsion of all Jews from Austria.
10. The first Jewish Sunday School in the United States was opened in Philadelphia on March 4, 1838 (*American Jewish Year Book*, vol. 33, p. 169).
11. *Ha-Yom*, the first daily Hebrew newspaper, which ushered in the modern period of the Hebrew press, was published for the first time on February 12, 1886.

    The growth of Zionism in the ninth decade of the 19th century is reflected in the three anniversaries which fall on Adar 7 (nos. 11, 12, 13).

    See Tishri 30:3.
12. The Zionist Order Benei Moshe was organized by Aḥad ha-Am on February 8, 1889.
13. The Menuḥah ve-Naḥalah company was organized in Warsaw, on February 27, 1890, to purchase and colonize land in Palestine.
14. Rabbi Elijah Benamozegh, influential Italian Jewish leader, author of *Em la-Mikra*, died on February 6, 1900.
15. Judah Steinberg, Hebrew writer of ḥasidic lore, died on February 9, 1908.

16. Rabbi Isaac Jacob Rabinovitz (Reb Itzele Ponevezher), talmudist, author of responsa *Zekher Yizhak*, died on February 7, 1919.
17. German elections, held on March 5, 1933, gave the Nazis control of the Reichstag, making it possible for Hitler to assume dictatorial powers.
18. The *Struma*, with 769 illegal Jewish immigrants aboard, was torpedoed by a Nazi submarine in the Black Sea on February 24, 1942.
19. Rabbi Hayyim Isaac Bloch, author of *Divrei Hibbah*, novellae and critical annotations on the Ritva, died on March 18, 1948 (Adar II).

ADAR 8

1. Rabbi Issachar Baer, author of *Arba'ah Hadashim*, died on March 4, 1648.
2. Jews of Barbados, British West Indies, were granted, on February 14, 1674, the privilege of taking an oath on the Old Testament and the right of giving testimony in a court of justice in cases relating to "trade and selling."

   The Jews of Barbados were the first in the New World to be permitted to take an oath in court on an Old Testament. This right was granted on Adar 8, 1674. The last remaining restriction on American Jews who could not take the official oath required of office-holders was removed by the state of Maryland, 151 years later, on Adar 8, 1825 (no. 4). The yahrzeit of Zacharias Frankel falls on the same day (no. 5). His first book, published in 1840, led to the revocation of the special oath required of German Jews.
3. Rabbi Aryeh Leib b. Jacob Joshua Falk, author of *Penei Aryeh*, novellae on the Talmud, died on March 6, 1789.

   He was the son of the author of *Penei Yehoshua* (Shevat 14:2).
4. The legislature of Maryland, on February 26, 1825, passed an act removing the requirement of taking a christological oath prior to the assumption of public office. A declaration of belief in reward and punishment in the hereafter was substituted.
5. Zacharias Frankel, theologian and scholar, president of the Rabbinical Seminary of Breslau, died on February 13, 1875.
6. Yeshiva Etz Chaim, the first elementary yeshivah with a secular department in the U.S., was established on March 15, 1886 (Adar II).

   Yeshiva Etz Chaim was merged in 1915 with Yeshivat Rabbi Isaac Elchanan to form the principal Orthodox rabbinic school in the U.S.
7. Benjamin Henry Ascher, Hebrew scholar and author, died on February 24, 1893 (JE).

8. Isaac Rabinowitz (Ish Kovno), Hebrew poet and Yiddish writer, died on March 9, 1900 (Adar II).
9. Isaiah Bershadsky, Hebrew novelist, died on March 11, 1908 (Adar II).
10. Deportation of Jews from Thrace began on March 15, 1943 (Adar II).
11. Levi Eshkol, prime minister of Israel, died on February 26, 1969.
     Levi Eshkol became prime minister of Israel on June 26, 1963, and led the nation during the Six Day War in 1967.

ADAR 9

1. Adar 9, traditional date of the first controversy between the schools of Shammai and Hillel, was observed as a fast-day in ancient times (*Megillat Ta'anit*, concluding chap.).
     The establishment of the rival schools of Shammai and Hillel was viewed with grave misgivings by the responsible rabbinic leadership of the 1st century. In the tragic period when the Sanhedrin was dominated by the Sadducees, the rabbinic academy was substituted for the Sanhedrin as the seat of supreme religious authority, with the exclusive right to declare official rabbinic doctrine. The scars left by the Sadducean schism were still visible on the Jewish scene at the time when the two rabbinic schools came into being. The emergence of rival schools raised the specter of a schism within the rabbinic camp. Each school had its mass following, contradictory decisions were handed down, and divergent customs were adopted. Had the two major schools chosen to fight for supremacy, and had they employed in their mutual antagonism the same weapons used by a previous generation of rabbis against the Sadducees, the results would have been disastrous. Fortunately, a more moderate view prevailed. It seems that the school of Hillel took the initiative in this direction (*Eruvin* 13b). The followers of each school, with a few rare exceptions, continued to treat each other with mutual respect, trust, and affection (*Eduyyot* 4:8). The Jewish people took in its stride the minor irritation resulting from the prevalence of divergent practices, as long as they did not affect the basic doctrines upon which the survival of Judaism depended. It was left to a subsequent generation to choose the view upon which to place the final stamp of approval.
2. Jews of the Papal States, with the exception of Rome and Ancona, were expelled by Pope Pius V on February 26, 1569.

3. Mordecai Marcus Meisel, philanthropist and communal leader of Prague, died on March 13, 1601 (Adar II).
4. *Israel's Herold*, the first German Jewish paper in the U.S., was published on March 3, 1849.
5. The German army marched into Austria on March 12, 1938 (Adar II) and celebrated the occasion with numerous attacks upon the Jewish population of 200,000.
   See note on Adar 10:6.
6. The Israeli army reached Eilat on the Gulf of Aqaba on March 10, 1949.
   The conquest of Eilat, vital to the viability of Israel, rounded out the boundary lines of Israel's Negev.
7. Daniel Persky, Hebrew educator, journalist, and author, died on March 15, 1962 (Adar II).

ADAR 10

1. Jews of Freiburg, Germany, were massacred on January 30, 1349, in the Black Death riots (JE).
2. Jews of Worms, Germany, set fire to their homes on March 1, 1349 (Adar II), and perished in the flames.
3. Rabbi Joseph Chajes of Lemberg, author of *Ben Porot Yosef*, died on February 14, 1685 (DYY).
4. David Brandeis of Jungbunzlau (Mlada Boleslav), Bohemia, designated Adar 10 Purim Povidl, to be annually celebrated by him and his descendants in commemoration of his deliverance on March 8, 1731.
   See note on Shevat 17:1.
5. Jews of the Austrian Empire were granted equal civil and political rights on March 4, 1849.
   The joyous anniversary of Adar 10 was subsequently overshadowed by the grim anniversary of Hitler's march into Austria on Adar 9, 1938.
6. Emperor Alexander II of Russia, on March 16, 1859 (Adar II), granted Jewish scholars, wholesale merchants, and manufacturers the right to reside outside of the Jewish Pale of Settlement.
7. Congress, on March 12, 1862, amended the chaplaincy law to permit Jewish clergymen to serve as army chaplains (Adar II).
   See Tammuz 19:6.
8. The Konitz affair, which led to anti-Jewish excesses in West Prussia, broke on March 11, 1900 (Adar II).

9. Joel Engel, noted composer of Jewish music, died on February 11, 1927.
10. The Suez ceasefire was not renewed by Egypt and lapsed on March 7, 1971.
11. The disengagement of Israeli and Egyptian forces was completed on March 4, 1974.
12. Israel and Egypt exchanged ambassadors on February 27, 1980.

ADAR 11

1. Pope Eugenius IV issued a bull on February 20, 1434, prohibiting anti-Jewish sermons.
2. The first dated printed Hebrew work, Rashi's commentary on the Pentateuch, was published in Reggio di Calabria, Italy, by Abraham Garton on February 18, 1475.

   Rashi's commentary on the Bible and Talmud and Rabbi Nathan's talmudic dictionary, the *Arukh,* are the two most invaluable works used by students of the Talmud. Both were completed in the year 1105 (see note on Kislev 15:2). With the advent of Hebrew printing, these two works were among the first to claim the attention of the publishers. Rashi's commentary was the first dated work to be published, the *Arukh* was the third.
3. The first printed edition of the complete Bible was published in Soncino, Italy, on February 23, 1488.
4. A violent earthquake shook Ferrara, Italy, on February 16, 1570. The Jewish community miraculously escaped danger.
5. Rabbi Hayyim Joseph David Azulai (Hida), early writer of history of rabbinic literature, author of *Shem ha-Gedolim,* died on March 1, 1806.
6. Isaac Franks, Jewish officer in the American Army during the Revolution, in whose home at Germantown George Washington had his temporary quarters, died on March 4, 1822.

   Jews were denied the right to bear arms or join military forces in most medieval European countries. However, as soon as they were granted equality they clamored for the right to help defend their country. Thus Asser Levy petitioned for the right to stand guard with the other burghers of New Amsterdam shortly after his arrival in the city. Trumpeldor at Tel Hai (no. 11) and Isaac Franks in the United States demonstrated the unselfish patriotism common to all freedom-loving people the world over.
7. Rabbi Samuel Strashun (Reshash) of Vilna, author of talmudic annotations, died on March 21, 1872 (Adar II).

8. Leopold Zunz, spiritual father of Reform Judaism, historian of Jewish literature and synagogal liturgy, died on March 18, 1886 (Adar II).
9. Po'alei Zion, the Labor Zionist organization, was organized underground in Poltava, Russia, on March 8, 1906.
   Po'alei Zion (no. 9) and He-Halutz (no. 10) share a common anniversary. Both significantly tie in with Tel Hai Day (no. 11), which evolved into Haganah Day.
10. He-Halutz, an organization for the training of pioneers for Palestine, was organized in Russia on February 23, 1918.
11. Joseph Trumpeldor was killed on March 1, 1920, while defending Tel-Hai against an Arab attack. Adar 11 was officially proclaimed Tel Hai Day.
12. Rabbi Joseph Rosen, the Illui of Ragachov, author of *Zofnat Paneah*, died on March 5, 1936.
13. Shmuel Yosef Agnon, Hebrew writer, recipient of the Nobel Prize for Literature, died on February 17, 1970.
14. The first class of the Brith Milah School, conducted at Mt. Sinai Hospital under the sponsorship of the Brith Milah Board and the New York Board of Rabbis, was graduated on February 17, 1970.

ADAR 12

1. Dedication of the Temple built by King Herod the Great at Jerusalem, 19 B.C.E. (*Zikhron Yemot Olam*).
2. The execution in the year 117 of Pappus and Julianus, two Jewish brothers of Laodicea, Syria, by order of the Roman Emperor Trajan, started a chain of events which led to the assassination of the emperor. Trajan Day was thereafter observed as a festival (*Ta'anit* 18b; *Megillat Ta'anit* 17a).
   The death of a tyrant does not normally lead to the introduction of a new festival into the Jewish calendar. The death of Trajan, however, meant more than just the passing of another oppressive ruler. The execution of Lucius Quietus by Trajan's successor, Hadrian, brought joy to Babylonian Jewry. Quietus was responsible for the destruction of the Jewish community of northern Mesopotamia. What was more important than this act of retribution was the permanent shift in the boundaries of the Roman Empire. The countries beyond the Euphrates were surrendered to the Persian Empire, thus leaving Babylonian Jewry under a more tolerant rule. This made possible the great development of the Babylonian Talmud and its academies.

3. The execution of Shemaiah and his brother Ahya on Adar 12 led to the abolition of the ancient festival of Trajan Day (*Ta'anit* 18b).
4. Bishop Pierre III Rostaing guaranteed protection to the Jews of Carpentras, France, on February 28, 1276, in return for a tax of one-thirteenth of the total seat rents of the synagogue.
5. Full civil rights were granted to Turkish Jews on February 18, 1856.
6. Abraham Shalom Friedberg (Bar Shalom), Hebrew scholar, died on March 21, 1902 (Adar II).
7. Isaac Moses Bader, Yiddish novelist, died on March 19, 1905 (Adar II).
8. Hitler, on March 1, 1942, ordered the Einsatzstab to establish a library of Jewish books and works of art to be used in the ideological war against Jews. 600,000 volumes of this library fell intact into the hands of the American Army.
9. The hideout of Emanuel Ringelblum, historian of the Warsaw ghetto and one of the leaders of the Jewish underground, was discovered by the Nazis on March 7, 1944. He, his family, and his Polish benefactors were executed a few days later.
10. A bomb, exploded by the British on Ben Yehudah Street, Jerusalem, on February 22, 1948, killed many Jews.
11. Zalman Shneier, distinguished Hebrew and Yiddish poet and writer, died on February 20, 1959.

ADAR 13

1. Fast of Esther.
2. The ten sons of Haman were hanged (Esther 9:7).
3. Judah Maccabee defeated and killed the Syrian general Nicanor, 161 B.C.E. (1 Macc. 7).
4. Rabbi Judah b. Samuel he-Hasid of Regensburg, popular writer on Jewish ethics, author of *Sefer Hasidim*, died on February 22, 1217.
5. The earliest charter of privileges, granting religious liberty and tolerance to Jews in the New World, was incorporated in a contract given by the Dutch West Indies Co. to David Nassi on February 22, 1652. This contact provided for the founding of a Jewish settlement in Curaçao, Dutch West Indies.
6. Aaron Levy, Revolutionary patriot and founder of Aaronsburg, Pa., died on February 23, 1815.
   See Tishri 12:5.
7. The Jewish Agricultural Society was organized on February 12, 1900.

8. The Jewish Theological Seminary of America obtained its charter on February 20, 1902.
    See note on Kislev 12:3.
9. Several thousand Jews of the ghetto of Minsk were killed by the Nazis on March 2, 1942.

ADAR 14

1. Circumcision of Moses.
    See Adar 7:1.
2. Purim (Esther 9:21).
3. Two thousand Jews were burned in Strasbourg, Germany, on February 14, 1349.
4. Marranos of Cordova, Spain, were massacred on March 14, 1473 (Adar II).
5. *Mekhirat Yosef*, the second-oldest published Yiddish play, was presented for the first time in Frankfort, Germany, on March 10, 1713.
6. Turkish soldiers killed 60 Jews in Bucharest, Rumania, on March 7, 1822.
7. Rabbi Abraham Simḥah of Amzislav, author of *Netia shel Simḥah*, died on March 5, 1833 (DDD).
8. Purim of Rhodes, a private festival, was instituted by the Jews of the island in commemoration of their deliverance from ritual-murder charges on February 18, 1840.
    See note on Shevat 17:1.
9. Mikveh Israel, home of the first Jewish agricultural school in Palestine, was founded on February 15, 1870.
10. Rabbi Dov Ber b. Isaac Meisels of Cracow, Polish patriot and communal leader, author of *Ḥiddushei Mahardam*, died on March 17, 1870 (Adar II).
11. Rabbi Gershon Tanḥum of Minsk, author of *Elano d'Hayei*, died on February 13, 1881.
12. Israel Shochat, dynamic leader of Jewish self-defense of the Yishuv, founder of Ha-shomer, arrived in Palestine on March 1, 1904.
13. Hadassah was founded by Henrietta Szold on March 3, 1912.
14. The Chief Rabbinate of Palestine was established on March 24, 1921 (Adar II).
15. Boris Schatz, founder of the Bezalel Art School in Jerusalem, died on February 21, 1932.

ADAR 15

1. Shushan Purim (Esther 9:21).
2. Giovanni Baptista, an apostate Jew, whose denunciation led to the burning of the Talmud, died on March 3, 1589.
3. The popular work *Menorat ha-Ma'or* by Rabbi Isaac Aboab, was printed for the first time in Mantua, Italy, on February 16, 1565.
4. Rabbi Ẓevi Hirsch Koidonover, author of *Kav ha-Yashar*, a book on ethics, died on March 23, 1712 (Adar II).
5. The first advertisement offering private Hebrew instruction in an American publication was inserted by Abraham Cohen in the *Pennsylvania Packet* on March 1, 1790.

   The first advertisement in an American publication, inserted by a Hebrew tutor, reflects the poor educational facilities available to the Jewish community in the early years after the establishment of the United States. The private tutor, who had dominated the field of elementary education in the Old World, soon emerged as an important educational functionary in the New World as well.
6. Jews of Sweden were emancipated on February 16, 1870.
7. Solomon Mandelkern, Hebrew poet, author of *Heikhal ha-Kodesh*, a biblical concordance, died on March 24, 1902 (Adar II).
8. David Ben-Gurion, head of the Israeli government, and Konrad Adenauer, head of the West German government, met for the first time on March 14, 1960, to discuss mutual problems.

ADAR 16

1. King Agrippa I began the construction of a gate for the wall of Jerusalem, 42 C.E. The day was designated a holiday (Zeitlin, *Megillat Ta'anit*).

   See Elul 7:2.
2. Jews were excluded from public offices and dignities in the Roman Empire on March 10, 418 (Adar II).

   The law excluding Jews from public office in the Roman Empire was published on Adar 16, 418. Emancipation was granted to most Italian Jews 1,430 years later. The destruction of the ghetto gates in Ferrara, Italy, on Adar 16, was a public manifestation of the new order (no. 7).
3. Emperor Henry III granted Judah b. Kalonymus and other Jews of Speyer protection of life and property on February 19, 1090.

4. Jews of New Amsterdam were denied the right to erect a synagogue on March 13, 1656.

   The denial of the petition of the Jews of New Amsterdam for permission to build a synagogue was the result of Peter Stuyvesant's efforts to transplant European religious prejudices in the New World. History made amends for this slip. The Rabbi Isaac Elchanan Theological Seminary, which was to provide religious leadership to a large segment of American Jewry, was incorporated on the anniversary of Stuyvesant's denial (no. 9). The United Synagogue of America, with which hundreds of Conservative congregations are affiliated, was also organized on the same anniversary (no. 10).

5. Emperor Maximilian II granted permission to Christophe Plantin, on February 21, 1665, to print Hebrew books in Antwerp.

6. Judah Leib b. Ze'ev, the first Jewish grammarian and lexicographer of modern times, died on March 12, 1811.

7. The ghetto pillars of Ferrara, Italy, were destroyed by the professors and students of the Athenaeum on March 21, 1848 (Adar II).

8. Rabbi Simeon Sofer, leader of Orthodox Jewry of Galicia, founder of a weekly publication *Maḥazikei ha-Dat*, died on March 25, 1883 (Adar II).

9. Rabbi Isaac Elchanan Theological Seminary, the first Orthodox Jewish rabbinical seminary in the United States, was incorporated in New York State on March 20, 1897 (Adar II).

10. The United Synagogue of America was organized on February 23, 1913.

11. Vladmir Jabotinsky announced, in Alexandria, Egypt, on March 2, 1915, the formation of a Jewish military force to fight in Palestine against the Turks.

    Three people volunteered on the day the force was formed: Vladimir Jabotinsky, Joseph Trumpeldor, and Hirsh L. Gordon. The British accepted the Jewish volunteers and formed them into a Jewish battalion officially designated as the Zion Mule Corps (Nisan 8:7).

12. Dr. Ludwig Fischer, landkommissar for Warsaw, was executed on March 8, 1947, for his part in the liquidation of the ghetto.

ADAR 17

1. The arrival of Josephus in the year 66 to assume command of the Jewish insurgent forces in the Galilee saved the local Jewish population from assault by the gentiles. The day was designated a holiday (Zeitlin, *Megillat Ta'anit*).

   The official outbreak of the rebellion against Rome took place, according to some historians, on Iyar 17 of the same year.
2. Rabbi Reuben Hoeshke of Prague, author of *Yalkut Reuveni*, an anthology of kabbalistic lore, died on April 3, 1673.
3. Rabbi Gedaliah Lipschutz, author of *Regel Yesharah*, died on February 24, 1826 (HY).
4. Rabbi David (Tevele) b. Moses of Minsk, Russia, author of *Bet David*, died on February 27, 1861 (DDD).
5. The Rumanian government, on March 26, 1902 (Adar II), passed an Artisan Bill, prohibiting Jews from engaging in handicrafts or trade.
6. The Bulgarian commissar for Jewish affairs, Alexander Belev, signed an agreement, on February 22, 1943, permitting Germany to deport 26,000 Jews to extermination camps.
7. The Jewish quarter of Old Jerusalem was besieged by Arabs on March 28, 1948 (Adar II).

   The Jews of the Old Quarter of Jerusalem were cut off from the Jewish community of New Jerusalem when access to the gates in the walls of Jerusalem was barred to them. Adar 16 was an ancient holiday commemorating Jewish construction and control of the gates in the Jerusalem wall (Adar 16:1).
8. Legal status was granted to the Jewish community of Spain on March 21, 1965 (Adar II), for the first time since the expulsion in 1492.

   See Kislev 25:20.
9. Yitzhak Dov Berkowitz, Hebrew and Yiddish writer, died on March 29, 1967 (Adar II).

ADAR 18

1. Rabbi Elijah b. Moses de Vidas completed his popular work on ethics, *Reishit Ḥakhmah*, on February 28, 1575 (Adar II).
2. Pope Benedict XIV, on February 28, 1747, reaffirmed a Church rule forcing Christianity upon a Jewish child who was baptized against the will of his parents and in violation of canonical law.
3. Rabbi Alexander Suskind of Horodno, kabbalist, author of *Yesod ve-Shoresh ha-Avodah*, a book on morals, died on Feburary 18, 1794 (JE).

4. David Emmanuel the first Jewish governor in the United States, was sworn in as governor of Georgia on March 3, 1801 (*AJHSP*, no. 17, p. 187).

Adar 18 is the anniversary of three important "firsts" in American Jewish history: the swearing in of the first Jewish governor; the publication of the first Anglo-Jewish periodical (no. 7); and the yahrzeit of the first Jew in the Foreign Service (no. 8).

See note on Tishri 11:7; Elul 18:6.

5. Napoleon I, on March 17, 1808, issued a decree suspending for a decade the emancipation of Jews in the French-occupied European countries.

6. The Jews of Mecklenburg, Germany, were emancipated on February 18, 1813.

7. The *Jew,* the first Anglo-Jewish periodical published in the U.S., appeared on March 1, 1823.

8. Mordecai Manuel Noah, author and communal leader and first American Jew to hold a diplomatic post, died on March 22, 1851 (Adar II).

9. A Russian imperial decree, issued on March 28, 1891 (Adar II), ordered the expulsion of all Jewish artisans, brewers, and distillers from Moscow.

10. Jews of Smyrna, Turkey, were attacked by Greeks on March 9, 1901, charging the Jews with ritual murder.

11. Joseph Meir Ya'avatz, translator of rabbinic literature into Yiddish, died on March 16, 1914.

12. The Jewish Infantry Brigade Group, organized by the British in World War II, was committed to active duty on March 3, 1945.

See Adar 16:11; Tammuz 17:15

13. Joseph Stalin died on March 5, 1953, the very day on which the Jewish doctors involved in the "Doctors' Plot" were to be brought to trial. His death disrupted plans for mass deportations of Russian Jews.

14. Eleven leaders of American yeshivot issued a rabbinic declaration, on March 1, 1956, prohibiting Orthodox participation in rabbinic or congregational organizations with which Reform or Conservative rabbis or congregations were affiliated. This declaration foreshadowed a new separatist orientation of a large segment of American Orthodox Jewry.

The ban was confirmed by the Union of Orthodox Rabbis (predominantly European-trained) and the Rabbinical Alliance (American-trained). The Rabbinical Council (Yeshiva University graduates) took no action on the ban, leaving affiliation with such mixed groups as the New York Board of Rabbis and the Synagogue Council to the discretion of the affiliate.

ADAR 19

1. Baruch Spinoza, philosopher, died on February 21, 1677. See Av 6:1.
2. Rabbi Jacob Kahana of Vilna, author of *Ge'on Ya'akov*, died on March 28, 1826 (Adar II).
3. Hayyim b. Naphtali Coslin, grammarian, author of *Maslul*, died on March 21, 1832 (Adar II).
4. Mordecai Spector, Hebrew and Yiddish novelist, died on March 15, 1925.
5. The restriction of the sale of Arab land to Jews in Palestine, published in the MacDonald White Paper, went into effect on February 28, 1940.

    The Balfour Declaration, which held out the promise of the establishment of a Jewish homeland in Palestine, was practically voided by the MacDonald White Paper. The capture of En-Gedi (no. 6), which terminated the War of Liberation of Israel on the anniversary of the MacDonald Paper, brought final fulfillment to the Balfour Declaration.
6. The capture of En-Gedi by Israel, on March 20, 1949, brought to a conclusion the military engagements of the War of Independence.

ADAR 20

1. The Messiah, accompanied by 30,000 pious men, will appear in an undisclosed year on Adar 20 (*Sefer Eliyahu*).
2. Honi ha-Me'agal's prayer for rain was answered on Adar 20 (*Megillat Ta'anit*).
3. *Havazzelet ha-Sharon*, a commentary on the Book of Daniel by Rabbi Moses Alshekh, was published for the first time on March 5, 1563.
4. Purim Fettmilch, a private Purim, was celebrated by the Jews of Frankfort on Adar 20 to commemorate the execution of their arch-enemy, Vincent Fettmilch on March 10, 1616.
5. Rabbi Joel Sirkes (Bah), author of the popular commentary *Bayit Hadash* on the *Tur* code, died on March 2, 1640.
6. Jacob Lumbrozo, a Jewish physician residing in Maryland, was indicted on February 23, 1658, on charges of blasphemy. He was pardoned on the accession of Richard Cromwell in England. See note on Adar 28:6.
7. Rabbi Moses Meir Perles of Prague, author of *Megillat Sofer*, died on March 30, 1739 (Adar II) (JE).
8. Rabbi Yom Tov Algazi (Maharit Algazi), author of popular commen-

tary on *Hilkhot Bekhorot ve-Ḥala* by Naḥmanides, died on February 22, 1802.
 9. Joseph Jonas, Jewish pioneer of the Ohio Valley, arrived in Cincinnati on March 8, 1817.
10. Commodore Uriah Phillips Levy, father of the law abolishing corporal punishment in the U.S. Navy, died on March 22, 1862 (Adar II).
11. The first Maccabiad was held at Tel Aviv on February 27, 1932.
12. Joseph Jaffe, Yiddish poet, died on February 21, 1938.

ADAR 21

 1. Purim of Narbonne was celebrated by the Jewish community of Narbonne to commemorate its escape from a rampaging mob on March 1, 1236 (JE).
    Purim of Narbonne is the oldest private Purim on record.
 2. Rabbi Elimelekh of Lizhansk, famous ḥasidic rabbi, author of *Noam Elimelekh,* died on March 11, 1787.
 3. Rabbi Isaac Elchanan Spektor, talmudic scholar and communal leader, author of responsa *Be'er Yiẓḥak,* died on March 6, 1896.
    Rabbi Isaac Elchanan Spektor, Adolf Crémieux (Shevat 27:8), and Sir Moses Montefiore (Av 13:5) were the three outstanding Jewish communal leaders of the 19th century.
 4. The American Jewish Congress was organized on March 26, 1916 (Adar II).
 5. The Italian Fascist Party was organized on March 23, 1919 (Adar II).
 6. Admiral Miklós Horthy, regent of Hungary, capitulated on March 16, 1944, to German demands for Nazi police control of Hungary and the deportation of Jews.
 7. The first three large convoys (Operation Naḥshon) broke through the siege of Jerusalem on April 1, 1948 (Adar II), bringing arms and food for the starving population.
 8. The German Bundestag, on March 25, 1965 (Adar II), voted to extend the statutory deadline on war-crimes prosecutions to January 1, 1970.
    Pressure of international public opinion forced the German government to extend the statue of limitations on the prosecution of Nazi war criminals, in spite of mounting internal opposition. The statute was extended again for ten more years on June 26, 1969 and signed into law on August 4, 1969. The new law set the statute of limitations at 30 years for all murders and war crimes. The right to prosecute war criminals expired at the end of 1979, 30 years after Germany's assumption of jurisdiction over such cases. The crime of genocide—the

liquidation or "ghettoization" of an ethnic or religious group—was exempted by the new law from the operation of statutory limitation. However, it was not made retroactive to the Nazi era because the inception of genocide as a legal crime postdated the Hitler period.

ADAR 22

1. Jews of Uberlingen, Switzerland, were massacred on February 11, 1349.
2. The third volume of the *Zohar* was printed for the first time in Mantua, Italy, on February 19, 1560.
3. Rabbi Elijah b. Solomon of Smyrna, Turkey, author of a popular book on ethics, *Shevet Musar*, died on February 21, 1729.
4. The Purim Association of the City of New York was organized on March 24, 1862 (Adar II), for the purpose of arranging annual Purim balls.
5. Anti-Jewish riots broke out in Lubny, Russia, on March 23, 1881.
6. Rabbi Jehiel Michal Epstein of Novogrudok, Russia, author of the popular code *Arukh ha-Shulḥan*, died on February 24, 1908.
7. The provisional government of Russia, on March 16, 1917, eliminated the restrictive Pale of Settlement to which Russian Jews had been confined under the czars. All other discriminatory laws were also voided.

    Russian anti-Jewish restrictions and exclusions date from the middle of the 16th century. Ivan the Terrible (1533–84) denied admission to Jewish merchants from Lithuania even for short visits for business purposes. The Pale of Settlement was established on December 23, 1791, limiting the right of Jewish residence to a specified number of provinces. The Pale continued to exist for 126 years until it was abrogated by the revolutionary government.
8. The convention of Aḥdut ha-Avodah, meeting at Kinneret, Palestine, passed a resolution on March 12, 1920, to establish Haganah, an underground Jewish defense organization.

    The decision to establish a Jewish self-defense organization was a response to the bloody events at Tel Ḥai (See Adar II:11; Nisan 21:14).
9. Rabbi Abraham Duber Shapiro, the last rabbi of the famous Jewish community of Kovno (Kaunas), Lithuania, author of responsa *Devar Avraham*, died on February 27, 1943.

    There were Jewish merchants and apparently a small Jewish community in Kovno in the 15th century. The Jews were expelled from Lithuania by Alexander Jagellon in 1495. They were permitted to return to Lithuania on Adar 24, 1503. The modern Jewish community of Kovno dated from that day. This community became one of the leading communities of Europe under the leadership of the world-renowned Rabbi Isaac Elchanan Spektor, who died on Adar 21, 1896. The last rabbi of Kovno was the prominent Rabbi Abraham Duber Shapiro, who died on Adar 22, 1943.

10. Israel and Lebanon signed an armistice agreement on March 23, 1949.

ADAR 23

1. The beginning of a seven-day practice period of a daily assembly of the Tabernacle (*Numbers Rabbah* 13; Jer. *Yoma* 1:1).
2. The beginning of the seven-day period of consecration of Aaron and his sons to the priesthood (Lev. 8:a, Rashi).
3. The Second Temple was dedicated in 516 B.C.E. (1 Esdras, 7).
4. Massacre of the Jews of Estella, Spain, on March 6, 1328. Rabbi Menahem b. Aaron ibn Zeraḥ (author of the code *Ẓeidah la-Derekh*), whose parents and four younger brothers were killed, survived, though critically wounded.
5. Moses Gideon Abudiente, Portuguese poet and Hebrew grammarian, died on February 24, 1688.
6. Rabbi Judah b. Eliezer (Yesod), talmudist and philanthropist, died on March 18, 1762.
7. Rabbi Isaac Meir Alter, talmudist and hasidic founder of the dynasty of Gur, author of *Hiddushei Horim*, novellae on the Talmud and code, died on March 10, 1866.
8. The Committee of Jewish Delegations, representing American, Canadian, and some European Jewish communities at the Peace Conference of Versailles, was organized on March 25, 1919 (Adar II).
9. David Raziel, the founder of the Jewish underground force Irgun, was killed in action in Iraq on March 12, 1942.

ADAR 24

1. Jews of Wurtzburg were massacred by the Crusaders on February 26, 1147.
2. Pope Nicholas V, on February 25, 1451, issued a bull banning all social intercourse between Christians and Jews.

The fear of Judaizing, in spite of the contempt in which Jews were held in medieval Europe, prompted numerous anti-Jewish laws. The anti-socializing bull of 1451 sought to minimize contact between Jew and Christian and thus prevent Jewish missionary activities. Jews guilty of Judaizing and Christian converts to Judaism were liable to the death penalty in most of the Catholic and Eastern Orthodox European countries.

See Adar 28:9; Tammuz 27:5.

3. Jews of Lithuania, on March 22, 1503, were granted permission to return to the country after a brief exile of 8 years (Adar II).
   See note on Adar 22:9.

4. Rabbi Isaac Eizik Margoliot, author of *Seder Gittin ve-Halizah*, died on February 17, 1525.

5. Rabbi Hayyim Algazi of Constantinople, author of *Nesivot ha-Mishpat*, died on March 19, 1640.

6. Lorenzo Bertran, was subjected to an auto-da-fé in Seville on March 31, 1799 (Adar II). He was the last person to be punished for Judaizing in Spain.

7. Jews of White Russia, on March 31, 1856 (Adar II), were forbidden to wear distinctive clothes which would set them apart from the rest of the population. Jewish women were forbidden by the same order to shave their heads.

8. Rabbi Eliezer Lipmann Silbermann, founder of *Ha-Maggid*, the first Hebrew weekly newspaper, died on March 15, 1882.

   Eliezer Lipmann Silbermann is considered the father of modern Hebrew journalism. The first known Hebrew periodical, *Peri Ez-Hayyim*, was printed in Amsterdam in 1728. Silbermann's *Ha-Maggid*, published in Lyck, East Prussia (now Poland), in 1857, was the first Hebrew weekly. *Ha-Zefirah*, published in Warsaw in 1862, became the first Hebrew daily newspaper. *Ha-Zofeh be-Erez ha-Hadashah*, published in New York in 1870, was the first Hebrew weekly in the United States. *Ha-Yom*, the first Hebrew daily newspaper in the U.S., was published on July 18, 1909. *Hadoar* began publication in New York in 1921 as a daily. It was unable to continue as a daily and was soon converted into a weekly. The first Yiddish daily newspaper in the world, the *Yidisher Tageblat*, was published in New York in 1885.

9. An attack on Petah Tikvah on March 1, 1886, was the first organized Arab assault on a Palestinian Jewish settlement (*Zikhronot Erez Yisrael*, vol. 1, p. 317).

10. Jews of Gluchor were massacred by Ukrainian mobs and Red guerilla forces on March 8, 1918.

11. German troops marched into Prague on March 15, 1939.

12. German troops occupied Hungary on March 19, 1944.

ADAR 25

1. King Nebuchadnezzar of Babylonia, conqueror of Jerusalem, died on Adar 25, 561, B.C.E. (Jer. 52:31; *Seder Olam* 28).

   Entries Adar 25:1 and 27:1 are based on *Seder Olam* (chap. 28) and its interpretation of the conflicting dates in Jeremiah 52:31 and 2 Kings 25:27.

2. King Philip Augustus of France, on March 14, 1181, ordered the seizure of all Parisian Jews attending Sabbath services and their detention for ransom.

3. Jews of Strasbourg were burned at the Jewish cemetery on February 14, 1349.

   See Shevat 28:3.

4. Jews of Carinthia, Austria, were expelled on March 9, 1496, and not readmitted until 1848.

5. Rabbi Hayyim b. David Abulafia, author of *Nishmat Hayyim*, died on March 27, 1775 (Adar II) (ATGY).

6. Rabbi Aaron Moses b. Abraham, son of a Swedish count who had converted to Judaism, rabbi of Amsterdam, and author of *Meliz Yosher*, died on March 19, 1803.

7. Wolf Breidenbach, Austrian champion of Jewish emancipation in Germany, died on February 28, 1829.

8. A petition initiated by Rev. William E. Blackstone was sent, on March 5, 1891, to President Harrison, requesting the aid of the U.S. government in the reestablishment of Palestine as a sovereign Jewish state (*AJHSP*, no. 36, p. 42).

   The petition was signed, among others, by Cyrus H. McCormick, J. Pierpont Morgan, William McKinley, John D. Rockefeller, Russell Sage, and Cardinal Gibbons. It was a spontaneous expression of American sympathy for Zionism, totally independent of Jewish Zionist activities. The petition was motivated by biblical influences and by intense indignation aroused by Russian pogroms.

9. Rabbi Isaac Mayer Wise, dominant figure in the Reform movement in America, died on March 26, 1900 (Adar II).

10. The World Mizrachi Organization was founded in Vilna, Russia, on March 4, 1902.

11. The discovery, on March 25, 1911, of the mutilated body of Andrei Yushinsky, near Kiev, Russia, led to the infamous trial of Mendel Beilis on ritual-murder charges.

12. Adolf Hitler was granted dictatorial powers by the German Reichstag on March 23, 1933.

13. David Ignatov, Yiddish writer, died on February 28, 1954.

ADAR 26

1. Pope Innocent IV, on March 9, 1244, issued a bull ordering the burning of the Talmud.
2. The Jewish community of Newport, R.I., on February 28, 1677, purchased a plot of land for a burial ground.

   Whenever Jews settled in a new land, the patterns of communal life soon began to emerge. The essential requirements of a new Jewish community were a synagogue, a school, and a cemetery. Thus, the first Jewish settlers of New Amsterdam bought a cemetery in 1656, two years after their arrival. The earliest record of a synagogue in New Amsterdam dates from about 1666. The Jewish community of Newport was established in 1658. Its first cemetery was acquired in 1677. The land for the Touro Synagogue was purchased in 1759, a full century after the establishment of the community.
3. Emperor Joseph II, on March 31, 1783 (Adar II), issued a decree granting Jews right of residence in Pest, Hungary.
4. Rabbi Aryeh Leib Yellin, author of *Yefeh Einayim*, died on April 2, 1886 (Adar II).
5. The Nazis, on March 6, 1940, issued an order barring Jewish physicians from treating Aryans and Aryan physicians from treating Jews.
6. Operation Nahshon, Haganah's first large-scale offensive, began on April 6, 1948 (Adar II).
7. Elisheva Bikhowsky, Hebrew poetess, Russian convert to Judaism, died on March 27, 1949.

ADAR 27

1. King Jehoiachin was released from a Babylonian prison, where he had been incarcerated for 36 years, since 597 B.C.E. (*Seder Olam.* 28). See note on Adar 25:1.
2. King Zedekiah, the last king of Judea, died in captivity in Babylonia, 561 B.C.E. (ibid.).
3. Jews were massacred by rioters in Stamford-fair, England, on March 7, 1190.
4. King Przemysl Ottocar II of Austria, on March 8, 1255, renewed an old charter granting favorable rights to Jews.
5. Rabbi Leone Modena (Aryeh Leib), scholar, liturgical poet, author of *Ari Nohem*, died on March 24, 1648 (OY).
6. Rabbi Isaac da Fonseca Aboab, first rabbi and first Jewish author in America, died on April 4, 1693 (Adar II).

Rabbi Aboab had to leave the flourishing Jewish congregation of Pernambuco, Brazil, in 1654, for fear of the advancing Portuguese army and the dreaded Inquisition. The latter was abolished 167 years later on the yahrzeit of the famous rabbi (no. 9).

7. Jews of Prague were exiled on March 31, 1745 (Adar II).
8. Citizenship was granted to Jews of Prussia, upon their adoption of family names, by a decree published March 11, 1812
9. The Portuguese Inquisition was abolished on March 31, 1821 (Adar II).

The Portuguese Inquisition was established on December 17, 1531, and was in existence 290 years.

10. Rabbi Joseph Saul Nathanson of Lemberg, author of Ner Ma'aravi, novellae on the Jerusalem Talmud, died on March 4, 1875.
11. Jacob Barit (Yankele Kovner), talmudist and communal leader, died on March 6, 1883.
12. Rabbi Eliezer (Leser) Landshuth, author of Amudei ha-Avodah, died on March 23, 1887.
13. Issachar Dov Ber Bampi, scholar and philanthropist, died on March 10, 1888.
14. Ferdinand Eberstadt, mayor of Worms, first Jewish mayor in Germany, died on March 10, 1888.
15. The Belzec death camp was opened on March 16, 1942.
16. Heinrich Himmler, on March 12, 1945, signed a pact with Dr. Felix Kerstein, a Swedish national and his personal physician, agreeing to stop the execution of Jews and to surrender the concentration camps with their inmates to the advancing allies.
17. 26 Jews were wounded on April 4, 1951 (Adar II), in Salzburg, Austria, in the first serious outbreak of postwar anti-Semitism.

There is an ironic twist to the date of the first Teutonic violent anti-Semitic outbreak in the postwar period. It fell on the anniversary of Himmler's agreement to desist from anti-Jewish violence (no. 16).

18. Hayyim Greenberg, essayist and journalist, Labor Zionist leader, died on March 14, 1953.
19. At a historic White House ceremony on March 26, 1979, Mr. Begin and Mr. Sadat signed a peace treaty.

ADAR 28

1. Antiochus V granted freedom of religion and political autonomy to the Jews of Palestine, 163 B.C.E. The anniversary of this date was designated a holiday (Zeitlin, *Megillat Ta'anit*).

   According to the Skolion, the holiday was observed in commemoration of the cancellation of a Roman decree prohibiting the rite of circumcision, the study of the Torah, and the observance of the Sabbath. Relief came as a result of a petition presented by Rabbi Judah b. Shammua and his colleagues to an influential Roman lady. Rabbi Judah b. Shammua, a disciple of Rabbi Meir, lived in the period of the Hadrianic persecutions. The Hadrianic decrees were voided by Emperor Antoninus Pius in the year 139.

2. Emperor Rudolph of Hapsburg, on March 4, 1277, granted a charter of rights to the Jews of Prussia.

3. Jews of Burgsdorf, Switzerland, were expelled on February 16, 1349.

4. Jews of Styria were expelled on March 12, 1496.

5. Purim of Cairo was observed annually on Adar 28 in commemoration of an escape from massacre on March 4, 1524.

6. Dr. Jacob Lumbrozo, first Jew to settle in Maryland, was amnestied on March 3, 1658, in honor of the accession of Richard Cromwell. He had been indicted on charges of the capital offense of blasphemy.

   The release of Dr. Lumbrozo from a Maryland jail brought to a happy conclusion this unique American case of prosecution of a Jew for blasphemy. Dr. Lumbrozo subsequently became one of the first Jews in North America to acquire American citizenship. The English Naturalization Act of 1740 (no. 7), which became law on the anniversary of the release of Lumbrozo, extended the privilege of citizenship to all Jews of America.

7. The English Naturalization Act, passed on March 19, 1740, granted to Jews the right of naturalization in the American colonies.

8. Rabbi Raphael Immanuel Ricchi, kabbalist and poet, author of *Mishnat Hasidim*, died on March 24, 1743.

9. A Christian woman of Hegenbein, Alsace, was compelled by Catholic authorities to do penance, on March 4, 1791, for kindling a fire on the Sabbath for a Jew.

10. Rabbi Samuel b. Nathan Ha-Levi, author of the popular work *Mahatzit ha-Shekel*, novellae on the code, died on March 27, 1827 (HY).

11. Leon Kobrin, Yiddish writer, died on March 31, 1946 (Adar II).

ADAR 29

1. Vincent Fettmilch, the anti-Jewish leader who was responsible for the massacre of many Jews, was hanged on March 10, 1616.
   See Adar 20:4; Elul 27:2.
2. Napoleon captured the city of Jaffa, Palestine, on March 6, 1799.
3. Naftali Herz Wessely of Hamburg, Hebraist, author of *Sefer ha-Middot*, died on February 28, 1805.
4. Rabbi Solomon Ha-Kohen of Radomsko, Poland, author of *Tiferet Shelomo*, died on March 16, 1866 (DDD).
5. The legal status of the Jewish communities of Austria was defined by the law of March 21, 1890. It provided for the establishment of a single religious community in each town with compulsory affiliation of every Jew.
6. Abraham Baer, author of *Ba'al Tifillah*, an anthology of Jewish liturgical melodies, died on March 7, 1894.
7. The American Red Magen David was organized on March 13, 1918.
8. Germany occupied Memel, Lithuania, on March 20, 1939. The entire Jewish community of 7,000 fled into the interior of Lithuania.
9. Dr. Cyrus Adler, scholar, president of the Jewish Theological Seminary, died on March 9, 1940.
10. The first Jewish immigrant to Israel to disembark at the Port of Eilat arrived on April 1, 1957, aboard an Israeli chartered vessel (Adar II).
    See Adar 9:6.

ADAR 30

1. Rabbi Simeon b. Zemah Duran (Rashbaz), talmudist and philosopher, author of responsa *Sefer ha-Rashbaz*, was born on March 7, 1361.
2. The headquarters of the Jewish Agency at Jerusalem was bombed on March 11, 1948, resulting in the death of many Jews. The Hebrew poet Leib Yaffe was among the victims.

NISAN 1

1. The erection of the Tabernacle was completed (Exod. 40:17; *Numbers Rabbah* 13).

   The construction work of the Tabernacle was completed, according to rabbinic tradition, on Kislev 25 (*Numbers Rabbah* 13).
2. Moses completed the consecration rites of Aaron and his sons (Lev. 9:1, Rashi).

   Aaron performed the first sacrificial rites on Nisan 1.
3. Death of Nadab and Abihu, sons of Aaron (*Megillat Ta'anit* 1).

   According to *Midrash Petirat Aharon*, the tragic deaths of Nadab and Abihu took place on Nisan 2.
4. The children of Israel arrived in Kadesh in the desert of Zin (Num. 20:1; *Seder Olam* 9).
5. The seven-year famine in the reign of King Jehoram of Israel (854–843 B.C.E.) came to an end with a rainfall on Nisan 1 (2 Kings 8:1; Joel 1:4; *Ta'anit* 5a).
6. King Hezekiah commenced the reconsecration of the Temple (2 Chron. 29:17).

   Hezekiah timed the reconsecration of the Temple with the anniversary of the Tabernacle.

   Both were scheduled to be ready for the first month of the year.
7. Cyrus was crowned "King of Babylonia and King of all lands," 538 B.C.E.

   The crowning of King Cyrus made possible the restoration of an autonomous Jewish community in Palestine and the rebuilding of the Temple. Ezra, who was to restore the primacy of religion in the life of the Jewish community, left Babylonia on the anniversary of Cyrus' coronation.
8. The plot of Bigthan and Teresh to assassinate King Ahasuerus was discovered by Mordecai (Apocrypha; Book of Esther).
9. Ezra and his followers left Babylonia for Jerusalem, 457 B.C.E. (Ezra 7:9).
10. The convocation summoned by Ezra on the problem of intermarriage adjourned, 456 B.C.E. (Ezra 10:16).

    The convocation came to an end on the first anniversary of Ezra's departure from Babylonia.

11. 3,000 Jews of Erfurt, Germany, were killed on March 21, 1349, in the Black Death riots.
12. The first dated edition of Maimonides' *Mishneh Torah* was published on March 23, 1490.
    This edition was published in Soncino. A prior undated edition was published before 1480 in Rome and is the eighteenth work on the incunabula list.
13. Meyer Hart, one of the founders of Easton, Pa., and its first merchant, took the oath of allegiance to the colonial government on April 3, 1764.
14. Rabbi Saul Shiskes of Vilna, author of *Shevil ha-Yashar* commentary on Alfasi, died on March 28, 1797.
15. Rabbi Joseph Hochgelehrter (Joseph Harif) of Zamosc, Poland, author of *Mishnat Hakhamim*, novellae on the Talmud, died on March 20, 1806.
16. Moses Hess, author of *Rome and Jerusalem*, died on April 6, 1875.
17. *Der Yiddisher Kemfer*, organ of American Labor Zionism, was published for the first time on March 27, 1906.
18. The German Reichstag conferred dictatorial powers on Hitler on March 28, 1933.
19. Germany invaded Norway and Denmark on April 9, 1940.
20. The Haganah repelled an Arab attack on Mishmar ha-Emek, on April 10, 1948.
21. A treaty of friendship between Israel and Liberia was signed on April 9, 1959. It was the first friendship treaty between Israel and an African country.

NISAN 2

1. Moses performed the first *parah adumah* (red heifer) rite (*Gittin* 60b, Rashi).
2. Jews of Mayence, Germany, were massacred on March 31, 1283.
3. King Ferdinand and Queen Isabella, on March 30, 1492, signed a decree expelling Jews from Spain.
   See Kislev 25:21.
4. Rabbi Benjamin b. Moses of Lemberg, talmudist, author of *Tavnit ha-Bayit*, died on March 18, 1580.
5. Jews of Basra, Persia, observed a private Purim, known as Yom ha-Nes, in commemoration of a happy event on March 14, 1774.
6. Anti-Jewish riots broke out in Jerusalem on April 1, 1881.
7. Menahem Begin visited Cairo, Egypt on April 2, 1979. It was the first visit by an Israeli Prime Minister to Egypt.

NISAN 3

1. Sa'ad al-Da'ulah, Jewish grand vizier under the Mongol ruler of Persia, Argun Khan, was assassinated on March 5, 1291.
2. A decree expelling Jews from Spain and Sicily was published on March 31, 1492.
3. The French-created Kingdom of Westphalia ordered its Jews to adopt family names on March 31, 1808.
4. Jews of Prussia were granted equality on April 6, 1848.
5. Ritual charges made on April 11, 1891, resulted in riotous pogroms on the island of Corfu.
6. In the Children's Action of March 27, 1944, Nazis raided the Kovno ghetto and removed all children for execution.

   Anti-Jewish persecutions were generally aimed at the people as a whole, regardless of age. There were instances, however, where children were singled out as the victims of a discriminating decree. Pharaoh's order to drown all male infants was the earliest example of this type of legislation.

   See Nisan 15:15; Adar 18:2.
7. The body of Baron Edmond de Rothschild was reinterred on April 6, 1954, at Zikhron Ya'akov, Israel, the wine-producing village which had been established with his financial aid.

   See Heshvan 24:5.
8. Aaron Leib Baron, Yiddish poet, died on April 6, 1954.

NISAN 4

1. Rabbi Ben-Zion Zarfati of Venice, talmudist, died on March 28, 1610.
2. Rabbi Judah Leib of Lublin, author of *Peri Shabbat*, died on April 2, 1748
3. Rabbi Jacob Zevi b. Gamaliel Konigsberg, author of a popular commentary on the Pentateuch, *Ha-Ketav ve-ha-Kabbalah*, died on March 31, 1865.
4. The first Young Men's Hebrew Association was organized in New York on March 22, 1874.
5. The first performance of a Goldfaden operetta in New York marked the establishment of the Yiddish theater in America on March 20, 1885.

   An earlier production of a Yiddish show in 1884 failed for lack of professional standards.
6. Anti-Jewish riots broke out in Dabrowa, Poland, on April 5, 1938.

7. Rabbi Hayyim Most, the Maggid of Kovno, was killed by the Nazis on March 28, 1944.
8. A convoy of physicians and scientists with their guards, totaling 75 persons, was ambushed on the way to Mt. Scopus on April 13, 1948.
9. Israel and Jordan signed an armistice agreement on April 3, 1949.

NISAN 5

1. Joshua sent scouts to survey Jericho and the surrounding territory (Josh. 2:1, Rashi).
2. Rabbi Abraham Joshua of Apta (Opatow), author of the popular hasidic book *Ohav Yisrael,* died on March 24, 1825.
3. Elijah Bardach, Hebrew scholar, author of *Akedat Yizhak,* died on April 11, 1864.
4. Rehovot, Palestine, was attacked by Arabs on March 22, 1893.
5. Anti-Jewish riots broke out in Nikolayev, Russia, on March 16, 1899.
6. Jews of Tel Aviv and Jaffa were expelled by the Turkish authorities on March 28, 1917.

    The deportation of the Jews of Tel Aviv took place eight years after the founding of that city (Nisan 20:9).
7. The Polish army, on April 5, 1919, executed 35 young Jews who had helped in the distribution of packages sent by the Joint to the Jewish community of Pinsk.

    The relief activities of the Joint Distribution Committee were used by Russians, in the declining years of Stalin, as a pretext for their anti-Semitic charges of disloyalty against Soviet Jews.
8. The official Nazi boycott of German Jewish merchants started on April 1, 1933.
9. 2,500 Jews of the district of Lublin were massacred and the rest of the Jews were deported on March 23, 1942.

    The ghetto of Lublin was established by the Nazis on March 24, 1941. It was liquidated on March 23, 1942.
10. The first oil tanker to call at the port of Eilat, Israel, arrived on April 6, 1957, and delivered Persian Gulf oil.
11. Menachem Begin visited Cairo, Egypt, on April 2, 1979. It was the first visit of an Israeli prime minister to Egypt.

NISAN 6

1. Rabbi Samuel Judah Katzenellenbogen, noted talmudist, died on March 25, 1597.
   Rabbi Katzenellenbogen was the father of Saul Wahl, who was reputed to have been king of Poland for a day.
2. Rabbi Isaac Drohobyczer, leading hasidic rabbi, died on April 6, 1794.
3. Kosher slaughtering was prohibited in Saxony on March 23, 1893. See note on Heshvan 13:5.
4. Moses Ha-Kohen Reicherson, Hebrew grammarian, died on April 3, 1903.
5. The Jewish Congress Organization Committee was formed in New York City on March 21, 1915.
6. Jews of Seredino Buda were massacred by Ukrainian mobs and Red guerilla bands on March 9, 1918.
7. The town of Afulah was founded in Palestine on March 31, 1925.
8. Rabbi Meir Dan Plotzki, author of *Kelei Hemdah*, commentary on the Pentateuch, died on March 27, 1928.
9. The Arab Yarmuk Army, under the command of Fawzi al-Kaukji, was defeated in the battle of Mishmar ha-Emek on April 15, 1948.
   The battle of Mishmar ha-Emek was the first major military engagement between Arab and Jewish forces prior to the establishment of Israel.

NISAN 7

1. Jews of York, England, committed mass suicide on March 16, 1190, rejecting an invitation to submit to baptism.
2. Jews of Weissensee, Germany, were massacred on March 25, 1303.
3. Rabbi Meir Schiff (Maharam Schiff), author of *Hiddushei Maharam Schiff*, novellae on the Talmud, died on April 13, 1644 (ATGY).
4. Duke Ferdinand, on March 23, 1714, published a decree ordering the expulsion of all Jews from Courland.
5. Rabbi Pinchas Zelig of Lask, author of *Ateret Paz*, comments on the Rosh, died on April 2, 1770.
6. The Hebrew University of Jerusalem was opened by Lord Balfour on April 1, 1925.
7. The government of Hungary issued a decree on March 31, 1944, ordering all Jews to wear a yellow star.

NISAN 8

1. The feast of King Ahasuerus, which had lasted for 180 days, came to an end (Esther 1:4; *Manot ha-Levi* by Solomon Ha-Levi Alkabez).
2. Rabbi Elijah Kalmankes of Lemberg, author of *Aderet Eliyahu*, died on April 13, 1636.
3. Rabbi Elijah Shapira of Prague, author of *Eliyahu Rabbah*, died on April 14, 1712.
4. Rabbi Benjamin Zev, author of *Ir Binyamin*, died on April 5, 1721.
5. The first rabbinic opposition to Ḥasidism was announced in Vilna, on April 11, 1772. A ḥerem, endorsed by the Gaon of Vilna, was published against the sectarians in 1777 and again in 1781.
6. Czar Alexander I of Russia, on March 25, 1817, recommended the formation of a Society of Israelitish Christians.
7. The Zion Mule Corps, consisting of Jewish volunteers from Palestine, was formed on March 23, 1915.

    The Zion Mule Corps was the first Palestinian Jewish military unit attached to a regular army in the Christian era. It was the forerunner of the Jewish Legion, which was formed in 1918 and committed to combat at Es-Salt, Transjordan. See note on Iyar 19:4.

NISAN 9

1. 57 Jews were killed in Bury St. Edmunds, England, on March 18, 1190.
2. Anti-Jewish riots broke out in Seville, Spain, on March 15, 1391. (JE)

    The anti-Jewish riots which broke out in Seville on Ash Wednesday of 1391 initiated a wave of violence which spread rapidly over the Iberian Peninsula and claimed 50,000 victims before the year was up. A substantial number of Jews escaped with their lives only at the cost of converting. This marked the emergence of Marranos, said to number 200,000, in the kingdoms of Aragon and Castile. They were to provide countless martyrs in the Old and New Worlds for centuries to come. See Tammuz 1:4.
3. Jews of Vienna, Austria, were accused of profaning the host. Many of those who refused to embrace Christianity were burned at the stake on March 12, 1421.
4. Rabbi Joseph b. Phinehas Haan of Cracow, author of *Yosef Ometz*, died on April 3, 1637.
5. The Jewish community of Carpentras, France, instituted a private

Purim on Nisan 9 to commemorate a miraculous escape from mob riots on March 26, 1692.

6. Rabbi David Pardo of Venice, liturgical poet, author of *Hasdei David*, was born on March 29, 1719.
7. The apostate Judah Monis, whose *Dikduk Lashon Ivrit* was the first Hebrew book published in New England, became instructor of Hebrew at Harvard College 3 months after his conversion to Christianity on March 27, 1722.
8. Rabbi Jacob Zevi Yales, author of *Melo ha-Roim*, novellae on the Talmud, died on March 28, 1825 (HY).
9. The Central Union of German Citizens of the Jewish Faith was organized on March 26, 1893, to protect the civil rights of German Jews.
10. The Jewish Colonial Trust, financial instrument of the Zionist movement, was incorporated in England on March 20, 1899.
11. Jacob De Haas, historian and Zionist leader, died on March 21, 1937.
12. Germany invaded Yugoslavia and Greece on April 6, 1941.
13. The Nazis, on April 6, 1941, established two ghettos in Radom, Poland.
14. A new road leading to Sodom, Israel, was dedicated on March 25, 1953.

NISAN 10

1. Death of Miriam (*Seder Olam* 10).

   According to *Midrash Petirat Aharon*, Miriam died and the well dried up on Nisan 1.
2. The mobile well, which supplied water to the Jews in the desert, dried up (ibid.).
3. The Jews, under the leadership of Joshua, crossed the Jordan and erected 12 monuments at Gilgal (Josh. 4:20).

   According to Rabbi Simon (*Sotah* 36a), the following events took place on that day: the Jews lined up on Mt. Ebal and Mt. Gerizim; the pertinent Torah portion relating to the blessings and curses was recited; Joshua erected an altar on Mt. Ebal and brought offerings; the entire Torah, with multilingual translations, was inscribed on it (Josh. 8:30–34); and Joshua composed the second paragraph of the after-meal grace (Berakhot 48b).
4. Rabbi Aaron of Neustadt (Blumlein), author of *Hilkhot Niddah*, was martyred in Vienna on March 13, 1421.
5. Emperor Charles V, on April 3, 1544, confirmed the privileges of Austrian Jews.

6. Rabbi Asher Anshel was martyred in Cracow on April 12, 1631.
7. Rabbi Judah Ashael b. David Eliezer del Bene, poet and philosopher, author of *Kisot le-Bet David*, died on April 2, 1678.
8. The first congregation of New Orleans, Shaare Chesed, was incorporated on March 25, 1828.
   This congregation was later renamed the Touro Synagogue.
9. The first train with Jewish deportees left Paris for Auschwitz on March 28, 1942.
10. Haganah captured Tiberias on April 19, 1948.

NISAN 11

1. The generation of Jews born in the desert submitted to the rite of circumcision upon entering Palestine (Josh. 5:3; *Seder Olam* 11).
2. Rabbenu Moses b. Nahman (Nahmanides), the greatest talmudic scholar of his generation, author of *Hiddushei ha-Ramban*, novellae on the Talmud, and outstanding Bible exegete, died on April 5, 1270 (HY).
3. Pope Pius IV, on March 24, 1564, authorized the printing of the Talmud in Mantua on condition that the word *Talmud* be omitted.
4. Rabbi Isaiah Horowitz (Shelah), distinguished kabbalist, author of *Shenei Luhot ha-Berit*, died on March 24, 1630 (HY).
5. The Dutch West India Co., on April 7, 1645, granted Michael Cardoso the right to practice law in Brazil, a privilege no Jew enjoyed at that time anywhere else.
6. Frederick the Great of Prussia, on April 17, 1750, issued a decree imposing oppressive restrictions upon Jews.
   The anti-Jewish policies of Frederick the Great foreshadowed the survival of anti-Semitism in the age of "Enlightenment."
7. Rabbi Simhah Bunim Rapaport of Wuerzburg, Germany, author of *Hiddushei Rashbaz*, died on April 9, 1816 (DYY).
8. The second Mill Street Synagogue of Congregation Shearith Israel was dedicated on April 17, 1818.
   The Mill Street Synagogue at that time was still the only synagogue in New York City.
9. The first two Nazi anti-Jewish decrees, barring Jews from public service and the legal practice, were published on April 7, 1933.
10. The Nazis established a ghetto in Kielce, Poland, on April 8, 1941.

NISAN 12

1. King Hezekiah fell critically ill (2 Kings 20:1, *Seder Olam* 23).
   According to *Seder Olam*, King Hezekiah was taken ill three days before the defeat of King Sennacherib (Nisan 15:9).
2. Ezra and his followers departed from the River Ahava on their way to Jerusalem, 457 B.C.E. (Ezra 8:31).
   Ezra's aliyah to Palestine started on Nisan 1 (no. 9). He arrived in Jerusalem four months later, on Av 1 (no. 5). One wonders why Ezra did not schedule the beginning of his journey after Passover. He might have wished to time his crossing of the River Ahava, from which point he no longer enjoyed the protection of the Persian authorities, with the anniversary of Joshua's historic crossing of the Jordan into Palestine on Nisan 10 (no. 3).
3. By a decree issued on April 11, 1302, the Jews of Barcelona, Spain, were ordered to kneel when meeting a priest with the sacraments.
4. 32 Jews of Meshed, Persia, were massacred on March 27, 1839. The remaining 100 families were forcibly converted to Islam.
   The tragic chapter of Marranoism in Spain had its inception in the events of Nisan 9, 1391 (no. 2). An obscure chapter of Islamic Marranoism, on a very small scale, had its inception in events at Meshed, Persia, on Nisan 12, 1839. 100 converted Jewish families continued to secretly observe most Jewish rites after their conversion. It was not until the establishment of Israel that many members of this secret Jewish community openly proclaimed their Judaism and emigrated to Israel.
5. The disappearance of Eszter Solymosi in Tisza-Eszlar, Hungary, on April 1, 1882, led to ritual charges resulting in a series of anti-Jewish riots.
6. The Russian revolutionary government, on April 4, 1917, granted equality to all Russian Jews for the first time in Russian history.
   In the first decade of the 20th century Russia had, under its effective control and domination, about 50 percent of the total world Jewish population. The grant of equality by the Russian revolutionary government affected, therefore, a major part of world Jewry. By the end of the second decade Russia had under its jurisdiction only about 18 percent of the total Jewish population.
7. Germany occupied Lemberg (Lwow) on March 30, 1942, and immediately imposed anti-Jewish restrictions.

NISAN 13

1. Haman published a decree calling for the extermination of all the Jews of the Persian Empire (Esther 3:12).
2. Esther ordered a three-day fast for all the Jews of Shushan (ibid. 4:16).
3. King Richard I granted a charter of rights to the Jews of England on March 22, 1190.
   See Nisan 7:1.
4. Rabbi Obadiah Bertinoro, author of a popular Mishnah commentary, arrived in Jerusalem on March 25, 1488.
5. Rabbi Joseph Caro, codifier, author of the authoritative *Shulhan Arukh*, died on March 24, 1575.
6. Rabbi David b. Solomon Altaras (Devash), author of *Kelalei ha-Dikduk*, died on March 29, 1714.
7. The New York State Convention at Kingston, N.Y., on April 20, 1777, guaranteed the free exercise of religion.
8. Rabbi Menahem Mendel of Lubavich, hasidic leader, author of responsa *Zemah Zedek*, died on March 29, 1866.
9. Rabbi Arnaud Aron, chief rabbi of Strasbourg, Alsace, author of *Prières d'un Coeur Israélite*, died on April 3, 1890.
10. The German Workers' Party, on April 1, 1920, was renamed the National Socialist German Workers' Party; this marked the emergence of the Nazi Party.

    The Nazi Party emerged on the anniversary of the day that Haman published his decree of extermination of the Jews (no. 1).
11. Rabbi Moses Avigdor Amiel, talmudist and eloquent preacher, author of *Derashot el-Ammi*, died on March 27, 1945.
12. Haganah occupied the city of Haifa, Palestine, on April 22, 1948.

NISAN 14

1. Cain and Abel brought sacrificial offerings (Yonaton b. Uziel, Gen. 4:3).

   Bereshit Rabbah (chap. 22) indicates two dates for the death of Abel—Kislev 25 and Sivan 6. It also states that he was less than three months old when he was killed. According to *Tanhuma* (Gen. 4:3), however, he was 40 years old.
2. The first Paschal lambs were sacrificed by the Jews in Egypt (Exod. 12:28).
3. Fast-day of the first-born (*Soferim* 21).

The fast of the first-born is mentioned in the Talmud (Jer. *Pesaḥim* 10:1), not as a generally accepted tradition, but rather as a voluntary practice of some individuals. The first authoritative source indicating that the fast had become a universally accepted tradition is *Masekhet Soferim* (chap. 21; ca. 8th cent.). The wording of the text: "One should not fast in the month of Nisan, with the exception of the first-born who fast on the eve of Passover. . . ." proves that the tradition of the fast had already been well established by the time the text was written. It may be assumed that this fast came into vogue in the 6th or 7th century.

4. Naomi and Ruth arrived in Bethlehem (Targum, Ruth 1:22).
5. Titus and the Roman army set up their camp before the walls of Jerusalem on May 8 (approximate), 70 C.E.

The broad implications of the struggle between Rome and Jerusalem, as a life-and-death conflict between two mutually antagonistic religious and social systems, was succinctly described by the Talmud: "If you are told that both [Caesarea and Jerusalem] are in ruins, do not believe it; both are prosperous, do not believe it; Caesarea is in ruins and Jerusalem prospers or Jerusalem is in ruins and Caesarea prospers, believe it" (*Megillah* 6a). The battle cry of the tug of war between Jerusalem and Rome changed its tone and slogans as the latter progressed from the temporal to the spiritual capital of the world, but the pull and stress continued unabated. The assault upon Vatican temporal absolutism was marked by the battering down of the gates of the Jewish ghetto (no.9). This was done on the anniversary of the siege of Jerusalem by ancient Rome (no.5). The first Roman assault upon Jerusalem was made on Tishri 30, 66 (no. 1). The foundation stone of the Knesset, symbol of restored Israel, was laid in Jerusalem on the anniversary of that event (no.5). Vespasian occupied the city of Gadara on Adar 4, 68, marking his triumphant march through Palestine (no.1). Roman Jews were declared free citizens by a French army on the anniversary of that march (no.6). King Agrippa I began the construction of a gate for the walls of Jerusalem on Adar 16, 42 B.C.E. (no.1). On the same day in 418, Jews were excluded from public office in the Roman Empire (no.2). On Iyar 7 Nehemiah dedicated the outer walls of Jerusalem (no.2). On the same day in the year 70, the Jews surrendered the outer walls of Jerusalem to the Romans (no.4). The Temple was set aflame on Av 10 (no.3). On the same date in 1556, Jews moved into the Roman ghetto (no.8).
6. Rabbi Moses b. Maimon (Rambam; also known as Maimonides), codifier and philosopher, was born on March 30, 1135.
7. 3,000 Jews of Erfurt were killed in the Black Death massacres on March 21, 1349.

8. The Pentateuch with a Yiddish translation was published in Cremona, Italy, on April 10, 1560.
9. Roman citizens, under the direction of the popular Ciceruacchio, pulled down the gates of the Roman ghetto, the most notorious medieval ghetto in Europe, on April 17, 1848.
10. Jews who had served in the Russian army received the right of residence in the province of Abo-Bjorneborg, Finland, upon its annexation to Russia on March 29, 1858.
11. Jews of Bavaria were granted equality on April 22, 1872.
12. The British army, with the participation of the Jewish battalion, captured Amman on March 27, 1918.
13. The uprising in the Warsaw ghetto broke out on April 19, 1943.
14. The Jewish underground in Belgium, aided by Christian railroad men, derailed a train with Jewish deportees bound for the extermination camps on April 19, 1943. Several hundred Jews were saved.
15. Abraham Reisen, Yiddish novelist and poet, died on March 30, 1953.
16. Rabbi Hayyim Heller, talmudist and biblical scholar, author of LeHikre ha-Halakhot, died on April 11, 1960.

NISAN 15

1. Sarah was brought to the house of Pharaoh (Gen.12:15, Yalkut Shimoni).
2. God made a covenant with Abraham (Gen. 15:18 Seder Olam 5).
   See note on Tishri 13:1.
3. The angels appeared to inform Abraham that a son would be born to Sarah (Gen. 18:10; Seder Olam 5).
4. Birth of Isaac (Rosh Ha-Shanah 10b).
5. Isaac summoned Esau and requested that he prepare a tasty meal for him and receive his blessing (Gen. 27:4; Yonatan b. Uziel; Pirkei de-Rabbi Eliezer 2).
   This tradition was apparently based on the wording of Isaac's blessing: "May God give you of the dew of heaven" (Gen. 27:28). The Talmud fixed Nisan 15 as the beginning of the harvest season and the end of the rainy season (Bava Mezia 106b). Thereafter rain is harmful but dew is beneficial.
6. Moses saw the burning bush (Exod. 3:2, Bahya, Bo).
7. The Egyptian first-born were slain (Exod. 12:29).
8. First day of Passover. The beginning of the Exodus (Exod. 12:37).
9. The Assyrian army of Sennacherib, which had threatened Jerusalem, was destroyed(2 Kings 19:35, Targum Rav Yosef; 2 Chron. 32:21).

10. Death of Job (Jer. *Sotah* 5:8).
11. Vashti was executed by order of King Ahasuerus (Esther 1:21; *Derash le-Purim*).
12. Queen Esther appeared before King Ahasuerus to plead for the Jews (Esther 5:1; *Seder Olam* 29).
13. The defenders of Masada committed suicide, 73 C.E. The last resistance to the Roman conquest of Palestine came to an end (Josephus, *Wars 7:9*).
14. The disappearance of Simon of Trent on March 23, 1475, led to the torture and death of many distinguished Jews of that community on charges of ritual murder.
15. An order issued on March 19, 1497, provided for the seizure of all Portuguese Jewish children, ages 4–14, for forcible conversion.
16. Jews of the principality of Orange, Burgundy, were expelled by Philibert of Luxembourg, on April 20, 1505.
17. Rabbi Jonah Teomim of Metz, France, author of *Kikayon de-Yona*, died on April 16, 1669.
18. Rabbi Abraham Kalmansk of Lemberg, author of *Eshel Avraham*, died on April 3, 1681.
19. Rabbi Elijah, the Gaon of Vilna, was born on April 23, 1720.
20. Rabbi Simḥon b. Joshua Moses Morforso, author of responsa *Shemesh Zedakah*, died on April 12, 1740.
21. Napoleon issued a proclamation to the Jews of Palestine on April 20, 1799, promising the "reestablishment of ancient Jerusalem," coupled with a plea for their support. This was the first promise by a modern government to establish a Jewish state.
22. An order expelling Jews from Moscow was published on April 23, 1891.
23. Vladimir Jabotinsky was sentenced by the British mandatory government of Palestine, on April 24, 1921, to 15 years of imprisonment for his participation in the Jewish self-defense corps.

NISAN 16

1. Second day of Passover.
2. Birth of Levi, third son of Jacob (*Midrash Tadshe*).
3. The supply of manna was exhausted on Nisan 16, six days after the Jews had crossed the Jordan into Palestine (*Kiddushin* 38a).
   See Adar 7:5.
4. The Omer was offered for the first time by the Jews in Palestine (Josh. 5:11; *Rosh Ha-Shanah* 13a).
5. An angel ordered Gideon to attack the Midianites (Judg. 6:19, Rashi).

6. King Saul's seven sons were killed (*Midrash Rabbah*, Naso, ch. 8).
7. King Hezekiah completed the rededication of the Temple (2 Chron. 29:17).
8. Haman was hanged (Esther 7:10; *Seder Olam* 29).
9. Mordecai was appointed chief minister by King Ahasuerus to replace Haman (Esther 8:2).
10. The alleged murder of William of Norwich, on March 21, 1144, led to the first charge of ritual murder against Jews in the Middle Ages.
    The timing of ritual libels with Passover is analyzed by Cecil Roth in his *Personalities and Events in Jewish History*, chap. 4.
    See notes on Sivan 20:2; Elul 24:4.
11. King Sigismund I of Poland issued a decree on March 28, 1537, granting a monopoly of importation and publication of Hebrew books to the Helitz brothers, who had established the first Hebrew printing press in Poland.
    The decree was issued following a widespread Jewish boycott of the firm as a result of the conversion of the brothers to Catholicism.
12. Jews of Genoa, Italy, were expelled on April 2, 1550.
13. Rabbi Ḥayyim b. Jacob Abulafia of Smyrna, author of *Eẓ ha-Ḥayyim*, died on March 29, 1744.
14. Anti-Jewish violence broke out in Budapest, Hungary, on April 19, 1848.
15. Moritz Lazarus, philosopher, died on April 13, 1903.
16. Rabbi Meyer Kayserling, historian, died on April 21, 1905.
17. Rioting Polish soldiers attacked the Jewish community of Lida, Russia, on April 16, 1919.
18. Arabs killed and wounded many Jews in Jerusalem on April 4, 1920.
19. Jacob P. Adler, outstanding Yiddish actor, died on March 31, 1926.
    The development of the Yiddish theater reached its peak in the United States. The concentration of over a million Yiddish-speaking people in the New York metropolitan area gave the Yiddish stage and press its golden age in the first three decades of the 20th century. Jacob P. Adler was one of the leading actors of that period.

NISAN 17

1. Third day of Passover.
2. Rabbi Reuben Hoeshke Katz of Prague, author of *Yalkut Reuveni*, a midrashic anthology, died on April 3, 1673.
3. Israel b. Moses Zamosc of Brody, Galicia, talmudist and mathematician, author of *Nezah Yisrael*, died on April 20, 1772.
4. Solomon Etting, prominent businessman of Lancaster, Pa., was the

first native American Jew to receive a limited authorization to function as a shoḥet. The certificate was dated April 1, 1782 (*AJHSP* no. 34).

The early American Jewish community, though mainly traditional, was too small to train its own religious functionaries and too distant to attract European scholars. The first "Kabbalah" (religious certification of qualification to function as a religious slaughterer) was granted in 1782 to Solomon Etting, a layman, who had to provide his own kosher meat.

5. The Jewish Welfare Board was founded on April 9, 1917, to meet the religious and cultural needs of Jewish personnel in the U.S. armed forces.
6. Mother Maria of Paris, a Russian nun who had saved many French Jews by providing them with hiding places, was killed by the Nazis in the Ravensbrueck camp on March 31, 1945 (Friedman, *Their Brothers' Keepers.*)
7. A rail line linking Beersheba with Israel's railway system was dedicated on March 29, 1956.

NISAN 18

1. Fourth day of Passover.
2. Pharaoh was informed that the Hebrew slaves had escaped (Exod. 14:5, Rashi).

   When Moses was sent to liberate the Jews from Egyptian slavery, he set out to attain three objectives: emancipation, religious education, and national independence (Exod. 6:7–8). The first objective was achieved with the exodus from Egypt. The next goal was reached at Mt. Sinai. The final aim was accomplished upon the military conquest of Palestine.
3. Rabbi Meir Abulafya Ha-Levi (Ramah), talmudist and liturgical poet, leading opponent of Maimonides, author of *Yad Ramah*, died on March 29, 1244.
4. A number of London Jews suffered martyrdom on April 2, 1279, following ritual charges.
   See Nisan 16:10.
5. Purim of the Bomb was celebrated by the Jews of Fossano, south of the Alps, to commemorate their escape from massacre on April 26, 1796.
6. Rabbi Gustav Gottheil, scholar and one of the founders of the Jewish Publication Society, died on April 15, 1903.

7. The Sons of Zion fraternal order was organized on April 19, 1908.
8. Po'al ha-Mizrachi, the religious Zionist labor movement, was founded on April 16, 1922.

NISAN 19

1. Fifth day of Passover.
2. Pharaoh set out in pursuit of the Jews (Exod. 14:5, Rashi).
    Adolf Hitler made his first appearance (no. 12) on the anniversary of the day on which the first anti-Semite in Jewish history set out in pursuit of the Jewish people.
3. Rabbi Isaac b. Baruch Albalia, mathematician and astronomer, author of *Kuppat ha-Rochlin*, novellae on the Talmud, died on April 8, 1094.
4. Rabbi Joshua Falk b. Alexander Katz of Lemberg, author of *Sefer Me'irat Einayim*, died on March 29, 1614.
5. The directors of the Dutch West India Co., on April 26, 1655, refused to grant permission to Governor Peter Stuyvesant to exclude Jews from New Amsterdam.
    Nisan 19 is a red-letter day in the history of the American Jewish community. The refusal of the Dutch West India Co. to permit the expulsion of the early Jewish settlers from New Amsterdam put an end to official efforts to bar Jews from North America. The Dutch West India Co. also specified that no restriction of trade be imposed upon the Jewish settlers. Thus it guaranteed not only the physical inviolability of the Jews but also their orderly economic development and progress. The only condition contained in the directive provided that "the poor among them shall . . . be supported by their own nation." This gave further impetus to the growth of Jewish philanthropy in the New World.
6. Moses Germanus (Johann Peter Spaeth), author, convert to Judaism, died on April 27, 1701.
7. Rabbi Raphael Meldola of Leghorn, Italy, author of *Mayim Rabbim*, died on April 17, 1748.
8. Hayyim (Hermann) Bloch, talmudic scholar and writer, author of *Mavo ha-Talmud*, was born on April 26, 1826.
9. Anti-Jewish riots broke out in Odessa, Russia, on April 10, 1871.
10. Rabbi Hayyim Bezalel Panet of Bielitz, Poland, author of *Derekh Yivhar*, died on April 2, 1877.
11. Adolf Hitler was born in Braunau-am-Inn, Austria, on April 20, 1889.
12. Rabbi Hayyim Leib Tiktinski, head of the Yeshivah of Mir for 49 years, died on March 30, 1899.

13. Anti-Jewish riots broke out in Zhitomir, Russia, on April 24, 1905.
14. The Polish army occupied Vilna and attacked its Jewish community on April 19, 1919.
15. Rabbi Menahem Zemba, author of *Zera Avraham*, was killed in the Warsaw ghetto on April 24, 1943.
16. Rabbi Meir Bar-Ilan, leader of Mizrachi, scholar and author, died on April 18, 1949.
17. Rabbi Jekuthiel Judah Greenwald, prolific writer of rabbinics and history, author of *Ach laZarah*, died on April 11, 1955.

NISAN 20

1. Sixth day of Passover.
2. Pharaoh and his pursuing army caught up with the Jews encamped at Pi-hahiroth by the sea (Exod. 14:5; Rashi)
3. Rav Hai Gaon, the last of the geonim of Pumpedita, author of responsa, died on March 28, 1038.
    The death of Rav Hai Gaon, the last of the geonim at Pumpedita, brought to a close the glorious epoch of Babylonian Jewry. For more than eight centuries Babylonia was the center of Jewish culture and creative scholarship. Its leaders provided the guidance and direction of Jewish religious development throughout the world. After the decline of Babylonian Jewry, the center of Jewish culture shifted in succeeding stages to North Africa, Germany, France, Spain, Italy, the Turkish Empire, and Eastern Europe. The post-Nazi period has witnessed the emergence of two new centers of Jewish learning—Israel and the United States.
4. The first Jewish settlers arrived in Amsterdam, Holland, on April 22, 1593.
5. Jews of Pressburg, Hungary, (now Bratislava, Czechoslovakia), were forced to flee their homes on April 6, 1809, when Napoleon's forces attacked the city.
6. Rabbi Ezekiel Panet, author of responsa *Mareh Yeḥezkel*, died on April 27, 1845.
7. The first issue of the *Jewish Daily Forward*, a daily Yiddish newspaper, was published on April 22, 1897.
8. Rumania barred Jews from professional and agricultural schools on March 31, 1899.
9. Tel Aviv, Palestine, was founded on April 11, 1909.

NISAN 21

1. Seventh day of Passover.
2. Jacob left Laban's home to return to Palestine (Gen. 31:17; Book of Jubilees).

   The inclusion of Laban's persecution of Jacob in the Haggadah is based on Deut. 26:5. This verse links the Laban episode with Jacob's trip to Egypt (according to midrashic interpretation). The tradition which assigns the same date to the flight from Laban's home and the flight across the Red Sea may have grown out of this association.
3. Pharaoh's decree against Jewish male infants was canceled on Nisan 21 (*Sotah* 12b).
4. Jews crossed the Red Sea. (Exod. 14:22; *Sotah* 12b).
5. Moses and the people of Israel sang the *Shirah* (*Sotah* 12b).
6. King Philip the Bold of France, on April 19, 1283, issued a decree prohibiting the repair of synagogues and the possession of the Talmud.
7. 26 Jews of Bacharach, Germany, were murdered on April 19, 1283. On the same day, 10 Jews were killed in Mayence, following blood ritual charges.
9. The entire ghetto of Nikolsburg (Mikulov),Moravia, was destroyed by fire on April 10, 1719.
10. Congregation Shearith Israel of New York dedicated the first synagogue built in North America on April 8, 1730.
11. Rabbi Daniel of Horodno, author of *Hamudei Daniel*, died on April 9, 1806.
12. Rev. Ferdinand Sarner became, on April 10, 1863, the first American rabbi to serve as a regimental chaplain with American forces.
    See Elul 23:3.
13. The Polna Affair, growing out of the discovery of a murdered Bohemian woman on April 1, 1899, led to ritual charges against Leopold Hilsner and attracted worldwide attention.
    See Heshvan 22:8.
14. Ha-Shomer early self-defense organization of Palestinian Jews, was organized on April 12, 1909.
15. Rabbi Benjamin Menasseh Levin, author of *Ozar ha-Geonim*, died on April 14, 1944.
16. The first transport of Jews of Athens, Greece, left for Auschwitz on April 14, 1944.

NISAN 22

1. Eighth day of Passover.
2. Isaac was circumcised on Nisan 22 (*Rosh Ha-Shanah* 10b).
3. Joshua began his march around Jericho (*Seder Olam* 11).
   The encirclement of Jericho, which led to its destruction within seven days, constituted the first Jewish military action in ancient Palestine. It was the opening phase in the attainment of the third objective of the exodus from Egypt—Jewish national independence (see note on Nisan 18:2). The first two objectives (freedom and Torah) were accomplished by Moses. Passover marks the achievement of freedom, Shavuot subsequently became the festival of the Torah. The third objective was never fully attained by Joshua due to his failure to conquer the entire land. No date can therefore be designated to mark the final completion of the third objective. The beginning of that phase, however, may be commemorated during the seven days allotted to Joshua for the conquest of Jericho, Nisan 22–28. Historical continuity in the observance of the first and third objectives is thus established.
4. 3,000 Jews of Prague were massacred on April 18, 1389.
5. Rabbi Judah Rosanes of Constantinople, author of *Mishneh La-Melekh*, popular commentary on Maimonides' code, died on April 13, 1727.
6. The new Austrian constitution of April 25, 1848, guaranteed freedom of the Jewish religion.
7. The Kishinev pogrom broke out on April 19, 1903. The massacres led to worldwide protests.
   The Kishinev pogrom sparked widespread efforts to organize Jewish self-defense. Ha-Shomer, an early Palestinian Jewish self-defense organization, was founded on Nisan 21, 1909.
8. Ludwik Lazar Zamenhof, originator of Esperanto, died on April 14, 1917.
9. Judah Loeb Cahan, author and collector of Jewish folklore, died on April 3, 1937.
10. The first enclosed and guarded ghetto was established by the Nazis in Lodz, Poland, on April 30, 1940.

NISAN 23

1. Titus tightened the siege of Jerusalem and stopped all infiltrations through his lines on May 17 (approximate), 70 C.E. See Nisan 14:5.
2. A fast-day was observed by the Jewish community of Cologne on Nisan 23 in commemoration of anti-Jewish violence on March 26, 1147, during the Second Crusade.
3. Rabbi Moses Trani (Mabit) of Safed, author of *Kiryat Sefer*, died on April 22, 1585 (J.E.).
4. Rabbi David Deutsch of Budapest, leader of Hungarian Orthodox Jewry, author of *Goren David*, died on April 26, 1878.
5. 47 Jews, among them Joseph Hayyim Brenner, labor leader and writer, were killed by Arabs in Jaffa on May 1, 1921.
6. The Biltmore Program, calling for an independent Jewish state in Palestine, was adopted by Zionists on April 10, 1942.
7. Haganah captured the strategic village of Katamon, southwest of Jerusalem, on May 2, 1948.
8. The Hebrew University, suspended during the hostilities with the Arabs, reopened in temporary quarters in Jerusalem on April 22, 1949.

NISAN 24

1. The Jews paused at Marah after their crossing of the Red Sea (Exod. 15:23).

   It was at Marah that the Jews paused on their first Sabbath in the desert (*Shabbat* 87b). According to the Talmud, Moses received preliminary instruction in this place, pertaining to a number of religious laws, in anticipation of the giving of the Torah on Mt. Sinai. Jews were enjoined for the first time to observe the seven Noahite laws, to honor their parents, and to rest on the Sabbath (*Sanhedrin* 56b). A talmudic passage in *Shabbat* (118b), however, implies that the Sabbath laws dated from their arrival in the "wilderness of Sin" on Iyar 15.
2. Rabbi Moses b. Abraham of Przemysl, Poland, author of *Matteh Moshe*, died on May 1, 1606.
3. Christians in France were forbidden, under pain of death, to shelter or converse with Jews, by order of Louis XIII on April 23, 1615.
4. Rabbi David Ha-Kohen of Jerusalem, author of *Da'at Kadoshim*, died on April 30, 1693.
5. The cornerstone of the Haifa Technion was laid on April 11, 1912.

6. Moses David Gisser, Yiddish poet and editor of *Nai-Land*, died in Santiago, Chile, on April 19, 1952.
7. Shmerke Katcherginsky, anti-Nazi underground fighter and Yiddish poet, was killed in an airplane crash on April 27, 1954.

NISAN 25

1. The Jews of the exodus arrived at Elim, where they discovered 12 springs. They remained there for 20 days (Exod. 15:27, Ibn Ezra).
2. Avigdor b. Isaac Kara of Prague, kabbalist and liturgical poet, died on April 10, 1439.
3. Private fast day of Rabbi Abraham b. Solomon Treves of Adrianople, author of *Birkhat Avraham*, in commemoration of a miraculous escape from drowning on March 27, 1505 (*Toledot ha-Poskim–Birkhat Avraham*).
4. Massacre of Marranos of Lisbon, Portugal, on April 19, 1506.
5. Soldiers, incited by ritual charges, rioted in Bucharest and killed 128 Jews on April 8, 1801.
6. The first Jewish American national organization of women, the United Order of True Sisters, was organized on April 21, 1846.
7. All civic limitations imposed on Jews of the German Empire were lifted on April 16, 1871.

    The end of German anti-Jewish civil restrictions in the year 1871 may be said to have brought to a conclusion the worst vestiges of medieval anti-Semitism. Ten years later, almost to the day, Germany opened the new epoch of modern anti-Semitism (Nisan 26:6). The cycle is completed by the anniversary of the opening of the Eichmann trial on Nisan 25 (no. 12).
8. Rabbi Ḥayyim Halberstam of Zanz, ḥasidic leader and talmudist, author of *Divrei Ḥayyim*, died on April 19, 1876.
9. Ha-Shomer ha-Ẓa'ir, socialist Zionist youth organization, was founded on April 25, 1919.
10. King Christian X of Denmark, on April 21, 1933, attended the celebration of the 100th anniversary of the Crystal Synagogue in Copenhagen to demonstrate his sympathy for the Jews.
11. All Austrian Jews were ordered to declare their property valued in excess of 5,000 reichsmarks, on April 26, 1938.
12. The trial of Adolph Eichmann on charges of genocide opened in Jerusalem on April 11, 1961.

NISAN 26

1. Death of Joshua (*Megillat Ta'anit* 1).
   The traditional yahrzeit of Joshua precedes by two days the traditional anniversary of his first military victory in Palestine (Nisan 28:1).
2. Abraham Nuñez Bernal was burned at the stake by the Inquisition of Cordova on May 3, 1655.
3. Rabbi Ephraim Navon of Constantinople, author of *Mahaneh Ephraim*, a book of responsa, died on April 18, 1735.
4. Jews of Arnhem, Holland, were granted permission to build a synagogue on April 17, 1765.
5. Rabbi Jacob Simhah of Kempna, author of *Sha'arei Simhah*, died on April 9, 1877.
6. A petition signed by 250,000 Germans was presented to the government on April 25, 1881, requesting the barring of foreign Jews from admission into Germany. This mass petition marked the opening of the epoch of modern German anti-Semitism.
   See note on Nisan 25:7.
7. Rabbi Joseph Lowenstein, historian, author of *Dor, Dor ve-Dorshav*, died on April 30, 1924.
8. 140 Palestinian Jews bound for Malta lost their lives when their ship was sunk by a German plane on May 1, 1943.
9. Israeli postal service was established on May 5, 1948.

NISAN 27

1. Anti-Jewish riots broke out in Seville, Spain, on April 5, 1464.
2. Adula of Tunis, who was forced into baptism, committed suicide in Rome on May 2, 1666, as the rites of conversion were about to begin (JE).
3. Rabbi Isaac Ashkenazi of Lemberg, author of *Taharot ha-Kodesh*, novellae on the tractate *Zevahim*, died on April 15, 1806.
4. Joseph Israel Benjamin (Benjamin II), globe-trotter and author, died on May 3, 1864.
5. Colonel Eliezer Margolin, on May 5, 1921, organized a defense corps in Jerusalem consisting of veterans of the Jewish Legion.
6. Anti-Jewish riots broke out in Palestine on April 19, 1936.
7. NISAN 27 was designated Holocaust Day, in commemoration of the martyred six million Jews and the fighters of the ghettos, by a resolution of the Knesset on April 12, 1951.

NISAN 28

1. Fall of Jericho (*Seder Olam* 11).
   See note on Nisan 22:3.
2. Fuerth, Bavaria, permitted the establishment of its first Jewish settlement on April 17, 1528.
3. Rabbi Shabbetai Sheftel Horowitz, son of the Shelah, author of *Vavei ha-Ammudim*, died on April 9, 1660.
4. Rabbi Raphael Ḥayyim Isaac Carigal, itinerant rabbi, died on May 5, 1777.
5. The Society for the Education of Poor Children and Relief of Indigent of the Jewish Persuasion in the City of New York was incorporated on April 11, 1831.
6. Widespread Russian pogroms started in Elisabethgrad on April 27, 1881.
7. Isidor Straus and his wife lost their lives in the sinking of the *Titanic* on April 15, 1912.
8. Felix Adler, founder of the Ethical Culture movement, died on April 24, 1933.
9. An Arab attack on Petaḥ Tikvah was repelled by the Jewish settlers on April 20, 1936.
   See Nisan 29:4.
10. Anti-Jewish riots broke out in Vilna, Poland, on April 29, 1938.
11. The peace treaty between Israel and Egypt went into effect on April 25, 1979.

NISAN 29

1. Nicolas Antione, a convert to Judaism, was burned at the stake in Geneva on April 20, 1632.
2. Rabbi Moses Samson Bacharach, author of *Shemen ha-Ma'or*, died on April 19, 1670.
   Rabbi Moses Bacharach was the father of the famous Rabbi Jair Ḥayyim Bacharach, author of the well-known book of responsa *Chavat Ya'ir* (Tevet 1:2). He was not related to Rabbi Judah Bacharach (Nisan 29:3), who died 176 years later on the yahrzeit of the former.
3. Rabbi Judah b. Joshua Heskiel Bacharach, guardian of the poor, author of *Nimukei Hagriv*, novellae on the Talmud, died on April 25, 1846.
   Rabbi Judah Bacharach was the seventh lineal descendent of Tobias Bacharach, the founder of a family which was to produce many

scholars. The founder was condemned on ritual charges and beheaded on September 19, 1659.
4. Three Jews were killed and many wounded on May 7, 1921, in Arab attacks on Petah Tikvah, Palestine.
5. The Hebrew poetess Rachel Sela (Blaustein) died on April 16, 1931.
6. The entire Crimea was declared by the Nazis "Free of Jews" on April 16, 1942.
7. U.S. forces liberated the Buchenwald concentration camp with its 20,000 inmates on April 12, 1945.
8. Izhak Ben-Zvi, second president of Israel, scholar and author, died on April 23, 1963.
9. On April 10, 1975, the government of Israel recognized Falashas as Jews under the law.

NISAN 30

1. Rabbi Joseph b. Meir Ha-Levi Ibn Migas, disciple and successor to Rabbi Isaac Alfasi, died on April 9, 1141.
2. Rabbi Jacob Berab, author and leader of the movement to restore Semiha (traditional ordination), died on April 3, 1546.
3. Rabbi Hayyim Vital, famous kabbalist, author of *Ez Hayyim*, died on May 3, 1620.
4. Eight Jews were martyred at Przemysl, Poland, on April 23, 1659.
5. Rabbi Abraham b. Saul Brode of Frankfort, author of *Hiddushe Geonim*, novellae on the Talmud, died on April 11, 1717.
6. Rabbi Jacob Emden (Ya'vez), scholar and controversial figure, author of *Bet Yaakov*, a standard prayerbook, died on April 19, 1776.
   Rabbi Jacob Emden was the son of Rabbi Zevi Ashkenazi (Iyar 1:8). Their careers and personalities were strikingly similar. Both were renowned scholars. Both were short-tempered and controversial figures. Both waged relentless war against the Shabbatean heresy. The yahrzeit of father and son is Rosh Hodesh Iyar.
7. The Polonie Talmud Torah was opened by Congregation Shearith Israel on May 2, 1802, marking a significant effort in the beginning of popular Jewish education in New York (*AJHSP* no. 34, p. 124).
   The first yeshivah in America was established on March 15, 1886 (Adar 8:6).
8. Jewish students were barred from German schools on April 26, 1933.

IYAR 1

1. Egypt was afflicted by the first biblical plague (*Seder Olam* 3).
2. An Israelite gathered wood on the Sabbath (*Yalkut*, Num. 15:32). This act marked the first public violation of the Sabbath (Ibid.).

   There are two traditional dates for the first Sabbath, Nisan 24 and Iyar 15 (see note on Nisan 24:1). Rabbi Simon's opinion that the wood-gatherer violated the Sabbath on Iyar 22 (*Yalkut* Num. 15:32), is in accord with the second tradition. The author of the hymm of Dayenu (Passover Haggadah), who lists the manna ahead of the Sabbath, also follows the second tradition.
3. Moses was ordered, in the second year of the exodus, to take a census of the Jewish people (Num. 1:1).
4. The foundation of the Second Temple was laid on Iyar 1, 537 B.C.E. (Ezra 3:8; 1 Esdras 5).

   According to Ezra (3:8), work on the Second Temple began "in the second year of their coming unto the House of God at Jerusalem in the second month . . . " Rabbinic interpreters occasionally assume that the failure to specify the day of the month is an indication that the event took place at the beginning of the month. The apocryphal Book of Esdras is more specific: "And they laid the foundation of the House of God in the first day of the second month, in the second year after they had come to Judea and Jerusalem" (1 Esdras 5). There are two biblical sources for the date of the beginning of the construction of the First Temple. The text in 1 Kings 6:1 reads: "And it came to pass . . . in the month of Ziv [Iyar], which is the second month, that he began to build the house of the Lord." Following the rule mentioned above, one may assume that the construction began on Iyar 1. However, the text in the later Book of Chronicles (2 Chron. 3:2) reads: "And he began to build in the second day of the second month." It is apparent that the beginning of the construction of the Second Temple was timed to coincide with the anniversary of the laying of the foundation of the Solomonic Temple. It is also apparent that there was still a tradition at the time of Zerubbabel that the construction of the Solomonic Temple had begun on Iyar 1.
5. Leo, Jewish court physician to Grand Duke Ivan III, the first physi-

cian to enter Russia from Western Europe, was executed on April 22, 1490.

6. *Iggeret Ba'alei Ḥayyim*, a book on zoology translated by Kalonymus, was printed for the first time in Mantua, Italy, on April 1, 1557.
7. Rabbi Nathan Shapiro of Horadno, author of *Mevo Shearim*, died on April 18, 1577.
8. Rabbi Zevi Hirsch b. Jacob Ashkenazi, controversial figure, author of book of responsa *Ḥakham Zevi*, died on May 2, 1718.
   See note on Nisan 30:6.
9. Rabbi Solomon b. Jacob Ayllon, hakham of the Sephardic congregation of Amsterdam, chief target in the Ḥakham Zevi controversy, died on April 10, 1728.

   The Sephardic Ḥakham Ayllon was violently attacked by the Ḥakham Zevi (Rabbi Zevi Hirsch Ashkenazi [no. 8] in the latter's relentless war on the Shabbatean heresy. Ayllon died on the tenth anniversary of the death of the Ḥakham Zevi.
10. Heinrich Himmler, chief of the Gestapo, established, on April 20, 1939, a new SS department for the creation of forced-labor camps.
11. The first attack by Egyptian irregular forces, comprising Muslim Brotherhood units, took place at Kefar Darom on May 10, 1948. They were repulsed with heavy losses.

IYAR 2

1. King Solomon began the construction of the Temple (2 Chron. 3:2).
   See note on Iyar 1:4.
2. Rabbi Baruch b. Samuel of Mayence, talmudist and liturgical poet, author of *Sefer ha-Ḥakhmah*, died on April 25, 1221.
3. Rabbi Kalman of Worms, one of the first of the prominent talmudic scholars of Polish Jewry, head of the Yeshivah of Lemberg, died on April 28, 1560.
4. Isaac Abrabanel, grandson of the famous Bible exegete of the same name, philanthropist and patron of science, president of the Jewish community of Ferrara, Italy, died on April 5, 1573 (JE).
5. Rabbi Menahem Mendel of Vitebsk, prime mover of the Ḥasidic aliyah to Palestine, author of *Peri ha-Arez*, died on May 9, 1788.
   See Sivan 1:8.
6. Abraham Baer Gottlober (Abag), Hebrew poet and author, died on April 12, 1899.
7. The Supreme Council of the Peace Conference recognized the Balfour

Declaration on April 20, 1920, and proclaimed Palestine a mandated territory under British administration.
See Iyar 6:12.
8. German forces marched into Holland on May 10, 1940.
The diary of Anne Frank, the young Dutch Jewish girl, attracted universal attention to the suffering of Jews in Nazi-occupied territories. Anne Frank died in the Belsen concentration camp. The British liberated Belsen (no. 9) on the fifth anniversary of the Nazi invasion of Holland.
9. The British army liberated the Belsen camp and its 40,000 inmates on April 15, 1945.
10. The city of Safed was taken by Haganah on May 11, 1948.
11. The port of Haifa was taken over by Haganah on May 11, 1948.
12. The Israeli freighter Ashdod passed through the Suez Canal on April 29, 1979, marking the opening of the canal to Israeli shipping.
13. Israel completed its withdrawal from Sinai on April 25, 1982.

IYAR 3

1. Rabbi Menahem b. Jacob of Worms, talmudic scholar and author of many liturgical poems, died on April 16, 1203.
2. A Spanish royal proclamation, issued on April 30, 1492, warned Jews that their departure must begin on May 1 and be completed by the end of July.
3. Portuguese Marranos who had reverted to Judaism were burned in Ancona, Italy, on April 13, 1556, by order of Pope Paul IV.
In all, 24 Jews were burned. The "acts of faith" were held on four days: April 13, April 15, June 15, and June 20. The atrocity of Ancona led the famous Dona Gracia of the House of Nasi to spearhead a boycott against the port of Ancona as a countermeasure to the pope's repressive policies. This marked the first Jewish effort, since the beginning of the diaspora, at a far-reaching, concerted drive by the free Jewish communities of the world to hit back at their enemies.
4. The cornerstone of the first public synagogue in Berlin was laid on May 9, 1712.
5. Rabbi Aryeh Leib b. Moses Zuenz of Plotsk, author of Ya'alat Hen, died on April 22, 1883.
6. Rabbi Isaac Farhi of Jerusalem, author of Marpe la-Ezem, died on May 11, 1853.
7. The establishment of Jewish congregations in Lower Austria was prohibited on April 27, 1857.
8. Gabriel Riesser, foremost fighter for emancipation of the Jews of Germany, died on April 22, 1863.

9. *Di Yidishe Gazeten*, first influential Yiddish newspaper in America was published on April 20, 1874.
10. Anti-Jewish riots broke out in Craiova, Rumania, on May 10, 1883.
11. Tel Aviv became the first all-Jewish municipality on May 11, 1921.
12. Mordecai Anielewicz, commander-in-chief of the uprising in the ghetto of Warsaw, was killed in action on May 8, 1943.
13. Bet-Shean was captured by Haganah on May 12, 1948.

IYAR 4

1. Solomon ibn Gabirol was born in Malaga, Spain, on April 21, 1021 (approximate).
2. Maimonides and his family left North Africa for Palestine on April 18, 1165. He designated the anniversary of this departure a private day of fast and prayer.
   See Heshvan 4:1.
3. Rabbi Meir b. Baruch's (Maharam of Rothenburg) body was released by the authorities for Jewish burial on April 19, 1306, 13 years after his death in prison.
   See Tishri 10:14. Rabbi Meir of Rothenburg was buried in the old Jewish cemetery of Worms. The tombstone, which marks his grave and the adjoining grave of Alexander Susskind, miraculously escaped the Nazi ravaging of the cemetery.
4. 30 Jews were killed in the riots in Cracow on April 12, 1464.
5. Jacob Bassevi of Treuenberg, a Court Jew, died on May 2, 1634.
6. Rabbi Jacob Sasportas, kabbalist, first rabbi of the Sephardic community in London after the resettlement, author of responsa *Ohel Ya'akov*, died on April 15, 1698.
7. Rabbi Joseph b. Meir Teomim of Frankfort on the Oder, author of *Peri Megadim*, popular commentary on the code, died on April 26, 1792.
8. Rabbi Joseph Baer Soloveichik, head of Yeshivah of Volozhin, member of an illustrious scholarly family, author of responsa *Bet ha-Levi*, died on May 1, 1892.
9. The Nazis issued a decree on April 27, 1944, providing for the establishment of ghettos for the Jews of Hungary.
10. Hans Biebow, Nazi administrator of the ghetto of Lodz, was executed on April 24, 1947.
11. The city of Jaffa surrendered to Haganah forces on May 13, 1948.
12. President Nasser of Egypt, on April 22, 1969, announced the abrogation of the U.N. cease-fire with Israel and the beginning of a war of attrition.

IYAR 5

1. David Joshua Oppenheim, famed philanthropist of Worms, died on April 21, 1692 (EJUD, Worms).
2. Napoleon retreated from Acre, Palestine, on May 10, 1799, giving up his dream of conquering the Near East.
3. A decree issued on April 30, 1800, prohibited the import by Russian Jews of books in any language.
4. Sebastian Brunner, Austrian Catholic anti-Jewish writer, instituted a libel suit against Ignaz Juranda, editor of *Ostdeutsche Post*, on April 27, 1860. The trial ended in an acquittal.
5. Joseph Rivlin laid the cornerstone of the first private home to be erected outside the walls of Jerusalem on April 16, 1869, marking the beginning of the modern Yishuv (*Zikhronot Eretz Yisrael*, 1:184).
6. Rabbi Meir b. Isaac Auerbach, chief rabbi of the Ashkenazi community of Jerusalem, author of *Imre Binah*, novellae on the code, died on May 8, 1878.
7. The Mizrachi Organization of America was founded at a conference which met in Cincinnati, Ohio, on May 1, 1914.
8. Isaac Katzenelson, Hebrew and Yiddish poet, known as the "Jeremiah of the Nazi period," was arrested on April 28, 1944. The following day he was deported to the Oswiecim (Auschwitz) extermination camp.
9. Israel was proclaimed an independent state on May 14, 1948.

   Iyar 5 marks the anniversary of the most significant event in modern Jewish history—the proclamation of the independence of Israel. Religious motives and messianic hopes were the mainspring of 18th century aliyahs. Anti-Jewish repression and massacres lent new impetus to the stream of immigrants to Palestine in the 19th and 20th centuries. Iyar 5 is the anniversary of many tragedies which form a somber backdrop against which the Proclamation of Independence stands out in greater brilliance. Thus we find on this day echoes of attacks on the Jewish creative genius (no. 3), of anti-Semitic agitations which prepared the ground for Nazism (no. 4), and of the horrible Nazi period (no. 8). All these events help place Yom ha-Azma'ut in its proper historic perspective.
10. The first legislative act of the provisional government of the State of Israel, passed on May 14, 1948, provided for the repeal of the British White Paper of 1939, which had restricted Jewish immigration and the acquisition of land in Palestine.

    The Haftarah on the Sabbath following the promulgation of the law of unrestricted Jewish immigration into Israel was the ninth chapter of Amos. It reads: "And I will return the captivity of my people Israel. And they shall build the waste cities and inhabit them . . . and they shall no more be plucked up out of their land which I have given them, saith the Lord thy God."

11. The last three settlements of the Ezyon Bloc surrendered to the Arabs on May 14, 1948.

12. Jordan's Arab Legion captured Atarot, a Jewish settlement north of Jerusalem, on May 14, 1948.

13. The U.S. granted Israel de facto recognition on May 14, 1948.

IYAR 6

1. Many Jews of Cordova, Spain, were massacred on April 19, 1013, by the soldiers of Suleiman ibn Al-Hakim.

2. Special privileges and immunities were granted to the Jews of Burgos, Spain, by Don Sancho el Bravo on April 23, 1295.

3. Rabbi Levi b. Gershom (Ralbag also known as Gersonides), philosopher and exegete, author of a popular commentary on the Pentateuch, died on April 20, 1344.

4. Jewish residents of Speyer, Germany, were expelled on May 5, 1435.

5. The council of Hanover, on May 3, 1588, ordered the severance of all business connections between Jews and Christians.

6. Rabbi Samuel b. David Moses Ha-Levi of Mezhirech, talmudist, author of the popular work *Nahalat Shivah*, died on April 24, 1681.

7. Joseph Jose Wertheimer, father of the Austrian court Jew, Samson Wertheimer, died on May 2, 1713.

8. Rabbi Isaac Ha-Levi Horowitz of Brody, talmudist, died on May 5, 1767.

9. Rabbi Joshua Ha-Kohen Perahyah, author of *Vayikra Yehoshua*, novellae on the code, died on May 10, 1810.

10. Anti-Jewish riots broke out in Kiev, Russia, on May 5, 1881.

    The Russian pogroms of 1881 led to the spread of Zionist ideas in Eastern Europe and the formation, in 1882, of Hovevei Zion, the first organized modern Zionist movement in the world. The subsequent publication in 1896, on the anniversary of the Kiev pogrom, of an English edition of Herzl's *Der Judenstaat* (no. 11), helped spread Zionism among the English-speaking, emancipated Jews.

11. An English edition of Herzl's *The Jewish State* was published for the first time on April 19, 1896.

12. The British mandate over Palestine went into effect on April 24, 1920. This date became known as San Remo Day.

    The coincidence of the dates of the publication of the English edition of Herzl's *The Jewish State* and the beginning of the British mandate over Palestine (no. 13), charged with the establishment of a Jewish home in Palestine, is noteworthy.

13. Sir Herbert Samuel, prominent British Jew, was appointed, on April 24, 1920, the first high commissioner of Palestine.

14. The French government prohibited the publication of alien propaganda material spreading racial hatred on April 25, 1939.

15. The British mandate over Palestine came to an end on May 15, 1948.

    The British mandate over Palestine went into effect on Iyar 6, 1920, and it came to an end exactly 28 years later on Iyar 6, 1948.

16. The armies of Egypt, Jordan, Syria, Iraq, and Lebanon invaded Israel on May 15, 1948.

17. The Arab Legion captured Neveh Ya'akov, the last Jewish settlement north of Jerusalem, on May 15, 1948.

18. Nelly Sachs, poetess, winner of Nobel Prize for Literature for her poems on the Holocaust, died on May 12, 1970.

IYAR 7

1. The serpent visited Eve (Jubilees 3:17).

    The Falasha sacred book *Teezaza Sanbat* (The Commandment of the Sabbath) fixes the date of the serpent's visit to Eve on Iyar 16. According to rabbinic tradition, the visit took place on Tishri 1 (see Tishri 1:3).

2. The new walls built by Nehemiah around Jerusalem (Neh. 12:27) were dedicated on Iyar 7, 443 B.C.E. This date was observed as a holiday in ancient times (Zeitlin, *Megillat Ta'anit*, chap. 2). See Elul 25:2.

    Nehemiah dedicated the outer wall of Jerusalem on Iyar 7. A little over 500 years later, the Jews surrendered the wall, on the same day, to the Romans (no. 4).

3. Vespasian laid siege to the fortified city of Jotapata in Galilee, 67 C.E. (Josephus, *Wars* 3:7).

    See Tammuz 1:2.

4. The Jewish defenders of Jerusalem surrendered the first wall of the city to the Romans on May 31 (approximate), 70 C.E. (Josephus, *Wars*, 5:7).

5. The Rindfleisch massacres of Jews began at Rottingen, Germany, on April 20, 1298, and spread through more than 150 Jewish communities.

6. *Midrash Tanhuma* was printed for the first time at Mantua, Italy, on April 30, 1563.

7. Rabbi Isaac b. Samuel Adarbi of Salonika, author of *Divrei Rivot*, died on April 24, 1577 (ATGY).
8. Asser Levy was admitted to burghership in New Amsterdam on April 20, 1657.
9. Hermann Cohen, founder of the Neo-Kantian school of philosophy, author of *The Religion of Reason from the Sources of Judaism*, died on April 19, 1918.
10. The first aliyah to the Negev began with the establishment of Kibbutz Gevulot on May 12, 1943.

   The aliyah to the Negev started officially on Iyar 7. The first three settlements, Gevulot, Revivim, and Bet Eshel, were experimentally established in 1943 to determine the feasibility of permanent settlements in the Negev. As a result of the information gathered in the experimental stage, eleven new settlements were established in the Negev on October 6, 1946, and an additional seven in 1947. These settlements served also as strongpoints to defend the Yishuv from attack by an enemy advancing from the south. The Egyptian army suffered its first defeat at Nirim (no. 12), one of the settlements established in 1946, on the anniversary of the first aliyah to the Negev.
11. Chaim Weizmann was elected first president of the State of Israel on May 16, 1948.
12. The Egyptian army suffered its first defeat at Nirim, in the Negev, on May 16, 1948.
13. The Egyptians entered Gaza on May 16, 1948.

IYAR 8

1. Jews of Speyer were massacred in the First Crusade on May 3, 1096 (JE. Crusades).
2. Venice became the first city in the world where the term *ghetto* was associated with the Jewish quarter, when the Jews were compelled, on April 10, 1516, to move into a restricted area (Roth, *Personalities and Events in Jewish History*, p. 232).

   The area was formerly the site of a foundry which manufactured weapons for the government of Venice. The Italian term for "new foundry" is *geto nuovo*. The first official document which uses the word *ghetto* to describe an area restricted to the residence of Jews exclusively was a papal edict dated February 27, 1562. (Teaff, *Getto-Ghetto; American Sephardi*, vol. 6, nos. 1–2).

3. Rabbi Menahem Monish Chajes of Vilna, died on May 13, 1636 (DYY).
4. Many Jews perished in anti-Jewish riots in Lemberg (Lwow), on May 3, 1667. The anniversary was proclaimed a fast-day (DDD).
5. Rabbi Isaiah b. Judah Berlin of Breslau, author of *Omer ha-Shikcha*, addenda to the code, died on May 13, 1799.
6. Joseph Abraham Steblicki, Ger Zedek of Nikolai,Upper Silesia, died on May 16, 1807 (JE).
7. Baron Maurice de Hirsch, famous philanthropist, died on April 21, 1896.
8. Russia recognized Israel on May 17, 1948.
9. Israeli forces captured Acre, Nebi Yusha, and Tel el-Kadi on May 17, 1948.

Napoleon was defeated in his Near Eastern campaign at Acre, Palestine, on Iyar 5, 1799 (no. 2). Israel captured Acre on Iyar 8, 1948.

IYAR 9

1. A three-month period of grace, given by the Portuguese to the Jews of Brazil to leave the country, terminated on April 26, 1654. Those who remained after this deadline were surrendered to the Inquisition.
2. Jews of Corfu were granted the right to practice law on May 7, 1680.
3. A letter of Empress Catherine II of Russia, dated May 11, 1764, opened the way for limited settlement of Jews in Riga.
4. Alter Druyanow, author of anthology of Jewish wit and folklore, died on May 10, 1938.
5. Poland, Czechoslovakia, Uruguay, and Nicaragua recognized Israel on May 18, 1948.
6. The Arab Legion captured the police fort on Mt. Scopus on May 18, 1948.
7. The army of Saudi Arabia joined on May 18, 1948, the other Arab armies in their invasion of Israel.
8. The Hebrew University–Hadassah Medical School was opened in New Jerusalem on May 17, 1959.

IYAR 10

1. The ark of the covenant was captured by the Philistines (*Megillat Ta'anit* 2).
2. Hophni and Phinehas, the sons of the high priest Eli, were killed by the Philistines (ibid).
3. The high priest Eli died on Iyar 10 (ibid).
4. Rabbi Isaac Alfasi (Rif), eminent codifier, died on April 20, 1103.
5. A storm at sea on April 24, 1165, threatened the ship aboard which Maimonides and his family had sailed for Palestine after their escape from North Africa. Maimonides set aside this anniversary as an annual private fast-day.
6. Rabbi Zevi Hirsch b. Abraham Katz was martyred in Lemberg (Lwow) on May 5, 1664.
7. Levi Sheftall presented to General George Washington, on behalf of Congregation Mikveh Israel of Savannah, Ga., an address, dated May 6, 1789, on the occasion of the latter's election to the presidency.
8. Rabbi Meir b. Zevi Margolis of Lemberg, author of responsa *Me'ir Netivim*, died on April 24, 1790.
9. Theodor Herzl, the founder of modern Zionism, was born on May 2, 1860.
   The proclamation of the independence of Israel was made five days short of Herzl's birthday.
10. Nathan Birnbaum, co-founder of the first national Jewish students' society, Kadimah, writer, and Orthodox leader, was born on May 16, 1864.
11. Anti-Jewish riots broke out in Shpola and Ananyev, Russia, on May 9, 1881.
12. Rabbi Hillel Lichtenstein, popular writer and Orthodox leader of Hungarian Jewry, died on May 18, 1891.
13. Shalom Rabinovitz (Shalom Aleichem), outstanding writer of Jewish humor, died on May 13, 1916.
14. The Warsaw ghetto was reduced to ashes and the uprising came to an end on May 15, 1943, after an active resistance of four weeks (Poliakov, *Harvest of Hate*, p. 235).
15. Isaac Katzenelson, Hebrew and Yiddish poet, perished in Auschwitz on May 3, 1944.
16. The provisional government council of Israel proclaimed, on May 19, 1948, a state of emergency.
17. The potash works on the northern end of the Dead Sea and the neighboring settlement, Bet ha-Aravah, were abandoned by Israel on May 19, 1948.

IYAR 11

1. Death of Methuselah (*Sanhedrin* 108b, Rabbi Joshua).
2. Noah was ordered to enter the ark within seven days (Gen. 7:4; *Sanhedrin* 108b).
   This entry is based on the opinion of Rabbi Joshua. According to Rabbi Eleazar, however, this event took place on Ḥeshvan 11.
3. Purim of Angora, a private communal Purim, was celebrated annually on Iyar 11.
4. The first printed edition of Mishnayot with Maimonides' commentary was published in Naples on May 8, 1492.
5. 1,500 Hebrew books and manuscripts were seized on April 11, 1510, in Frankfort, Germany, for confiscation by the authorities.
6. Rabbi Menahem Zion of Altona, Germany, author of *Neḥamat Zion*, died on April 23, 1679.
7. The Judenordnung of May 7, 1789, provided for the abolition of discriminatory laws enacted against the Jews of Galicia, Austria.
8. Rabbi Samuel Judah Leib b. David Kauder, author of responsa *Olat Shmuel*, died on May 6, 1838.
9. Anti-Jewish riots broke out in Wasilkow and Konotop, Russia, on May 10, 1881.
10. Judah Philip Benjamin, American statesman, died on May 6, 1884.
11. Akiva Fleischman, journalist and novelist, died on May 21, 1929.
12. The famous Tolmatsky Synagogue of Warsaw was dynamited on May 16, 1943, by order of General Jürgen Stroop.
    The dynamiting of the famous Tolmatsky Synagogue marked the last German "major operation" in the liquidation of the Warsaw ghetto uprising.
13. Chaim Zhitlowsky, Yiddish writer and journalist, died on May 16, 1943.
14. Yehoshua Ḥana Rawnitzki, Hebrew writer and collaborator of Bialik, died on May 4, 1944.
15. Count Folke Bernadotte was named mediator in the Israel-Arab War on May 20, 1948.
16. The Israeli air force went into action for the first time in Israel's War of Independence on May 20, 1948.
17. The Syrian army, which had advanced to Deganyah, was halted and repulsed on May 20, 1948.
    The defeat of the Syrians at Deganyah was Israel's first significant victory in the War of Independence. It came on the anniversary of the end of the Warsaw ghetto uprising (no. 12).
18. Germany established diplomatic relations with Israel on May 13, 1965.

Germany established diplomatic relations with Israel 20 years after its unconditional surrender, at the end of World War II, and 17 years after the establishment of the State of Israel.
19. The Reconstructionist Rabbinical College ordained its first graduate on May 13, 1973.

IYAR 12

1. Roman legions under Titus breached the middle wall of Jerusalem on June 5 (approximate), 70 C.E. (Josephus, *Jewish Wars* 5 : 8). A counter-attack by the Jews restored the wall to their command.
2. Pope Innocent IV refused, on April 15, 1250, to grant permission to the Jews of Cordova, Spain, to build a new synagogue.
3. Pope Boniface IX granted liberal privileges to the Jews of Rome on April 15, 1402.
4. Rabbi Samuel Shmelke Horowitz of Nikolsburg, Moravia, hasidic leader, author of *Divrei Shmuel*, died on May 9, 1778.
5. David Woolf Marks, father of Anglo-Jewish Reform movement, died on May 3, 1909.
6. The name"Tel Aviv" was adopted officially by the new settlement near Jaffa on May 21, 1910.

    The name was derived from Nahum Sokolow's Hebrew translation of Herzl's *Altneuland*. See Iyar 16:11
7. Tel Aviv was sacked by the Arabs on May 4, 1917. Djemal Pasha announced that it was the intention of the Turkish government to purge Palestine of its Jewish population.

    Tel Aviv was sacked by the Arabs on the anniversary of the official adoption of the name "Tel Aviv" (no. 6).
8. Israel was admitted as the 59th member nation of the U.N. on May 11, 1949.

    Israel was admitted to the U.N. on the anniversary of Turkey's declaration, in 1917, of its intention to free Palestine of the entire Jewish population.
9. Egypt blocked the Gulf of Aqaba to Israeli shipping on May 22, 1967.

IYAR 13

1. A Church synod, meeting in Vienna, ordered distinctive garb for Jews on May 10, 1267.
2. By a decree issued on May 10, 1427, all Jews were ordered expelled from Berne, Switzerland.
   Expulsions of Jewish communities continued unabated throughout the 15th century. The following is a partial list of expulsions in the 15th century: Treves, 1419; duchy of Austria, 1421; Cologne, 1424; Zurich, 1436; archbishopric of Hildesheim, 1457; Schaffhausen, 1472; Mayence, 1473; Warsaw, 1483; Geneva, 1490; Thurgau, 1491; Spain, Sicily, Sardinia, and Lithuania, 1492; Mecklenburg and Arles, 1493; Portugal, 1497; Nuremberg 1499; Provence, 1500.
3. Rabbi Moses Darshan, author of *Torat Asham*, died on May 14, 1726 (DDD).
4. Rabbi Nethanel Weil of Prague, author of *Korban Nethanel*, commentary on the Rosh, died on May 20, 1769 (HY).
5. Rabbi Joseph of Piltz, author of *Maaseh Choshev*, died on May 8, 1800.
6. Jews of Leipzig, Saxony, were permitted to organize themselves into a religious community on May 18, 1837 and to establish a synagogue.
7. The U.N. Security Council ordered a cease-fire in the Israeli-Arab war on May 22, 1948.
8. Nasser repudiated the cease-fire between Egypt and Israel on May 1, 1969.

IYAR 14

1. The Jewish community of Bisenz, Austria (now Bzenec, Czechoslovakia), was massacred on May 2, 1605.
2. Rabbi David of Kadni, author of *Ateret Rosh*, died on April 26, 1793 (DDD).
3. Po'alei Zion (Labor Zionist Organization) held its first convention in America on April 29, 1904.
4. Thousands of books written by Jewish and liberal non-Jewish authors were publicly burned by the Nazis on May 10, 1933.
5. Berlin was declared "Judenrein" on May 19, 1943.
   Berlin was declared free of Jews on the tenth anniversary of the day when Berlin was declared free of the influence of Jewish authors.
6. Ramat Rahel, the gateway to modern Jerusalem, was repossessed by Israel on May 23, 1948. The battle for Jewish control of the Jordan Valley was successfully concluded on the same day.

7. The settlement Yad Mordecai in the Negev was captured by the Arabs on May 23, 1948.
8. The only advance of the Arab Legion beyond the city walls of Old Jerusalem into Jewish Jerusalem was halted in front of the Notre Dame Monastery on May 23, 1948.
   The commander of the Arab Legion, Sir John Bagot Glubb (Glubb Pasha), considered the failure of the attack on the Notre Dame Monastery the worst defeat suffered by the legion throughout the war.
9. Israel captured Ras en-Nakura, on the Lebanese border, on May 23, 1948.
10. Adolf Eichmann, charged with the implementation of the "final solution" of the Jewish problem, was captured in Buenos Aires, Argentina, on May 11, 1960.
    Adolf Eichmann was in charge of all transportation required for the shipment of Jews to the extermination camps. The height of his career was reached in Hungary in 1944, when he managed to transport 400,000 Jews to the gas chambers in less than five weeks.

IYAR 15

1. The ancient Israelites reached the desert of Sin (Exod. 16:1; *Shabbat* 87b).
2. The supply of matzah, taken along by the Jews upon their exodus from Egypt, was exhausted (Yonatan b. Uziel, Exod. 16:2).
3. The quail came down in the desert on the evening of Iyar 15 to supply the Israelites with meat (Exod. 16:13; *Seder Olam* 5).
4. The yahrzeit of Rabbi Meir Ba'al Ha-Nes is annually observed by Jews of Tiberias on Iyar 15.
5. The first auto-da-fé in Saragosa, Spain, was held on May 10, 1484.
6. Empress Catherine I of Russia expelled all Jews from the Ukraine by a decree dated May 7, 1727.
7. Anti-Jewish riots broke out in Rostov on the Don, Russia, on May 22, 1883.
8. Benito Mussolini was executed by Italian partisans on April 28, 1945.
9. South Africa recognized Israel on May 24, 1948.
10. The Egyptian army captured Yad Mordecai on May 24, 1948.

IYAR 16

1. Manna fell for the first time in the desert of Sin (*Seder Olam* 5; *Kiddushin* 38a, Rashi).
2. Moses composed the initial benediction of the grace to be recited after meals (*Berakhot* 48b).
3. The Roman legion under Florus plundered Jerusalem and killed 3,600 Jews, 66 C.E. (Josephus, *Wars*, 2:15).
4. Titus recaptured the middle wall of Jerusalem and razed it on June 9, (approximate), 70 C.E. (Josephus, *Jewish Wars* 5:8).
5. Rabbi Meir b. Gedaliah of Lublin (Maharam of Lublin), author of a popular commentary on the Talmud, died on May 3, 1616.
6. Antonio Homem, Jewish martyr, was burned at the stake in Lisbon, Portugal, on May 5, 1624.
7. The constitution of the YMHA movement was adopted on May 3, 1874.
8. Anti-Jewish riots resumed in Odessa, Russia, on May 15, 1881.
9. David Gordon, early Zionist, editor of the periodical *Ha-Maggid*, died on May 21, 1886.
10. Anti-Jewish riots broke out in Algeria on May 18, 1897.
11. Construction began on the first 100 houses to be built in Ahuzat Bayit (to be known later as Tel Aviv) on May 7, 1909.
    See Iyar 12:7.
12. *Der Stürmer*, vicious Nazi daily, published, on May 1, 1934, a special supplement dedicated to the revival of the discredited blood-ritual charge.
13. The Nuremberg anti-Jewish laws went into effect in Hungary on May 5, 1939.
14. The U.S. 7th Army liberated the Dachau concentration camp on April 29, 1945.
15. Rabbi Chaim Tchernowitz (Ish Z'air), scholar, author of *Toledot haHalakhah*, died on May 15, 1949.

IYAR 17

1. The serpent persuaded Eve to eat from the fruit of the Tree of Knowledge (Book of Jubilees).
   According to talmudic sources, the Tree of Knowledge episode took place on the first day of creation (*Sanhedrin* 38b). See Iyar 7:1.
2. Beginning of the biblical flood (Gen. 7:11; Rabbi Joshua, *Sanhedrin* 108b)

According to Rabbi Eleazar (*Rosh Ha-Shanah* 11b), the flood commenced on Heshvan 17.

3. The Roman garrison under Florus, on its way to seize the Temple, was attacked by Jewish defense forces and compelled to retreat, 66 C.E.

The Jews destroyed the ramp which connected the Temple to the citadel where the Roman guards were quartered. This first open clash marked, according to Prof. Klausner, the opening of the Jewish rebellion against Rome. Prof. Zeitlin dated the outbreak of the rebellion to June 8, 65 (Sivan 14:1).

4. Jews of England were thrown into prison on May 10, 1278, on charges of coining.
5. Samuel Oppenheimer, banker and court Jew, died on May 3, 1703.
6. Rabbi Ezekiel Landau of Prague, author of the popular *Noda bi-Yehudah*, died on April 29, 1793.
7. Rabbi Moses Hayyim Ephraim of Sadilkov, author of *Degel Mahaneh Ephraim*, hasidic dissertations, died on May 12, 1800.
8. Professor Zevi Shapiro, early Zionist, first to propose the establishment of the Jewish National Fund and a Hebrew University in Jerusalem, died on May 9, 1898.
9. Ozer Blaustein, Yiddish novelist, died on April 27, 1899.
10. The Nazis, on May 14, 1941, interned 3,600 naturalized Jews of Russian origin.
11. Adolf Hitler, mass murderer of the Jewish people, committed suicide on April 30, 1945.

IYAR 18

1. Lag ba-Omer.
2. Traditional yahrzeit of Rabbi Simon b. Yohai.
3. Rabbi Moses Isserles (Rama), codifier, died on May 1, 1572.
4. The Jewish community of Ettingen, Germany, set aside Iyar 18 as a day of thanksgiving for their escape from blood-ritual charges in the year 1690.
5. Betty Hart, the first American female convert to Judaism, was married to Moses Nathans on May 18, 1794, (Marcus, *Essays in American Jewish History*, p. 92).

There were prior conversions to Judaism in America. Elisabeth Whitlock was converted in 1760–61. Ann Sarah Irby, a Huguenot, was converted prior to December 26, 1784. However, both of them were denied burial in Jewish cemeteries, indicating that the conversions had failed to meet Orthodox requirements.

6. Rabbi Elijah Levensohn (Kretinger), talmudist and Orthodox leader, died on April 29, 1888.
7. The Bezalel Art School was opened in Jerusalem on May 13, 1906.
8. Histadrut Ivrit of America was organized on May 21, 1916, for the promotion of Hebrew culture in the United States.
9. The Israeli Defense Army—Zeva Haganah le-Israel (Zahal for short)—was established by law on May 27, 1948.
10. The Arabs blew up Hurbat Rabbi Yehudah he-Hasid, the historic Jewish synagogue in Old Jerusalem on May 27, 1948.
11. The Jewish community of Old Jerusalem surrendered to Jordan's Arab Legion on May 27, 1948.
12. The first degrees of Doctor of Medicine were awarded to 62 graduates of the Hebrew University—Hadassah Medical School on May 13, 1952.

IYAR 19

1. Rabbi Meir b. Baruch of Rothenburg (Maharam), outstanding talmudic authority of his generation, author of commentary on the Talmud and book of responsa, died in the fortress of Ensisheim on April 27, 1293.
   See Tishri 10:14; Iyar 4:3; note on Tammuz 4:2.
2. Moses Eidlitz, talmudist and mathematician, author of *Melekhet Mahshevet*, died on May 17, 1786.
3. Right of citizenship was denied to Jews of the canton of Aargau, Switzerland, on May 5, 1809. Emancipation was delayed until January 1, 1879.
4. Berek Joselewicz, famed commander of the Jewish Legion created by General Tadeusz Kosciuszko of the Polish revolutionary army, was killed in action on May 5, 1809.
   A Jewish regiment, consisting of 1,000 men, was created in 1651 and incorporated into the Polish army which was engaged in fighting the murderous bands of Chmielnicki. In 1794 General Tadeusz Kosciuszko, of Polish and American fame, created a Jewish regiment in an effort to enlist Jewish aid in his aim to reestablish an independent Poland (Elul 22:2).
5. Samuel Altari, leader of Italian Jewry, died on May 20, 1889.
6. Rabbi Alexander Kohut, orientalist, author of *Arukh ha-Shalem*, died on May 25, 1894.
7. Oscar S. Straus, philanthropist, first Jew to occupy a cabinet post in the American government, died on May 3, 1926.

8. Paul Josef Goebbels, Nazi minister of propaganda, disseminator of anti-Semitic literature throughout the world, committed suicide on May 1, 1945.
9. By a government decree issued on May 28, 1948, Haganah was converted into the regular Israeli army.
10. Israeli forces captured the Arab village of Zar'in on Mt. Gilboa on May 28, 1948.
11. Iraqi military forces captured the settlement of Ge'ulim on May 28, 1948.

IYAR 20

1. Jews left the vicinity of Mt. Sinai in the second year of the exodus, after a pause of 11 months and 20 days (Num. 10:11).

    The last biblical injunction, prior to the departure of the Jews from the vicinity of Mt. Sinai on Iyar 20, deals with the blowing of the trumpets on festive days, upon decamping and assembling in the desert and in the event of war. The duty of blowing the trumpets was assigned to the priests (Num. 10: 1–10). The role of the priest as a chaplain in the armed forces was thus established (see Maimonides, *Hilkhot Melakhim* 7). The earliest participation of Jews in chaplaincy service in modern times dates from the Civil War. The law authorizing Jewish military chaplains was passed on Tammuz 19, 1862 (no. 6). See Nisan 21:11.
2. 13 Jews of Troyes, France, were condemned to the stake by the Inquisition on April 24, 1288, on charges of ritual murder.
3. Jews of Venice were denied, on May 14, 1637, the right to practice law.
4. D. M. Dyte, an English Jew, saved the life of King George III on May 15, 1800.
5. A community of Jewish slaves, captured over a period of two centuries and held for ransom by the Knights of St. John on the island of Malta, was officially dissolved on May 15, 1800 (Roth, *Personalities and Events in Jewish History*).
6. Isaac Halevy (Rabinowitz) of Hamburg, historian, spokesman of traditionalist opponents of Bible criticism, author of *Dorot ha-Rishonim*, died on May 16, 1914 (HY).
7. Joshua Barzilai (Eisenstadt), Hebrew writer, active member of Hovevei Zion, died on May 2, 1918.
8. The Rothschild-Hadassah University Hospital and Medical Center was opened on Mt. Scopus, Jerusalem, on May 9, 1939. See Iyar 9:8; 18:11.

9. The Nazis, on May 7, 1942, decreed the execution of all pregnant Jewish women in the ghetto of Kovno.
10. The Israeli army crossed into Lebanon on May 29, 1948, and scattered the Arab forces concentrated on the border.
11. The village of Sedeh Boker was founded in Israel on May 15, 1952, on an ancient Nabatean site never before inhabited by Jews.

IYAR 21

1. The Jewish agricultural settlement, Alliance, was founded in New Jersey on May 10, 1882.
2. A pogrom broke out in Minsk, Russia, on May 26, 1905.
3. Karl Frank, Nazi protector of Bohemia-Moravia, was executed in Prague on May 22, 1946.

IYAR 22

1. The first Sabbath, the observance of which was made obligatory for all Jews, was dated Iyar 22 in the first year of the Exodus. It was violated by some Jews who had gone to collect manna (Exod. 16:27; Seder Olam 5).
2. The first printed edition of the Pentateuch with the commentary of Ibn Ezra was published in Naples, Italy, on May 3, 1488.
3. All Hebrew books found in the Papal States were seized and confiscated on May 28, 1731.
4. Rabbi Zevi of Vilna, author of Bet Leḥem Yehudah, died on May 7, 1733.
5. Rabbi Aaron b. Solomon Amarillo, author of responsa Penei Aharon, died on May 25, 1772.
6. Rabbi Judah Leib, author of Likkutei Maharil, novellae on the Talmud, died on May 29, 1826.
7. David b. Moses Fraenkel, editor of Sulamith, first Jewish monthly in the German language, died on May 18, 1865.
8. The Rumanian government, on May 22, 1919, published a decree granting citizenship to all native-born Jews.
9. The Jewish autonomous region in Birobidzhan was founded by Russia on May 7, 1934.
10. The Nazi deportation of Jews from greater Hungary to the extermination camps began on May 15, 1944.

IYAR 23

1. The Jews of the Exodus arrived at Rephidim (Exod. 17:1; *Seder Olam* 5).

   According to tradition, the Jews arrived at Rephidim on Sunday, Iyar 23, and sojourned there one week. They left Rephidim on Sunday, Sivan 1, and arrived the same day in the wilderness of Sinai (*Shabbat* 86b). It was a momentous week which was to witness the first foreign attack upon Jewish national existence.
2. Moses smote the rock to provide water for the people (Exod. 17:6 *Seder Olam* 5).
3. Simon the Hasmonean drove the Syrians and their allies, the Hellenized Jews, out of the citadel, their last stronghold in Jerusalem, in 142 B.C.E. The anniversary of the defeat of the Hellenists was observed as a holiday in ancient times (*Megillat Ta'anit* 2; 1 Macc. 13:41).
4. Jews of Worms were massacred by Crusaders on May 18, 1096.
5. The Russian government, on May 26, 1848, issued a decree providing for the establishment of a rabbinical committee to be attached to the Ministry of the Interior.

   This measure was part of the government's policy which aimed at the compulsory assimilation of Russian Jewry. It was issued on the anniversary of an ancient holiday which marked the defeat of the assimilationist Hellenist Jews.
6. Aaron Zevi Friedman, the Ba'al Shem of America, author of *Tuv Ta'am*, a defense of ritual slaughtering methods, died on May 17, 1876.
7. Judah Leib Kantor, Hebrew writer, editor of *Ha-Yom*, died on May 26, 1916.
8. The Zion Mule Corps was disbanded on May 26, 1916.
9. Amman, the capital of Jordan, was bombed by Israel's air force on June 1, 1948.
10. The Arab states and Israel agreed to a cease-fire on June 1, 1948.

    By the time of the first truce, Israel had already scored substantial victories over the Syrian and Egyptian armies, though greatly outnumbered by the enemy. The biblical portion of that week includes the following verses: "And I will bring peace in the land . . . and you shall chase your enemies . . . and five of you shall chase a hundred . . ." (Lev. 26:6–8).

IYAR 24

1. Joseph Jonas, the first known Jew to settle in Ohio, died on May 5, 1869.

   Joseph Jonas arrived in Cincinnati in 1817 and became the leading figure of the Jewish community. He organized the first Jewish congregation of Cincinnati.
2. The Jewish community of Brisk (Brest-Litovsk), Lithuania, was pogromized on May 29, 1905.
3. Mordecai David Brandstaetter, Hebrew novelist, died on May 14, 1928.
4. The Mauthausen concentration camp was liberated on May 7, 1945.

   The Mauthausen camp had housed 225,000 inmates in the course of its existence. Of this total, 200,000 were exterminated.

   See Elul. 22:6.
5. Germany surrendered unconditionally to the Allies on May 7, 1945.
6. Viktor Brack, department chief of Hitler's Chancellery, supervisor of the installation of gas chambers in Poland, was executed on June 2, 1948.
7. An Israeli attack on Egyptian positions at Ashdod, on June 2, 1948, marked the turning point in the war between Israel and Egypt.

   The battle forced Egypt to change its military strategy. It gave up its plans to attack Tel Aviv and made the isolation of the Negev from the rest of Israel its prime objective.

IYAR 25

1. Crusaders reached Cologne on May 30, 1096, and found the gate to the city closed by order of the bishop. Of all the Jewish communities in the path of the Crusaders, Cologne's Jews were the only ones to escape total destruction.
2. King Edward I of England, on May 23, 1275, ordered the cessation of persecution of Jews of Bordeaux, France.
3. 1,200 Jews of Toledo, Spain, were killed on May 7, 1355, by the troops of Count Henry of Trastámara (later King Henry II of Castile).
4. Rabbi Israel of Krems was appointed *hochmeister* (chief rabbi) of Germany by Emperor Rupert III on May 3, 1407. He was the first rabbi to hold this position.
5. Rabbi Benjamin Ozer of Zolkiev, author of *Even ha-Ozer*, novellae on the Talmud, died on May 25, 1710.
6. Rabbi Jacob Lorberbaum of Lissa, author of the popular *Netivot ha-Mishpat*, commentary on the code, died on May 25, 1832.

7. Alliance Israélite Universelle of Paris was organized on May 17, 1860, for the purpose of defending Jewish civil rights throughout the world (*AJHSP*, no. 26).
8. Nahum Sokolow, early Zionist leader, author, and founder of Hebrew journalism, died on May 17, 1936.

IYAR 26

1. Saadiah Gaon, head of the talmudic academy of Sura, famous talmudist and philosopher, author of *Emunot ve-Deot*, first philosophical presentation of Judaism, died on May 16, 942.

   Rav Saadiah Gaon was the outstanding scholar of his age. A recognized authority on the Talmud, he was also a profound student of philosophy and philology. In a generation when the heretical Karaite sect had made substantial inroads into rabbinic Judaism, Rav Saadiah Gaon was compelled to fight the battle for traditionalism on many fronts. He fought to establish unity within the ranks of rabbinic Judaism by saving the authority and scholastic primacy of the ancient Babylonian academies. His vigorous anti-Karaite campaign, which was later resumed by Maimonides, dealt a severe blow to the anti-rabbinic movement.
2. Hundreds of Jews were massacred in Brussels, Belgium, on May 22, 1370.
3. Rabbi Moses Hayyim Luzatto, kabbalist and Hebrew poet, author of *Mesillat Yesharim*, popular moralist work, died on May 6, 1747.
4. Jews of Frankfort on the Main, Germany, were permitted for the first time to appear in public at the coronation of Joseph II on May 28, 1764.
5. The first Jewish public school in Hungary was opened by special edict of Emperor Joseph II on May 17, 1784.
6. Levy Solomons, one of the founders of the Canadian Jewish community, died on May 18, 1792.
7. The Russian provisory regulations (the "May Laws") were issued by Czar Alexander III on May 15, 1882, providing for the banning of Jewish residence in rural districts within the Pale of Settlement and more stringent economic restrictions.
8. The Hebrew newspaper *Davar*, organ of the Palestinian labor movement, was founded on May 20, 1925.
9. Rabbi Joshua Hayyim Kasovsky, editor of the monumental *Mishnah Concordance*, died on May 23, 1960.
10. War broke out between Israel and the Arab nations on June 5, 1967. The important Egyptian base at El-Arish, in the Sinai Peninsula, was captured by the Israeli army on the same day.

IYAR 27

1. Demetrius II, in the year 143 B.C.E., relinquished to the Jews of Palestine the crown money which he had annually levied. This marked his recognition of the independence of Judea under Simon the Hasmonean (Zeitlin, *Megillat Ta'anit*).

   This period of independence, which marked the Second Commonwealth, lasted 70 years. It was terminated by the Roman general Pompey in the year 63 B.C.E. (Tammuz 9:2). The month of Iyar has become the month of Jewish Independence. Independence was granted to the Hasmoneans on Iyar 27 (no. 1). Jews rebelled against Rome and proclaimed their independence on Iyar 17 (no. 3). Modern Israel proclaimed its independence on Iyar 5 (no. 9).

2. Rabbi Abraham Samuel Bacharach, talmudist and poet, died on May 26, 1615.

3. The annual period of pilgrimage of Kurdistani Jews to the tomb of the prophet Nahum at Mosul begins on Iyar 27.

4. Isaac Hirsch Weiss, scholar and historian, author of *Dor Dor Ve-Dorshav*, died on June 1, 1905.

5. Simḥa Alter Gutmann (S. Ben-Zion), Hebrew poet and writer, died on June 2, 1932.

6. The foundation of the harbor of Tel Aviv, was laid on May 28, 1938.

7. The Theresienstadt concentration camp was liberated on May 10, 1945.

8. Israeli armed forces captured Yavneh on June 5, 1948.

9. Jacob Fichman, Hebrew poet and writer, died on May 17, 1958.

10. The Israeli army captured the city of Gaza on June 6, 1967. The Jordanian cities of Latrun, overlooking the old road to Jerusalem, and Qalqîlya were also captured on the same day.

11. The U.N. Security Council unanimously ordered a cease-fire in the Middle East War on June 6, 1967.

IYAR 28

1. Maimonides observed Iyar 28 as a private festival in honor of his discovery of the ancient scroll of the Torah written by Ben Asher.

2. Rabbi Isaac b. Joseph of Corbeil, author of the code *Sefer Mizvot Katan (Semak)*, died on April 29, 1280.

3. The first Hebrew printing press in Poland, located in the city of Cracow, published its first book *Sha'arei Duro*, a code of dietary laws by Rabbi Isaac b. Reuben, on May 13, 1534.

4. Rabbi Aryeh Leib Epstein, of Konigsberg, Prussia, author of *Or ha-Shanim*, died on June 6, 1775.
5. Meir Halevi Letteris, Hebrew scholar and poet, died on May 19, 1871.
6. Theodor Herzl was received in audience by the sultan of Turkey at Yidlizkiosk on May 17, 1901.
7. The Turkish government, on May 20, 1917, authorized the return of the Jews who had been expelled from Jaffa and Tel Aviv, Palestine.
8. The White Paper of the McDonald government of Britain, which reversed the policy of the Balfour Declaration, was published on May 17, 1939.
   The McDonald White Paper nullified, in effect, the aims and legal commitment of the Balfour Declaration. It was published on the anniversary of Herzl's historic audience with the sultan (no. 6), at which time Herzl had failed to secure the cooperation of Turkey in the establishment of a Jewish homeland in Palestine.
9. The "Road of Valor" to Jerusalem was completed by Israel on June 6, 1948.
10. The remains of Oscar Grusenberg, the successful defender of Beilis against blood-ritual charges, were interred in Israel on May 15, 1950.
11. Adolf Eichmann, head of the Jewish department of the Gestapo, the first Nazi to be condemned by the Jewish state, was hanged on May 31, 1962.
12. Israel captured the Old City of Jerusalem on June 7, 1967, uniting the city for the first time since the establishment of the state. It also captured, on the same day, Jericho, Bethlehem, and Sharm-el-Sheikh, and lifted the blockade of the Gulf of Aqaba. The entire Jordanian bulge on the western bank of the Jordan came under Israeli control.
13. Hostilities between Israel and Jordan came to an end on June 7, 1967, upon their acceptance of the cease-fire demanded by the Security Council of the U.N.

IYAR 29

1. Death of the Prophet Samuel (*Megillat Ta'anit*, concluding chap.).
   According to the version of the *Tur* (*Orah Hayyim*, 580), Samuel died on Iyar 28.
2. The Romans completed the construction of banks around Jerusalem in preparation for the final assault on the third wall on June 22 (approximate), 70 C.E. (Josephus, *Jewish Wars*, 5:11).
   The completion of the banks around Jerusalem on Iyar 29 opened

the way for the capture of the city by the Romans. The opening of the "Burma Road" to Jerusalem on Iyar 28 saved the city from capture by the Arabs (no. 9).

3. Jews of Sicily were forbidden, on May 12, 1393, to display any funeral decorations in public.

4. Marranos of Segovia, Spain, were massacred on May 16, 1474.

5. Sebastian Munster, the first Christian to publish a complete edition of the Bible in Hebrew, died on May 23, 1552.

6. Sigismund III of Poland barred Jews from living in Riga and the province of Livonia on May 31, 1593.

7. Rabbi Abraham b. Isaac and six other Jews were martyred in Cracow on May 23, 1637 (DDD).

8. Rabbi Gabriel Dessauer, author of *Yad Gavriel*, died on June 1, 1878.

9. The Egyptian army captured Niẓẓanim on June 7, 1948.

10. Israel, Egypt, and Syria accepted the cease-fire ordered by the Security Council on June 8, 1967.

SIVAN 1

1. The flood waters began to recede (Gen. 8:3, Rashi).
2. Jacob departed from Hebron for Egypt to visit his son Joseph (Book of Jubilees).

   According to the Book of Jubilees, Abraham was informed on Sivan 1 of the eventual enslavement of his descendants by the Egyptians. Jacob's departure for Egypt is alleged in the same source to have taken place on the anniversary of that date.
3. The Israelites arrived in the wilderness of Sinai (Exod. 19:1, Rashi).
4. Korah and his followers vanished into the depth of the earth (*Zikhron Yemot Olam*).

   This entry is not corroborated by earlier sources. According to Abraham ibn Ezra, the rebellion of Korah took place in the wilderness of Sinai (Num. 16:1). The Jews arrived at Sinai on Sivan 1. Even if we were to assume that Korah rebelled on the day of arrival, the punishment did not come before the following day (v. 16). According to *Midrash Tanhuma (Korah* 4), Korah's rebellion took place after the defection of the scouts. The scouts were dispatched by Moses on Sivan 29 in the second year of the exodus, and they returned on Av 9. The exact time of the rebellion was not determined.
5. Simhah b. Isaac Ha-Kohen of Worms was killed by Crusaders in a church on May 25, 1096, for stabbing the bishop's nephew while pretending to submit to compulsory baptism.
6. Massacre of the Jews of Worms who took refuge in the castle during the First Crusade on May 25, 1096. See Iyar 23:4.
7. The Polonies Talmud Torah of Congregation Shearith Israel of New York was reorganized on May 27, 1808, as a day school with secular and religious curricula. It became the first Jewish day school in America.
8. Rabbi Israel Ashkenazi of Shklov, leader of the aliyah of the disciples of the Gaon of Vilna to Palestine, died on May 13, 1839.

   The dynamic force of early Hasidism clashed head-on with the dynamic force of Ashkenazic traditionalism generated by the Gaon of Vilna. The momentum of both movements created the two major aliyahs of the pre-Zionist times. Rabbi Israel of Shklov arrived in

191

Palestine in 1808. In 1815 he moved to Jerusalem, where he founded the modern Ashkenazic community. The location of his grave was unknown for a long time. It was discovered in 1964, 125 years after his death, in Tiberias.

See Iyar 2:5.

9. The Hebrew periodical *Ha-Maggid* was published for the first time on June 4, 1856.
10. The discovery by Solomon Schechter of a fragment of the original Hebrew text of Ecclesiasticus on May 13, 1896, attracted worldwide attention to the famous Cairo Genizah.
11. Hayyim Selig Slonimski, inventor, founder of Hebrew weekly *Ha-Zefirah*, first Hebrew organ devoted to science, died on May 15, 1904.
12. Renewed fighting broke out on the Israeli-Syrian frontier on June 9, 1967.
13. Israel reached the eastern bank of the Suez Canal at 1:00 A.M. on June 9, 1967.

SIVAN 2

1. Moses ascended Mt. Sinai (Exod. 19:3, Rashi).
2. Crusaders massacred the Jewish community of Neuss, Prussia, on May 26, 1096.
3. Pope Benedict XIII condemned the Talmud in a bull issued on May 11, 1415.
4. Rabbi Aryeh Leib Berlin of Cassel, Germany, author of talmudic annotations, died on May 21, 1814.
5. Marshal Ion Antonescu, prime minister of Rumania, and Mihai Antonescu, president of council, under whose regime numerous Jewish communities were massacred, were executed on June 1, 1946.
6. Israel captured El-Quneitra, Syria, on June 10, 1967, and smashed the well-fortified Syrian positions in the mountains facing Galilee.

SIVAN 3

1. Moses returned to Mt. Sinai to report the public declaration of the Jewish people, affirming their desire to accept the Law (Exod. 19:8, Rashi).
2. Beginning of Sheloshet Yemei Hagbalah.

The Sheloshet Yemei Hagbalah are the Three Days of Preparation, during which the Jews were to purify themselves and abstain from

uncleanliness in anticipation of the revelation on Mt. Sinai. According to Rashi, the injunction instituting the Sheloshet Yemei Hagbalah
was issued on Sivan 4 (Exod. 19:9).

3. Vespasian captured Jericho and killed its inhabitants 68 C.E. (Josephus, *Wars,* 4:8).
4. Crusaders massacred the Jews of Mayence on May 27, 1096.
5. Maimonides and his family reached Acre, Palestine, on May 16, 1165,
after a hazardous voyage from North Africa. Maimonides observed
the anniversary of his arrival as a holiday.
6. Rabbi Joseph b. Immanuel Ergas, Italian kabbalist, author of *Divrei
Yosef,* died on May 9, 1730.
7. Anti-Jewish riots broke out in Warsaw on May 16, 1790.
8. Rabbi Samuel Adler, scholar and author, died on June 9, 1891.
9. The Syrian army captured Mishmar ha-Yarden on June 10, 1948.
10. Israel and the invading Arabs agreed to a cease-fire on June 10, 1948,
to go into effect on the following day.
11. Colonel David Marcus, the American Jewish defender of Jerusalem,
was killed at Abu Ghosh on June 10, 1948, six hours before the first
cease-fire was to go into effect.
12. The aliyah of Iraqi Jews began on May 19, 1950.
    The first deportation of Palestinian Jews to Babylonia took place in
597 B.C.E. The bulk of Palestinian Jewry followed them to Babylonia 11
years later, in 586 B.C.E. The first return of some Babylonian Jews to
Palestine took place in 539 B.C.E. The majority, however, remained in
Babylonia, where they were destined eventually to make a major
contribution to Judaism through the creation of the Babylonian Talmud and the Geonic responsa. It was not until 1951, 2,548 years after
the arrival of the first Jewish deportees in Babylonia, that this ancient
Jewish community began its own liquidation through an aliyah to
Israel.
13. Israel and Syria signed a cease-fire agreement on June 11, 1967.

SIVAN 4

1. Moses wrote the first part of the Torah, from Genesis to the revelation
on Mt. Sinai, in the first year of the Exodus (Exod. 24:4, Rashi).
2. Over 500 Jews were forcibly baptized in Clermont-Ferrand, France,
on May 18, 576.
3. The first printed edition of the Book of Job, with the commentary of
Rabbi Levi b. Gershom (Ralbag), was published in Ferrara, Italy, on
May 16, 1477.

4. Pope Sixtus IV issued an order, on May 2, 1481, calling on all Christian princes to send back to Spain the Jews who had fled from the Inquisition.
5. Bogdan Chmielnicki's anti-Polish warfare, which resulted in the massacre of more than 300,000 Jews, broke out on May 25, 1648. (Hanover, *Yeven Mezulah* 4).
6. Rabbi Solomon b. David de Oliveira, poet and grammarian, author of *Eẓ Ḥayyim*, died on May 23, 1708.
7. *Die Welt*, a weekly periodical published by Theodor Herzl, and later the official organ of the World Zionist movement, appeared for the first time on June 4, 1897.
8. The municipality of Minsk, Russia, recognized Yiddish as a second official language on May 25, 1917.
9. Representative Louis T. McFadden of Pennsylvania delivered a Nazi-type attack on Jews as a race on May 29, 1933. It was the first anti-Semitic speech made in Congress.

   McFadden published his speeches in the *Congressional Record* and then used his congressional frank to disseminate thousands of reprints through anti-Semitic organizations. The exposure of McFadden's fraudulent past led to his defeat by the electorate and to an end of his public anti-Semitic career.
10. The first truce in Israel's War of Independence went into effect on June 11, 1948.
11. Oswald Pohl, chief of the economic office of the SS, in charge of the work projects for inmates of concentration camps; Otto Ohlendorf, responsible for the murder of 90,000 Ukrainian Jews, and Colonel Paul Blobel, organizer of the massacre of the Jews of Kiev, were hanged on June 8, 1951.
12. The *Dolphin*, the first Israeli ship to sail through the Gulf of Aqaba after the suspension of hostilities with Egypt, arrived at Eilat on June 12, 1967.

SIVAN 5

1. Reuben found mandrakes (*dudaim*) in the field (Gen. 30:14; *Alshikh*).
   The tradition that the incident of the *dudaim* took place on Sivan 5 has no historical evidence. However, it is indicated clearly in the text that it occurred in that season of the year: "and it was in the days of the wheat harvest." It is also indicated that the conception of Issachar took place at the same time (Gen. 30:16). It is therefore obvious that the two traditional dates of Issachar's birth—Av 4 (Book of Jubilees) and Av 10 (*Midrash Tadshe*) are inconsistent with this conclusion.

2. Moses built an altar and erected 12 monuments at the foot of Mt. Sinai (Exod. 24:4; Rashi).
3. Rabbi Judah b. Dama, one of the Ten Martyrs, was executed by the Romans (*Midrash Esfah*).
4. Vespasian left Caesaria to lay siege to Jerusalem, 68 C.E. (Josephus, *Jewish Wars* 4:10).
5. Jews of Bacharach, Germany, were massacred by the Crusaders on May 29, 1096.
6. Hundreds of Jews of Brussels, Belgium, were burned alive, and the remainder were banished from the country on May 22, 1370.
7. Portuguese Marranos were granted permission to settle in Brazil on May 21, 1577.
8. Rabbi Gershom Ashkenazi of Metz, author of *Avodat ha-Gershuni*, died on June 9, 1693.
9. Rabbi Isaac Vita Cantarini, poet and writer, author of *Pahad Yizhak*, died on June 8, 1723.
10. The brothers Hayyim and Joshua Reizes of Lemberg, famous for their piety and scholarship, were tortured and executed on May 12, 1728, on charges of influencing the apostate Jan Filipowicz to return to Judaism.
11. Marshal Mniszek issued a decree, on May 25, 1784, ordering the expulsion of Jews from Warsaw and its environs.
12. Solomon Ludwig Steinheim, champion of Jewish emancipation in Germany, outstanding philosopher and author, died on May 19, 1866.
13. *Haemet*, a Hebrew socialist periodical, was published in Vienna on May 17, 1877.
    The publisher, Aaron Samuel Liebermann, died by his hand at Syracuse, N.Y. on November 8, 1880.
14. Henry Ford's *Dearborn Independent* began a serialization of the *Protocols of the Elders of Zion* on May 22, 1920.
    Sivan 30:3.
15. Israel bombed and destroyed the Iraqi nuclear reactor in Baghdad on June 7, 1981.
    See Sivan 6:14.

SIVAN 6

1. First day of Shavuot.
2. Enoch ascended to heaven (Ginzberg, *Legends of the Jews*, 1:137).
3. Moses was placed by his mother in a basket and was left floating on the river (*Sotah* 12b).

   This entry follows the view of Rabbi Aha bar Hanina. According to Rabbi Hanina bar Papa, the infant Moses was placed on the river on Nisan 21 (*Sotah* 12b).
4. The Ten Commandments were proclaimed on Mt. Sinai (*Shabbat* 86b).
5. Uriah divorced Bathsheba (*Shalshelet ha-Kabbalah*).
6. Pilgrimage day of Mesopotamian Jews to the tomb of the prophet Ezekiel.
7. Mar Isaac and Rebecca chose martyrdom in a church of Cologne, Germany, during the First Crusade, on May 30, 1096.
8. Pope Paul III issued a bull against blood-ritual accusations on May 12, 1540.
9. Naturalization papers, dated May 26, 1697, were given to Simon Valentine by the colony of South Carolina.

   Asser Levy was admitted to burgher rights in New Amsterdam on April 21, 1657. Burghership secured his right to keep a store and carry on a trade in New Amsterdam. It is South Carolina which won the distinction of being the first community in America where Jews were given the right to vote. In Europe, the distinction of being the first country to give full rights of citizenship to Jews belongs to the Kingdom of Naples, where Ferrante I issued a charter on March 13, 1468, granting Jews full rights of citizenship (Roth, *History of the Jews of Italy*, p. 276).

   See Elul 8:5.
10. The first Jewish sermon preached and published in America was delivered by Rabbi Hayyim Isaac Carigal in the Newport Synagogue on May 28, 1773.
11. Israel Jacobson introduced an organ for the first time at a Reform service in Berlin on June 8, 1810.
12. A pogrom broke out in Rostov, Russia, on May 24, 1882.
13. A pogrom broke out in Lodz, Poland, on June 9, 1905.
14. A large number of Jews of Baghdad were massacred on June 1, 1941.
15. The first transport of Hungarian Jews for the extermination camps left on May 28, 1944. See Iyar 22:10.
16. Rumania and Finland recognized Israel on June 13, 1948.
17. Rabbi Abraham Mordecai Alter, head of the Hasidic dynasty of Gur, died on June 13, 1948.

SIVAN 7

1. Second day of Shavuot.
2. Moses ascended Mt. Sinai to receive the first Tablets of the Law (Exod. 32:1; Rashi).
3. Death of King David (Jer. Talmud, *Haggigah* 2:3).
4. Crusaders dragged Rabbenu Jacob b. Meir Tam from his home in Ramerupt, France, on May 8, 1147, and left him critically wounded in a field.
5. Rabbi Hayyim b. Bezalel, author of *Sefer ha-Hayyim*, died on June 2, 1588 (DYY).
6. Pope Innocent XI suspended the Portuguese Inquisition on May 27, 1679, due to its severe treatment of Marranos.
7. Abraham (Valentine) Potocki, a convert to Judaism (*ger zedek*), was burned at the stake on May 24, 1749.
8. Rabbi Jacob Daniel (Olmo) of Ferrara, author of *Eden Arukh*, died on May 26, 1757 (DDD).
9. Rabbi Israel b. Eliezer Ba'al Shem Tov (also known as Besht), founder of Hasidism, died on May 22, 1760.
10. Rabbi Hayyim Abraham b. Moses Israel of Ancona, Italy, author of *Bet Avraham*, died on May 16, 1785 (ATGY).
11. Jews of Canada were accorded equal political rights with Christians on June 5, 1832.
12. Rabbi Hayyim Isaac Mussafia of Jerusalem, author of *Hayyim va-Hesed*, died on June 10, 1837.
13. Thomas Jones, English publisher, convert to Judaism, died on May 25, 1882.
14. Metullah, the northernmost settlement of Israel, was founded on May 19, 1896.
15. Jacob Ezekiel, Jewish historian, whose efforts led to the enactment of an amendment to the Virginia state law, placing observance of the Jewish Sabbath on a level with Sunday, died on May 16,1899.
16. Dropsie College for Hebrew and Cognate Learning was incorporated on May 20, 1907.
17. Anti-Jewish riots in Brest-Litovsk, Poland, resulted in serious injuries to hundreds of Jews and major property damage on May 17, 1937.
18. The Soviet government informed the Jewish community, on June 6, 1957, that it would permit the opening of a yeshivah in Moscow for the training of rabbis.

    The permission of the Soviet government to open a yeshivah in Moscow was announced on Shavuot, the anniversary of Matan To-rah. The coincidence of the timing, with its symbolic significance, might have been designed to impress world Jewry. However, the yeshivah was intended merely to serve window-dressing purposes. The laymen's council of the yeshivah was dissolved in 1961. The bulk of the yeshivah students had come from Georgia. After the Passover vacation of 1962 these students were denied permits by the local government to return to Moscow. Thus the yeshivah, reduced to a handful of students, could no longer hope to provide rabbis for Russian Jewry.

SIVAN 8

1. Anti-Jewish riots broke out in Emden, Prussia, on May 30, 1762.
2. Riots in Safed, Palestine, took a toll of many Jewish lives on June 15, 1834.
   The Safed pogrom in 1834 was not an isolated incident in the history of the town's Jewish community. Ever since Safed became a prominent center of Jewish culture in the 16th century, it was frequently ravaged by Arabs, Bedouins, and Turkish soldiery. In addition to these human assaults, the community was devastated many times by earthquakes. Only three years after the pogrom of 1834, Safed was practically wiped out by a major earthquake on January 1, 1837. In spite of these many mishaps, the existence of its Jewish community was never interrupted.
3. A pogrom broke out in Bialystok, Russia, on June 1, 1906.
4. Kinneret, the first workers' settlement, was founded in Palestine on June 7, 1908.
5. Dr. Shemaryahu Levine, popular Hebrew writer and orator, died on June 9, 1935.
6. The extermination camp of Auschwitz was opened on June 14, 1940.
   In the course of the existence of the notorious camp at Auschwitz, two and a half million people were exterminated there and another half-million died of disease and starvation.
7. Heinrich Himmler ordered the liquidation of all Polish ghettos on June 11, 1943.
8. A disengagement agreement was reached between Israel and Syria on May 29, 1974.

SIVAN 9

1. Titus set up battering rams in position to assault the walls of Jerusalem, on July 1 (approximate), 70 C.E.
   See Iyar 29:2.
2. The bishop of Strasbourg formed an alliance, on May 17, 1338, for the pursuit of the Armleder assassins who were responsible for the massacring of many Jews of Alsace.
3. An uncontrolled fire at Posen (Poznan) cost the lives of many Jews on June 11, 1590.
4. Rabbi Moses Rivkes of Vilna, author of Be'er ha-Golah, annotations on the code, died on June 4, 1672 (HY).
5. The first synagogue in Lisbon, Portugal, since the expulsion of 1497, was dedicated on May 23, 1904.
6. Anti-Jewish riots broke out in Warsaw, Poland, on June 8, 1938.
7. The republic of Croatia issued an order, on June 4, 1941, depriving all Jews of their property and compelling them to wear a yellow badge with the letter Z.
8. The ancient Jewish community of Khonia, Crete, dating from Roman times, came to an end on May 31, 1944, when the ship Danai, into which all the Jews had been herded, was towed out of the port of Iraklion 12 miles to sea and sunk.

SIVAN 10

1. Emperor Theodosius II issued a decree, on May 30, 429, ordering all collections made in the diaspora and Palestine for the nasi's fund to be henceforth turned over to the royal Treasury.
   Jews of the diaspora had helped maintain the Temple through special "shekel" contributions annually made by world Jewry. After the destruction of the Temple, voluntary contributions were collected for the maintenance of the Palestinian patriarchate. The order of Theodosius II dried up these funds and brought to an end the illustrious office of the nasi.
2. 60 Jews were murdered in Breslau, Silesia, on May 28, 1349, in riots which followed a disastrous fire which had destroyed part of the city.
3. Jews of Austria were imprisoned and expelled from the country on May 23, 1420.
4. A great number of Jews of Styria, Austria, were burned on May 11, 1421, and the balance were expelled from the country.
5. The printing of the first edition of the code, Tur Orah Ḥayyim, was completed in Mantua, Italy, on June 2, 1476.

The *Tur*, a very popular code, written by Rabbi Jacob b. Asher in the 14th century, formed the basis for the *Shulḥan Arukh*, written by Rabbi Joseph Caro in the 16th century. The latter became, and remains to this day, the undisputed standard code of Judaism. The first printed edition of the *Tur* was published in the 15th century one month after the yahrzeit of Rabbi Alfasi whose decisions it incorporated (Iyar 10:4).

6. Rabbi Eliezer Rokeah of Amsterdam, kabbalist, author of *Maasseh Rokeaḥ*, died on June 5, 1740.
7. Brith Abraham, third oldest fraternal order in the U.S., was organized on June 12, 1859.
8. Kalonymus Ze'ev Wissotzky, famous Russian Jewish philanthropist, died on May 24, 1904.
9. Reuben Siegel laid the cornerstone of the first house in Tel Aviv, Palestine, on May 30, 1909.

SIVAN 11

1. The Great Elector, Frederick William of Prussia, on May 20, 1671, permitted 50 Jewish families who had been expelled from Vienna to settle in his dominion.
2. Rabbi Abraham Geron of Adrianople, author of *Tikkun Soferim*, died June 4, 1751.
3. A fire broke out on May 29, 1795, in Padua, Italy. The community set aside a private Purim to be annually observed on Sabbath Toledot in commemoration of their escape from disaster.
4. Purim Urbino was annually celebrated on Sivan 11 in commemoration of an escape from massacre by the timely intervention of the civil government upon the withdrawal of the French army on June 14, 1798.
5. A resolution introduced in the U.S. House of Representatives on June 2, 1879, requested the president to have all international treaties which impair the rights of American citizens because of religion amended to secure equal rights (*AJHSP*, no. 41, p. 168).

   This resolution marked the first action taken by Congress affecting Russo-American relations. It was prompted by Russian discriminatory policies against American Jews.
6. The town of Bene-Berak was founded in Palestine on June 13, 1924.
7. Heinrich Himmler, chief of the Gestapo, committed suicide on May 23, 1945.

SIVAN 12

1. The Festival of the First Fruits (Shavuot) is observed by the Falashas on Sivan 12 (Leslau, *Falasha Anthology*).

   The Falashas observe Shavuot on Sivan 12 because it is the fiftieth day after the conclusion of Passover. Thus they agree with the rabbinic interpretation of the term *Sabbath*, mentioned in the biblical injunction to count 50 days (Lev. 23:15), as a reference to the festival of Passover rather than the day of the Sabbath. However, according to the Falasha tradition, the counting is to begin on the conclusion of the festival of Passover and not at the end of the first day of the festival.
2. Rabbi Isaac b. Samson Ha-Kohen, author of *Kizzur Mizrachi*, a compendium of annotations to Rashi's commentary on the Bible, died on May 30, 1624.
3. An edict admitting Jews into Berlin was published on May 21, 1671.
4. The American Jewish Historical Society was organized on June 7, 1892.
5. Israel Michel Rabinowitz, Franco-Jewish author of *Legislation Civile du Talmud*, died on May 27, 1893.
6. Agudat Yisrael, leading Orthodox organization, was founded at Kattowitz (Katowice), Poland, on May 28, 1912.
7. Anti-Jewish riots broke out in Tarnopol, Poland, on June 11, 1938.
8. The governments of Panama and Costa Rica recognized Israel on June 19, 1948.
9. The cornerstone of the Albert Einstein College of Medicine of Yeshiva University, the first medical school under Jewish auspices in America, was laid on June 13, 1954.

SIVAN 13

1. Laban caught up with Jacob at Mt. Gilead (Gen. 31:23; Book of Jubilees).

   Jacob fled from Laban's home, according to the Book of Jubilees, on Nisan 21. According to the same source, Laban caught up with him on the Sivan 13. A period of 52 days thus elapsed between these two events. This is obviously contradicted by the biblical account, which relates: "And it was told to Laban on the third day that Jacob was fled. And he took his brethren with him, and pursued after him seven days' journey; and they overtook him in Mt. Gilead" (Gen. 31:22–23). Thus only ten days at most elapsed between the two events.

2. 30 Jews of Posing, Hungary, charged with blood-ritual, were burned on May 27, 1529.

3. Rabbi Ephraim b. Jacob Katz, author of responsa *Sha'ar Ephraim*, died on June 3, 1678.

4. Manuel (Isaac Hayyim) Teixeira de Sampaio, philanthropist and communal leader, principal agent of Queen Christina of Sweden, died on June 5, 1705.

5. Rabbi Abraham b. David Yizhaki, author of responsa *Zera Avraham*, died on June 10, 1729.

6. Elisabeth Jane Charlemont, countess of Caulfield, a convert to Judaism, died on May 31, 1882.

7. Shalom Schwarzbard, on May 26, 1926, assassinated S. V. Petlura, former ataman of the Ukrainian Republican army, whose followers were responsible for 493 pogroms in which 50,000 Jews lost their lives.

8. Reinhard Heydrich, chief Nazi exterminator of European Jewry, was fatally injured by a bomb near Lidice, Czechoslovakia, on May 29, 1942. He died six days later.

9. 20 Jews were killed by the explosion of a bomb thrown in the Jewish quarter of Cairo, Egypt, on June 20, 1948.

10. The central system of the underground water supply was dedicated in the northern Negev in Israel on June 17, 1951.

11. Martin Buber, philosopher and author, died on June 13, 1965.

12. Yizhak Rabin, the first native-born Israeli to become prime minister of Israel, assumed office on June 3, 1974.

SIVAN 14

1. Jewish insurgent forces captured the fortress of Antonia in Jerusalem on June 8 (approximate), 65. This battle marked the outbreak of the Jewish revolt against Rome (Zeitlin, *Megillat Ta'anit*, 3).

   According to Prof. Klausner, the rebellion against Rome dates from the attack on the Roman garrison under Florus, on Iyar 17, 66 B.C.E. See note on Iyar 17:3.

2. The first attack on the Jewish community of Frankfort on the Main, Germany, took place on May 25, 1241. The Jewish quarter was destroyed and most of the Jews were massacred.

3. Emperor Maximilian of Germany rescinded on May 23, 1510, a previously issued order to burn all Hebrew books found in Cologne and Frankfort, Germany.

Jewish culture depended upon the availability of books and manuscripts. The burning of Jewish books by civil and ecclesiastical authorities inevitably led to a decline of the creative genius of the Jewish people. Emperor Maximilians' rescinding, on Sivan 14, 1510, of a previous order condemning Jewish books to the flames was a great victory for the Jewish spirit. Sivan 14 is also the yahrzeit of Rabbi Ḥayyim of Volozhin (no. 7), founder of the Yeshivah of Volozhin, which inaugurated a new cultural era in the history of Lithuanian Jewry.

4. Saul Cohen Ashkenazi, philosopher, author of *She'elot*, died on May 28, 1523.
5. An auto-da-fé in Barcelona claimed the lives of 24 Jews on May 24, 1588.
6. Rabbi Moses Brandeis Charif, talmudist, died on June 24, 1761.
7. Rabbi Ḥayyim b. Isaac of Volozhin, founder of the famed Yeshivah of Volozhin, author of *Nefesh ha-Ḥayyim*, died on June 14, 1821.
8. Anti-Jewish riots broke out in Przemysl, Poland, on June 13, 1938.
9. The Allies marched into Rome on June 5, 1944. Jews emerged from their hiding places and the gate of the great synagogue was opened.
10. The Rhodes conference on the Israeli-Arab war opened on June 21, 1948.

SIVAN 15

1. Birth of Judah (*Midrash Tadshe*).
2. Laban and Jacob erected a monument at Gilead (Book of Jubilees; Gen. 31:46).
3. The sons of John Hyrcanus the Hasmonean captured the city of Beth-Shean and the Valley of Jezreel in the war against Antiochus IX (Zeitlin, *Megillat Ta'anit* 3).
4. The Crusaders laid siege to Jerusalem on June 7, 1099.
5. Rabbi Joseph b. Benjamin Samegah of Venice, talmudist and kabbalist, author of *Mikrae Kodesh*, died on June 6, 1629.
6. King John Casimir of Poland, on June 8, 1664, denied the Jews of Vilna the right to deal in non-Jewish books.
7. Rabbi Isaac of Poznan, author of responsa *Be'er Yitzḥak*, died on June 3, 1689 (HY).
8. The last restrictions on the Jews of Denmark were lifted with the adoption of the constitution on June 5, 1849.
9. Samuel Ḥayyim Landau, one of the organizers of the Torah va-Avodah movement, died on June 3, 1928.

10. Anshel Schorr, Yiddish playwright, died on May 31, 1942.
11. The Israeli legation in Moscow issued the first immigration visa for Israel to Mrs. Tova Lerner, a Soviet Jewish citizen, on June 19, 1951.

   The hope that the permission granted to the first Soviet Jew to emigrate to Israel was a portent of a liberalized Russian policy has not materialized. Nikita Khrushchev, the First Secretary of the Communist Party, told Dr. Jerome David, an American scientist, on August 27, 1957, that "the time may come when all Jews who wish to settle will be able to do so." This was a propaganda statement issued for foreign consumption. The foreign policy of a dictatorship has no public opinion to answer to and is never moved by considerations of merit or justice.

   In the hope of obtaining favorable trade terms from the U.S., Russia relaxed restrictions on emigration of Soviet Jews in the seventies. By the end of the decade the restrictions were reimposed. About a quarter of a million Jews left in that decade.
12. Israeli forces crossed into Lebanon on June 6, 1982, to destroy P.L.O. military bases.

SIVAN 16

1. Jacob left Mt. Gilead after Laban's departure and met the angels at Mahanaim (Book of Jubilees; Gen. 32:2).

   Gilead was a gateway to the countries north and east of Palestine. It was from Mizpeh of Gilead that Jephthah advanced ·to attack the Ammonites (Judg. 11:29). Beersheba was the gateway to the countries south and west of Palestine. It was on Sivan 16, according to Jubilees, that Jacob proceeded from Gilead to Palestine after having secured himself from attack by Laban. It was on the same day, about 33 years later, according to Jubilees, that Jacob left Beersheba for Egypt, after receiving divine assurance of protection from attack by the people in that region (no. 2).
2. God appeared to Jacob at Beersheba and said: "Fear not to go down to Egypt, for I will make thee there a great nation" (Book of Jubilees; Gen. 46:3).
3. The beginning of a substantial Jewish settlement in Massachusetts was made on June 6, 1716, with the arrival of the ship *Restoration* from London with several Jewish merchants aboard.
4. French planes, loyal to the Vichy government, bombed Tel Aviv and killed 20 Jews on June 11, 1941.

SIVAN 17

1. Noah's ark came to rest on Mt. Ararat (Gen. 8:4, Rashi).
2. The Hasmoneans captured Migdal Zur and founded a Jewish settlement there. The anniversary of this event was observed as a holiday (*Megillat Ta'anit* 3).
3. The Inquisition was introduced into Mexico on June 6, 1536. It attained autonomous jurisdiction in 1571.
4. Rabbi Eleazer b. David Fleckeles of Prague, author of *Teshuva me-Ahavah*, a book of responsa, died on June 22, 1826 (HY).
5. The first Russian Jewish congregation in America, Bet Hamidrash HaGadol, was organized on June 4, 1852. It met in a garret at 83 Bayard Street, New York City (*AJHSP*, no. 9, p. 64).

   The early Jewish settlers of America were mainly of Spanish and Portuguese extraction. They were followed by German Jewish immigrants who came in the early part of the 19th century (see Tishri 14:7). These Jews later became the founders of the Reform movement in the United States. East European Jews came next, in the second half of the 19th century. They became the founders of the Ashkenazic Orthodox congregations in the U.S. The first East European congregation was organized 50 years after the establishment of the first Hebrew German Society. The Conservative movement came into being approximately 50 years later. A rigid social exclusiveness kept the various elements of American Jewry apart. The ultimate integration of American Jews within the broad cultural pattern of the country led to the weakening of intramural exclusiveness within the Jewish community. Free social intercourse among all elements of Jewry has also brought about intercongregational cooperation. The Synagogue Council of America, representing all the three wings, was founded on Sivan 17, 1925 (no. 8), the anniversary of the founding of the first East European Orthodox congregation in the U.S. The post-Hitlerian era has revived a separatist tendency, based exclusively on religious considerations. This trend has affected also some of the older American Orthodox groups.
6. Rabbi Aaron b. Asher of Karlin, hasidic leader, author of *Beit Aharon*, died on June 23, 1872.
7. Zevi Gershoni, Yiddish journalist, editor of the first Yiddish periodical in America, *Di Post*, died on June 17, 1897.
8. The Synagogue Council of America, composed of representatives of Orthodox, Conservative, and Reform congregations and rabbinical groups, was organized on June 9, 1925.

SIVAN 18

1. The City of Acre was captured by Muslims on May 18, 1291, bringing to an end the Christian Kingdom of Palestine.
   The persecution of medieval Jewry in England dates from the 12th century, with the launching of the Crusades. The persecutions led to the expulsion of the Jewish community in 1290. The vestiges of the Crusaders' Kingdom in Palestine came to an end in 1291.
2. Rabbi Abraham Rapoport of Lemberg, head of the Yeshivah of Lemberg, author of "Eitan ha-Ezrahi", died on June 7, 1651.
3. The Union of Orthodox Jewish Congregations of America was organized on June 8, 1898.
   The Union of Orthodox Jewish Congregations was organized on the 18th of Sivan. The Synagogue Council of America was organized on the 17th of Sivan (no. 8). The first East-European Orthodox Congregation was also founded on the 17th of Sivan (no. 5).
4. The German military commander of occupied France, on June 3, 1942, ordered all Jews to wear a yellow Star of David with the inscription "Juif" on it.
5. On June 21, 1943, Heinrich Himmler ordered the extension of a decree providing for the liquidation of all Polish ghettos to include also the Russian ghettos.
6. The liquidation of the ghetto of Lvov began on June 21, 1943, and was completed on June 27th.
7. The Law of the Exercise of the Civil Right to Religious Freedom was passed by Spain's Cortes on June 26, 1967.
   The law granted to Jews and Protestants the right of public worship for the first time since Ferdinand and Isabella proclaimed Catholicism as Spain's only religion. By the terms of this law, Jews were authorized to mark their places of worship and to advertise their religious services. The number of Jews in Spain at the time of the passage of the law was estimated at 6,000.

SIVAN 19

1. The first Jewish hospital in America, Jews' Hospital of New York, admitted its first patient on June 5, 1855.
   The Jewish community of Berlin maintained a small hospital in the 16th century. The Jewish community of Rome had its own hospital in the 17th century. The first Jewish hospital in England was opened in 1743. The first French Jewish hospital was opened in 1836. Russian

Jewry maintained 112 hospitals prior to World War I. Some East European countries restricted the right of Jews to build hospitals and also restricted the number of Jewish patients admitted into public hospitals. When a Bucharest Jew died in 1896 because he was denied admission to the city hospital, the Jewish community petitioned the government for permission to build its own hospital. The petition was denied.

2. Rabbi Samuel Mohilewer, pioneer of Russian Zionism, co-founder of Rehovot, Palestine, died on June 9, 1898 (HY).
3. Anti-Jewish riots broke out in Jassy, Rumania, on May 28, 1899.
4. Hayyim Rosenblueth, pioneer of Yiddish poets in America, died on May 29, 1956.
5. Isaac Simbar, Hebrew writer, died on June 18, 1957.

SIVAN 20

1. 34 Jewish men and 17 Jewish women were burned at the stake in Blois, France, on May 26, 1171, in the first ritual-murder charge on the European continent.
2. The fast of Sivan 20 was decreed by Rabbenu Tam in memory of the martyrs of Blois who were burned on charges of ritual murder.

   The fast of Sivan 20 was originally ordained by Rabbenu Tam in the 12th century to commemorate the first blood-ritual charges in France and the subsequent burning of the innocent Jewish victims in Blois. The fast was observed in France, in the German province of the Rhine, and most likely also in England. The same day was also declared a fast-day in Poland in the year 1650 to commemorate the Chmielnicki pogroms (no. 3). Sivan 20 was designated a memorial day because it was the anniversary of the massacre of the Jews of Niemirow, early in the uprising. The fact that this day had already been observed as a fast-day in the 12th century, and that special prayers had already been composed for the occasion, was an important factor in the selection of this date.

   See Nisan 16:10.
3. 6,000 Jews of Niemirow, Poland, perished in the Chmielnicki massacres on June 10, 1648. The anniversary of this day was set aside by Polish Jewry as a day of fasting and mourning.
4. Reinhard Heydrich, head of the Nazi security police charged with the extermination of millions of Jews, died on June 5, 1942, following injuries suffered several days earlier in the explosion of a bomb.
5. Israel annexed the Old City of Jerusalem on June 28, 1967, and united it with New Jerusalem.

SIVAN 21

1. Miriam was afflicted with leprosy and confined for seven days (*Seder Olam* 8).

   According to some biblical chronologists, Miriam was afflicted on Sivan 23. The Talmud, however, states that she was afflicted on Sivan 22 (*Ta'anit* 29a).
2. Sultan Mohammed II, the conqueror of Constantinople, granted equal rights to Jews and other non-Muslim subjects of the Ottoman Empire on May 29, 1453.

   The liberal policy of the Turkish government toward its Jewish population was announced upon the capture of Constantinople on Sivan 21, 1453. This policy providentially provided one of the principal havens of refuge for the mass of immigrants who were to pour into Muslim countries 40 years later, after the expulsion from Spain in 1492.
3. Isaac Miranda, the first Jewish settler of Lancaster, Pa., was appointed deputy judge of the Court of Vice-Admiralty on June 10, 1727. It was the first judicial office held by a Jew in the colonies.

   Miranda had converted to Christianity several years before his appointment.
4. Harvard College created the Hancock Professorship of Hebrew and Oriental Languages on June 12, 1765.
5. Rabbi Samuel b. Issachar Baer Freund, author of *Zera Kodesh*, died on June 18, 1881.
6. Rabbi Aryeh Leib Horowitz of Stanislav (Stanislawow, Russia) author of responsa *Harei Besamim*, died on June 10, 1909.

SIVAN 22

1. Pope Clement VII ordered the Jews of Carpentras, France, on June 13, 1525, to wear distinctive yellow hats.
2. Rabbi Jehiel Michel of Niemirow, Poland, author of *Shivrei Luḥot*, was killed by Chmielnicki Cossacks on June 12, 1648.

   See Sivan 20:3
3. The directors of the West India Co. instructed Governor Peter Stuyvesant, on June 14, 1656, to suggest to the Jews of New Amsterdam that they restrict their residence to a self-imposed ghetto where they might exercise their religion in the privacy of their homes; to permit Jews to trade along the South River (Delaware River); and to grant

them the right to own real estate in New Amsterdam (*AJHSP*, no. 10, p.48).

A petition by the Jews of New Amsterdam for permission to build a synagogue was denied by the local authorities on Adar 16, 1656. History made amends for this mistake. The United Synagogue of America was founded on Adar 16, 1913. The early Jewish community of New Amsterdam never succeeded in obtaining a permit to build a synagogue during the 10 years of its existence under Dutch rule. On September 7, 1664, New Amsterdam became New York. We do not know when the first public synagogue was dedicated. There is positive proof, however, of the existence of a synagogue in 1697.

4. Rabbi Judah Loeb b. Asher Margoliot of Frankfort, author of *Or Olam*, first Judeo-Polish author to write on natural philosophy, died on June 14, 1811.

5. *Ha-Zofeh ba-Arez ha- Hadashah*, the first Hebrew periodical published in America, appeared for the first time in New York on June 11, 1871. See Av 4:5.

6. *Die Yidishe Velt*, a Yiddish daily newspaper, was founded in New York on June 27, 1902.

7. Dr. Chaim Arlosoroff, leader of the Palestine Labor Party, was assassinated on June 16, 1933. His death led to intense civil strife within the Jewish community.

SIVAN 23

1. King Jeroboam stopped the Jews of the northern kingdom from bringing *bikkurim* (first fruits) to Jerusalem. This date was observed as a fast day (*Megillat Ta'anit* 3).

2. Mordecai issued a royal decree calling upon Jews to defend themselves against attack (Esther 8:11).

   This is the oldest record of an organized Jewish self-defense in the diaspora.

3. Rabbi Jacob Pollack of Prague , outstanding talmudist of his age, died on June 18, 1541.

4. Jews of Poznan (Posen), Poland, were rescued on June 23, 1696, from a mob set to avenge the murder of a soldier. A peasant woman, seized carrying the victim's clothes, confessed to her son's murder (Bernfeld, *Sefer ha-Dema'ot*, vol. 3)

5. Fast-day of the Jewish community of Pesaro, Italy, in commemoration of the murder of Jews on June 7, 1798, following the retreat of Napoleon's army.

6. Rabbi Joshua Heller of Telshi, Lithuania, author of *Divrei Yehoshua*, died on June 2, 1880.
7. The U.S. Bureau of Naturalization, on July 1, 1929, issued a new form of application, requiring persons seeking naturalization to state their race as well as nationality.
8. The last British armed forces left Israel on June 30, 1948.
9. Authority over the port of Haifa was taken over by Israel on June 30, 1948.
10. The U.S. Supreme Court, on June 25, 1962, outlawed the reading of the New York State Regents' Prayer in public schools as a violation of the constitutional separation of Church and State.
11. Ephraim Lisitzky, Hebrew poet, died on June 25, 1962.

SIVAN 24

1. Rabbi Moses b. Solomon Ha-Kohen of Mainz, German tosafist, died on May 31, 1198 (DDD).
2. Rabbi Abraham Mintz of Padua, author of *Seder Gittin Ve-Ḥaliẓah*, died on May 27, 1535.
3. The Jewish Publication Society of America was organized on June 3, 1888.

    The first Anglo-Jewish periodical in the United States, the *Jew* was published in 1823. The need for Anglo-Jewish publications to meet the requirements of native English-speaking American Jews became apparent in the early decades of the 19th century. However, it was not until the organization of the Jewish Publication Society in 1888 that concrete steps were initiated in the cultural and religious struggle to provide educational material for the increasing numbers of English-speaking native Jews.
4. Pinhas Yosenofsky, Yiddish poet, died on June 25, 1954.

SIVAN 25

1. Geviha ben Pesisa, Jewish delegate, emerged victorious from his debate with the Samaritans in the presence of King Alexander the Great (*Megillat Ta'anit* 3).
2. Trajan, commander of the 10th Legion, conquered the Galilean fortress city of Japha in the year 67 and killed 15,000 Jews (Josephus, *Jewish Wars* 3:7;31).
3. Rabbis Simon b. Gamaliel, Ishmael b. Elisha, and Ḥanina Segan

ha-Kohanim were martyred by the Romans (*Megillat Ta'anit*, concluding chap.) These sages are listed among the Ten Martyrs.

4. Massacre of the Jews of Erfurt, Germany, on June 16, 1221. The anniversary of this massacre was observed as a fast-day. The liturgical poet, Samuel b. Kalonymus was one of the martyrs.
5. Rabbi David Mirles of Berlin, author of *Korban ha-Edah*, popular commentary on the Jerusalem Talmud, died on June 17, 1762.
6. Jews were granted permission to settle in the Kiev province of Russia, by order of Empress Catherine II, dated June 23, 1794.
7. The Russian General Nikolai Pavlovich Ignatyev was dismissed from office on June 12, 1882, for his part in the pogroms of 1881.
8. Rabbi Ḥayyim b. Mordecai Sofer of Pest, Hungary, author of *Maḥaneh Ḥayyim*, died on June 28, 1886.

SIVAN 26

1. Rabbi Baruch Rapoport of Fürth, Germany, scholar and ascetic, died on June 14, 1746.
2. Rabbi Pesahya b. David was martyred in Cracow on June 29, 1799 (DYY).
3. Rabbi Zevi Hirsh Horowitz of Frankfort, author of *Mahane Levi*, died on June 30, 1818 (HY).
4. Fra Vincenzo Soliva, inquisitor of Ancona, Italy, published a decree, on June 24, 1843, forbidding Jews to reside in any municipality which had not established a ghetto.
5. Rabbi Isaac b. Ḥayyim, head of the Yeshivah of Volozhin, author of *Mile de-Avot*, died on June 16, 1849.
6. Leib Malach, Yiddish writer, died on June 16, 1936.
7. The German army was defeated at El-Alamein, North Africa, on June 11, 1942, ending the threat to Palestine.

The defeat of General Erwin Rommel at El-Alamein brought to an end the worst crisis facing the Jewish community of Palestine in World War II. The turning point came one day short of the first anniversary of the Nazi attack on Russia, which led to the destruction of a great part of Russian Jewry.

SIVAN 27

1. Miriam ended the seventh day of her confinement (*Seder Olam*).
2. The Roman general Cerealis stormed the Samaritan stronghold on Mt. Gerizim and killed 11,600 men, 67 C.E. (Josephus, *Jewish Wars* 3:7).
3. Rabbi Ḥanina b. Teradyon, one of the Ten Martyrs, was burned at the stake (*Megillat Ta'anit* concluding chap.).
4. Rabbi Akiva was imprisoned by the Romans, ca. 132 (Maharam of Rothenburg, *Sefer ha-Minhagim*).

   Maharam of Rothenburg, the source for the date of Rabbi Akiva's imprisonment, alleged that Sivan 27 was observed as a fast-day in commemoration of the execution of Rabbi Ḥaninah b. Teradyon and the imprisonment of Rabbi Akiva. In modern times this date has also become a memorial for the exterminated Lithuanian Jewry (no. 13).
5. The second expulsion of the Jews of France took place on June 24, 1322.

   See Kislev 9:1.
6. Construction of the Bevis Marks Synagogue, the oldest Jewish house of worship in London, England, began on June 24, 1699.
7. Rabbi Meir Eisenstadt of Worms, author of *Or ha-Ganuz*, commentary on the Talmud and code, died on June 6, 1744.
8. Purim of Florence was celebrated by the Jewish community of Florence, Italy, to commemorate an escape from massacre on June 9, 1790.
9. Rabbi Mordecai b. Asher Klatzko, author of *Tekhelet Mordecai*, a book of responsa, died on July 2, 1883.
10. Rabbi Jacob b. Mordecai Prager, author of responsa *She'elot Yaakov*, died on June 17, 1898.
11. A libel suit against Dr. A. Zander of Switzerland, editor of the periodical *Iron Broom*, for allegations pertaining to the *Protocols of the Elders of Zion*, ended on June 21, 1933, upon the defendant's admission of guilt.

    A similar retraction of charges based on the *Protocols* was made by Henry Ford on Sivan 30, 1927 (no. 3).
12. Germany invaded Lithuania and Latvia in its opening attack on Russia on June 22, 1941.
13. Sivan 27 has been designated a Memorial Day by the survivors of Lithuanian Jewry.
14. Michael Licht, Yiddish poet, died on June 10, 1953.

SIVAN 28

1. The ancient Hebrews arrived at the wilderness of Paran (*Seder Olam* 8).
2. Solomon b. Joel Dubno of Amsterdam, poet and student of the Masorah, died on June 26, 1813.
3. Yeshivat Hakhmei Lublin, an academy for the training of rabbis and teachers, was opened by its founder, Rabbi Meir Shapira, on June 24, 1930.
4. The famous Yeshivah of Slobodka, Lithuania, closed its door on June 23, 1941.

   The two outstanding yeshivot of Lithuania were in Slobodka and Telz. Both institutions came to an end within a day of the Nazi invasion of Lithuania (no. 5).
5. Germany occupied Telz, Lithuania, on June 23, 1941.

SIVAN 29

1. Moses sent 12 scouts to survey Palestine (*Seder Olam* 8).
2. Rabbi Shmuel Shmaryah of Ostrovce, author of *Zikhron Shmuel*, died on June 13, 1847(HY).
3. The first public warning of rising anti-Semitism in the U.S. was given by Henry Ward Beecher in a sermon entitled "Jew and Gentile," delivered on June 24, 1873.
4. The Jewish community of Nizhni Novogrod was pogromized on June 22, 1884. It was the first Russian pogrom outside of the Jewish Pale of Settlement.
5. The Lovers of Zion, a pre-Zionist American group, was organized on June 29, 1897.

   The American early Zionist group was founded on the anniversary of the departure of the 12 scouts to Palestine in preparation for the ultimate settlement of the land (no. 1). It was on the same anniversary that the Russian government prohibited all Zionist activities (no. 6).
6. Russia prohibited Zionist meetings and the collection of funds for Zionist purposes on June 24, 1903.
7. Germany occupied Kovno (Kaunas) and Vilna, Lithuania, on June 24, 1941.
8. The Jewish male population of Gorzhdy (Gargzdai), Lithuania, was exterminated by the Nazis on June 24, 1941.
9. Yosele Shumacher, whose disappearance from Israel had attracted worldwide attention, was found in Brooklyn on June 30, 1962.

SIVAN 30

1. Rabbi Moses Najara of Damascus, author of *Lekah Tov*, died on June 1, 1581.
2. The residence tax imposed on Hungarian Jews was abolished on June 24, 1846.
3. In a letter to Louis Marshall, dated June 30, 1927, Henry Ford retracted and apologized for the publication of the spurious *Protocols of the Elders of Zion* in the *Dearborn Independent*.
   See Sivan 27:11; Sivan 29:3.
4. Numerous Jews were killed in a pogrom at Jassy, Rumania, on June 25, 1941.
5. The British mandatory government of Palestine arrested a hundred leaders of the Yishuv on the "Black Sabbath," June 29, 1946.

TAMMUZ 1

1. Jacob and his family arrived in Goshen, Egypt (Book of Jubilees). Tammuz 1, according to the Book of Jubilees, is the anniversary of the establishment of the first Jewish voluntary diaspora. A moshav established on this day in modern Palestine, in the year 1940 (no. 10), was appropriately given the name of She'ar Yashuv ("the remnant will return").
2. The fortress city of Jotapata in the Galilee was demolished by Vespasian, and its 40,000 Jewish inhabitants were slain, 67 C.E. (Josephus, *Jewish Wars* 3:7).

   See Iyar 7:3.
3. The wall surrounding the citadel of Antonia in Jerusalem fell after an assault by the Roman legion on June 23 (approximate), 70 C.E. (Josephus, *Jewish Wars* 6:1).

   The fall of Jotapata (no. 2) led to the defection of Josephus and the end of the large-scale organized resistance in Galilee. The capture of the citadel of Antonia in Jerusalem on the anniversary of the fall of Jotapata led to the Roman assault on the walls of the Temple Court from the north.
4. A riotous mob led by the queen mother's confessor, Ferrand Martinez, killed many Jews in Seville, Spain, on June 4, 1391. The riots spread throughout the country (EJVD).
5. Emperor Maximilian issued a decree on June 21, 1498, permitting the citizens of Nuremberg, Bavaria, to expel its Jewish community.
6. Rabbi Aaron Abba ha-Levi b. Pinehas, head of the Yeshivah of Lemberg, died on June 20, 1641 (DDD).
7. Rabbi Kalonymus Kalman Halevi Epstein of Cracow, author of *Ma'or va-Shemesh*, popular hasidic work, died on June 26, 1827.
8. Rabbi Solomon Kluger of Brody, talmudist, author of *Sefer ha-Hayyim*, comments on the code, died on June 10, 1869 (HY).
9. Philipp Schey, Baron von Koromla, first Jew in Hungary to be made an Austrian nobleman, died on June 28, 1881.
10. The moshav She'ar Yashuv was founded in Palestine on July 7, 1940.
11. Germany occupied Shavl (Siauliai), Lithuania, on June 26, 1941.
12. Lithuanian Facists massacred 2,300 Jews in Kovno (Kaunas), Lithuania, on June 26, 1941. Rabbi Ossovsky was decapitated in his home.

215

TAMMUZ 2

1. Rabbi Samuel b. Jehiel of Cologne was killed by the Crusaders on June 25, 1096.
2. Johann Gottfried Eichhorn, orientalist and biblical scholar, died on June 27, 1827.
3. The *Maccabean*, first Zionist publication in America, was founded at the convention of the Zionist Societies of America in Philadelphia on June 19, 1901.
4. Palestine was rocked by an earthquake on July 2, 1927.
5. Rabbi Sheraga Faivel Horowitz, one of the heads of the Yeshivah of Slobodka, was killed by the Nazis on June 27, 1941.
6. Bialystok, Poland, fell to the Germans on June 27, 1941.
7. The first truce of the Israeli-Arab war ended on July 9, 1948.

TAMMUZ 3

1. Joshua commanded the sun to "stand still upon Gibeon" (Josh. 10:12; *Seder Olam* 11).
2. Sabinus, the first Roman soldier to scale the last wall in front of the Tower of Antonia in Jerusalem, was killed by the Jewish defenders on July 25 (approximate), 70 c.e. (Josephus, *Jewish War*, 6:1).
3. Anti-Jewish riots spread throughout Castile and Aragon, Spain, on June 6, 1391.
   See Tammuz 1:4.
4. A petition by Rabbi Menasseh ben Israel for official permission to practice Judaism in England was granted by the Council of State on June 25, 1656 (Roth, in *Commentary*, June 1956, p. 513).
   Tammuz 3 is a significant date in the history of English and Russian Jewries. The official approval of the practice of Judaism in England became the basis for the tolerant policy toward Jews in the far-flung British Empire. Russian permission for the establishment of Jewish printing presses in the 19th century (no. 5) stimulated the widespread cultural output of East European Jewry.
5. Emperor Alexander II granted permission to Russian Jews on July 1, 1862 to open printing establishments for the printing of Jewish books.
6. Rabbi Bernard Illowy, first Orthodox rabbi with a Ph.D. degree from a European university to settle in America, died on June 22, 1871.
   Rabbi Illowy was ordained by the famous Rabbi Moses Sofer of Pressburg, Hungary (now Bratislava, Czchoslovakia). Although the latter was opposed to secular education, Rabbi Illowy broke with the

Pressburg tradition and proceeded to get an education in Germany and Italy, where he received his Ph.D. He emigrated to the U.S. in 1852. His first rabbinic position was with Congregation Shaare Zedek of New York. Thereafter he held posts in Philadelphia, St. Louis, Syracuse, Baltimore, New Orleans, and Cincinnati. He was a firm opponent of the Reform movement.

7. 1,500 Jews were killed in Kovno (Kaunas), Lithuania, on the night of June 28, 1941.

8. German and Rumanian soldiers killed 11,000 Jews in Kishinev, in a two-day pogrom which started on June 28, 1941.
See Nisan 22:7.

9. Lydda Airfield was captured by the Israeli army on July 10, 1948.

TAMMUZ 4

1. Rabbenu Jacob b. Meir (Tam), leading French Tosafist, died on June 9, 1171.

2. A public debate between Rabbi Jehiel of Paris and the apostate Nicholas Donin, which was to decide the fate of the confiscated volumes of the Talmud, began on June 25, 1240, at the court of Louis IX of France, in the presence of Queen-Mother Blanche.

The confiscated Talmud volumes were burned two years later, on Tammuz 6 (no. 3). The theological debate brought disastrous results to French Jewry. Impoverished economically, it now experienced a rapid cultural decline, an exodus of talmudic scholars and the removal of the Yeshivah of Paris. The debate (Vikku'aḥ) began in the week when the biblical portion of Balak is read on the Sabbath. The Haftarah portion that day is from the prophet Micah and includes the following verse: "For the Lord has a controversy with his people and he will dispute with Israel" (Mic. 6:2). Among Rabbi Jehiel's distinguished disciples who had witnessed the disastrous burning of the Talmud in Paris on June 6, 1242, was Rabbi Meir of Rothenburg (no. 3). He subsequently commemorated the tragedy with a stirring elegy—Sha'ali Serufah—immortalized in our liturgy. Shocked by this misfortune and the ever-rising wave of persecutions, Rabbi Meir urged European Jews to emigrate to Palestine. In 1286, Rabbi Meir and his family set out for the Holy Land. He was recognized by an apostate Jew in Lombardy and imprisoned on the anniversary of the fateful debate in Paris.
See Iyar 19:1.

3. Rabbenu Meir of Rothenburg (Maharam) was imprisoned in the fortress of Ensisheim on June 19, 1286.
4. 40 Jews were killed in Oberwesel on charges of ritual murder on June 19, 1286.
5. The Jewish community of Berne, Switzerland, forfeited all its financial claims against the non-Jewish citizenry by a decree published on June 30, 1294. This was followed up by an order of expulsion.
6. 1,000 Jews of Tulchin, Poland, were tortured and massacred by Cossacks on June 24, 1648.
7. Rabbi Moses Mizraḥi, author of *Admat Kodesh*, died on June 20, 1749 (ATGY).
8. Rabbi Phinehas Ha-Levi Ish Horowitz, outstanding talmudic scholar, author of *Hafla'ah*, novellae on the tractate *Ketubbot*, died on July 1, 1805.
9. Moses b. Ẓaddik Belinfante, journalist and author of Jewish school texts, died on June 29, 1827.
10. The Jewish male population of Drobian (Darbenai), Lithuania, was massacred by the Nazis on June 29, 1941.
11. The cities of Lydda (Lod) and Ramallah were captured by the Israeli army on July 11, 1948.
12. Ra's al-Ayin, with its pumping station, which supplied water to Jerusalem, was captured by the Arabs on July 11, 1948.
13. The Arab siege of the children's settlement of Ben Shemen was lifted on July 11, 1948.
14. Jerusalem was bombed from the air for the first time in its history on July 11, 1948.

TAMMUZ 5

1. Ezekiel made his first appearance as a prophet in the year 502 B.C.E. (Ezek. 1:2).

   The emergence of prophecy in the diaspora was the earliest manifestation of the ability of Judaism to survive in an alien atmosphere.
2. The inner (third) wall in front of the Tower of Antonia in Jerusalem was captured by the Romans. The Jewish defenders retreated to the Temple Court area on July 26 (approximate), 70 C.E. (Josephus, *Jewish Wars* 6:1).
3. Jews of Xanten, Germany, committed mass suicide on June 28, 1096.
4. Rabbi Yom Tov Lipmann Heller, author of *Tosefot Yom Tov*, was imprisoned on June 26, 1629. The anniversary of his arrest was designated by him a private fast-day for himself and his descendants.

5. The explosion of a powder magazine at Breslau, Germany (now Wroclaw, Poland), on June 21, 1749, led to riots in which many Jews lost their lives. The day was designated a fast-day.
6. Tammuz 5 was set aside as a memorial fast-day for the estimated 50,000 Ukrainian Jews who had lost their lives in Uman and other cities on June 20, 1768, in the Haidamack uprising under Gonta and Zheleznyak.

   Jews of Uman were massacred again on June 19, 1788.
7. Wolf Ha-Kohen Kaplan, Hebrew poet, died on June 14, 1888.
8. Mark Antokolski, Jewish sculptor, died on July 10, 1902.
9. Moses Aaron Dropsie, communal leader and scholar, president of Gratz College, died on July 8, 1905.
10. Mass extermination of Jews by Nazis began on June 20, 1942, at the Auschwitz camp (Poliakov, *Harvest of Hate*, p. 201).

    The beginning of the mass extermination of Jews on Tammuz 5 provides a historical basis for the designation of this date as a memorial day for victims of the Nazis. Entries 2–6 highlight the tragic background of Tammuz 5 in Jewish history.
11. The deportation of Hungarian Jews to extermination camps was temporarily halted by Regent Miklós Horthy on June 26, 1944.
12. A bloody pogrom at Kielce, Poland, the first post-Nazi massacre of Polish Jews, broke out on July 4, 1946.

TAMMUZ 6

1. The Tower of Antonia, which dominated the Temple Court area, was taken by the Romans on July 27 (approximate), 70 C.E. (Josephus, *Jewish War* 6:1).
2. Crusaders massacred the Jews of Mehr on June 29, 1096.
3. 24 wagonloads of talmudic volumes and 200 other rabbinic manuscripts were burned at Paris on June 6, 1242.

   See note on Tammuz 4:2.
4. The first native white male child of Georgia, Philip Minis, was born to Abraham and Leah Minis on July 7, 1734. (UJE, Georgia).
5. Rabbi Israel Jacob Algazi of Jerusalem, author of *Kehilat Ya'akov*, died on July 4, 1756 (DDD).
6. Empress Catherine II of Russia issued an order, dated July 4, 1794, restricting the area where Jews were permitted to trade.
7. Rabbi Gershom Mendes Seixas, early American patriot, died on July 2, 1816.

   The yahrzeit of Rabbi Seixas falls on the birthday of an older compatriot, Philip Minis (no. 4). Though the former was a native of New York and the latter of Georgia, they might have met. Rabbi Seixas's brother, Lieut. Abraham Seixas, was a Georgia resident.

8. Michel Berr, the first Jew to practice law in France, died on July 4, 1843.
9. *Ha-Karmel*, early Hebrew publication, appeared for the first time on June 26, 1860.
10. The Jewish male population of Nayshtat (Kudirkos-Naumiestis), Lithuania, was executed by the Nazis on July 1, 1941.
11. Germany occupied Riga, Latvia, on July 1, 1941.
12. An organized pogrom erupted in Jassy, the cradle of Rumanian anti-Semitism, on July 1, 1941. About 5,000 Jews lost their lives.
13. The Migdal Zedek quarry was captured by the Israeli army on July 13, 1948.
14. Israeli commandos, in a daring and spectacular raid on July 4, 1976, rescued about 100 Jewish passsengers held hostage at Uganda's airport of Entebbe.

TAMMUZ 7

1. Rabbi Saul of Amsterdam, author of *Binyan Ariel*, died on June 19, 1970 (DDD).
2. Ukrainian rioters attacked and killed Jewish refugees in Brailov, Podolia, on July 5, 1919.

    The Ukrainian anti-Jewish riots in 1919 were inspired by the leader of the Ukrainian nationalists, Simon Petlyura. He was subsequently assassinated by a young Jew. The Nazis exploited the assassination of Petlyura to instigate new pogroms in the Ukraine. The pogrom in Lemberg (Lwow) (no. 4), labeled "Action Petlyura," took place on the anniversary of the pogrom in Brailov (no. 2).
3. President Franklin D. Roosevelt called an international conference at Evian-les-Bains, France, on July 6, 1938, to consider the "displaced persons" problem.

    The negligible results of the Evian Conference highlight the passive role of the Western world in face of sordid Nazi crimes.
4. The Action Petlyura pogrom in Lemberg (Lwow), instigated by the Nazis on July 2, 1941, took the lives of many Jews.
5. 320 Jews of Yurburg, Lithuania, headed by their rabbi, Reuben Rubenstein, were executed by the Nazis on July 2, 1941.
6. The Jewish Brigade, attached to the British army in World War II, was formed on June 22, 1942.
    See Tammuz 17:15.

7. Israel bombed Cairo on July 14, 1948.
8. Moshe Sharett, Zionist leader, second prime minister of Israel, died on July 7, 1965.

Moshe Sharett was influential in the formation of the Jewish Brigade (no. 6). He died on the anniversary of its founding.

TAMMUZ 8

1. Pope Boniface VIII entered Rome on June 23, 1295, and spurned the Torah scrolls presented to him by the Roman Jewish community.
2. The first printed edition of the commentaries of Rabbi Bahya b. Asher on the Pentateuch was published in Naples, Italy, on July 3, 1492.
3. The first printed edition of *Sefer ha-Manhig*, a book of customs and prayers, by Rabbi Abraham ibn Hayarchi, was published in Constantinople on June 7, 1519.
4. Jews were expelled from the territory of Genoa on June 15, 1567.
5. Rabbi Daniel b. Perahyah Ha-Kohen, scholar and astronomer, died on June 16, 1575 (ATGY).
6. The first printed edition of *Bet Hadash* (Bah), popular commentary by Rabbi Joel Sirkes on the *Tur* code, was published on June 28, 1640.
7. Queen-Mother Maria Christina of Spain abolished the Spanish Inquisition on July 15, 1834.

The last auto-da-fé was held on April 1, 1826, in Valencia, Spain.
8. A pogrom broke out in Bialystok, Russia, on July 3, 1903.
9. Morris Rosenfeld, Yiddish poet, died on June 22, 1923.

TAMMUZ 9

1. King Nebuchadnezzar's army breached the walls of Jerusalem and entered the city, 586 B.C.E. (Jer. 39:2).

According to the Babylonian Talmud (*Rosh Ha-Shanah* 18b), Tammuz 9 was one of the four commemorative fast-days established by the Babylonian Jewish community.
2. Pompey captured Jerusalem in the year 63 B.C.E. and killed 12,000 Jews (Zeitlin, *Megillat Ta'anit*, p. 27). This was the first military confrontation between Rome and Judea.

According to Josephus (*Antiquities* 14:4), Pompey captured the city "in the third month, on the day of the fast." This fixes the date of the assault in the month of Sivan. The only known ancient fast-day in Sivan is the fast of Sivan 23 (*Megillat Ta'anit*, concluding chap.).

Tammuz 9 was similarly a fast-day prior to the reconstruction of the Second Temple, but it was discontinued after the construction of the Temple. Some historians assumed that the fast referred to by Josephus was Yom Kippur, which may properly be called "the day of the fast" without any further specific designation.

3. Anti-Jewish riots started in Wiener-Neustadt, Austria, on June 21, 1230. The assault continued for 11 days.

4. Two Dutch ships arrived, on June 22, 1646, in the port of Recife, Brazil, and brought temporary relief to the beleaguered city and its endangered Jewish community besieged by the Portuguese.

5. Ernest Bloch, famous composer of Jewish sacred music, died on July 15, 1959.

6. Rabbi Judah Maimon, author and scholar, first Israeli minister of religious affairs, and founder of Mosad ha-Rav Kook, died on July 11, 1962.

TAMMUZ 10

1. King Zedekiah was captured by the Babylonians in the plains of Jericho, 586 B.C.E. (Jer. 39:4–5).

2. Tammuz 10 concludes the Fast of Tammuz, observed by Falashas over a ten-day period (Leslau, *Falasha Anthology*).

    The Falashas were familiar with biblical dates and the dates in the Book of Jubilees. According to the latter, Adam was exiled from the Garden of Eden on Tammuz 1. This event might have started off a period of sorrow which culminated with the fast of Tammuz 9.

3. 12 Jews of Cologne, including Rabbi Isaac b. Simson, were martyred on June 15, 1266.

4. Fire-fast was observed by the Jewish community of Frankfort on the Main, Germany, on Tammuz 10, in commemoration of the escape of the Jewish quarter from damage in the large conflagration which broke out on July 16, 1720.

5. A fast-day of the Jewish community of Algiers was observed on Tammuz 10 to commemorate the siege of the city by Spanish forces on June 19, 1774.

6. A conference of Reform rabbis, which opened at Frankfort on the Main, Germany, on July 15, 1845, adopted a resolution to eliminate from the prayerbook all "prayers for the restoration of a Jewish State."

    The classic anti-Zionism of the early Reform movement preceded the birth of Zionism. The naive faith in the liberal orientation and progress of modern society was to be shattered within the century by their host-country.

7. The Witwatersand gold fields Jewish Association, the first organization of South African Jews, was organized on July 2, 1887.

   The first congregation in South Africa was founded in Cape Town in 1841.

8. The Central Conference of American Rabbis (Reform) was organized on July 9, 1889.

   See no. 6; note on Tammuz 24:9.

9. Nazareth was captured by the Israeli army on July 17, 1948.

10. The 50-year-old Jewish community of the Belgian Congo, Africa, comprising 2,500 souls, fled from the country on July 5, 1960, in the wake of riots which broke out following the proclamation of independence.

TAMMUZ 11

1. Purim of Tammuz was celebrated by the Jews of Algiers on Tammuz 11 to mark their escape from attack by a Spanish army on June 20, 1774.

2. Colonel Alfred Dreyfus, victim of French anti-Semitism and militarism, died on July 12, 1935.

3. Ein Kerem and Hartuv were occupied by Israel on July 18, 1948.

4. Sholem Asch, Yiddish novelist, died on July 10, 1957.

TAMMUZ 12

1. Jews of Wiener-Neustadt, Austria, were massacred on June 23, 1298.

2. Pope Boniface VIII issued a bull on June 13, 1299, which allowed Jews denounced to the Inquisition the right to have the names of their accusers revealed to them.

   By the terms of an order issued by the Inquisition on November 18, 1297, accused Jews were not entitled to demand a confrontation with their accusers. The denial of the right of confrontation was also one of the worst features of European totalitarianism and of McCarthyism in modern America. Extremism, religious or political, produces the same evils. It is ironical that the Roman Emperor Trajan, one of the most tyrannical persecutors of early Christianity, specifically rejected anonymous charges as inconsistent with equity and fair play. He directed all magistrates to allow every person accused of practicing

Christianity the right to face his accuser (Gibbon, *Decline and Fall of the Roman Empire*, chap. 16).

See Tammuz 8:1.

3. Rabbi Jacob b. Asher, author of the code *Turim*, died on July 8, 1340 (HY).

   See Tammuz 17:8.

4. Rabbi Aaron ibn Hayyim (the second), author and talmudist, perished in an earthquake at Smyrna, Turkey, on July 10, 1688.

5. Edgar Mortara, a Jewish child of Ancona, Italy, was taken forcibly from his parents by order of the bishop of Bologna on June 24, 1858. The abduction became a cause célébre, stirring worldwide protests.

6. The Berlin Congress, on July 13, 1878, voted for equal rights for the Jews of Rumania.

7. Nazis executed 5,000 Jews in the fortress of Kovno (Kaunas), Lithuania, on July 7, 1941.

8. Rabbi Elchanan Wasserman, author of *Ohel Torah*, head of the Yeshivah of Baranowicze, Russia, was martyred by the Nazis on July 7, 1941.

9. The second truce in Israel's War of Independence went into effect on July 19, 1948.

TAMMUZ 13

1. Jews of Ifhauben, Austria, were massacred on June 24, 1298.

2. The first printed edition of the Pentateuch with Nahmanides' commentary was published on July 2, 1490.

3. The first printed edition of *Ha-Hinnukh* by Rabbi Aaron mibeit Levi of Barcelona, an exposition of the 613 biblical commandments, was published on June 26, 1523.

4. Rabbi Mordecai Ze'ev Ettinger, author of *Haggahot al ha-Shas*, died on June 30, 1863.

5. The North German Federation, on July 3, 1868, passed a law abolishing restrictions based on creed.

6. The Anglo-Jewish Association was founded on July 2, 1871.

   The Anglo-Jewish Association, which was organized in England in 1871, was patterned after the Alliance Israélite Universelle, founded by French Jewry 11 years earlier. Both Jewish communities had been emancipated and enjoyed full civil rights. Having won equality for themselves, they set out to extend protection to Jewish communities in other lands still subjected to discrimination and oppression.

7. The Union of American Hebrew Congregations, the national organization of Reform congregations, was founded on July 8, 1873.

8. The Home Construction Co. was organized on July 6, 1906, to build homes on a site outside Jaffa, later known as Tel Aviv.
9. The Jew badge was decreed for all Jews in the Baltic States on July 8, 1941.
10. Minsk, Russia, was captured by the Germans on June 28, 1942. Approximately 40,000 Jews were trapped in the city.

TAMMUZ 14

1. The Sadducean Code was abolished under the leadership of Rabbi Simeon b. Shetaḥ, in the reign of Salome Alexandra, 76–67 B.C.E. (*Megillat Ta'anit* 4).
2. 250 Jews were killed in Rothenburg on the Tauber, Germany, on June 25, 1298.
3. 30 Jews of Schaffhausen, Switzerland, who had been charged with ritual murder, were burned at the stake on June 25, 1401.
4. King George Podiebrad of Bohemia issued an order, on June 20, 1464, forbidding Jews to reside in Brux or within a mile of it.
5. The first printed edition of the talmudic tractate *Ḥullin* was published on June 13, 1489.

   The tractate *Ḥullin* was published by Joshua Solomon Soncino, the first publisher in the 15th century to print talmudic volumes. The first published volume was the tractate *Berakhot*, printed in 1483. The tractate *Beẓah* was published simultaneously. These were followed by *Megillah* (1485), *Shabbat* (1489), *Bava Kama* (1489), *Ḥullin* (1489), and *Niddah* (1489). Gershom Soncino published *Sanhedrin* in 1497.
6. Rabbi Joseph b. Moses Trani (Maharit) of Safed, author of responsa, died on July 16, 1639.
7. Francis Salvador, a plantation-owner of South Carolina, the first Jew to lose his life in the American Revolution, was killed on July 1, 1776.
8. Dr. F. W. Donovan, a convert to Judaism, married Deborah Salomon, a granddaughter of the financier Haym Salomon, on July 15, 1840. Dr. Donovan is the first recorded American male convert to Judaism (Marcus, *Essays in American Jewish History*, p. 93).
   See Iyar 18:5.
9. Federation of American Zionists, the first national American Zionist organization, was organized on July 4, 1898.
10. Berlin Jews were attacked by Nazi gangs on July 15, 1935.

TAMMUZ 15

1. Hur, the son of Miriam, was killed when he attempted to dissuade the Israelites from demanding a golden calf (*Shemot Rabbah* 48; DDD).

   Tradition assigns to Hur the distinction of being the first Jewish martyr to die in defense of his faith. The second entry on this date records the death of another martyr who died in defense of the faith approximately 3,000 years after Hur's martyrdom.

   According to DYY Hur was killed on Tammuz 16.
2. Isabel Nuñez Alvarez, owner of a building used as a synagogue in Madrid, Spain, was burned at the stake on July 4, 1632.
3. Rabbi David Tevle b. Jacob Ashkenazi of Aussee, Bohemia, author of *Bet David*, died on July 16, 1734.
4. Rabbi Hayyim b. Moses Attar of Jerusalem, author of *Or ha-Hayyim*, died on July 7, 1743 (HY).
5. *Sulamith*, the first Jewish monthly magazine in German, was published on July 1, 1806.
6. The first public Reform service was conducted at Seesen, Germany, on July 17, 1810.
7. A band of Druse Arabs attacked the Jewish community of Safed on July 8, 1838.
8. The Hebrew Education Society of Philadelphia, one of the oldest societies of its kind in the U.S., was organized on July 16, 1848.
9. Isaac Benjacob, bibliographer, author of *Ozar ha-Sefarim*, died on July 2, 1863.
10. The United Synagogue of London was established by act of Parliament on July 14, 1870.
11. The *Jewish Morning Journal*, the first Yiddish morning newspaper in the U.S., started publication in New York on July 2, 1901.
12. Sir Herbert Samuel was installed as the first British high commissioner of Palestine on July 1, 1920.
13. The 17th World Zionist Congress met at Basle, Switzerland, on June 30, 1931. The Revisionists seceded from this congress.

TAMMUZ 16

1. Aaron made a golden calf (*Seder Olam* 6).
   See Tishri 7:3.
2. A bull issued by Pope Gregory IX, on July 21, 1239, ordered the confiscation of all manuscripts of the Talmud.
3. Czarina Anne ordered the expulsion of all Jews from Little Russia (Ruthenia) on July 11,1740.

4. Rabbi Mordecai Dayan, author of *Mor Dror*, died on July 2, 1855 (DDD).
5. Zevi Hirsch Filipowski, mathematician and linguist, editor of *Ha-Asif*, died on July 22, 1872.
6. Italian professors issued a 10-point program on July 15, 1938, foreshadowing the adoption of Nazi anti-Semitism by Italian Fascism.
7. Rabbi Aaron Bokst and leading members of the Jewish community of Shavl (Siauliai), Lithuania, were executed by the Nazis on July 11, 1941.

TAMMUZ 17

1. Fast of Tammuz 17.
2. The beginning of *bein ha-mezarim*, a three-week period of semi-mourning for the destruction of the Temple.
3. Moses broke the Tablets of the Law (Exod. 32:19; *Ta'anit* 28b).
4. King Manasseh placed a graven image of Asherah in the Temple (2 Kings 21:7; *Ta'anit* 28b).
5. The Tower of Antonia, overlooking the Temple Court, was demolished by the Romans on August 8 (approximate), 70 C.E. (Josephus, *Jewish War* 5:7).
6. The *korban tamid* was discontinued in the second Temple on August 8 (approximate), 70 C.E. (*Ta'anit* 28b; Josephus, *Jewish War* 6:2).
7. Rabbi Meir b. Isaac, tosafist, died on June 22, 1312 (DDD).
8. Rabbi Judah b. Asher (son of Rosh), talmudist and moralist, author of *Iggeret ha-Tokhahah*, died on July 4, 1349.
9. 4,000 Jews were killed in Toledo, Spain, on June 20, 1391 (JE, Spain).
   The anti-Jewish riots which broke out on the fast-day of Tammuz 17, 1391, in Toledo and Jaén, Spain, spread rapidly to many Spanish Jewish communities. The riots reduced the once prosperous and powerful Jewish community to poverty and impotence. The end of this community came a century and one year later on Tishah be-Av.
10. Jews of Jaén, Spain, were massacred on June 20, 1391.
11. The Jewish quarter of Prague was burned and looted on June 22, 1559.
12. The American colonies declared their independence on July 4, 1776.
    The American Declaration of Independence, with its momentous potential for the future of Jewry, marks a ray of light against the tragic background of Tammuz 17. Similarly, Columbus' journey into history (Av 10:7) brightened the darkness of Tishah be-Av.
13. The gates of the Jewish ghetto of Venice, Italy, were torn down July 11, 1797.

The first restricted area to which the name *ghetto* was attached was in Venice, Italy (Roth, *Personalities and Events*, p. 230).
14. The Rabbinical Assembly of the Jewish Theological Seminary was organized on July 4, 1901.
15. The volunteers of the Jewish Battalion in World War I were sent to the fighting front on June 27, 1918.
    See Adar 18:12.
16. The Nazis, on July 4, 1939, established a Union of the Jews of Reich with which all Jews had to affiliate.
    The union was to be responsible for the education of Jewish children, social security, and emigration.
17. 4,000 Jews of the ghetto of Bialystok were shot on July 12, 1941.
18. The Nazis decreed the liquidation of the Kovno (Kaunas) ghetto on July 8, 1944.
19. Libya ordered the confiscation of Jewish property on July 21, 1970.

TAMMUZ 18

1. Moses destroyed the golden calf (Exod. 32:20; *Seder Olam* 6; Rashi, *Ta'anit* 30b).
2. King Louis IX of France (St. Louis) decreed, on June 19, 1269, that all Jews must wear the distinctive yellow badge. France was the first European state to implement the order of the Fourth Lateran Council of 1215.
    The yellow badge, introduced by St. Louis of France, became known as the "badge of shame" (*ot ha-kalon*). This humiliating decree was published on the anniversary of the day when Moses had destroyed the golden calf (no. 1). Moses observed that "the people's shame now stands exposed" (Rashi, Exod. 32:25).
3. The Jewish community of Morgentheim, Austria, was massacred on June 30, 1298.
4. Rabbi Samuel b. Joseph Schotten of Frankfort, author of *Kos Yeshuot*, comments on the Talmud, died on July 7, 1719.
5. Rabbi Abraham Maskielson of Minsk, Russia, author of *Maskil le-Eitan*, talmudic novellae, died on July 19, 1848 (DDD).
6. Purim of Candia, in commemoration of a salvation in 1583.
7. Rehovot, Palestine, was attacked by Arabs on July 23, 1913.
8. Jonah Rosenfeld, Yiddish writer, died on July 9, 1944.
9. Moses Basin, Yiddish poet, author of an anthology of 500 years of Yiddish poetry, died on July 10, 1963.

TAMMUZ 19

1. Moses ascended Mt. Sinai for the second time. He remained there for 40 days, pleading for the Jews who were guilty of the sin of the golden calf (Rashi, Exod. 33:11).
2. Kalonymus saved the life of King Otto II, in the battle of Cotrone against the Saracens, on July 13, 982.
3. Rabbi Aaron Samuel Koidonover of Cracow, author of *Birkat Shmuel*, a commentary on the Bible, died on June 30, 1676.
4. Rabbi Meir b. Joseph Teomim of Lemberg, author of *Birkat Yosef*, died on July 18, 1773 (DYY).
5. The *American Israelite*, an Anglo-Jewish weekly, was founded by Rabbi Isaac Mayer Wise on July 15, 1854, for the purpose of promoting Americanism and the principles of Reform Judaism.
6. Legislation abolishing discrimination against the service of Jewish chaplains in the military forces of the U.S. became law on July 17, 1862.
7. The first 14 members of Bilu, Russian Jewish pioneers of pre-Zionist days, reached Jaffa, Palestine, on July 6, 1882.
8. Alfred Dreyfus was rehabilitated on July 12, 1906, and restored to the army with full honors.
   The Dreyfus Affair was a motivating force in Herzl's Zionist orientation. The rehabilitation of Dreyfus came on the eve of Herzl's second yahrzeit (Tammuz 20:4).
9. Professor Israel Friedlander, noted Hebrew scholar, was killed on July 5, 1920, while on a relief mission to Ukrainian Jews.
10. The American Jewish Joint Agricultural Corp., the operating agency of the Joint in Russia, was organized on July 21, 1924.
11. 6,000 Lithuanian Jews were killed in the Viszalsyan camp on July 14, 1941, after they had been ordered to appear at a Herzl Day celebration.
12. The Jewish population of Utyan (Utena), Lithuania, was exterminated on July 14, 1941.
13. Rabbi Isaac Halevi Herzog, the first chief rabbi of Israel, author of *Divrei Yiẓḥak*, talmudic dissertations, died on July 25, 1959.

TAMMUZ 20

1. Rabbi Nathan Nata b. Moses Hannover, author of *Yeven Mezulah*, a chronicle of the Chmielnicki massacres, was killed on July 14, 1683.
2. Rabbi Menahem Mendel Auerbach of Krotoschin, Posen, author of *Ateret Zekenim*, died on July 8, 1689.
3. Orders issued by General Ulysses S. Grant, barring Jews from entering the military department under his command, were revoked on July 7, 1863 (*AJHSP*, no. 17, p. 71).
4. Theodor Herzl, founder of Zionism, died on July 3, 1904.

    Herzl Day was appropriately selected by the Yishuv as the occasion for marking the progress of the aims of Zionism. Many new settlements were founded on that date. The Settlement Law, a basic goal of Zionism, was also passed on the same day (no. 9). To the Nazis Herzl Day was an incentive to greater barbarism and sadistic outbursts, and 25 Lithuanian communities were massacred on Herzl Day, 1941. Jewish inmates of concentration camps were forced, in many instances, to stage self-degrading spectacles in "celebration" of the occasion. Balfour Day was similarly exploited by Nazis for the purpose of demonstrating their barbarism. See Tammuz 19:11 Heshvan 4:8.

5. The 16th World Zionist Congress met at Zurich, Switzerland, on July 28, 1929.
6. Jews of Telz (Telsiai), Lithuania, including the heads of the Yeshivah of Telz, Rabbis Abraham Isaac Bloch and Azriel Rabinowitz, were killed by the Nazis on July 15, 1941.
7. Jews of Kovno (Kaunas), Lithuania, began to move into the ghetto in Slabodka on July 15, 1941.
8. Nazis liquidated the Kovno ghetto on July 11, 1944.

    The liquidation of the ghetto of Kovno took place on the anniversary of its opening (no. 7).

9. The Knesset passed the Settlement Law on July 5, 1950, granting every Jew the absolute right to settle in Israel.
10. A Fair Sabbath Law, covering the entire state of New York, was signed into law on July 20, 1965.

    See Tishri 12:10.

TAMMUZ 21

1. Rabbi Tanḥum b. Joseph Yerushalmi, the "Ibn Ezra of the Orient," Bible exegete and grammarian, died on June 20, 1291 (ATGY).
2. The expulsion of all Marranos residing at Ghent, Belgium, was ordered by decree, dated July 17, 1549.
3. Don Henrique, regent of Brazil, issued a decree on June 20, 1567, barring Jews from settling in Brazil.
4. Rabbi Elijah Ba'al Shem, kabbalist and poet, author of *Mihlal Yofi*, commentary on *Shir ha-Shirim* (the Song of Songs), died on July 13, 1637 (DDD).
5. Don Lope de Vera y Alarcon, Spanish nobleman, convert to Judaism, widely known as Judah the Believer, was martyred on July 25, 1644 (see Roth, *Personalities and Events in Jewish History*, p. 182).

   The martyrdom of Don Lope created a stir in many countries. The Inquisition continued, however, to kill innocent people for a long time to come. The last victim of the Spanish Inquisition lost his life on the 182nd anniversary of the martyrdom of Don Lope (no. 8).
6. Jews of Savannah, Ga., reestablished Congregation Mikveh Israel on July 7, 1787. It was originally founded in the year 1733 (JE, Georgia). See Tammuz 28:5.
7. Many Jews lost their lives in Vilna on July 8, 1795, in riots following the Polish rebellion. The anniversary of this date was set aside as a communal fast-day.
8. The last victim of the Inquisition on the Iberian Peninsula was executed in Valencia, Spain, on July 26, 1826.
9. Rabbi Solomon Polyatchek, head of the Yeshivah of Lide and Rabbi Isaac Elchanan Theological Seminary, author of posthumous work, *Ḥiddushei ha-Iluy*, talmudic dissertations, died on July 9, 1928.
10. Ḥayyim Naḥman Bialik, Hebrew poet, died on July 4, 1934.
11. An uprising broke out in the Jewish ghetto of Bendin, Poland, on July 6, 1942.
12. Simon Rawidowicz, Hebrew writer and scholar, died on July 20, 1957.
13. The law prohibiting the raising of swine in Jewish settlements in Israel went into effect on July 13, 1963.

    According to a Jerusalemite tradition, the raising of swine in Palestine was originally prohibited by talmudic sages on Tammuz 17. The modern prohibition passed by the Israeli government went into effect on Tammuz 21.
14. The remains of 25 members of the Zealot community of Masada, who died by suicide in the year 73, were interred with full honors at the foot of the rock-fortress on July 7, 1969.

TAMMUZ 22

1. Marranos were permitted to leave Portugal by a decree dated June 30, 1557.
2. Rabbi Moses Cordovero (Remak), famous kabbalist, author of *Pardes Rimonim*, died on June 25, 1570.
3. Jews of New Amsterdam petitioned the authorities on July 27, 1655, for permission to open a cemetery. After an initial denial, a lot was granted on July 14, 1656.
4. Shabbetai b. Joseph Bass of Prague, pioneer of Jewish bibliography, author of *Siftei Yeshenim*, died on July 21, 1718.
5. Rabbi Solomon b. Meir Karlin, hasidic leader and talmudist, was killed in the Polish rebellion against Russia on July 12, 1792.
6. The poet Henry Wadsworth Longfellow visited the Jewish cemetery in Newport, R.I., on July 9, 1852. Shortly thereafter he wrote the poem. "The Jewish Cemetery at Newport."

    Longfellow visited the Jewish cemetery of Newport on the anniversary of the historic petition for the opening of the first Jewish cemetery in North America (no. 3).
7. *Revue des Études Juives*, a journal dedicated to research in Judaism, was founded on July 1, 1880.
8. Benito Mussolini was dismissed from office on July 25, 1943. His downfall was followed by the cancellation of the Fascist anti-Jewish laws.
9. Rabbi Abraham Grodzensky, author of *Ḥokhmat ha-Musar*, was buried alive in the hospital of the Kovno ghetto on July 13, 1944.
10. Rabbi Bertram W. Korn was promoted on July 1, 1975, to rear admiral in the Chaplains Corps, U.S. Naval Reserve, making him the first Jewish flag officer in the chaplaincy.

TAMMUZ 23

1. Crusaders captured Jerusalem on July 15, 1099.
2. Duke Frederick II of Austria granted a model charter to all Jews in his territory on July 1, 1244.
3. Pope Paul IV, on July 12, 1555, issued a bull reintroducing all restrictive Church laws against the Jews of Rome.
4. Jacob Barsimson, the first Jewish settler in North America, left for New Amsterdam on July 8, 1654.

    See Elul 9:2. The strange arm of coincidence has fused the anniversaries of the destruction of Jerusalem and the opening up of the New

World as a place of refuge for persecuted Jews. If the Puritans and Mormons viewed the sprawling American continent as the new Promised Land, the Jew surely was entitled to view it as the new Land of Promise. The first known Jew to arrive in the New World sailed on Tammuz 23, the anniversary of the capture of Jerusalem by the Crusaders (no. 1). See also note on Tammuz 17:12.

5. Chmielnicki hordes attacked Vilna on July 28, 1655, and killed many Jews. Rabbi Shabbetai ha-Kohen (Shakh), the famous talmudist, was among the refugees who had fled the city.

   Vilna, the "Jerusalem of Lithuania," was attacked on the anniversary of the Crusader attack on Jerusalem.

   See Tammuz 21:7.

6. Rabbi Ezekiel b. Abraham Katzenellenbogen of Altona, Prussia, author of *Knesset Yehezkel*, died on July 9, 1749.

7. Sir David Salomons, first Jewish lord-mayor of London, died on July 18, 1873.

8. Mattityahu Shoham (Poliakewicz), Hebrew poet, died on July 2, 1937.

9. The Jews of Shkudvil (Skaudvile), Lithuania, including Rabbi Abraham Isaac Perlman, author of *Penei Avraham,* were killed by the Nazis on July 18, 1941.

10. The armistice agreement between Israel and Syria was signed on July 20, 1949.

11. Hillel Bavli, Hebrew poet, died on July 7, 1961.

TAMMUZ 24

1. Crusaders herded the Jews of Jerusalem into a synagogue on July 16, 1099, and set it aflame. All the Jews perished in the fire.

   Jerusalem remained under the control of the Crusaders for 88 years. Jews were barred from the city throughout that period.

2. Anti-Jewish riots broke out in Cordova, Spain, on July 13, 1148.

3. The second edition of *Sefer Mizvot Katan (Smak)*, a popular code by Rabbi Isaac b. Joseph, was published in Cremona, Italy, on July 2, 1556.

4. Issachar Ha-Levi Bermann of Hanover, Prussia, noted philanthropist, died on July 9, 1730.

5. The People's Representatives Hentz and Goujon issued a decree, on July 22, 1794, ordering the arrest of all priests, rabbis and cantors in the district of Schlettstadt and Altnirch, Alsace.

6. The Union of Jewish German Congregations (in America) was founded on July 3, 1869.
7. The Prussian Diet removed the ineligibilities of Jews for public office on July 3, 1869.
8. Rabbi Jacob Joseph, chief rabbi of the Russian Orthodox communities of New York, died on July 29, 1902.
9. The Union of Orthodox Rabbis of the United States and Canada was organized on July 29, 1902.

The national organization of Orthodox rabbis was the last of the three religious groupings to make its appearance on the American scene. The Central Conference of American Rabbis (Reform) was organized in 1889 (Tammuz 10:8). The Rabbinical Assembly (Conservative) was organized in 1901. On the congregational level the chronological order of organization was as follows: The Union of American Hebrew Congregations (Reform) was founded in 1873, the Union of Orthodox Jewish Congregations was founded in 1898, the United Synagogue (Conservative) was founded in 1913. A predecessor of the Union of American Hebrew Congregations, the Union of Jewish German Congregations, was founded in 1869.

10. The 7th Zionist Congress met in Basle, Switzerland, on July 27, 1905.

The 7th Zionist Congress marked the withdrawal from the Zionist Organization of the Territorialists, headed by Israel Zangwill.

11. Mendel Beilis, whose trial in Russia on ritual charges attracted worldwide attention, died on July 7, 1934.

TAMMUZ 25

1. Jews of Lithuania received a Charter of Privilege on July 1, 1388.
2. Rabbi Isaiah b. David Leib, author of *Ma'aseh le-Melekh*, commentary on Maimonides, died on July 20, 1730.
3. Rabbi Aryeh Leib b. Asher Gunzberg of Metz, prominent talmudist, author of the popular book of responsa, *Sha'agat Ayreh*, died on July 3, 1785.
4. Napoleon, on July 20, 1808, issued a decree requiring all Jews of the French Empire to adopt family names.

The first country to introduce compulsory adoption of family names for its Jewish population was Austria. It was enacted as part of the sweeping reforms of Emperor Joseph II in 1785. The French-created Kingdom of Westphalia followed with a similar decree in 1808. Napoleon extended the decree, in the same year, to all of France. Poland made family names compulsory in 1821, and Russia, in 1844.

5. Rabbi Moses Teitelbaum of Ujhely, Hungary, founder of a hasidic dynasty, author of *Yismah Moshe*, comments on the Bible, died on July 14, 1841.
6. Anti-Jewish rioters attacked the funeral procession of Rabbi Jacob Joseph, chief rabbi of New York, on July 30, 1902.

TAMMUZ 26

1. Rabbi Aaron Berechiah b. Moses of Modena, kabbalist, author of *Ma'aver Yabek*, died on July 28, 1639 (DDD).
2. Rabbi Solomon Ganzfried, author of the popular code, *Kizzur Shulhan Arukh*, died on July 29, 1886 (HY).

   According to an estimate of Rabbi Gershom Bennet, the author's son-in-law, there were close to a quarter of a million copies of the *Kizzur* throughout the world at the time of Rabbi Ganzfried's death.
3. Rabbi Benjamin Szold, American author and scholar, died on July 31, 1902.
4. The moshav Kefar Bialik was founded in Palestine on July 9, 1934. See Tammuz 21:10.
5. Jews of Upina, Lithuania, including Rabbi Isaac Jaffe, were executed by the Nazis on July 21, 1941.
6. Israeli airmen over the Suez front shot down four Migs flown by Russian pilots on July 30, 1970. The brief engagement marked the first encounter between Israeli and Russian military forces.

TAMMUZ 27

1. Pope Innocent III promulgated, on July 15, 1205, a Church doctrine which held Jews doomed to perpetual servitude and subjugation due to the crucifixion of Christ.

   The first official effort to remove this classic charge of deicide was made in a document presented to the Vatican II ecumenical council on November 8, 1963.
2. The third expulsion of Jews from France was decreed on June 24, 1322.
3. A Charter of Privileges was granted to the Jews of Ancona on June 29, 1535 (*Jewish Quarterly Review*, vol. 4, p. 225).
4. Daniel Bueno Henriques became the first Jew of Barbados, British West Indies, to be granted letters of denization on July 24, 1661.
5. Baruch Leibov was burned at the stake in St. Petersburg, Russia, on

July 15, 1738, on charges of proselytizing. Alexander Voznitsyn, a Russian naval officer whom he had converted to Judaism, was burned at the same time.

6. Rabbi Solomon b. Moses of Chelm, author of *Mirkevet ha-Mishnah*, commentary on Maimonides, died on July 20, 1781 (ATGY).
7. Jews of Holstein, Germany, were granted equality on July 14, 1863.
8. Rabbi Israel Joshua Trunk of Kutno, Poland, author of *Yeshuat Yisrael*, died on July 11, 1893.
9. Jews of Bialystok, Russia, were pogromized on July 30, 1905.
10. The new harbor of Haifa, Palestine, was opened to traffic on July 21, 1933.

TAMMUZ 28

1. 41 Jewish martyrs were burned at the stake in Breslau (Wroclaw) on July 4, 1453. The remainder of the Jewish population was expelled.
2. The printing of the first complete edition of Rabbi Jacob b. Asher's *Tur* code was finished on July 3, 1475, at Piove di Sacco, Italy.
3. 53 marranos appeared at an auto-da-fé in Madrid, Spain, held on July 4, 1632.
4. A decree ordering the expulsion of all Jews from Brussels was issued on July 18, 1716.
5. Jewish settlers, bringing with them a Torah and other religious articles, arrived from London on July 11, 1733, on the second ship to reach Savannah, Ga.

   The availability of religious articles made it possible for the new arrivals to organize Congregation Mikveh Israel within a month after their arrival. The congregation dissolved in 1740. Services were resumed in 1750 and continued sporadically until they were reorganized on a more permanent basis in 1774. Jewish life was once again disrupted with the occupation of Savannah by the British in 1778. Congregation Mikveh Israel was reestablished on July 7, 1787 (Tammuz 21:6).
6. Jews of Hebron, Palestine, were attacked by the army of Ibrahim Pasha on July 25, 1835.
7. The Council of the League of Nations confirmed Britain's mandate to administer Palestine on July 24, 1922.
8. Rabbi Bezalel Dzimitrofsky and the leading members of the community of Yanishok (Joniskis), Lithuania, were executed by the Nazis on July 23, 1941.
9. 5,000 Jews of Rovno, Polish Ukraine, were executed by the Nazis on July 13, 1942.

TAMMUZ 29

1. Rabbi Shelomoh Yizhaki (Rashi), celebrated talmudic commentator and Bible exegete, died on July 13, 1105.

   Rashi was one of the outstanding intellectual giants produced by medieval Jewry. As the commentator of the Talmud par excellence, he has no peer in the long post-talmudic history. His comments illumine the most complex and obscure passages of the Talmud with logic and incisive analysis. The popularity of his work may be gauged from the fact that the first dated printed Hebrew book was his commentary on the Pentateuch.

2. Rabbi Abraham b. David Portaleone of Mantua, physician and philosopher, author of *Shiltei ha-Gibborim,* a detailed description of the structure of the Temple and the priestly vestments, died on July 29, 1612 (DDD).

3. Rabbi Immanuel b. David Frances of Mantua, Hebrew poet and scholar, was born on July 22, 1618.

4. Annual fast-day of the Hevra Kaddisha of Dubno, Poland.

   The fast was decreed to commemorate the death of 400 infants decimated in an outbreak of an epidemic. The community attributed the plague to an inadvertent disturbance by the Hevra Kaddisha of the remains of Rabbi Jacob Yaska on July 26, 1729.

5. Rabbi Moses of Zalshin, author of *Tikkun Shabbat,* died on July 10, 1831.

6. German elections, held on July 30, 1878, gave the reactionary element a dominant voice in the Reichstag. This date is considered the birthday of modern German anti-Semitism.

7. 15 Jews charged with the ritual murder of Eszter Solymosi of Tiszaeszlar, Hungary, were acquitted on August 3, 1883.

8. Rabbi Jacob Saul Elyashar, head of the Sephardic community of Jerusalem, author of responsa *Ma'aseh Ish,* died on July 22, 1906.

9. *Ha-Yom,* the first Hebrew daily newspaper printed in America, was published for the first time on July 18, 1909.

   See note on Adar 24:8.

10. Vladimir Jabotinsky, founder of the Revisionist Zionist movement, author and leader, died on August 4, 1940.

11. The entire Jewish male population of Grodz, Lithuania, was executed by the Nazis on July 24, 1941.

12. Raoul Wallenberg, a Swedish national who had saved hundreds of Hungarian Jews from Nazi deportation, was reported by Russia to have died in the Lublyanka prison in Moscow on July 17, 1947.

13. The Yarkon water project, which supplies water to parts of the Negev, was officially opened on July 19, 1955.

AV 1

1. Peaks of high mountains emerged above the receding flood waters (Gen. 8:5, Rashi).
2. Egypt was afflicted with the plague of frogs *(Seder ha-Dorot)*.
3. Aaron, the first high priest, died on Av 1 (Num. 33:38; *Seder Olam* 10).
4. Elazar, son of Aaron, the second high priest, died on Av 1 (DDD).
5. Ezra and his followers arrived in Jerusalem, 457 B.C.E. (Ezra 7:9).
6. Pope Innocent IV issued a bull against blood-ritual charges on July 5, 1247.
   See Tammuz 29:7
7. The Book of Proverbs, with the commentaries of Levi b. Gershom (Gersonides) and Menahem Meiri, was published in Leira, Portugal, on July 25, 1492.
8. A printed edition of the popular work *Halikhot Olam*, talmudic dissertations by Rabbi Jeshua b. Joseph Ha-Levi, was published in Constantinople on July 8, 1510.
9. Rabbi Hillel b. Naphta Zevi of Altona, author of *Bet Hillel*, novellae on the code, died on July 7, 1690 (HY).
10. Purim of Ibrahim Pasha was celebrated by the Jews of Hebron, Palestine, in commemoration of their deliverance in 1832.
    See Tammuz 28:6.
11. Nachman Krochmal, philosopher, known as the Mendelssohn of the East, author of *Moreh Nevukhei ha-Zeman*, died on July 31, 1840.
12. Abraham Benisch, journalist and theologian, pre-Herzlian Zionist, died on July 31, 1878.
13. An armed revolt broke out in the Treblinka extermination camp on August 2, 1943. Part of the plant was destroyed by fire.
    The revolt at Treblinka was one of several similar outbreaks in extermination camps which were staged by inmates encouraged by the turning of the tide in the military fortunes of the German armies. These uprisings and the outbreaks in ghettos refute the malicious charges that the Jews were docile and willing accomplices in their own extermination. Among those who were killed in the uprising at

Treblinka was Rudolf Masaryk, nephew of the founder of the Czech Republic. He had voluntarily gone to the Treblinka extermination camp in order to be close to his Jewish wife.

14. The British seized the ship *Exodus 1947*, bearing illegal immigrants to Palestine, on July 18, 1947. The seizure resulted in three deaths and the wounding of over 100 immigrants.

The *Exodus 1947* carried 4,000 illegal immigrants. Its stirring defiance of the might of the British navy and its ultimate compulsory return to Germany, a land haunted by memories of gas-chambers and crematoria, formed one of the most dramatic and heroic episodes in postwar Jewish history.

AV 2

1. Titus commenced battering operations against the wall of the Temple Court on August 22 (approximate), 70 C.E. (Josephus, *Jewish War* 6:4).
2. The Inquisition was established in Rome by Pope Clement IV on July 26, 1267.
3. Pope Gregory X, on July 7, 1274, confirmed a bull of 1272, banning blood-ritual charges.

Papal bulls banning ritual accusations were obviously ineffective. The bull of Pope Gregory X, issued on Av 2, 1274, was preceded by a similar bull by Pope Innocent IV issued on Av 1, 1247. About three centuries later, Pope Paul III issued a bull on May 12, 1540, banning blood accusations. That bull, too, failed to halt the flood of ritual libels in Christendom.

See Tishri 9:9.

4. Rabbi Aaron b. Moses Teomim of Worms, talmudic scholar, author of *Mate Aharon*, died on July 8, 1690.
5. The last auto-da-fé ordered by the Inquisition of Peru was held on July 17, 1806.
6. The remains of Rabbi Isaac b. Sheshet (Ribash), famous talmudist and author of responsa (d. 1408), were removed from his grave by order of the government of Algiers and reinterred on July 12, 1896.
7. The German army occupied the city of Vilkomierz (Ukmerge), Lithuania, on July 26, 1941.
8. The first train with Jewish deportees from Holland left for an extermination camp on July 16, 1942.
9. The French police rounded up 13,000 Jews in occupied Paris on July 16, 1942, including 4,500 children, for deportation. Only 30 adults survived the roundup.

AV 3

1. 10,000 Jews of Polannoe perished on July 22, 1648, in the Chmielnicki massacres (Hanover, *Yeven Mezulah*, chap. 7).
2. Shiye Mordecai Lifshits, father of modern Yiddishism, died on August 2, 1878.
3. The first shipload of Russian Jewish immigrants, opening the mass immigration of Russian Jews following the pogroms of 1881, arrived in New York on July 29, 1881.

   Av 3 is an important anniversary in American Jewish history. It marks the beginning of the mass immigration of East European Jews to America. But for these immigrants, the native Jewish community would have remained numerically small, thoroughly assimilated, predominately Reform, and anti-Zionist in outlook. Yiddish journalism and theater were among the first beneficiaries of the changing scene. It is noteworthy that Av 3 is also the yahrzeit of Shiye Lifshits (no. 2), who is considered by many to be the father of modern Yiddishism.
4. The liquidation of the ghetto of Sosnowiec, Poland, was begun by the Nazis on August 4, 1943, in a sustained action of mass executions which lasted for eight days.
5. Israel and Syria signed an armistice agreement on July 29, 1949.

AV 4

1. Nehemiah began to build a wall around Jerusalem, 444 B.C.E. (Neh. 6:15).
2. Rabbi Solomon ibn Adret (Rashba) proclaimed a ban of excommunication on July 26, 1305, forbidding the study of metaphysics and philosophy by students under 30.

   The ban by Rabbi Solomon ibn Adret assumed historic significance due to the widespread controversy between traditionalists and students of philosophy. Another historic ban was proclaimed 351 years later on Av 6 against the philosopher Spinoza (Av. 6:1).
3. Rabbi Menahem Azariah da Fano (Rama), kabbalist and talmudist, author of *Alfasi Zuta*, died on August 13, 1620.
4. Rabbi Abraham b. David of Lemberg, author of a commentary on Alfasi, died on July 20, 1624 (DYY).
5. The first Yiddish periodical in the United States, *Di Post*, was published in New York on August 1, 1870.

6. The Jewish male population of Aniksht (Anyksciai), Lithuania, was executed by the Nazis on July 28, 1941.
7. Jews of Vilkovishk (Vilkaviškis), Lithuania, were exterminated by the Nazis on July 28, 1941.
8. The Russian army liberated the Lublin concentration camp on July 24, 1944.
9. The first envoy of Soviet Russia arrived in Israel on August 9, 1948.

AV 5

1. Pope Clement VI issued a bull on July 5, 1345, forbidding forcible baptism of Jews.

   The Roman Curia ruled, on October 22, 1597, that a Jewish child baptized without the permission of his parents, as required by canonical law, must be brought up as a Catholic. This ruling required the removal of the child from its parents. Pope Benedict XIV confirmed this decision 250 years later in a bull issued on February 28, 1747.
2. 1,800 Marranos were released from the prisons of the Portuguese Inquisition on July 10, 1548.
3. Rabbi Isaac Luria (Ari) of Safed, founder of an influential school of Kabbalah, died on July 15, 1572 (HY).
4. Anti-Jewish riots broke out in Posen (Poznan), Poland, on July 24, 1716.
5. Rabbi Meir b. Saul Barby of Pressburg, author of *Sefer Hiddushei Halakhot*, died on July 28, 1789.
6. Rabbi Ze'ev Lesh, author of *Kedushat Yisrael*, died on August 9, 1807.
7. Anti-Jewish riots broke out in Budapest, Hungary, on August 8, 1883, following the acquittal of Jews charged with the ritual murder of Eszter Solymosi.
8. Rabbi Israel Hildesheimer, author and leader of German Orthodox Jewry, died on July 12, 1899.

   Rabbi Israel Hildesheimer and his senior colleague, Rabbi Samson Raphael Hirsch (Tevet 27:4), were the architects of modern German Jewish Orthodoxy. With the rise of emancipation in many countries, an inevitable clash between modernists and traditionalists rocked West European Jewry and American Jewry and finally threatened the hold of Orthodoxy upon East European Jewry. Traditionalists insisted on the total exclusion of secular culture. Rabbis Hirsch and Hildesheimer, however, were convinced that such exclusion was impractical and ineffective in an emancipated community.

242   DAY BY DAY IN JEWISH HISTORY

9. Rabbi Ḥayyim Ozer Grodzinski, communal leader, author of responsa *Aḥi'ezer*, died on August 9, 1940.
10. A cease-fire went into effect on the Egyptian, Jordanian, and Lebanese fronts on August 7, 1970.

   The agreement, the result of an American initiative, provided for the beginning of peace talks between Israel, Egypt, and Jordan, with Dr. Gunnar V. Jarring acting as the U.N. intermediary. The only session under this agreement was held on August 25. Israel withdrew from the talks on September 6, due to Egyptian violation of the cease-fire. The talks were resumed on January 5, 1971.

AV 6

1. The elders of the Jewish community of Amsterdam excommunicated Baruch Spinoza on July 27, 1656.
2. Rabbi Issachar Dov Baer of Zloczow, hasidic leader, author of *Mevasser Ẓedek*, died on August 6, 1810 (HY).
3. A bill for the emancipation of the Jews of England passed its third reading in the House of Commons on July 22, 1833.

   The bill was rejected by the House of Lords and not approved until July 31, 1845.

AV 7

1. King Nebuchadnezzar occupied Solomon's Temple, 586 B.C.E.
   Some historians date the destruction of the First Temple in the year 587 B.C.E.
2. Jews of Valencia, Spain, were massacred on July 9, 1391. The massacre destroyed this important Jewish community.
3. August Rohling, notorious slanderer of Jews and the Talmud, brought charges of defamation against Rabbi Joseph Samuel Bloch of Vienna on August 10, 1883. Rohling's failure to prove his charges led to his unmasking.
4. The execution of the last czar of Russia, Nicholas II, on July 16, 1918, brought to an end a tyrannical dynasty which was guilty of many crimes against the Jewish minority.
5. Keren Hayesod (Palestine Foundation Fund) was established on July 22, 1920.
6. Hermann Goering ordered Reinhard Heydrich on July 31, 1941, to "take all preparatory measures . . . required for the final solution of

the Jewish question in the European territories under German influence." This order launched the official and systematic Nazi policy of mass extermination of Jews.

Historians may never be able to pinpoint the exact date when the Nazi plans for the extermination of the Jews were first formulated and set into motion. For the purpose of historical observance of the tragic Nazi period, the following dates are significant: Tishri 23, 1939 (October 6)—Hitler foreshadowed the doom of East European Jewry; Av 7, 1941 (July 31)—Goering ordered the launching of the Nazi extermination program; Tammuz 5, 1942 (June 20)—the first mass extermination of Jews took place at Auschwitz. One may also add that the order for the deportation of Jews from the Warsaw ghetto, the largest ghetto under Nazi control, was announced on Av 8, 1942 (no. 7), a year after Goering's decree activating the measures "for the final solution of the Jewish question."

7. The first diplomatic envoy of the United States arrived in Israel on August 12, 1948.

AV 8

1. Civil war broke out in Jerusalem in the year 66 between the activists and peace party.

   The activists were in control of the Temple Court and the Lower City at the time of the outbreak of the civil war. The struggle continued for 9 days (See Av 17:1) and ended in the defeat of the forces of King Agrippa.

2. Jews of Frankfort, Germany, perished on July 24, 1349, in the Black Death massacres.

3. Jews of Worms, Germany, succeeded in repelling an attack on the Jewish quarter on July 14, 1614.

4. The Jewish community of Vienna, Austria, was expelled on July 25, 1670.

5. Emperor Joseph II of Austria issued an ordinance on July 23, 1787, requiring Jews to take permanent family surnames.

6. The Jewish Agency for Palestine was founded on August 14, 1929.

7. The order of mass transportation of Jews from the ghetto of Warsaw was announced on July 22, 1942.

   The order of deportation of Jews from the Warsaw ghetto was aimed at the liquidation of the largest Jewish ghetto under Nazi control. The deportations started on the eve of Tishah be-Av and continued for 53 days, reaching a climax on the eve of Rosh Ha-

Shanah with the deportation of 90,000 Jews. The action removed 300,000 Jews to extermination camps.
8. A plane bound for Israel was shot down by Bulgaria on July 27, 1955, resulting in the loss of 58 lives.

AV 9

1. Fast of Tishah be-Av (Zech. 8:19).
2. The 12 scouts dispatched by Moses to survey Palestine returned with an unfavorable report (*Ta'anit* 29a).
3. The exodus generation was condemned to die in the desert (Deut. 1:35; *Ta'anit* 26b). More than 15,000 died annually on Av 9 (Jer. Talmud, *Ta'anit* 3:7).
4. Nebuzaradan set fire to the Temple, 586 B.C.E.
5. The Romans destroyed the Second Temple on August 29 (approximate), 70 C.E.
   See note Av 14:1.
6. Messiah was born on the day of the destruction of the Temple (Jer. Talmud, *Berakhot* 2:4).
7. The Romans plowed up the site of the Temple to convert it into a Roman colony, 71 C.E. (*Ta'anit* 26b).
8. Betar, the last independent outpost under Bar Kokhba, fell to the Romans on August 5 (approximate), 135 (*Ta'anit* 26b).
9. King Edward I of England ordered the expulsion of all Jews on July 18, 1290.
10. Joseph Trèves, liturgical poet, died on July 10, 1429.
    Joseph and Jochanan (no. 11) were brothers.
11. Rabbi Johanan b. Mattathias Trèves, talmudist, chief rabbi of France, died on July 21, 1439.
12. The period of expulsion of the Jews from Spain commenced on August 2, 1492.
13. The ghetto of Florence, Italy, was inaugurated on July 31, 1571 (Roth, *The History of the Jews of Italy*, p. 311).
14. Shabbetai Zevi, the pseudo-Messiah, was born in Smyrna, Turkey, on July 23, 1626.
15. 3,000 Jews perished on July 28, 1648, in Konstantynow, in the Chmielnicki massacres (Hanover, *Yeven Mezulah*, chap. 9).
16. The last group of Jews left Vienna on July 26, 1670, following an order of expulsion from Austria.
17. Rabbi Isaac Spitz, author of *Birkat Yizhak*, commentary on the Pentateuch, died on July 23, 1768.

18. Rabbi Abraham Isaac Castello, poet, died on August 1, 1789.
19. Two Jews, Bromet and DeLemon, were elected members of the Second National Assembly of Holland on August 1, 1797.
20. Rabbi Jacob Isaac Horowitz, hasidic leader (haHozeh miLublin), author of *Divrei Emet,* died on August 15, 1815.
21. The Hungarian revolutionary government granted emancipation to the Jews of Hungary on July 28, 1849.
22. Petach Tikvah, the "mother of settlements," was founded in Palestine on August 8, 1878.
23. The Turkish government barred immigration of Russian and Rumanian Jews into Palestine on July 25, 1882, and banned the sale of Palestinian land to Jews (Yaari, Zikhronot Erez Yisrael 36).
24. The Russian government prohibited the collection of funds or the publication of appeals for financial assistance to Jewish emigrants on August 13, 1891.
25. World War I broke out on August 1, 1914.
26. Rivka Galin, Yiddish poetess, died on August 8, 1935.
27. A decree expelling all Jews from Hungarian Ruthenia was issued on August 2, 1941.
28. David Pinsky, Yiddish playwright and journalist, died on August 11, 1951.

AV 10

1. Birth of Issachar (*Midrash Tadshe*).
2. The First Temple was destroyed by a fire which had started on the preceding evening, 586 B.C.E. (*Ta'anit* 29a).
3. The Second Temple was set aflame on August 30 (approximate), 70 C.E. (Josephus, *Jewish War* 6:4).
4. Jews of France were arrested on July 22, 1306, and ordered to leave the country.
   They were readmitted on July 28, 1315.
5. Hundreds of Jews of Catalonia were murdered on July 7, 1358.
6. Rabbi Menahem b. Aaron ibn Zerah, talmudist, author of *Zeidah la-Derekh,* an abridged code, died on July 19, 1385.
7. Columbus set sail for the new world on August 3, 1492.
   The coincidence of the departure of the Jews from Spain and the sailing of Columbus for the new world was noted by the explorer himself in his diary. There was another coincidence linking the two events. The decree expelling the Jews from Spain was publicly announced on April 30, 1492. On the same day Columbus was given the royal commission to equip a fleet for the voyage.

8. Jews of Rome were compelled to move into a ghetto on July 26, 1555, by order of Pope Paul IV.
9. Joseph Nasi, the duke of Naxos, communal leader, early Zionist and colonizer, died on August 2, 1579.
10. Rabbi Samuel Filorintin, author of *Olat Shemuel*, died on July 26, 1719 (DYY).
11. Prussian Jewry was granted civil equality on July 23, 1847.
12. The British Aliens Act, which reflected anti-Jewish bias by limiting free immigration into England, was enacted into law on August 11, 1905.
13. The cornerstone of Herzliah, the first Hebrew gymnasium (secondary school) in the world, was laid in Tel Aviv on July 28, 1909.
14. David Frischmann, Hebrew poet and short-story writer, died on August 4, 1922.
15. The 1st World Congress for the Promotion of the Hebrew Language and Culture met in Jerusalem on July 24, 1950.

AV 11

1. Anti-Jewish riots broke out in Arnstadt, Germany, on August 5, 1264.
2. Anti-Jewish riots broke out in Breslau, Silesia (now Wroclaw, Poland), on July 25, 1360, following a major conflagration. Many Jews were killed and the remainder was expelled.
3. The edict of expulsion of Bohemian Jewry was revoked by Empress Maria Theresa on August 5, 1748.
4. Rabbi Simḥah b. Abraham, linguist and poet, died on August 2, 1784.
5. The Common Council of New York City suppressed the butcher license of Nicholas Smart, a non-Jew, on August 15, 1796, for affixing Jewish seals to nonkosher meats. This action marked the earliest intervention of the law in protection of kashrut (*AJHSP*, no. 25, p. 32).

   New York was the first state to prohibit the sale of nonkosher meat which was represented as kosher. The statute became law in 1915 and was upheld by the U.S. Supreme Court in 1924.
6. Emperor Francis I issued an order, on August 3, 1797, permitting Jews of the "Countries of the Bohemian Crown" who had volunteered for service in the army to marry outside the restricted quota of marriages allowed to Jews.
7. Many Jews of Jassy, Rumania, perished in the flames which enveloped the Jewish quarter on August 4, 1827.
8. Rabbi Isaac Blaser, leader of the Musar movement, author of *Peri Yiẓḥak*, died on July 22, 1907 (HY).

9. The Israeli pound became legal tender on August 16, 1948.
10. Arab forces blew up the Latrun pumping station on August 16, 1948, cutting off Jerusalem's water supply.
11. Rebecca Kohut, writer and social worker, died on August 13, 1951.

AV 12

1. The famous disputation between Naḥmanides and the apostate Pablo Christiani opened on July 20, 1263.
2. 38 Jews were burned at the stake in Berlin, Prussia, on July 19, 1510, by order of Elector Joachim I.
3. The Russian government removed the ban on Hebrew and Yiddish periodicals on July 21, 1918.
4. The moshav Magdi'el, (now part of the larger township of Hod ha-Sharon) was founded in Palestine on August 12, 1924.
5. The Russian army liberated the city of Kovno (Kaunas), Lithuania, on August 1, 1944.
6. Peretz Hirschbein, Yiddish playwright, died on August 17, 1948.
7. The 23rd Zionist Congress, the first after the proclamation of the State of Israel, convened in Jerusalem on August 14, 1951.

AV 13

1. Jews of Wurzburg, Germany, were massacred on July 23, 1298.
2. Rabbi Nathan Shapiro of Cracow, kabbalist, author of *Megale Amukot*, died on July 20, 1633 (HY).
3. Rabbi Mordecai b. Abraham Benet of Nikolsburg, author of *Biur Mordecai*, died on August 12, 1829.
4. Rabbi Abraham Abele Poswoler, talmudist, leader of Lithuanian Jewry, died on July 27, 1836 (DYY).
5. Sir Moses Montefiore, outstanding philanthropist and Jewish leader, died on July 25, 1885.
6. A handful of Jewish survivors of the Kovno ghetto, among them Rabbi Ephraim Oshri, author of *Ḥurban Litte*, emerged from a hideout bunker in the ghetto on August 2, 1944.
7. New Zealand recognized Israel on July 27, 1950.

AV 14

1. Arabs wrested control of most of Palestine from the Byzantine Emperor Heraclius, in the decisive battle of the Yarmuk on July 23, 636.
   The three major religions successively lost their supremacy in the Holy Land in the month of Av. Judaism suffered its setback on Av 9, 70 (nos. 4 and 5); Christianity, on Av 14, 636, and Islam, on Av 26, 1920 (n. 3). Judaism was dominant for about 13 centuries, Islam about 11 centuries, and Christianity about four and one-half centuries.
2. Pope Gregory X issued a bull against blood-ritual accusations on July 17, 1272.
3. Pope Nicholas III issued a bull on August 4, 1278, providing for compulsory attendance of Jews to hear conversionist sermons by Christian clergymen.
4. The Jewish community of Bischofsheim on the Tauber, Germany, perished on July 24, 1298, in the Rindfleisch massacres.
5. Antonio Fernandez Carvajal made history on August 17, 1655, when he became the first Jew to receive English denizenship.
6. 407 Jews of Zhitomir, Russia, were executed by the Nazis on August 7, 1941.
7. 10,000 Jews of Minsk, Russia, were liquidated by the Nazis on July 28, 1942.

AV 15

1. The last of the exodus generation, which was barred from entering Palestine, died in the desert (*Bava Batra* 121a).
2. Intertribal marriage was permitted to post-exodus generations (*Ta'anit* 30b).
3. Permission was given to the young men of the tribe of Benjamin to marry young women of other tribes, and thus the tribe of Benjamin was saved from extinction (Judg. 21:21; *Bava Batra* 121a).
4. An ancient folk-festival was celebrated on Av 15 by the youth of Palestine, featuring annual dances for young men to choose prospective brides (*Bava Batra* 121a).
5. King Hosea restored the pilgrimage to Jerusalem by putting an end to the interference of King Jeroboam (Bava Batra 121a).
6. Av 15 was designated "wood-bearing day" and observed as a religious holiday by Jews who brought contributions of wood to the Temple (*Megillat Ta'anit* 5).
7. Romans permitted the burial of Jewish victims who had been killed in

the fortress of Betar in the Bar Kokhba rebellion, 138 C.E. (*Bava Batra* 121b).

8. The power of the Almohades, a fanatic Muslim sect which had persecuted the Jews of Spain, was broken in the battle of Las Navas de Tolosa in Spain on July 16, 1212.
9. Jews of Great Poland were authorized by King Sigismund I, on August 8, 1541, to elect a chief rabbi.
10. The Jewish community of Cochin, India, received, on Av 15, 1686, a large shipment of prayerbooks, rabbinic works, and Torah scrolls from Amsterdam. This date was designated an annual holiday.
11. Baron Lionel de Rothschild became the first Jew to be seated in the British Parliament, on July 26, 1858, after a new version of the oath was agreed upon, omitting the reference to Christianity.
12. The 10th World Zionist Congress met in Basle, Switzerland, on August 9, 1911. It was the first Zionist congress to conduct its sessions in Hebrew.
13. The cornerstone of the Hebrew University of Jerusalem was laid on July 24, 1918.
14. A religious youth center, Tiferet Bahurim, was secretly opened in the Kovno (Kaunas) ghetto on July 29, 1942.
15. An uprising broke out in the Bialystok ghetto on August 16, 1943. Regular German army forces suppressed the uprising on August 20.

AV 16

1. *Sefer ha-Harkavah*, a Hebrew grammar by Elijah Levita (Bahur), was published in Rome on July 24, 1518.
    Elijah Levita was the author of *Bove-Bukh*, the first published Yiddish book.
2. Rabbi Jacob Raphael Hezekiah Hazak (Forti), author of *Meginnei Erez*, popular commentary on the *Tur* code, died on July 27, 1782.
3. The Jewish Theological Seminary of Breslau, Germany (now Wroclaw, Poland), was opened on August 10, 1854.
    The Jewish community of Breslau dated from the 12th century. It shared the tragic fate of German Jewry during the Black Death riots and the subsequent waves of persecution. Its existence came to an end with an expulsion order, confirmed by the king in 1455, banning Jews from Breslau "forever." Four hundred years later the Jewish community of Breslau celebrated the opening of its Theological Seminary, which made that city a seat of Jewish culture and scholarship. The seminary was destroyed by the Nazis in 1938.

4. The British Mandatory Government ordered, on August 13, 1946, the removal of all illegal immigrants bound for Palestine to Cyprus.

AV 17

1. Jewish activists attacked the Roman garrison and the Jewish loyalists entrenched in the Citadel of Antonia, 66 C.E.
2. The extended Fast of Av, observed by the Falashas commencing with Av 1, is terminated on Av 17 (Leslau, *Falasha Anthology*).

   Falashas observe two extended fast periods in commemoration of the destruction of the Temple. The first is the Fast of Tamos (Tammuz 1–10). The second is the Fast of Av (Av 1–17). In spite of the explanations offered for these two periods, one cannot escape the conclusion that they have come about as a result of some early confusion regarding general Jewish practice. A reversal of the months, setting the fast periods as Tammuz 1–17 and Av 1–10 would be in accord with Jewish history.
3. Rabbi Asher b. Shlomo Zalman of Vilna, author of *Mayim Adirim*, died on August 21, 1796 (DYY).
4. Jacob Abraham de Mist, Dutch commissioner general, proclaimed religious equality for all persons residing in the colony of Cape of Good Hope, South Africa, on July 25, 1804.
5. The arrival of 120 Jewish families in Buenos Aires, Argentina, on August 14, 1889, marked the birth of the modern Argentinian Jewish community.

   See Heshvan 26:4.
6. Isidor Bush, publisher of *Israel's Herold* (German), first Jewish weekly in the U.S., died on August 5, 1898.
7. Arabs attacked Jews throughout Palestine on August 23, 1929. Many students of the Yeshivah of Hebron, among them 12 Americans, were killed.
8. The laying of oil pipes from Eilat to Haifa was completed on August 3, 1958.

   See Shevat 25:10.

AV 18

1. The *ner ma'aravi* was extinguished in the Temple in the reign of King Ahaz. (*Megillat Ta'anit* concluding chapter).

   The ancient fast of Av 18 is attributed in *Megillat Ta'anit* to the extinction of the "western light" *(ner ma'aravi)* of the menorah in the reign of King Ahaz. There may be several reasons for the significance attached to the extinction of the "western light." The *ner ma'aravi* was the only light of the seven-branched menorah which was supposed to burn day and night. This perpetual flame was a "testimony" that the Shekhinah (Divine Presence) dwells in the midst of Israel (*Menaḥot* 86b). The extinction of the "western light" in the days of King Ahaz was an indication of the departure of the Shekhinah from Israel and a warning of dire consequences to follow. One may also suggest a halakhic explanation for the fast of Av 18. The flame of the *ner ma'aravi* was used daily to rekindle the other six lights. Thus no new flame was ever introduced. On the occasion that the *ner ma'aravi* did go out, a flame was taken from the fire on the altar of the burnt offering (the copper altar) to light the *ner ma'aravi* and thence the rest of the menorah. King Ahaz had illegally removed the copper altar, which had been built by King Solomon, and replaced it with one modeled after an Assyrian altar (2 Kings 16:10–15). As a result of this desecration there was no legal method of rekindling the "western light" after its extinction, and the perpetual flame was thus interrupted.
2. Rabbi Jacob Culi, talmudist and Bible exegete, author of *Me-Am Lo'ez*, died on August 9, 1732 (JE).
3. The 4th Zionist Congress met in London, England, on August 13, 1900.
4. Gerhart Riegner, representative of the World Jewish Congress in Switzerland, was informed by a German industrialist, on August 1, 1942, that Hitler had ordered the extermination of all European Jews. It was the first reliable report of the impending mass murder of Jews to reach Western Europe.

   Riegner sent two reports through diplomatic channels to Rabbi Stephen Wise in New York and Mr. Sidney Silverman in Liverpool on August 8, 1942. The State Department suppressed the report until August 28, when the British draft had reached Rabbi Wise. (Morse, *While Six Million Died*, chap. 11).
5. The liquidation of the ghetto of Bialystok was started by the Nazis on August 19, 1943, and was completed 8 days later.
6. The millionth immigrant, since the establishment of the State of Israel, arrived on July 31, 1961.

AV 19

1. 200 Jews lost their lives in the massacre of the population of Béziers, France, on July 22, 1209.
2. The Jewish community of Mitchenick, Poland, was expelled by the Russian military authorities on August 11, 1914, in World War I. It was the first in a long series of expulsions which uprooted Polish and Lithuanian Jewries.

   Many of the major expulsions of large Jewish communities took place in the month of Av. See Av 8:4; Av 9:9; Av 9:12; Av 10:4; Av 25:1.
3. Rabbi Joseph Hayyim Sonnenfeld, leader of Palestine's Orthodox Jewry, died on August 21, 1932.
4. A systematic Nazi extermination of the Jews of Dvinsk (Daugavpils), Latvia, began on August 12, 1941.
5. Bar-Illan University, the first secular institution of higher learning under religous auspices in Israel, was founded on August 7, 1955.

AV 20

1. Titus ordered the raising of banks in preparation for the attack on Mt. Zion, on September 9 (approximate), 70 C.E. (Josephus, *Jewish War*, 6:8).
2. The first printed edition of the *Zohar* (the basic book of kabbalist interpretation of the Bible) was published on August 4, 1558.

   The publication of the *Zohar* in the year 1558 popularized the study of Kabbalah and stimulated the spread of mysticism and messianic movements.
3. Rabbi Joseph Steinhardt of Fürth, Germany, author of responsa *Zikhron Yosef*, died on August 5, 1776 (HY).
4. Jacob Epstein, Polish Jewish banker and philanthropist, died on August 16, 1843.
5. Anti-Jewish riots broke out in Zola-Egerszeg, Hungary, on August 23, 1883, following the acquittal of the Jewish defendants charged with the murder of Esther Solymosi.
6. Nahman Nathan Coronel of Jerusalem, annotator of rare rabbinic manuscripts, died on August 6, 1890.

AV 21

1. Rabbi Jacob Koppelman of Breisgau, author of *Omek Halakhah*, died on August 13, 1610 (HY).
2. Jonas Abrabanel of Amsterdam, Hebrew poet, died on August 11, 1667 (JE).
3. B'nai Jeshurun, the first Jewish congregation of Newark, N.J., was founded on August 20, 1848.
4. Hirsch Bernstein, journalist, founder of the first Yiddish periodical (Die Post) and the first Hebrew publication (HaZofeh beErez haHadashah) in the United States, died on August 1, 1907.
5. Rabbi Hayyim Soloveichik of Brisk (Brest Litovsk) outstanding talmudic scholar and teacher, author of *Hiddushei Rabbenu Hayyim Halevi*, died on July 30, 1918.
6. Israel Zangwill, Anglo-Jewish novelist, died on August 1, 1926.
7. Adolf Hitler assumed the powers of head of state and commander-in-chief of the armed forces upon the death of Paul von Hindenburg on August 2, 1934, making his dictatorship absolute and complete.
8. The 19th World Zionist Congress met in Lucerne, Switzerland, on August 20, 1935. Henrietta Szold proposed at this congress the plan for saving Jewish youngsters through Youth Aliyah.
9. Jews of Austria were ordered, by a Nazi decree of August 18, 1938, to adopt Israel and Sarah for their first names.
10. The first train with Jewish deportees from Belgium to Auschwitz left on August 4, 1942.
11. 24 of the foremost Yiddish writers of Russia, including David Bergelson, Itzik Fefer, and Perez Markish, were executed by the Soviet government on August 12, 1952. These executions marked the liquidation of Yiddish culture in Russia.
    See Tevet 15:4.

AV 22

1. A violent earthquake rocked Palestine on July 23, 501. The city of Acre was totally destroyed.
2. Rabbi Mordecai b. Hillel, famed talmudist and author of halakhic compendium, perished in Nuremberg with his wife and five children on August 1, 1298, in the Rindfleisch massacres.
3. 16 Jews were burned at an auto-da-fé in Toledo, Spain, on July 30, 1488.
4. Rabbi Raphael b. Samuel Meyuhas, author of *Peri ha-Adamah*, died on August 22, 1781.

5. Abraham Moshe Dillon (Zuchowicki), Yiddish poet, died on August 3, 1934.
6. Jews of Kovno (Kaunas), Lithuania, were herded into the ghetto of Slobodka on August 15, 1941.
7. Joop Westerweel, Dutch poet and educator, was executed by the Nazis on August 11, 1944, for assisting Jews to escape from Nazi arrests.

AV 23

1. Rabbi Benjamin Aaron of Cracow, author of *Maseat Binyamin*, died on August 15, 1610 (HY).
2. A pogrom broke out in Zhitomir, Russia, on August 24, 1905.
      Among the victims of the first Zhitomir pogrom in April 1905 was a Russian student (N. Blinov) who had helped defend the Jews. See Av 22:7

AV 24

1. The Hasmoneans replaced the Hellenic code with a Pharisaic code. The anniversary of this date was observed as a festival in ancient times (*Megillat Ta'anit* 5).
2. The first printed edition of the talmudic tractate *Niddah* was published on July 22, 1489.
3. Bogdan Chmielnicki, Cossack leader, murderer of 300,000 Jews, died on August 16, 1675.
4. Rabbi Ephraim Zalman Margolioth of Brody, author of *Bet Ephraim*, comments on the code, died on August 4, 1828.
5. The Jewish agricultural colony of Woodbine, N.J., was established on August 28, 1891.
      The establishment of a Jewish agricultural colony at Woodbine, N.J., was one of several attempts of the Baron de Hirsch Fund to found Jewish agricultural settlements in North and South America. The failure of most of these projects confirmed the pessimistic view of early Zionists regarding the practicability of Jewish farming in areas divested of historical and religious sentiments linking the Jew to the soil. The history of the Jewish autonomous province of Birobidzhan was no exception. According to a Belgrade Radio report announced on August 26, 1951 (the 60th anniversary of the founding of the Woodbine colony), the autonomous province was abolished by Russia and incorporated into the province of Khabarovsk.

6. The 13th World Zionist Congress met in Karlsbad, Bohemia, on August 6, 1923. A resolution to open a Hebrew University in Jerusalem was approved by this congress.
7. The Italian government issued an order barring Jewish teachers from public grade and high schools on August 21, 1938.
8. Berl Katznelson, leader of the Jewish labor movement in Palestine and first editor of *Davar*, died on August 13, 1944.

AV 25

1. Pope Innocent IV, on July 23, 1253, approved the expulsion of the ancient Jewish community of Vienne, France.
   See Av 1:6; Av 8:4.
2. King Louis X, on July 28, 1315, invited all French Jews who had been expelled from the country to return to France.
3. Rabbi Isaiah Menahem b. Isaac of Cracow (Mendel Avigdors) originator of *Hetter iskah*, a legal formula permitting the lending and borrowing of money on interest, died on August 16, 1599.
4. Rabbi Samuel David Ottolengo of Venice, kabbalist, author of *Kiryah Ne'emanah*, died on August 22, 1718.
5. Jacob b. Abraham Koppel, leader of Hungarian Jewry and influential *shtadlan*, died on August 26, 1799.
6. Many Jews of Copenhagen lost their lives in the British bombardment of the city on August 29, 1807. The anniversary of this date was set aside as a memorial day.
7. Solomon Plessner, eminent preacher and scholar, opponent of German Reform Judaism, died on August 28, 1883.
8. Jozef Israels, Jewish painter, died on August 19, 1911.
9. The Nazis removed 500 Jews from the Kovno (Kaunas) ghetto for execution on August 18, 1941.
   See Av 12:5; Av 13:6.
10. The Amsterdam hideout of Anne Frank, whose diary attracted worldwide attention, was discovered by the Nazis on August 4, 1944.

AV 26

1. A group of 70 people, led by the disciples of the Gaon of Vilna, arrived in Palestine on August 8, 1809.
2. The Sheriff's Declaration Bill of August 21, 1835, authorized Jews of England to hold the ancient and important office of sheriff.
3. The Turkish government renounced its sovereignty over Palestine

and recognized the British mandate by the terms of the Treaty of Sèvres signed on August 10, 1920.

4. The 20th World Zionist Congress met in Zurich on August 3, 1937.
5. Anti-Jewish riots broke out in Bransk, Poland, on August 23, 1938.
6. 10,000 Jews were sent from the Borislav ghetto to the Belsen extermination camp on August 9, 1942, in the first mass deportation of Jews to the gas chambers.

   The first mass deportation of German Jews to East European ghettos took place on October 15, 1941 (Tishri 24:3). The first Nazi mass extermination of Jews took place on June 20, 1942 (Tammuz 5:10).

AV 27

1. Queen Bona Sforza of Poland confirmed for the Jews of Pinsk, on August 18, 1533, all the rights already granted to the Jews of Lithuania.

   The economic and political condition of the Jews of Lithuania in the 16th century was generally much more favorable than that of Polish Jewry. Though the Polish king was the ruler of both countries, the Polish nobility frequently defied his wishes and authority. Queen Bona's exceptional liberality is not to be attributed merely to her name ("good"). As an Italian princess of liberal leanings she continued to follow her natural inclinations. One also must not overlook the fact that she was extremely greedy for money and happily accepted it from all donors.
2. S. A. Bierfield was lynched by the Klan in Franklin, Tenn., on August 15, 1868, in the first such incident involving a Jew (Schappes, *Documentary History of the Jews in the U.S.*, p. 515).
3. Mathilda Schechter, founder of the National Woman's League of the United Synagogue, died on August 27, 1924.

AV 28

1. Moses came down following his second ascent to the top of Mt. Sinai (*Bava Batra* 121a, Rashbam).
2. Jews of Brunn (Brno), Moravia, were expelled by King Ladislaus on August 22, 1454.
3. Rabbi Joshua Hoeschel b. Joseph Harif, head of the Yeshivah of Cracow, author of *Meginnei Shelomo*, died on August 16, 1648.

4. The Council of Four Countries, a semi-autonomous congress of Po- lish Jewry, met for the last time at Pilica, Poland, on August 17, 1762.

   The Council of Four Countries was the autonomous governing body of Polish Jewry, sanctioned by the Polish government. It was organized in 1580 and dissolved in 1764 when the Polish Diet ordered the dissolution of all Jewish general congresses. The Poles called this council the "Jewish Parliament."
5. Rabbi Naphtali Zevi Judah Berlin, head of the Yeshivah of Volozhin, author of *Haamek She'alah*, died on August 10, 1893.
6. The 12th World Zionist Congress met in Carlsbad, Czechoslovakia, on September 1, 1921.
7. The 14th World Zionist Congress met in Vienna Austria, on August 18, 1925.

AV 29

1. Moses hued out of stone the second Tablets in preparation for his third ascent to Mt. Sinai on the following morning (Exod. 34:4).

   According to *Seder Olam*, this event took place on Av 28.
2. Jews of Holland were emancipated on September 2, 1796.
3. Isaac Crémieux, Solomon Munk, and Sir Moses Montefiore, on Au- gust 28, 1840, secured from the Khedive Mohammed Ali of Egypt, the release of the nine surviving Jewish prisoners of Damascus who had been charged with a blood ritual.
4. Rabbi Samuel Salant, chief rabbi and leader of the Ashkenazic com- munity of Jerusalem, died on August 16, 1909.
5. Moshe Leib Halpern, Yiddish poet, died on August 31, 1932.
6. The 18th World Zionist Congress met in Prague, Czechoslovakia, on August 21, 1933.
7. The Nazis passed a law, on August 26, 1938, ordering all Jews to take the names Israel or Sarah.

   Most Nazi discriminatory regulations were revivals of medieval anti-Jewish decrees. The compulsory adoption of the two biblical names of Israel and Sarah was a historic "first," spawned in the fertile brain of the propaganda minister, Goebbels. Both names have a common root—*sar*, a person of power and influence or one who governs. The sadist Nazi doctor, who bore the biblical name of Jozef (Joseph), was apparently unaware that the name *Israel* was given to the patriarch Jacob "because you wrestled with me and your power prevailed."
8. Abraham Cahan, Yiddish writer and editor of the "Forward," died on August 31, 1951.

AV 30

1. Moses ascended Mt. Sinai to receive the second Tablets of the Law (Exod. 33:11, Rashi).
2. Ḥayyim Farhii, financial secretary of the pasha of Acre and benefactor of the Jews of Safed, was killed on August 21, 1819 (Yaari, *Zikhronot Erez Yisrael,* 100).
3. The 6th World Zionist Congress met in Basle, Switzerland, on August 23, 1903.

   It was the last Zionist Congress at which Theodor Herzl presided. The British proposal for Jewish colonization of a part of Uganda, approved at this congress, split the Zionist movement. See Tammuz 6:14.
4. The 11th World Zionist Congress met in Vienna, Austria, on September 2, 1913.

   A resolution to establish a Hebrew University in Palestine was approved at this congress. The outbreak of World War I prevented its immediate implementation.
5. Isaac Sadeh, "father" of Palmach, Jewish commando forces in the Arab-Israel war, died on August 21, 1952.

ELUL 1

1. Beginning of the third biblical plague (*Zikhron Yemot Olam*).
2. Prophet Haggai exhorted Zerubbabel in 520 B.C.E., to commence the construction of the second Temple (Hag. 1:1). See Kislev 24:1.
3. Elul 1 marked the beginning of the fiscal year for the purpose of determining tithes of cattle (*Rosh Ha-Shanah* 2a).
4. Elul 1 was observed by Persian Jews as a day of pilgrimage to the traditional tomb of Sarah, the daughter of Asher.
5. Rabbi David b. Abraham Maimuni ha-Nagid, grandson of Maimonides, died on August 6, 1301(HY).
6. Jews of Palma, Majorca, were massacred on August 24, 1391.
7. Anti-Jewish riots broke out in Prague on August 22, 1400, taking a toll of 77 lives.
8. The anniversary of the Maccabeans, annually observed by Christian churches on August 1, was celebrated for the last time in the year 1505. Thereafter the festival became known as the Feast of St. Cuthbert.
9. Elul 1 was designated Purim de los Christianos by Jews of Tangier ...d Tetuán in commemoration of the defeat of King Sebastian of Portugal in the "Battle of the Kings" on August 4, 1578 (Goodman, *Purim Anthology* 21).
10. The World Zionist Organization was founded at the 1st World Zionist Congress, which opened in Basîe, Switzerland, on August 29, 1897.
11. The first meeting of the representatives of Palestine's Jewry opened in Zikhron Ya'akov on August 24, 1903.

    The first meeting of the representatives of Palestine's Jewry took place on the anniversary of the opening of the 1st World Zionist Congress and the founding of the World Zionist Organization (no. 10).
12. The 21st World Zionist Congress met in Geneva, Switzerland, on August 16, 1939. It was the last congress before the outbreak of World War II.
13. Metropolitan Andreas Szeptycki, archbishop of Lemberg (Lwow), Poland, provided, on August 14, 1942, hiding places for Jewish children and for the storing of Torah scrolls.

ELUL 2

1. 160 Jews of Chinon, France, led by Rabbi Eliezer b. Joseph, were burned on August 21, 1321, on charges of poisoning of wells.
2. The Charter of King Casimir IV Jagellon, defining the rights of the Jews of Poland and Lithuania, was granted on August 14, 1447. (Dubnow, *History of Jews in Russia and Poland*, vol. 1, chap. 2)
3. Pope Julius III ordered the confiscation and burning of the Palestinian and Babylonian Talmuds on August 12, 1553.

   The banning of the Talmud was officially justified by the claim that it contained anti-Christian statements. The real reason, however, was the belief that the destruction of talmudic Judaism would hasten the conversion of Jews to Christianity.
   See Tishri 1:17.
4. The first printing of the code *Shulḥan Arukh, Oraḥ Ḥayyim* was completed in Biriyah, near Safed, Palestine, on August 19, 1555.
5. Rabbi Samuel Aboab (Rasha), author of *Devar Shemuel*, died on August 22, 1694.
6. General Salicetti, commissioner of the French Directory, issued a decree, on September 5, 1796, granting the Jews of Bologna, Italy, equal rights with all other citizens.
7. The 15th World Zionist Congress met in Basle, Switzerland, on August 30, 1927.

ELUL 3

1. Rabbi Menahem b. Solomon Meiri, outstanding medieval commentator on the Talmud, author of *Beit ha-Beḥirah*, was born on August 22, 1240.
2. Jews of Budapest, Hungary, received permission from the government on August 17, 1787, to conduct religious services in private homes, with the proviso that no rabbi was to officiate at such services.
3. Rabbi Abraham Ẓevi Eisenstadt of Utina (Uttian) Lithuania, author of *Pitḥei Teshuvah*, popular addendum to the code, died on August 21, 1868 (HY).
4. Rabbi Abraham Isaac Kook, talmudic scholar and philosopher, author of *Ḥokhmat ha-Kodesh*, first chief rabbi of the Ashkenazic community of Palestine, died on August 31, 1935.

   Rabbi Kook died on the anniversary of his arrival in Jerusalem, Elul 3, 1919.
5. The first news of Nazi mass extermination reached the outside world

on August 16, 1942, when a group of Polish women who had been exchanged for German war prisoners arrived in Palestine. See Av 18:4.

ELUL 4

1. Jews of Barcelona, Spain, were massacred on August 5, 1391.
   The massacre of the Jewish community of Barcelona was one of a series of convulsive riots that spread throughout Spain over a period of three months, beginning in Seville on June 6, 1391. When the disturbance had spent its force, Spanish Jewry was left in a helpless and impoverished state. The first proposal for the introduction of an Inquisition into Spain was made on the 70th anniversary of the massacre of the Jews of Barcelona (no. 2).
2. Alfonso de Espina, bishop of Osma, urged the establishment of an Inquisition in Spain on August 10, 1461.
3. Rabbi Moses b. Abraham Provençal of Mantua, author of *BeShem Kadmon*, died on July 29, 1576 (ATGY).
4. A decree issued on September 5, 1750, provided for the annual search of every Jewish home in Paderborn, Prussia, for stolen or "doubtful" goods.
5. Rabbi Samuel Bodheim, leader of the extreme wing of the German Reform movement, pioneer in the field of modern Jewish homiletics, died on August 22, 1860.
6. Professor Heinrich Graetz, outstanding Jewish historian, died on September 7, 1891.
7. The 8th World Zionist Congress met in the Hague, Netherlands, on August 14, 1907. It adopted "Ha-Tikvah" as the official Zionist hymn. See Tishri 23:8.
8. Rabbi Meir Simḥah Hakohen, author of *Or Sameaḥ*, novellae on Maimonides, died on August 14, 1926.
9. The Jewish community of Posvol, Lithuania, was massacred by the Nazis on August 27, 1941.

ELUL 5

1. Miriam Bella, sister of Rabbi Moses Isserles (Rama) and wife of Phinehas Horowitz, head of community of Cracow, famed for her piety and scholarship, died on August 15, 1619.
2. Solomon Zalman Geiger, author of *Divrei Kohelet*, died on September 5, 1875.

3. Albert Siegfried Bettelheim, journalist and author, convicted by a Georgia jury of murder amidst anti-Semitic outbursts and shouts of "Hang the Jew," was lynched on August 15, 1915.
4. The 38th, 39th and 40th Battalions of the Royal Fusiliers, consisting of British, Palestinian, and American Jewish volunteers, was formed on August 23, 1917.

   The Jewish elements of the Royal Fusiliers comprised three battalions—the 38th, 39th, and 40th. The 38th consisted of Anglo-Jewish volunteers, the 39th of American Jewish volunteers, and the 40th of Palestinian Jewish volunteers. Due to pressures by influential Anglo-Jewish assimilationist circles, the units were not officially designated as "Jewish" and the wearing of Jewish insignia was forbidden. Most of the volunteers, however, attached the Star of David to their uniforms. According to official statistics published in 1919, there was a total of 5,000 volunteers, 28 percent from England, 30 percent from Palestine, and 34 percent from America.
5. Petlyura's Ukrainian army massacred Jews of Kiev on August 31, 1919.

   See Sivan 13:7.
6. Mussolini canceled the civil rights of Italian Jews and ordered the expulsion of all foreign-born Jews on September 1, 1938.

   See Heshvan 5:8, 23:10
7. Rabbi Simon Huberband, young historian and chronicler, died in the Warsaw ghetto on August 18, 1942.

ELUL 6

1. Menahem, a leader of seditious Zealots, permitted Agrippa's forces to withdraw from Jerusalem, 66 C.E. The Roman soldiers who fell into their hands were killed (Josephus, *Jewish War* 2:17).

   See Sivan 14:1.
2. Rabbi Yom Tov Lipmann Heller of Cracow, author of *Tosefot Yom Tov*, popular commentary on the Mishnah, died on August 19, 1654 (OY).

   There are a number of alternate dates: August 2(HY), August 17 (DDD) and September 7 (JE).
3. Rabbi Shabbetai of Orlo, author of *Shevet Ahim*, died on August 16, 1820 (DDD).
4. Rabbi Moses Mintz of O-Buda, Hungary, author of responsa *Maharam Mintz*, died on August 15, 1831.
5. Rabbi Jekuthiel Judah Teitelbaum, founder of Yeshivath Yitav Lev in Sighet, Hungary (now Rumania), author of *Yitav Lev*, a commentary on the Pentateuch, died on September 8, 1883.

6. *Ha-Refuah*, Palestine's first medical journal, was published on August 20, 1920.
7. Louis Marshall, American Jewish communal leader, died on September 11, 1929.
8. Italian planes bombed Tel Aviv on September 9, 1940, and killed 117 people.

    Italy adopted Nazi anti-Jewish laws on Elul 5, 1938. Its planes bombed Tel Aviv, a nonmilitary target, on Elul 6, 1940.

ELUL 7

1. Amram remarried Jokhebed (*Sotah* 12a; *Seder ha-Dorot*).
2. King Agrippa I dedicated the new gate of the Jerusalem wall, 42 C.E. (*Megillat Ta'anit* 6). The anniversary of this date was observed in ancient times as a holiday.
3. The high priest Hananiah and his brother, Hezekiah, were killed by order of Menahem, leader of the activist party, 66 C.E. (Josephus, *Jewish War* 2:17).
4. Menahem, leader of the activist party, was executed by order of Eliezer, head of the war party and son of a slain high priest, 66 C.E. (ibid.).
5. 6,000 Jews of Mayence, Germany, set fire to their homes on August 22, 1349, and perished in the flames.
6. Rabbi Joseph Stadthagen, author of *Divrei Zikharon*, died on September 5, 1715.
7. Jews of Hanover were granted equality on September 5, 1848.
8. The Jewish Colonization Association (ICA) was founded by Baron Maurice de Hirsch on September 10, 1891.

    The Jewish Colonization Association provided financial assistance to the Jews who established the agricultural colony of Moisésville in Argentina. See Av 17:5.
9. Nahman Syrkin, founder of Labor Zionism and Yiddish writer, died on September 6, 1924.
10. General Jürgen Stroop, commander of the Nazi forces which had razed the Warsaw Ghetto, was executed on September 8, 1951.

ELUL 8

1. The walls of the upper city of Jerusalem were battered down by the Romans and all resistance came to an end on September 27 (approximate), 70 C.E. The leaders of the resistance, Simon and John of Giscala (Gush Halav) were captured (Josephus, *Jewish War* 6:9).

   On Elul 6 and 7, 66 C.E. activist rebels under the leadership of Menahem fought their way into the upper city of Jerusalem to flush out the moderate rebels and the Roman garrison stationed in Herod's palace. Four years later, on Elul 8, 70 C.E., the Romans battered down the walls of the upper city, completing the conquest of Judea and Jerusalem.
2. The execution, on August 21, 1379, by Jewish authorities of Joseph Picho, an informer, led to the repeal of Jewish jurisdiction in criminal cases in Castile.
3. 17 Jews were burned at the stake in Schweidwitz, Silesia, on August 13, 1453.
4. David Gans, talmudic scholar and scientist, author of *Zemah David*, died on August 25, 1613.
5. Dr. Jacob Lumbrozo was granted letters of denization in Maryland on September 10, 1663.
6. Emperor Alexander III appointed a commission on September 2, 1881, to study the "injurious influences of Jews upon the Russian native population."
7. Ritual slaughtering was prohibited in Switzerland on August 20, 1893.

ELUL 9

1. Birth of Dan (*Midrash Tadshe*).
2. Rabbi Moses b. Nahman (Nahmanides) arrived in Jerusalem on September 1, 1267, and soon thereafter reestablished a Jewish community (Kohler, *A Treasury of Jewish Letters*, 225).

   After the defeat of Bar Kokhba in the year 135, the Romans razed Jerusalem and built a smaller city on its site which they named Aelia Capitolina. Jews were barred from residing in this city. A Jewish community was reestablished in 637 and continued to exist until Jerusalem fell to the Crusaders in 1099. A new community was established again in 1187, but it was forced to dissolve in 1260 when the Tartars overran the city. Nahmanides renewed the community seven years later. It enjoyed an uninterrupted existence until 1948

and was reestablished in 1967, 700 years after the arrival of Nahmanides.
3. Jews of Cologne, Germany, set fire to their homes and perished in the flames on August 24, 1349, to escape compulsory baptism.
4. Jews of Gerona, Spain, were massacred on August 10, 1391.
5. A papal edict of August 17, 1592, prohibited Jews from admitting Christians into synagogues.
6. Jacob Barsimson, the first known Jew to settle in North America, arrived in New Amsterdam on August 22, 1654.
7. Rabbi Aaron Chorin of Arad, Hungary, author of *Emek ha-Shavah*, died on August 24, 1844.
8. Dedicatory services were held on September 9, 1867, in the first synagogue built in modern times by the Jewish community of Basle, Switzerland.
9. The 3rd Zionist Congress met in Basle, Switzerland, on August 15, 1899.
10. Rabbi Zadok Rabinowitz of Lemberg, hasidic leader and prolific writer, author of *Peri Zadok,* an encyclopedic commentary on the Pentateuch, died on September 3, 1900 (HY).
11. Jewish teachers and students were barred from Italian educational institutions by a decree dated September 5, 1938.
12. Hungarian Jewish deportees were massacred in Kamenets-Podolski, Russia, on September 1, 1941.
13. Jews of Shavl (Siauliai), Lithuania, were confined to a ghetto on September 1, 1941.
14. 7,000 Jews were massacred in Marijampole, Lithuania, on September 1, 1941.
15. The wearing of a yellow star became obligatory for all Jews in the Reich on September 1, 1941.
16. SS Officer Toth, who was responsible for the liquidation of the ghetto of Cracow, was condemned to death on September 5, 1946, by the Polish People's Court in Cracow.

ELUL 10

1. Noah opened the window of the ark and sent out the raven (Rashi, Gen. 8:5).
2. The ghetto of Buda was attacked by a riotous mob on August 20, 1684. In gratitude for their deliverance from serious injury, the community designated Elul 10 Buda Purim.

3. The 2nd Zionist Congress met in Basle, Switzerland, on August 28, 1898.

   The Zionist Party and the Jewish Socialist Party, the Bund, were both formed in 1897. The former looked to Palestine for a solution of the Jewish problem. The latter looked to emancipation and equality in the diaspora through socialism for an ultimate solution. The clash between the two Jewish groups was harsh and bitter from the very outset. Due to this ideological collision, splinter groups were formed with a view toward a fusion of the two dynamic forces. The result was Socialist Zionism. The 2nd Zionist Congress had Socialist Zionist delegates participating for the first time. Two years later the Workmen's Circle was founded in America on the anniversary of the 2nd congress (no. 4).

4. The Workmen's Circle was organized on September 4, 1900.

5. Rabbi Isaac Jacob Reines, head of the yeshivah of Lida and one of the founders of Mizrachi, died on August 20, 1915.

   See Elul 11:7.

6. The Supreme Court of Israel was inaugurated in Jerusalem on September 14, 1948.

ELUL 11

1. The first printed edition of *Lashon Limudim*, a Hebrew grammar by David b. Yaḥya, was published in Constantinople on August 31, 1506.

2. Rabbi Joseph Caro completed his popular commentary on the *Tur* code on August 23, 1542.

3. King Sigismund II, Augustus, granted limited self-government to the Jews of Great Poland on August 13, 1551.

4. The Jewish Community of Neutitschlin (Novy Jicin), Moravia, was expelled on August 30, 1563.

5. Rabbi Isaiah Horowitz (Shelah) and fifteen other rabbis were imprisoned in Jerusalem on September 13, 1625, and held for ransom.

6. Rabbi Aaron Zelig of Zalkova, author of *Amudei Shesh*, died on September 3, 1740 (DDD).

7. The liquidation of the Minsk and Lida ghettos began on September 11, 1943, and was completed three days later.

8. Operation Magic Carpet, which transported 45,000 Yemenite Jews to Israel, was officially concluded on August 24, 1950.

ELUL 12

1. One of the earliest recorded Church censorships of Hebrew writings was ordered by King James I of Aragon on August 19, 1263.
   Russia was the last feudal government to introduce censorship of Hebrew books. It was decreed on October 17, 1796 (Tishri 15:9). The ban on Hebrew and Yiddish periodicals was lifted by the revolutionary government of Russia on July 21, 1918 (Av 12:3).
2. Pope Clement XII renewed the restrictive anti-Jewish laws of the Roman Jewish community on September 2, 1732.

ELUL 13

1. Rabbi Moses b. Jacob Ziprish of Lemberg, author of *Seder Gittin*, died on August 24, 1608 (DYY).
2. Governor Dongan was petitioned by the Jews of New York on September 12, 1695, for liberty to exercise their religion in public.
   The Charter of Liberties granted by James I of England on October 30, 1683, limited the free exercise of religion to Christians only. Accordingly, Governor Dongan declined the Jewish petition.
3. Rabbi Elijah Schick (Elinke Lider), popular preacher, author of *Ein Eliyahu*, died on September 2, 1876.
4. Joshua Heschel Shorr, founder of the Hebrew periodical, *He-Halutz*, died on September 2, 1895.
5. Hersh Danielevitz (Hershele), Yiddish poet, died on September 5, 1941.
6. A round-up of 7,000 stateless Jews in the Vichy Free Zone of France began on August 26, 1942.
7. Nazis closed all synagogues and schools in the ghetto of Kovno on August 26, 1942.
8. U.N. mediator Count Folke Bernadotte was assassinated on September 17, 1948.

ELUL 14

1. The oldest existing ketubbah written in the Western Hemisphere was dated Elul 14, 1643. It was executed in Surinam (Paramaribo) at the marriage of Ḥakham Yiẓḥak Meatob to Yehudit.
2. Congregation Shearith Israel of New York laid the foundation stone of the first synagogue structure in North America, on Mill Street, New York City on September 8, 1729.

3. In a letter dated August 29, 1939, Chaim Weizmann informed the prime minister of England that the Jews of Palestine would stand by Great Britain and fight on the side of the democracies.
4. The Nazis issued a decree, on September 17, 1940, depriving Jews of all their moveable and immoveable property.
5. Jews of Vilna, Poland, were confined to a ghetto on September 6, 1941.
6. 1,668 Jews of Radomysl, Poland, were executed by the Nazis on September 6, 1941.
7. The Knesset passed Israel's draft law on September 8, 1949, making it obligatory for every Jewish youth in Israel to serve a term in the military forces.

   Israel's draft law, passed on Elul 14, 1949, was the first such law since the loss of Jewish independence. Jews were ineligible for military service in the medieval period. With the coming of emancipation they were gradually incorporated in all national armies. The most shocking draft law affecting Jews was enacted by the Russian government on Elul 15, 1827 (no. 5). Under the provisions of that law, Jewish minors were drafted into battalions of cantonists. They were educated until the age of 18 and thereafter had to serve in the army for 25 years. It is estimated that 100,000 Jewish boys became cantonists and that at least half of them were baptized.
8. The first Knesset building was dedicated in Jerusalem on August 30, 1966.

ELUL 15

1. Rabbi Moses Alashkar of Cairo, talmudist and liturgical poet, author of *Ge'on Ya'akov*, commentary on the code, died on August 15, 1535 (HY).
2. The Jewish community of Trèves, Prussia, observed a fast on Elul 15 to commemorate a period of persecution which began on September 6, 1675.
3. The right to worship in public was denied to Jews by the Common Council of New York on September 14, 1685.

   Jewish residents of New York were denied the right of public worship on Elul 15, 1685. On Elul 14, 44 years later, New York Jewry laid the foundation of the first synagogue structure in New York and North America (no. 2).
4. Rabbi Akiva Eger the Elder of Pressburg, author of *Mishnah de-Rabbi Akiva*, died on September 18, 1758 (HY).

5. The Russian government issued a decree, on September 7, 1827, providing for the draft of Jewish boys at the age of 12 and their placement in cantonist schools for military education.

    See note on Elul 14:7.

6. Rabbi Isaco Samuel Reggio (Yashar), founder of the Rabbinic Seminary of Padua, author of *Ha-Torah ve-ha-Pilosofyah*, died on August 29, 1855.

7. The study of Hebrew as a modern language was introduced for the first time into the public schools of New York on September 8, 1930.

    Hebrew was taught at Harvard College almost from the very inception of the school in 1636.

8. Manfred von Killinger, who had forced Rumania to adopt Nazi anti-Jewish laws, committed suicide on September 3, 1944.

9. The Camp David summit talks, which produced two framework documents on an Egyptian-Israeli peace agreement and Palestinian self-rule, ended on September 17, 1978.

ELUL 16

1. Rabbi Isaac Shapiro, talmudist, head of the Yeshivah of Cracow, died on September 4, 1582.

2. Rabbi Naphtali Spitz, author of *Male Razon,* died on September 17, 1712.

3. By a decision of the Supreme Court of Poland, announced on September 14, 1753, Jews were granted permission to reside in the Starochinka district of Kovno.

4. Leon Mandelstamm, Russian Hebrew poet, died on September 12, 1889.

5. The forged *Protocols of the Elders of Zion* were serially published for the first time in the Russian paper *Znamia,* beginning with the issue of August 26, 1903.

    The spurious *Protocols of the Elders of Zion* were exploited by anti-Semites throughout the world in their dissemination of anti-Jewish slanders. Articles based on the *Protocols* were serialized in Henry Ford's *Dearborn Independent,* beginning with May 22, 1920. Thirty years after the original publication of the work at Kishinev, Congressman Louis T. McFadden spread the charges contained in the *Protocols* in the *Congressional Record* (Sivan 4:9).

6. Hitler issued Directive No. 1 on August 31, 1939, ordering an attack on Poland to begin at dawn of the next day.

7. The Nazis issued a decree on September 19, 1940, forbidding employment of non-Jewish women in Jewish homes or businesses.
8. The entire Jewish community of Meretsch (Merkine), Lithuania, was massacred on September 8, 1941.
9. Illegal Jewish immigrants who had been exiled by the British mandatory authorities to the island of Mauritius were admitted into Palestine on August 25, 1945.

ELUL 17

1. Noah released the dove from the ark to test the depth of the floodwaters (Gen. 8:5, 8 Rashi).
2. The Roman garrison in Jerusalem was destroyed by the Judean insurgents in the year 66 C.E. Judea was cleared of Roman forces. The anniversary of this date was designated a holiday (*Megillat Ta'anit* 6; Klausner, *Historia shel ha-Bayit ha-Sheni*, vol. 5, chap. 11).
   See Sivan 14:1.
3. 2,000 Jews of Caesaria were massacred by the native population at the instigation of the Roman procurator, Florus, who had fled from Jerusalem, 66 C.E. (Josephus, *Jewish War* 2:18).
4. Vincent Fettmilch and his mob invaded Frankfort on the Main, Germany, on August 22, 1614, and sacked the Jewish quarter.
5. Isaac Cohen Belinfante, poet and preacher, died on September 7, 1781 (JE).
6. The Jewish community of Shedlitz, Russia, was pogromized on September 7, 1906.
7. Rabbi Ḥayyim Hirschensohn, prolific writer, author of *Malki ba-Kodesh*, died on September 15, 1935.
8. The anti-Semitic Nuremberg racial laws were passed by the Nazis on September 15, 1935.
9. World War II broke out on September 1, 1939.
10. The ghetto of Lodz was evacuated on September 5, 1944.
11. Abraham Slutcki, Yiddish poet, died on September 13, 1957.

ELUL 18

1. Amalekites defeated the Jews who had stormed their mountain stronghold in defiance of Moses' order (Num. 14:45).
   According to Seder haDorot (2449) the scouts who maligned Palestine died on Elul 17. The Amalekite attack took place on the next day (Num. 14:40).

2. Simon the Hasmonean was elected high priest and governor of the Jews, marking the new independence of the Jewish nation, 141 B.C.E. (1 Macc. 14).

   The election of Simon the Hasmonean on Elul 18, 141 B.C.E., as high priest and governor of Judea marked the completion of the struggle for political independence and the beginning of the hereditary Hasmonean dynasty. Rome extended its recognition of this dynasty two years later. Exactly 206 years after the election of Simon, on Elul 17, 65 C.E., the last of the Hasmonean dynasty, King Agrippa II, a vassal of Rome, was expelled from Jerusalem by insurgent Jewish nationalist forces (no. 2).

3. Falashas designated Elul 18 "The Festival of the Eighteenth" to commemorate the death of the patriarchs Abraham, Isaac, and Jacob (Leslau, *Falasha Anthology*).

4. Rabbi Judah Loew b. Bezalel (Maharal of Prague), author and creator of the legendary "Golem of Prague," died on September 17, 1609 (ATGY).

5. Rabbi Isaac Chajes, author of *Api Ravrevi*, a code in verse, died on September 4, 1613 (HY).

6. Mordecai Manuel Noah, on September 1, 1825, issued a manifesto urging Jewish emigration to the projected Jewish colony, Ararat, which was to be established on Grand Island in New York State.

7. Moses Aaron Shatzkes, of Kiev, Russia, author of *Ha-Mafte'ah*, died on August 24, 1899.

8. The first Jewish self-defense organization in Palestine was founded on September 14, 1908.

9. A compulsory education law was passed in Israel on September 12, 1949.

10. Israel agreed to accept reparation payments by West Germany for losses caused by the Nazis on September 8, 1952.

ELUL 19

1. The first printed edition of *Minhagei Maharil*, a popular book on customs and ceremonies by Rabbi Jacob Moellin, was published on August 25, 1556.

   See Elul 21:3.

2. The first edition of the *Zohar* on the Book of Exodus was printed on August 22, 1559.

3. Rabbi Hayyim Benveniste, codifier, author of the monumental work *Knesset ha-Gedolah*, died on September 8, 1673 (HY).

   According to JE, September 6, 1673.

4. Ashkenazim of Jerusalem began the reconstruction of the ruined synagogue of Rabbi Judah Hasid on September 1, 1836.
5. Anti-Jewish riots broke out in Stockholm, Sweden, on September 3, 1852.
6. The Italian government removed the restrictions of the Roman ghetto on September 15, 1870.
   On October 2, 1870, Rome was annexed to United Italy.
7. England and France declared war on Germany on September 3, 1939.
8. Jews of Czestochowa, Poland, were massacred on September 3, 1939.
9. An anti-Semitic speech by Charles A. Lindbergh, delivered over the radio on September 11, 1941, marked the introduction of anti-Semitism in American public life as a means for attainment of political ends.

ELUL 20

1. Charles VI issued a decree on September 17, 1394, ordering the expulsion of Jews from France.
   See Av 10:4; Kislev 9:1.
2. The first printed edition of the Psalms, with Kimhi's commentary, was published in Bologna, Italy, on August 29, 1477.
3. Rabbi Judah Aryeh Moscato, poet and philosopher, author of *Kol Yehudah*, commentary on the *Kuzari*, died on September 19, 1590.
   According to EJUD, 1593.
4. Eliakum Zunser, Yiddish folk-singer and composer, died on September 22, 1913.
5. Germany occupied Kalisz, a Polish city with a Jewish population of 30,000, on September 4, 1939.
6. The ghetto of Mir, Poland, was liquidated by the Nazis on September 2, 1942.
7. Rabbi Joseph S. Kahaneman of Ponevezh (the Ponevezher Rav), dynamic communal leader of Lithuanian Orthodoz Jewry, founder of Kiryat ha-Yeshivah at Bene-Berak, Israel, died on September 3, 1969.
8. Shlomo Bickel, Yiddish literary critic, editor, and author, died on September 3, 1969.

ELUL 21

1. Many Jews of London, England, lost their lives in anti-Jewish riots which broke out during the coronation of King Richard I on September 3, 1189.
2. Rabbi Jacob of Orléans, prominent French tosafist, was killed in London, England, in the anti-Jewish riots which broke out on September 3, 1189.
3. Rabbi Jacob b. Moses ha-Levi Moellin of Mayence, author of the popular work *Minhagei Maharil*, died on September 13, 1427 (ATGY). See Elul 19:1.
4. Tomás de Torquemada, chief of the Spanish Inquisition and principal instigator of the expulsion of the Jews from Spain, died on September 8, 1498.
5. Rabbi Jonathan Eybeschuetz, of Prague, author of *Kereti u-Feleti*, controversial figure, died on September 18, 1764.
6. Anti-Jewish riots broke out in Polish Silesia on September 17, 1938. The riots continued until September 22.
7. Piotrków, Poland, a city with a Jewish population of 17,000, was occupied by Germany on September 5, 1939. The first ghetto in Poland was established in this city.

ELUL 22

1. Purim de los Ladrones (Purim of Bandits) was celebrated by the Jews of Gumeldjina, near Adrianople, Turkey, on Elul 22 to commemorate their escape following an attack by bandits on September 15, 1786.
2. General Tadeusz Kosciuszko appointed Berek Joselewicz commander of the Jewish regiment fighting with the Polish revolutionary army on September 17, 1794. It was the first Jewish fighting force in modern times.
3. Jews of Homel, Russia, were massacred on September 14, 1903.
4. Germany occupied Cracow, Poland, on September 6, 1939.
5. 9,000 Jews of Slonim, Russia, were executed by the Nazis on September 14, 1941.
6. Colonel Franz Ziereis, commander of the notorious Mauthausen camp, was killed in an attempted escape on August 31, 1945.

ELUL 23

1. Noah kept the dove in the ark for 6 days before dispatching it on the next morning. (Rashi, Gen. 8:5).
2. Cornelio da Montalcino, a monk who had converted to Judaism, was burned at the stake in Rome on September 4, 1553. (Roth, *The History of the Jews of Italy*, chap. 7).
3. Rabbi Jacob Frankel, head of Philadelphia's Congregation Rodeph Shalom, was appointed a military hospital chaplain on September 18, 1862. He was the first American rabbi in the U.S. Chaplaincy (Korn, *American Jewry and the Civil War*, 77).
   See Nisan 21:11
4. Germany occupied the cities of Aleksandrów, Zgierz, and Łódź, Poland, on September 7, 1939.
   See Shevat 29:5.
5. 800 Jewish women of Shkudvil (Skaudvile), Lithuania, were executed by the Nazis on September 15, 1941.
6. Slovakia adopted the Nuremberg Laws on September 15, 1941.
7. The Nazis liquidated the ghetto of Vilna on September 23, 1943.

ELUL 24

1. David married Bath-Sheba *(Shalshelet ha-Kabbalah)*.
2. Zerubbabel and the people of Judea began the clearing of the Temple site in preparation for the building of the Second Temple in 520 B.C.E. (Hag. 1:15).
3. The fortified city of Gamala, Palestine (in lower Golan), joined the insurrection against Rome, 67 C.E. (Josephus, *Jewish War* 4:1).
   See Tishri 23:4.
4. The discovery, on August 29, 1255, of the body of the child Hugh of Lincoln, led to ritual accusations and the hanging of many prominent Jews of England.
5. The establishment of a Jesuit Order in Lemberg (Lwow), Poland, on September 1, 1592, marked the beginning of the persecution of the city's Jews.
6. Anti-Jewish riots broke out in Endingen and Lengnau, Switzerland, on September 21, 1802.
7. Judah Leib Gordon, Hebrew poet, died on September 16, 1892.
8. David Wolfson, second president of the World Zionist Organization, died on September 15, 1914.
9. Rabbi Israel Meir Kagen, author of *Ḥafeẓ Ḥayyim*, founder of the

Yeshivah of Radin, talmudist and moralist, died on September 15, 1933.

N. Rabbi Israel Meir Kagen, known the world over as the Ḥafeẓ Ḥayyim, was the most revered person of his generation. His emphasis on ethics and moralism and his exemplary life made him a legendary figure in his lifetime. Even the Communist officials of Russia treated him with great deference and respect.

10. The Nazis ordered the liquidation of the Bialystok ghetto on September 6, 1942.
11. Rabbi Ben-Zion Meir Ḥai Uziel, chief rabbi of the Sephardic community of Israel, author of *Mishpetei Uziel* died on September 4, 1953.

ELUL 25

1. The beginning of the Creation (*Seder ha-Dorot*).
2. Nehemiah completed the building of the walls around Jerusalem, 444 B.C.E. (Neh. 6:15).

   The construction work began on Av 4 and was completed 52 days later on Elul 25.
3. A party of 23 Jews from Recife, Brazil, arrived in New Amsterdam on the *St. Catherine* on September 7, 1654. They became the pioneers of New York's Jewish community (*AJHSP*, no. 18, p. 3).

   The first known Jew to settle in North America arrived 16 days earlier, on August 22, 1654. (See Elul 9:6).
4. Rabbi Joseph Babad of Sniatyn, Poland, author of popular *Minḥat Ḥinnukh*, a commentary on the classic *Ḥinnukh*, died on September 7, 1874.
5. Rabbi Moses Aronson, one of the earliest East European rabbis to settle in America, author of *Pardes ha-Ḥakhmah*, a book of sermons, died on September 25, 1875.
6. Solomon Zainwil Rapaport (S. An-Ski), playwright, author of *Der Dibbuk*, died on September 8, 1920.
7. Henry Kissinger, America's first Jewish secretary of state, was sworn in on September 22, 1973.

ELUL 26

1. The second day of the Creation of the world. God made the "firma-ment in the midst of the waters and let it divide the waters from the waters" (Gen. 1:6). He also created angels (*Midrash Bereishit Rabbah* 1), the manna, and Miriam's well (*Pirkei de-Rabbi Eliezer* 3).
2. Jews of Zurich, Switzerland, were charged on September 21, 1348, with the perpetration of the Black Death epidemic. Some were burned on February 22, 1349, and the rest were expelled.
3. Peter Stuyvesant and the New Amsterdam Council passed a resolu-tion on August 28, 1655, barring Jews from military service.
    The resolution to bar Jews from the guard duty performed by the burghers of New Amsterdam was passed one day after the first anniversary of the arrival of the first group of Jewish settlers from Brazil (Elul. 25:3). See Ḥeshvan 5:2.
4. Hodel, the daughter of Moses Kikinish, a wealthy Jew of Lemberg (Lwow), Poland, was martyred on September 21, 1710, after falsely confessing to blood-ritual charges in order to save the lives of other Jews.
5. The Congress for the Safeguarding of Non-Jewish Interests, which opened at Dresden, Germany, on September 10, 1882, was the first international conference assembled to promote anti-Semitism.
    The conference was attended by close to 300 delegates. They repre-sented anti-Semitic parties in Germany, Austria, Moravia, Hungary, and Russia.
6. The Jewish community of Shirvint (Sirvintos), Lithuania, was massa-cred by the Nazis on September 18, 1941.

ELUL 27

1. Third day of the Creation of the world. The waters were gathered together forming seas and oceans and dry land appeared. The earth brought forth grass and fruit-bearing trees (Gen. 1:9–12).
2. Jews of Frankfort on the Main, Germany, were expelled by Vincent Fettmilch on September 1, 1614.
    See Adar 20:4.
3. The General Assembly of New York passed a resolution on Septem-ber 23, 1737, that "persons of the Jewish religion be not admitted to vote for representatives in this colony."
4. British commissary officer Aaron Hart, who rode through the ancient

city gate of Montreal on September 8, 1760, at the time of the French surrender, was the first Jew known to have settled in Canada.

5. Rabbi Elhanan b. Samuel Ashkenazi, author of *Sidrei Taharah*, died on September 27, 1780 (DDD).
6. Rabbi Nathan Adler, kabbalist and rosh-yeshivah, author of *Mishnah de-Rabbi Natan*, died on September 17, 1800.
7. Rabbi Shalom Roke'aḥ founder of the hasidic dynasty of Belz, died on September 10, 1885.
8. Rabbi Zevi Benjamin Hirsch Auerbach, leader of Orthodox Jewry in Germany, author of *Berit Avraham*, died on September 30, 1872.
9. The ghetto of Zhitomir, Russia, was liquidated by the Nazis on September 19, 1941.
10. Germany captured Kiev, Russia, on September 19, 1941.
11. Jews of Kislovodsk, Russia, were massacred on September 9, 1942.

ELUL 28

1. Fourth day of the Creation of the world. God created the sun and the moon and the stars (Gen. 1:14–16).
2. Rabbi Baruch b. Isaac Albalia, disciple of Alfasi, died on September 18, 1126.
3. Czar Peter the Great of Russia entered the synagogue of Mstislavl, Poland, on September 13, 1708, and issued orders to hang 13 of his soldiers who had participated in anti-Jewish riots (Dubnow, *History of the Jews in Russia and Poland*, vol. 1, p. 248).
4. The first synagogue in South Africa, Tikvat Israel, was dedicated in Cape Town on September 15, 1849.
5. The forcible baptism on September 29, 1864, of Joseph di Michele Coen, a Jewish boy of Rome, stirred a wave of protests in many European countries.
6. Gedera, Palestine, was attacked by Arabs on September 12, 1901.
7. President Warren G. Harding, on September 21, 1922, signed a Joint Resolution of Congress expressing approval "of the establishment in Palestine of a National Home for the Jewish People."

ELUL 29

1. Fifth day of the Creation of the world. The Lord created all the living creatures which swarm in the waters and the fowl which fly above the earth (Gen. 1:20).
2. Rabbi Aryeh Leib Darshan and many leading Jews of Posen (Poznan), Poland, were imprisoned and tortured following blood-ritual charges made against them on September 5, 1736.
3. Jews of France were emancipated on September 28, 1791. France was the first European country to enact such liberal legislation.

   The anniversaries of the last day of the Jewish calendar reflect both the pathos and the hopefulness of Jewish history. The emancipation of the Jews of France (no. 3) heralded the dawn of a new era of freedom. A century and a half later, Europe was in the grip of Hitler, who swept away the progress made in 150 years of emancipation and threatened the extinction of the Jewish people (nos. 7, 9, 10). The very depth of Jewish tragedy set in motion counterforces which were to culminate in the creation of the State of Israel. The Jewish Brigade, fighting under its own flag (no. 11) ultimately became the backbone of the Haganah and other self-defense bodies which were to achieve independence for the Jews of Palestine.

4. Jews of Austria were barred from acquiring land by a law passed on October 2, 1853.
5. Jacob Lipschitz, Orthodox writer and biographer, died on October 2, 1921.
6. The founding of the Palestine Philharmonic Society was announced on September 20, 1933.
7. Germany occupied Miclec, Poland, on September 13, 1939, and massacred its entire Jewish population.
8. Hillel Zeitlin, religious philosopher, scholar and writer, was killed by the Nazis on September 11, 1942.
9. The ghetto of Stolin, Poland, the seat of the Karliner Ḥasidim, was liquidated on September 11, 1942, with the mass execution of its 11,000 Jewish residents.
10. The mass deportation of Jews from the ghetto of Warsaw, which was started on the eve of Tishah be-Av (Av 8:7), reached its climax 53 days later, on the eve of Rosh Ha-Shannah, September 11,1942, with the deportation of 90,000 Jews. During this period a total of 300,000 Jews were sent to extermination camps.
11. The establishment of a Jewish fighting force, recruited from the Jews of Palestine, was approved by Britain on September 17, 1944.

12. Alexander Ziskind Rabinowitz (Azar), Hebrew writer, died on September 7, 1945.
13. Remnants of the Jewish community of Plungyan (Plunge), Soviet Lithuania, consisting of 18 families, were pogromized, on September 14, 1948, by a mob inflamed by rumors of a ritual murder.

Civil Dates

JANUARY

1—Tevet 1:8; 1:9; 10:11; 13:1; 13:3; 14 :1; 14:2; 20:7; 20:8; 24:4; Shevat 3:1; 7:1; 10:1

2—Tevet 1:16; 4:5; 6:3; 10:16; 16:1; 20:6; 23:5; 25:3; 27:3; 28:8; 29:7; Shevat 2:2

3—Tevet 2:9; 9:8; 17:2; 26:7; 29:5

4—Tevet 13:6; 22:4; 25:2; 25:4; Shevat 1:5; 1:7; 4:1; 5:2; 9:1

5—Tevet 9:12; 13:7; 19:1; 20:11; 26:5; 28:5; Shevat 6:3

6—Tevet 24:2; 27:6; 29:10; Shevat 4:6

7—Tevet 6:4; 16:2; Shevat 8:3

8—Shevat 1:4; 7:2

9—Tevet 10:10; 10:12; 10:13; 11:4; 12:5; Shevat 3:5; 6:6; 19:1

10—Tevet 18:6; 22:2; 28:4; 28:9; Shevat 7:6

11—Tevet 14:8; 15:3; 18:3; Shevat 2:4; 5:8

12—Tevet 16:4; 18:5; 23:6; 26:6; Shevat 5:11; 6:5

13—Tevet 10:6; 12:8; 15:4; 19:6; 23:3; 23:4; 26:8; 29:4; Shevat 4:2; 7:5; 10:2

14—Tevet 23:1; Shevat 11:2; 12:6; 17:2; 23:3

15—Tevet 28:6

16—Tevet 24:5; Shevat 5:10; 7:3; 14:2

17—Tevet 23:10; 25:5; 26:2; 29:2; Shevat 5:4

18—Tevet 19:3; 23:7; 24:9; Shevat 3:7; 12:3; 18:4; 18:5

19—Tevet 18:7; 20:9; Shevat 3:7

20—Tevet 27:5; Shevat 2:5; 2:6; 3:3; 4:4; 17:6

21—Tevet 29:8; Shevat 6:1; 8:7; 13:5; 21:2; 21:5

22—Tevet 23:8; 27:1; Shevat 1:9; 5:7; 5:9; 6:4; 11:1; 11:4; 14:3; 16:2; 20:6; 21:6; Adar 2:2

23—Tevet 23:2; 26:3; Shevat 18:2; 23:8; 24:2; Adar 1:3

24—Tevet 23:9; 24:7; Shevat 1:6; 4:5; 7:4; 9:4; 10:3; 18:3; 18:6

25—Tevet 20:11; 24:8; Shevat 1:10; 5:5; 10:4; 15:4; 15:7; 17:5

26—Tevet 25:7; 28:3; Shevat 8:10; 12:5; 24:3; Adar 6:4

27—Tevet 27:2; 29:3; Shevat 8:9; 9:6; 22:3; Adar 1:2; 6:3
28—Tevet 27:7; Shevat 1:8; 2:3; 3:5; 10:6; 13:3; 13:6; 23:5; 24:4
29—Tevet 29:6; Shevat 10:7
30—Shevat 3:8; 3:9; 10:5; 13:4; Adar 10:1
31—Shevat 9:2

FEBRUARY

1—Shevat 8:5; 8:6; 12:1; 16:5; 21:7; 25:10; 29:4; Adar 1:14
2—Shevat 8:4; 15:6; 17:3; 21:1; 25:4; 27:9; 30:5; Adar 1:10; 6:5
3—Shevat 4:3; 5:1; 5:6; 13:7; 16:1; 23:6; 23:7; 25:1; 25:9; 28:9; 29:2; Adar 2:4
4—Shevat 8:8; 14:1; 17:1; 20:3; 21:3; 26:3; 28:6; 30:2
5—Shevat 9:3; 13:2; 18:1; 18:8; 20:2; 30:3
6—Shevat 12:4; 13:1; 24:12; 28:2; Adar 1:8; 4:4; 7:7; 7:14
7—Shevat 9:5; 15:3; 29:1; Adar 2:7; 4:3; 7:16
8—Shevat 19:2; 25:3; 29:5; Adar 3:6; 7:12
9—Shevat 12:2; 15:5; 16:3; 23:2; 27:7; Adar 1:19; 7:15
10—Shevat 16:7; 17:4; 24:8; 25:5; Adar 3:7
11—Shevat 24:4; 26:2; 28:4; Adar 1:4; 2:5; 10:9; 22:1
12—Shevat 19:4; 29:6; Adar 7:11; 13:7
13—Shevat 19:3; 24:7; 24:9; 27:5; Adar 2:1; 4:8; 6:9; 8:5; 14:11
14—Shevat 15:8; 16:6; 27:8; 30:1; 30:4; Adar 5:1; 8:2; 10:3; 14:3
15—Shevat 20:5; 24:6; 27:4; Adar 14:9
16—Shevat 22:6; 24:10; 28:5; Adar 6:12; 11:4; 15:3; 15:6; 28:3
17—Shevat 18:7; 27:6; Adar 11:13; 11:14; 24:4
18—Shevat 29:3; Adar 1:22; 6:6; 11:2; 12:5; 14:8; 18:3; 18:6
19—Shevat 22:2; 22:5; 27:1; Adar 1:6; 2:6; 4:9; 6:11; 16:3; 22:2
20—Shevat 23:10; 23:11; 26:1; Adar 1:7; 1:9; 1:18; 4:6; 6:7; 12:11; 13:8
21—Shevat 28:3; 29:7; Adar 3:10; 7:8; 14:15; 16:5; 19:1; 20:12; 22:3
22—Shevat 24:11; 25:6; 27:2; 27:3; 28:8; Adar 5:4; 12:10; 13:4; 13:5; 16:10; 17:6; 20:8
23—Shevat 25:2; Adar 11:3; 11:10; 13:6; 16:10; 20:6
24—Shevat 25:7; 30:6; Adar 7:18; 8:7; 17:3; 22:6; 23:5
25—Shevat 28:7; Adar 8:12; 24:2
26—Adar 8:4; 8:11; 9:2; 24:1
27—Adar 1:5; 7:9; 7:13; 10:12; 17:4; 20:11; 22:9
28—Adar 1:15; 4:7; 12:4; 18:1; 18:2; 25:7; 25:13; 26:2; 29:3
29—Adar 2:9

MARCH

1—Adar 10:2; 11:5; 11:11; 12:8; 14:12; 15:5; 18:7; 18:14; 21:1; 24:9
2—Adar 13:9; 16:11; 20:5
3—Adar 4:2; 9:4; 14:13; 15:2; 18:4; 18:12; 28:6
4—Adar 1:21; 3:3; 3:8; 3:9; 8:1; 10:5; 10:11; 11:6; 25:10; 27:10; 28:2; 28:5; 28:9
5—Adar 1:11; 1:12; 7:17; 11:12; 14:7; 18:13; 20:3; 25:8; Nisan 3:1
6—Adar 6:8; 8:3; 21:3; 23:4; 26:5; 27:11; 29:2
7—Adar 3:2; 3:4; 3:5; 6:14; 10:10; 12:9; 14:6; 27:3; 29:6; 30:1
8—Adar 5:3; 5:5; 10:4; 11:9; 16:12; 20:9; 24:10; 27:4
9—Adar 2:8; 8:8; 18:10; 25:4; 26:1; 29:9
10—Adar 1:17; 2:10; 4:5; 9:6; 14:5; 16:2; 20:4; 23:7; 27:13; 27:14; 29:1
11—Adar 1:20; 8:9; 10:8; 21:2; 27:8; 30:2
12—Adar 2:3; 10:7; 16:6; 22:8; 23:9; 28:4; Nisan 9:3
13—Adar 6:10; 9:3; 16:4; 29:7; Nisan 10:4
14—Adar 14:4; 15:8; 25:2; 27:18; Nisan 2:5
15—Adar 8:6; 8:10; 9:7; 19:4; 24:8; 24:11; Nisan 9:2
16—Adar 10:6; 18:11; 21:6; 22:7; 27:15; 29:4; Nisan 5:5; 7:1
17—Adar 6:13; 14:10; 18:5
18—Adar 7:19; 11:8; 23:6; Nisan 2:4; 9:1
19—Adar 12:7; 24:5; 24:12; 25:6; 28:7; Nisan 6:6; 15:15
20—Adar 16:9; 19:6; 29:8; Nisan 1:15; 9:10
21—Adar 11:7; 12:6; 16:7; 17:8; 29:5; Nisan 1:11; 6:5; 9:11; 14:7; 16:10
22—Adar 18:8; 20:10; 24:3; Nisan 4:4; 5:4
23—Adar 15:4; 21:5; 22:5; 22:10; 25:12; 27:12; Nisan 1:12; 5:9; 6:3; 7:4; 8:7;
    15:14
24—Adar 14:14; 22:4; 27:5; 28:8; Nisan 5:2; 11:3; 11:4; 13:5; 19:15
25—Adar 16:8; 21:8; 23:8; 25:11; Nisan 6:1; 7:2; 8:6; 9:14; 10:8; 13:4
26—Adar 17:5; 21:4; 25:9; 27:19; Nisan 9:5; 9:9; 23:2
27—Adar 25:5; 26:7; 28:10; Nisan 1:17; 3:6; 6:8; 9:7; 12:4; 13:11; 14:12; 25:3
28—Adar 17:7; 18:9; 19:2; Nisan 1:14; 1:18; 4:1; 4:7; 5:6; 9:8; 10:9; 16:11; 20:3
29—Adar 17:9; Nisan 9:6; 13:6; 13:8; 14:10; 16:13; 17:7; 18:3; 19:4
30—Adar 20:7; Nisan 2:3; 14:6; 14:15; 19:12
31—Adar 24:6; 24:7; 26:3; 27:7; 27:9; 28:11; Nisan 2:2; 3:2; 3:3; 4:3; 6:7; 7:7;
    16:19; 17:6; 20:8

APRIL

1—Adar 21:7; 29:10; Nisan 2:6; 5:8; 7:6; 12:5; 13:10; 17:4; 21:13; Iyar 1:6
2—Adar 26:4; Nisan 2:7; 4:2; 5:11; 7:5; 10:7; 16:12; 18:4; 19:10
3—Adar 17:2; Nisan 1:13; 4:9; 6:4; 9:4; 10:5; 13:9; 15:18; 17:2; 22:9; 30:2

4—Adar 27:6; 27:17; Nisan 12:6; 16:18
5—Nisan 4:6; 5:7; 8:4; 11:2; 27:1; Iyar 2:4
6—Adar 26:6; Nisan 1:16; 3:4; 3:7; 3:8; 5:10; 6:2; 9:12; 9:13; 20:5
7—Nisan 11:5
8—Nisan 11:10; 19:3; 21:10; 25:5
9—Nisan 1:19; 11:7; 17:5; 21:11; 26:5; 28:3; 30:1
10—Nisan 1:20; 14:8; 19:10; 21:9; 21:11; 23:6; 25:2; 29:9; Iyar 1:9
11—Nisan 3:5; 8:5; 12:3; 14:16; 19:17; 20:9; 24:5; 25:12; 28:5; 30:5; Iyar 11:5
12—Nisan 10:6; 15:20; 21:14; 27:7; 29:7; Iyar 2:6; 4:4
13—Nisan 4:8; 7:3; 8:2; 16:15; 22:5; Iyar 3:3
14—Nisan 8:3; 21:15; 21:16; 22:8
15—Nisan 6:9; 18:6; 27:3; 28:7; Iyar 2:9; 4:6; 12:3
16—Nisan 15:17; 16:17; 18:8; 25:7; 29:5; 29:6; Iyar 3:1; 5:5
17—Nisan 11:6; 11:8; 14:9; 19:7; 26:4; 28:2
18—Nisan 19:16; 22:4; 26:3; Iyar 1:7; 4:2
19—Nisan 10:10; 14:13; 14:14; 16:14; 18:7; 19:14; 21:6; 21:7; 22:7; 24:6; 25:4; 25:8; 27:6; 29:2; 30:6; Iyar 4:3; 6:1; 6:11; 7:9
20—Nisan 13:7; 15:16; 15:21; 17:3; 19:11; 28:9; 29:1; Iyar 1:10; 2:7; 3:9; 6:3; 7:5; 7:8; 10:4
21—Nisan 16:16; 25:6; 25:10; Iyar 4:1; 5:1; 8:7
22—Nisan 13:12; 14:11; 20:4; 20:7; 23:3; 23:8; Iyar 1:5; 3:8; 4:12
23—Nisan 15:19; 15:22; 24:3; 29:8; 30:4; Iyar 6:2; 11:6
24—Nisan 15:23; 19:15; 19:16; 28:8; Iyar 4:10; 6:6; 6:12; 6:13; 7:7; 10:5; 10:8; 20:2
25—Nisan 22:6; 25:9; 26:6; 28:11; 29:3; Iyar 2:2; 6:14
26—Nisan 18:5; 19:5; 19:8; 23:4; 25:11; 30:8; Iyar 4:7; 9:1; 14:2
27—Nisan 19:6; 20:6; 24:7; 28:6; Iyar 3:7; 4:9; 5:4; 17:9
28—Iyar 2:3; 5:8; 15:8
29—Nisan 28:10; Iyar 2:12; 14:3; 16:14; 17:6; 18:6
30—Nisan 22:10; 24:4; 26:7; Iyar 3:2; 5:3; 7:6

MAY

1—Nisan 23:5; 24:2; Iyar 4:8; 5:7; 13:8; 16:12; 18:3; 19:8
2—Nisan 23:7; 27:2; 30:7; Iyar 1:8; 4:5; 6:7; 10:9; 14:1; 20:7; Sivan 4:4
3—Nisan 26:2; 27:4; 30:3; Iyar 6:5; 8:1; 8:4; 10:15; 12:5; 16:5; 16:7; 17:5; 19:7; 22:2; 25:4
4—Iyar 11:14; 12:7
5—Nisan 26:9; 27:5; 28:4; Iyar 6:4; 6:8; 6:10; 10:6; 16:6; 16:13; 19:3; 19:4; 24:1
6—Iyar 11:8; 11:10; 26:3

7—Nisan 29:4; Iyar 9:2; 11:7; 15:6; 16:11; 20:9; 22:4; 22:9; 24:4; 25:3
8—Iyar 3:12; 5:6; 11:4; Sivan 7:4
9—Iyar 2:5; 3:4; 10:11; 12:4; 17:8; 20:8; Sivan 3:6
10—Iyar 1:11; 2:8; 3:10; 5:2; 6:9; 9:4; 11:9; 13:1; 13:2; 14:4; 15:5; 17:4; 21:1; 27:7
11—Iyar 2:10; 2:11; 3:6; 3:11; 9:3; 12:8; 14:10; Sivan 2:2; 10:4
12—Iyar 3:13; 7:10; 17:7; 29:3; Sivan 5:10; 6:8
13—Iyar 4:11; 8:3; 8:5; 10:13; 11:18; 11:19; 18:7; 18:12; 28:3; Sivan 1:8; 1:10
14—Iyar 5:9; 5:10; 5:11; 5:12; 5:13; 13:3; 17:10; 20:3; 24:3
15—Iyar 6:15; 6:16; 6:17; 10:14; 16:8; 16:15; 20:4; 20:5; 20:11; 22:10; 26:7; 28:10; Sivan 1:11
16—Iyar 7;12; 7:13; 8:6; 10:10; 11:12; 11:13; 20:6; 26:1; 29:4; Sivan 3:5; 3:7; 4:3; 7:10; 7:15
17—Nisan 23:1; Iyar 8:8; 8:9; 9:8; 19:2; 23:6; 25:7; 26:5; 27:9; 28:6; 28:8; Sivan 5:13; 7:17; 9:2
18—Iyar 9:5; 9:6; 9:7; 10:12; 13:6; 16:10; 18:5; 22:7; 23:4; 26:6; Sivan 4:2; 18:1
19—Iyar 10:16; 10:17; 14:5; 28:5; Sivan 3:12; 5:12; 7:14
20—Iyar 11:15; 11:16; 11:17; 13:4; 19:5; 26:8; 28:7; Sivan 7:16; 11:1
21—Iyar 11:11; 12:6; 16:9; 18:8; Sivan 2:3; 5:7; 12:3
22—Iyar 12:9; 13:7; 15:7; 21:3; 22:8; 26:2; Sivan 5:6; 5:14; 7:9
23—Iyar 14:6; 14:7; 14:8; 14:9; 25:2; 26:9; 29:5; 29:7; Sivan 4:6; 9:5; 10:3; 11:7; 14:3
24—Iyar 15:9; Sivan 6:12; 7:7; 10:8
25—Iyar 19:6; 22:5; 25:5; 25:6; Sivan 1:5; 1:6; 4:5; 4:8; 5:11; 7:13
26—Iyar 21:2; 23:5; 23:7; 27:2; Sivan 6:9; 7:8; 13:7; 20:1
27—Iyar 18:9; 18:10; Sivan 1:7; 3:4; 7:6; 12:5; 13:2; 24:2
28—Iyar 19:9; 19:10; 19:11; 22:3; 26:4; 27:6; Sivan 6:10; 6:15; 10:2; 12:6; 14:4; 19:3
29—Iyar 20:10; 22:6; 24:2; Sivan 4:9; 5:5; 8:8; 11:3; 13:8; 19:4; 21:2
30—Iyar 25:1; Sivan 6:7; 8:1; 10:1; 10:9; 12:2
31—Iyar 7:4; 28:11; 29:6; Sivan 9:8; 13:6; 15:10; 24:1

JUNE

1—Iyar 23:10; 27:4; 29:8; Sivan 2:4; 6:14; 8:3; 30:1
2—Iyar 24:6; 24:7; 27:5; Sivan 7:5; 10:5; 11:5; 23:6
3—Sivan 13:3; 13:12; 15:7; 15:9; 18:4; 24:3
4—Sivan 1:9; 4:7; 9:4; 9:7; 11:2; 17:5; Tammuz 1:4
5—Iyar 12:1; 26:10; 27:8; Sivan 7:11; 10:6; 13:4; 14:9; 15:8; 19:1; 20:4
6—Iyar 27:10; 27:11; 28:9; Sivan 7:18; 15:5; 16:3; 17:3; 27:7; Tammuz 6:3
7—Iyar 28:12; 28:13; 29:9; Sivan 8:4; 12:4; 15:4; 18:2; 23:5; Tammuz 8:3

8—Iyar 29:10; Sivan 4:11; 5:9; 9:6; 14:1; 15:6; 18:3
9—Iyar 16:4; Sivan 1:12; 1:13; 5:8; 6:13; 8:5; 17:8; 19:2; 27:8; Tammuz 4:1
10—Sivan 2:5; 3:9; 3:10; 3:11; 7:12; 13:5; 20:3; 21:3; 21:6; 27:14; Tammuz 1:8
11—Sivan 3:13; 4:10; 8:7; 9:3; 12:7; 16:4; 22:5; 26:7
12—Sivan 4:12; 10:7; 21:4; 22:2; 25:7
13—Sivan 6:16; 6:17; 11:6; 12:9; 13:11; 14:8; 22:1; 29:2; Tammuz 12:2; 14:5
14—Sivan 8:6; 11:4; 14:7; 22:3; 22:4; 26:1; Tammuz 5:7
15—Sivan 8:2; Tammuz 8:4; 10:3
16—Sivan 22:7; 25:4; 26:5; 26:6; Tammuz 8:5
17—Sivan 13:10; 17:7; 25:5; 27:10
18—Sivan 19:5; 21:5; 23:3; Tammuz 5:6
19—Sivan 12:8; 15:11; Tammuz 2:3; 4:3; 4:4; 7:1; 10:5; 18:2
20—Sivan 13:9; Tammuz 1:6; 4:7; 5:6; 5:10; 11:1; 14:4; 17:9; 17:10; 21:1; 21:3
21—Sivan 14:10; 18:5; 18:6; 27:11; Tammuz 1:5; 5:5; 9:3
22—Iyar 29:2; Sivan 17:4; 27:12; 29:4; Tammuz 7:6; 8:9; 9:4; 17:7; 17:11
23—Sivan 17:6; 23:4; 25:6; 28:4; 28:5; Tammuz 1:3; 8:1; 12:1
24—Sivan 14:6; 26:4; 27:5; 27:6; 28:3; 29:3; 29:6; 29:7; 29:8; 30:2; Tammuz 4:6; 12:5; 13:1; 27:2
25—Sivan 23:10; 23:11; 24:4; 30:4; Tammuz 2:1; 3:4; 4:2; 14:2; 14:3; 22:2
26—Sivan 18:7; Tammuz 1:7; 1:11; 1:12; 5:4; 5:11; 6:9; 13:3
27—Sivan 22:6; Tammuz 2:2; 2:5; 2:6; 17:15
28—Sivan 20:5; Tammuz 1:9; 3:7; 5:3; 8:6; 13:10
29—Sivan 26:2; 29:5; 30:5; Tammuz 4:9; 4:10; 6:2; 27:3
30—Sivan 23:8; 23:9; 26:3; 29:9; 30:3; Tammuz 4:5; 13:4; 15:13; 18:3; 19:3; 22:1

JULY

1—Sivan 9:1; 23:9; Tammuz 3:5; 4:8; 6:10; 6:11; 6:12; 14:7; 15:5; 15:12; 22:7; 22:10; 23:7; 25:1
2—Sivan 27:9; Tammuz 2:4; 6:7; 7:4; 7:5; 10:7; 13:2; 13:6; 15:9; 15:11; 16:4; 23:8; 24:3
3—Tammuz 8:2; 8:8; 13:5; 20:4; 24:6; 24:7; 25:3; 28:2
4—Tammuz 5:12; 6:5; 6:6; 6:8; 6:14; 14:9; 15:2; 17:8; 17:12; 17:14; 17:16; 21:10; 28:1; 28:3
5—Tammuz 7:2; 10:10; 19:9; 20:9; Av 1:6; 5:1
6—Tammuz 7:3; 13:8; 19:7; 21:11
7—Tammuz 1:10; 6:4; 7:8; 12:7; 12:8; 15:4; 18:4; 20:3; 21:6; 21:14; 23:11; 24:11; Av 1:9; 2:3; 10:5
8—Tammuz 5:9; 12:3; 13:7; 13:9; 15:7; 17:18; 20:2; 21:7; 23:4; Av 1:8; 2:4
9—Tammuz 2:7; 10:8; 18:8; 21:9; 22:6; 23:6; 24:4; 26:4

10—Tammuz 3:9; 5:8; 11:4; 12:4; 18:9; 29:5; Av 5:2; 9:10
11—Tammuz 4:11; 4:12; 4:13; 4:14; 9:6; 16:3; 16:7; 17:13; 20:8; 27:8; 28:5
12—Tammuz 11:2; 17:17; 19:8; 22:5; 23:3; Av 2:6; 5:8
13—Tammuz 6:13; 12:6; 19:2; 21:4; 21:13; 22:9; 24:2; 28:9; 29:1
14—Tammuz 7:7; 15:10; 19:11; 19:12; 20:1; 25:5; 27:7; Av 8:3
15—Tammuz 8:7; 9:5; 10:6; 14:8; 14:10; 16:6; 19:5; 20:6; 20:7; 23:1; 27:1; 27:5;
    Av 5:3
16—Tammuz 10:4; 14:6; 15:3; 15:8; 24:1; Av 2:8; 2:9; 7:4; 15:8
17—Tammuz 10:9; 15:6; 19:6; 21:2; 29:12; Av 2:5; 14:2
18—Tammuz 11:3; 19:4; 23:7; 23:9; 28:4; 29:9; Av 1:14; 9:9
19—Tammuz 10:5; 12:9; 18:5; 29:13; Av 10:6; 12:2
20—Tammuz 20:10; 21:12; 23:10; 25:2; 25:4; 27:6; Av 4:4; 12:1; 13:2
21—Tammuz 17:19; 19:10; 22:4; 26:5; 27:10; Av 9:11; 12:3
22—Tammuz 16:5; 24:5; 29:3; 29:8; Av 3:1; 6:3; 7:5; 8:7; 11:8; 19:1; 24:2
23—Tammuz 18:7; 28:8; Av 8:5; 9:14; 9:17; 10:11; 13:1; 14:1; 22:1; 25:1
24—Tammuz 27:4; 28:7; 29:11; Av 4:8; 5:4; 8:2; 10:15; 14:4; 15:13; 16:1
25—Tammuz 3:2; 19:13; 21:5; 22:8; 28:6; Av 1:7; 8:4; 9:23; 11:2; 13:5; 17:4
26—Tammuz 5:2; 21:8; Av 2:2; 2:7; 4:2; 9:16; 10:8; 10:10; 15:11
27—Tammuz 6:1; 22:3; 24:10; Av 6:1; 8:8; 13:4; 13:7; 16:2
28—Tammuz 20:5; 23:5; 26:1; Av 4:6; 4:7; 5:5; 9:15; 9:21; 10: 4; 10:13; 14:7
29—Tammuz 24:8; 24:9; 26:2; 29:2; Av 3:3; 3:5; 15:14; Elul 4:3
30—Tammuz 25:6; 26:6; 27:9; 29:6; Av 21:5; 22:3
31—Tammuz 26:3; Av 1:11; 1:12; 7:6; 9:13; 18:6

AUGUST

1—Av 4:5; 9:18; 9:19; 9:25; 12:5; 18:4; 21:4; 21:6
2—Av 1:13; 3:2; 9:12; 9:27; 10:9; 11:4; 13:6; 21:7
3—Tammuz 29:7; Av 10:7; 11:6; 17:8; 22:5; 26:4
4—Tammuz 29:10; Av 3:4; 10:14; 11:7; 14:3; 20:2; 21:10; 24:4; Elul 1:9
5—Av 9:8; 11:1; 11:3; 17:6; 20:3; Elul 4:1
6—Av 6:2; 20:6; 24:6; Elul 1:5
7—Av 5:10; 14:6; 19:5
8—Tammuz 17:5; 17:6; Av 5:7; 9:22; 9:26; 15:9; 18:4; 26:1
9—Av 4:9; 5:6; 5:9; 15:12; 18:2; 26:6
10—Av 7:3; 16:3; 26:3; 28:5; Elul 4:2; 9:4
11—Av 9:28; 10:12; 19:2; 21:2; 22:7;
12—Av 7:7; 12:4; 13:3; 19:4; 21:11;
13—Av 4:3; 9:24; 11:11; 16:4; 18:3; 21:1; 24:8; Elul 8:3; 11:3
14—Av 8:6; 12:7; 17:5; Elul 1:13; 2:2; 4:7; 4:8
15—Av 11:5; 22:6; 23:1; 27:2; Elul 5:1; 5:3; 6:4; 9:9; 15:1

16—Av 11:9; 11:10; 15:15; 20:4; 24:3; 25:3; 28:3; 29:4; Elul 1:12; 3:5
17—Av 12:6; 14:5; 28:4; Elul 3:2; 9:5
18—Av 25:9; 27:1; 28:7; Elul 5:7
19—Av 18:5; 25:8; Elul 2:4; 12:1
20—Av 21:3; 21:8; Elul 6:6; 8:7; 10:2; 10:5
21—Av 17:3; 19:3; 24:7; 26:2; 29:6; 30:5; Elul 2:1; 3:3; 8:2
22—Av 2:1; 22:4; 25:4; 28:2; Elul 2:5; 3:1; 4:5; 7:5; 9:6; 17:4; 19:2
23—Av 17:7; 26:5; 30:3; Elul 5:4; 11:2
24—Av 23:2; Elul 1:6; 1:11; 9:3; 9:7; 11:8; 13:1; 18:7
25—Elul 8:4; 16:9; 19:1
26—Av 25:5; 29:7; Elul 13:6; 13:7; 16:5
27—Elul 4:9
28—Av 24:5; 25:7; 29:3; Elul 10:3; 26:3
29—Av 9:5; 25:6; Elul 1:10; 14:3; 15:6; 20:2; 24:4
30—Av 10:3; Elul 2:7; 11:4; 14:8
31—Av 29:5; 29:8; Elul 3:4; 5:5; 11:1; 16:6; 22:6

SEPTEMBER

1—Av 28:6; Elul 5:6; 9:2; 9:12; 9:13; 9:14; 9:15; 17:9; 18:6; 19:4; 24:5; 27:2
2—Av 29:2; 30:4; Elul 8:6; 13:4; 20:6;
3—Elul 9:10; 11:6; 15:8; 19:5; 19:7; 19:8; 20:7; 20:8; 21:1; 21:2
4—Elul 10:4; 16:1; 18:5; 20:5; 23:2; 24:11
5—Elul 2:6; 4:4; 5:2; 7:6; 7:7; 9:11; 9:16; 13:5; 17:10; 21:7; 29:2
6—Elul 7:9; 14:5; 14:6; 15:2; 22:4; 24:10
7—Elul 4:6; 15:5; 17:5; 17:6; 23:4; 25:3; 25:4; 29:12; Tishri 3:6; 10:14
8—Elul 6:5; 7:10; 14:2; 14:7; 15:7; 16:8; 18:10; 19:3; 21:4; 25:6; 27:4
9—Tishri 1:17; 1:26; 5:5; Av 20:1; Elul 6:8; 9:8; 27:11
10—Tishri 6:2; Elul 7:8; 8:5; 26:5; 27:7
11—Tishri 1:21; 1:22; 1:27; Elul 6:7; 11:7; 19:9; 29:8; 29:9; 29:10
12—Tishri 1:20; 1:24; 1:28; 3:5; 4:6; 7:4; Elul 13:2; 16:4; 18:9; 28:6
13—Tishri 1:18; 2:11; 5:3; Elul 11:5; 17:11; 21:3; 29:7
14—Tishri 6:4; Elul 10:6; 16:3; 18:8; 22:3; 22:5; 29:13
15—Tishri 2:7; 3:7; 6:1; Elul 17:7; 17:8; 22:1; 23:5; 23:6; 24:8; 24:9; 28:4
16—Tishri 6:5; 12:3; Elul 24:7
17—Tishri 8:4; 10:15; Elul 13:8; 14:4; 15:9; 16:2; 18:4; 20:1; 21:6; 22:2; 27:6;
   29:11
18—Tishri 1:25; 13:5; Elul 15:4; 21:5; 23:3; 26:6; 28:2
19—Tishri 2:5; 3:8; 6:6; 10:13; 15:6; Elul 16:7; 20:3; 27:9; 27:10
20—Tishri 3:3; 11:6; 16:10; Elul 29:6
21—Tishri 1:19; 2:8; 5:4; 10:16; 25:1; Elul 24:6; 26:2; 26:4; 28:7

22—Tishri 1:16; 1:23; 1:29; 8:5; 11:5; 29:3; Elul 20:4; 25:7
23—Tishri 2:10; 4:2; 9:9; Elul 23:7; 27:3
24—Tishri 4:3; 4:4; 9:6; 13:9; 14:4
25—Tishri 2:4; 12:4; 13:6; 19:5; Elul 25:5
26—Tishri 5:6; 12:9; 27:2
27—Tishri 15:13; 21:6; 23:6; Elul 8:1; 27:5
28—Tishri 4:5; 7:6; 14:5; 15:10; 18:6; 28:3;
29—Tishri 16:4; 16:12; 19:10; 25:2; Elul 28:5
30—Tishri 8:3; 9:10; 9:11; 10:18; 10:21; 12:10; 19:9; 22:6; 22:7; 23:5; Elul 27:8

OCTOBER

1—Tishri 9:8; 15:7; 15:12; 16:6; 25:3
2—Tishri 3:9; 9:7; 10:17; 11:8; 14:3; 19:8; 28:2; Elul 29:4; 29:5
3—Tishri 4:7; 4:8; 7:5; 7:8; 12:8; 16:5; 17:3; 25:5; 27:3
4—Tishri 2:9; 3:4; 6:3; 10:19; 12:5; 13:7; 14:9; 25:13; 27:4; Ḥeshvan 19:1
5—Tishri 14:11; 14:12; 24:5; 25:4; 29:2;
6—Tishri 10:24; 11:4; 18:5; 18:9; 23:9
7—Tishri 10:23; 12:6; 20:4; 21:8; 22:4; 24:2; 25:8
8—Tishri 20:2; 23:8; 25:9; Ḥeshvan 12:1
9—Tishri 6:7; 10:22; 13:3; 13:10; 19:4; 25:14; Ḥeshvan 3:2; 3:6; 9:3
10—Tishri 7:7; 10:20; 11:7; 14:7; 15:14; Ḥeshvan 5:4; 5:11; 6:4
11—Tishri 16:13; 25:6; Ḥeshvan 11:4
12—Tishri 13:4; 16:8; 21:4; 21:11; 28:6; 29:5; 30:2; Ḥeshvan 2:2; 4:1; 6:1
13—Tishri 16:9; 17:7; 18:8; 19:6; 20:5; 21:10; 22:5; 26:2; Ḥeshvan 1:4; 8:2; 8:3;
     12:3; 22:2
14—Tishri 11:9; 15:16; 18:10; 18:12; 19:11; 30:5; Ḥeshvan 1:5; 8:10
15—Tishri 14:6; 15:11; 16:7; 19:3; 24:3; 24:4; Ḥeshvan 2:5; 6:2; 10:3; 23:2
16—Tishri 13:8; 14:10; 15:8; 16:11; 17:4; 17:6; 20:6; 21:13; 25:7; 25:11;
     Ḥeshvan 5:5; 7:7; 11:6; 16:11
17—Tishri 15:9; 18:3; 21:7; 26:3; 28:1; Ḥeshvan 4:2; 4:5; 5:7; 9:1; 12:9
18—Tishri 14:8; 15:17; 17:5; 18:7; 19:7; Ḥeshvan 1:3; 11:10
19—Tishri 17:2; Ḥeshvan 3:4; 6:6; 10:7; 12:2; 12:4; 14:4
20—Tishri 21:12; 25:12; 28:5; 29:7; Ḥeshvan 1:6; 15:7; 22:1; 24:1
21—Tishri 18:11; Ḥeshvan 2:3; 5:1; 5:8; 13:2
22—Tishri 19:12; 20:3; 23:7; 26:4; 26:7; Ḥeshvan 1:7; 9:6; 14:1; 15:4
23—Tishri 18:4; 21:5; 27:5; 27:8; Ḥeshvan 1:8; 2:6; 2:7; 3:7; 12:7; 13:3; 19:3;
     20:2
24—Tishri 28:4; 29:4; Ḥeshvan 3:3; 3:9; 4:4; 5:6; 11:9; 15:11; 17:10
25—Tishri 22:8; 26:5; Ḥeshvan 4:7; 9:2; 14:7; 17:5
26—Tishri 27:6; Ḥeshvan 1:9; 10:6; 10:8; 13:5; 13:6; 15:3; 20:5; 25:2

27—Tishri 24:6; 25:10 27:1; Ḥeshvan 7:2; 13:9
28—Ḥeshvan 2:8; 3:8; 6:3; 7:3; 7:4; 13:4; 15:9
29—Tishri 26:6; Ḥeshvan 4:9; 5:3; 8:9; 18:5; 19:5; 23:11; 24:7
30—Tishri 27:7; 30:4; Ḥeshvan 5:9; 8:8; 13:7; 13:8; 14:6; 19:6; 25:4; 26:1; 26:3
31—Tishri 29:6; Ḥeshvan 2:4; 3:5; 9:4; 11:5; 12:8; 15:5; 26:10; 26:11

NOVEMBER

1—Tishri 30:3; Ḥeshvan 8:7; 13:1; 22:5; 24:2; 27:6
2—Ḥeshvan 4:8; 10:9; 11:7; 16:3; 16:8; 17:4; 17:7; 17:8; 24:5; 28:8
3—Ḥeshvan 5:10; 7:1; 14:5; 20:4; 21:2; 24:4; 29:4; 29:6; Kislev 9:1
4—Ḥeshvan 6:7; 22:11; 30:5
5—Ḥeshvan 2:9; 3:10; 5:2; 7:5; 8:4; 11:8; 16:1; 16:4; 16:5; 20:3; 20:8; Kislev
    1:9; 1:10; 19:2
6—Ḥeshvan 4:6; 10:5; 11:11; 16:6; 16:7; 18:2; 20:7; 21:3; 26:8; 29:3
7—Ḥeshvan 8:6; 12:5; 18:3; 22:10; Kislev 1:5; 2:2; 3:5; 8:1; 12:1
8—Ḥeshvan 6:8; 16:9; 22:12; 27:2; 27:4; 29:1; 30:1
9—Ḥeshvan 6:5; 7:6; 8:5; 15:8; 16:2; 19:7; 21:1; 21:5; 22:3; 28:5; 29:5; Kislev
    4:2; 6:3
10—Ḥeshvan 9:5; 12:6; Kislev 5:3; 6:13; 7:5; 18:2
11—Ḥeshvan 10:4; 16:10; 20:6; 23:7; 23:9; 26:2; 26:4; 29:2
12—Ḥeshvan 14:2; 14:3; 15:6; 17:6; 18:4; 19:4; 23:6; 28:4; 30:4; Kislev 1:4;
    13:2
13—Ḥeshvan 18:1; 22:4; Kislev 1:6; 3:6; 9:7; 14:3
14—Ḥeshvan 22:8; 22:9; Kislev 5:8; 10:2; 11:5
15—Ḥeshvan 21:4; 22:7; 28:2; Kislev 2:3; 3:9; 23:1
16—Ḥeshvan 15:10; 23:5; 28:3; Kislev 1:8; 4:8; 11:8; 17:2; 20:2
17—Ḥeshvan 10:2; 21:6; 23:10; Kislev 1:3; 6:4; 10:7; 13:3
18—Ḥeshvan 17:9; 28:6; Kislev 6:11; 15:3; 19:1; 20:5; 24:5
19—Ḥeshvan 23:8; Kislev 1:12; 3:7; 6:1; 8:2; 9:3; 12:3
20—Ḥeshvan 19:2; 24:3; 26:7; 28:7; Kislev 1:11; 2:4; 2:7; 6:5; 6:8; 10:8; 11:7;
    17:4; 20:3
21—Ḥeshvan 22:6; 26:12; Kislev 6:6; 11:1; 12:5; 13:9; 16:2
22—Kislev 4:7; 5:4; 8:4; 10:3; 13:6; 18:3; 18:8
23—Ḥeshvan 23:4; 26:6; 27:3; 28:1; Kislev 3:4; 3:8; 3:10; 11:6; 13:5
24—Ḥeshvan 26:5; Kislev 4:9; 12:4; 14:6; 15:2
25—Ḥeshvan 24:6; 27:5; 30:3; Kislev 1:7; 5:12; 14:2; 14:4; 21:2; 21:3; 22:2;
    23:3; Tevet 3:1
26—Ḥeshvan 25:3; 30:2; Kislev 6:9; 6:10; 10:5; 19:3; 20:4; 26:3
27—Kislev 4:3; 9:5; 11:3; 11:4; 18:5; 19:4; 23:6; 26:4
28—Ḥeshvan 26:9; Kislev 5:11; 9:4; 12:6; 16:1; 16:4; 17:8; 22:6; 24:9

29—Kislev 2:8; 6:7; 8:3; 17:1; 17:11
30—Kislev 5:2; 10:4; 17:12; 22:5; 23:4; 28:2

DECEMBER

1—Kislev 4:4; 4:5; 6:12; 12:2; 17:6; 18:7; Tevet 1:7
2—Kislev 2:5; 9:2; 11:2; 21:6; 24:7; 26:5; 29:2
3—Kislev 6:2; 7:6; 17:10; 19:5; 25:15; 30:2; 30:3
4—Kislev 5:5; 5:6; 14:7; 22:1; 26:11; 26:12; Tevet 2:4
5—Kislev 3:11; 16:3; 18:4; 19:6; 23:2; 26:6; 29:2; Tevet 1:13
6—Kislev 4:6; 5:7; 7:9; 20:6; 22:8; 23:9; 24:3; 25:13; 25:16; 29:3; 29:4; Tevet 1:11; 12:2
7—Kislev 5:9; 5:10; 17:9; 18:1; Tevet 7:1
8—Kislev 17:3; 18:9; 21:4; 23:5; 23:8; 25:12
9—Kislev 7:8; 9:6; 10:1; 13:4; 16:5; 16:6; 18:11; 20:8; 24:10; 27:6; Tevet 7:3; 7:4
10—Kislev 22:11; 27:10; Tevet 6:5; 8:4
11—Kislev 18:6; 27:4; 27:11; Tevet 1:10
12—Kislev 10:6; 13:7; 13:8; 17:5; 17:7; 21:5; 22:9; 24:4; 25:7; 27:3; 29:5; Tevet 2:6; 5:2; 7:2; 17:1
13—Kislev 22:3; 22:10; Tevet 5:6; 20:1
14—Kislev 20:9; 25:9; 26:8; 27:8; 30:4; Tevet 1:14; 1:17; 4:7; 11:5
15—Kislev 15:4; 25:18; Tevet 2:8; 8:6; 11:1; 12:4; 12:6
16—Kislev 14:8; 25:20; 25:21; 26:9; 29:7; Tevet 4:6; 9:9; 14:3
17—Kislev 25:11; 29:8; 29:9; Tevet 2:3; 8:2; 17:4
18—Kislev 20:5; 25:10; Tevet 13:2; 18:1
19—Kislev 27:7; Tevet 9:10; 9:11; 15:1; 17:6; 20:2
20—Kislev 18:10; 27:5; 29:6; 29:10; Tevet 7:6; 9:5; 10:9; 15:2
21—Kislev 20:7; 21:7; 22:7; 24:6; 24:8; 26:15; 28:3; Tevet 14:6; 17:3
22—Kislev 24:13; 25:17; Tevet 2:2; 2:7; 3:2; 14:7; 20:3; 21:3
23—Kislev 25:8; 26:7; 28:4; Tevet 2:5; 18:2; 19:5
24—Kislev 24:12; Tevet 9:6; 9:13; 13:4
25—Kislev 23:7; 23:10; 25:6; 25:14; Tevet 3:3; 4:1; 6:2; 15:6; 25:1; 26:1
26—Kislev 24:11; Tevet 5:3; 8:3; 8:5; 10:7; 12:7; 14:5; 16:3; 20:10; Shevat 3:2; 6:2
27—Kislev 25:19; Tevet 9:7; 12:3; 13:5; 24:3; 25:6
28—Kislev 26:10; Tevet 7:5; 10:8; 11:6; 18:4; Shevat 8:2
29—Kislev 27:9; Tevet 5:5; 16:5; 19:7; 20:5; 21:2; 21:5; 24:6; 26:4
30—Tevet 4:2; 9:4; 10:14; 17:7; 17:8; 19:2; 28:7
31—Tevet 4:3; 5:4; 11:2; 15:5; 17:5; 19:4; 21:6; 27:4

Table of Years

76—Tammuz 14:1
63—Tammux 9:2
53—Kislev 26:2
19—Adar 12:1
4—Kislev 7:2

C.E.

37—Tevat 10:6
41—Shevat 22:1
42—Adar 16:1; Elul 7:2
65—Tishri 3:2; Sivan 14:1
66—Tishri 13:2; 26:1; 30:1; Heshvan 8:1; Adar 17:1; Iyar 16:3; Av 8:1; 17:1; Elul 6:1; 7:3; 7:4; 17:2; 17:3
67—Tishri 23:4; Iyar 7:3; Sivan 25:2; 27:2; Tammuz 1:2; Elul 24:3
68—Adar 4:1; Sivan 3:3; 5:4
70—Nisan 14:5; Iyar 7:4; 12:1; 16:4; 29:2; Sivan 9:1; Tammuz 1:3; 3:2; 5:2; 6:1; 17:5; 17:6; Av 2:1; 9:5; 10:3; 20:1; Elul 8:1
71—Av 9:7
73—Nisan 15:13
135—Tishri 9:1; 9:2; 9:3; Av 9:8
138—Av 15:7
331—Kislev 1:3
415—Tishri 28:1
418—Adar 16:2
429—Sivan 10:1
466—Tishri 11:4
468—Tevet 7:1
486—Tevet 18:1
499—Kislev 13:1
501—Av 22:1
506—Adar 4:2
511—Tishri 10:13
553—Adar 2:1
576—Sivan 4:2
636—Av 14:1
641—Heshvan 29:1
921—Tevet 11:1
942—Iyar 26:1
982—Tammuz 19:2
1012—Shevat 3:1
1013—Tishri 23:5
1021—Iyar 4:1

1033—Tevet 12:2
1038—Nisan 20:3
1066—Tevet 9:4
1090—Adar 16:3
1094—Nisan 19:3
1095—Kislev 26:3
1096—Iyar 8:1; 23:4; 25:1; Sivan 1:5; 1:6; 3:4; 5:5; 6:7; Tammuz 2:1; 5:3; 6:2
1099—Sivan 15:4; Tammuz 23:1; 24:1
1103—Iyar 10:4
1105—Kislev 15:2; Tammuz 29:1
1126—Elul 28:2
1135—Nisan 14:6
1141—Nisan 30:1
1144—Nisan 16:10
1147—Adar 24:1; Nisan 23:2; Sivan 7:4
1148—Tammuz 24:2
1158—Kislev 7:3
1164—Adar 1:2
1165—Heshvan 4:1; 9:1; Iyar 4:2; 10:5; Sivan 3:5
1171—Sivan 20:1; Tammuz 4:1
1181—Adar 25:2
1187—Tishri 28:2
1189—Elul 21:1; 21:2
1190—Shevat 28:2; Adar 27:3; Nisan 7:1; 9:1; 13:3
1197—Kislev 22:1; Adar 6:3
1198—Kislev 26:4; Sivan 24:1
1199—Tishri 8:3
1203—Iyar 3:1
1204—Tevet 20:1
1205—Tammuz 27:1
1209—Av 19:1
1210—Heshvan 13:1
1212—Av 15:8
1216—Tevet 6:1
1217—Adar 13:4
1221—Iyar 2:2; Sivan 25:4
1227—Tevet 9:5
1230—Tammuz 9:3
1235—Shevat 10:1
1236—Adar 21:1
1237—Kislev 18:1
1239—Tammuz 16:2

1240—Adar 7:6; Tammuz 4:2; Elul 3:1
1241—Sivan 14:2
1242—Tammuz 6:3
1244—Adar 26:1; Nisan 18:3; Tammuz 23:2
1247—Av 1:6
1250—Iyar 12:2
1253—Av 25:1
1255—Adar 27:4
1263—Heshvan 8:2; 8:3; Av 12:1; Elul 12:1
1264—Av 11:1
1265—Kislev 11:1
1266—Tammuz 10:3
1267—Tishri 1:16; Shevat 23:2; Iyar 13:1; Av 2:2; Elul 9:2
1269—Tammuz 18:2
1270—Heshvan 1:3; Nisan 11:2
1272—Heshvan 12:1; Av 14:2
1274—Av 2:3
1275—Iyar 25:2
1276—Adar 12:4
1277—Adar 28:2
1278—Heshvan 10:2; Shevat 9:1; Iyar 17:4; Av 14:3
1279—Nisan 18:4
1280—Iyar 28:2
1283—Nisan 2:2; 21:6; 21:7
1285—Heshvan 11:4
1286—Tammuz 4:3; 4:4
1288—Iyar 20:2
1290—Heshvan 3:2; Av 9:9
1291—Nisan 3:1; Sivan 18:1; Tammuz 21:1
1293—Iyar 19:1
1294—Tammuz 4:5
1295—Iyar 6:2; Tammuz 8:1
1296—Heshvan 22:1
1298—Heshvan 12:2; Iyar 7:5; Tammuz 12:1; 13:1; 14:2;
1299—Tammuz 12:2
1301—Elul 1:5
1302—Nisan 12:3
1303—Nisan 7:2
1305—Av 4:2
1306—Iyar 4:3; Av 10:4
1307—Tishri 10:14; Adar 4:3
1312—Tevet 25:1; Tammuz 17:7

1315—Av 25:2
1321—Tishri 2:4; Elul 2:1
1322—Sivan 27:5; Tammuz 27:2
1327—Heshvan 9:2
1328—Adar 23:4
1334—Heshvan 9:3
1338—Shevat 23:3; Sivan 9:2
1340—Tammuz 12:3
1344—Iyar 6:3
1345—Av 5:1
1348—Kislev 23:1; Shevat 8:2; Elul 26:2
1349—Tishri 16:4; Kislev 17:1; 23:2; 24:3; Shevat 19:1; Adar 2:2; 10:1; 10:2; 14:3;
    22:1; 25:3; 28:3; Nisan 1:11; 14:7; Sivan 10:2; Tammuz 17:8; Av 8:2; Elul
    7:5; 9:3
1354—Tevet 9:6
1355—Iyar 25:3
1357—Kislev 22:2
1358—Av 10:5
1360—Av 11:2
1361—Adar 30:1
1366—Heshvan 6:1
1369—Tevet 26:1
1370—Heshvan 16:1; Iyar 26:2; Sivan 5:6
1375—Shevat 3:2
1379—Elul 8:2
1380—Kislev 17:2
1385—Av 10:6
1388—Tammuz 25:1
1389—Nisan 22:4
1391—Tishri 14:3; Nisan 9:2; Tammuz 1:4; 3:3; 17:9; 17:10; Av 7:2; Elul 1:6; 4:1;
    9:4
1392—Tishri 14:3
1393—Shevat 6:1; Iyar 29:3
1394—Tishri 10:15; Kislev 9:1; Elul 20:1
1396—Heshvan 20:2
1400—Elul 1:7
1401—Tammuz 14:3
1402—Iyar 12:3
1407—Heshvan 25:2; Iyar 25:4
1413—Adar 4:4
1415—Sivan 2:2
1420—Tevet 18:2; Sivan 10:3

1421—Nisan 9:3; 10:4; Sivan 10:4
1424—Shevat 6:2
1427—Iyar 13:2; Elul 21:3
1428—Shevat 17:1; 18:1
1430—Tishri 16:5; Shevat 7:1
1434—Adar 11:1
1435—Iyar 6:4
1439—Nisan 25:2; Av 9:11
1442—Shevat 21:1
1447—Elul 2:2
1450—Tishri 29:2
1451—Tishri 25:1; Adar 24:2
1453—Sivan 21:2; Tammuz 28:1; Elul 8:3
1454—Av 28:2
1461—Elul 4:2
1464—Nisan 27:1; Iyar 4:4; Tammuz 14:4
1466—Tevet 29:2; Shevat 3:3
1468—Ḥeshvan 5:1
1473—Adar 14:4
1474—Iyar 29:4
1475—Adar 11:2; Nisan 15:14; Tammuz 28:2
1476—Sivan 10:5
1477—Sivan 4:3; Elul 20:2
1497—Kislev 27:3
1480—Tishri 23:6
1481—Adar 7:7
1482—Adar 6:4
1483—Ḥeshvan 4:2; 12:3; Tevet 20:2
1484—Kislev 24:4; Shevat 17:2; Adar 6:5; Iyar 15:5
1485—Tishri 6:1; Ḥeshvan 6:2; Kislev 7:4; Tevet 21:2
1487—Tishri 3:3
1488—Tevet 15:1; Adar 6:6; 11:3; Nisan 13:4; Iyar 22:2; Av 22:3
1489—Kislev 24:5; Tevet 3:1; Tammuz 14:5; Av 24:2
1490—Adar 1:3; Nisan 1:12; Iyar 1:5; Tammuz 13:2
1491—Ḥeshvan 26:1; Kislev 23:3; Adar 1:4
1492—Tishri 21:4; Ḥeshvan 3:3; Tevet 11:2; Shevat 24:2; Nisan 2:3; 3:2; Iyar 3:2;
        11:4; Tammuz 8:2; Av 1:7; 9:12; 10:7
1493—Tishri 10:16; 14:4
1494—Tishri 28:3
1496—Kislev 29:2; Tevet 15:2; Adar 25:4; 28:4
1497—Kislev 5:1; 20:2; Nisan 15:15
1498—Tammuz 1:5; Elul 21:4

1503—Tevet 9:7; Adar 24:3
1505—Nisan 15:16; 25:3; Elul 1:8
1506—Nisan 25:4; Elul 11:1
1508—Tishri 29:3
1509—Tishri 14:5
1510—Iyar 11:5; Sivan 14:3; Av 1:8; 12:2
1514—Adar 1:5
1515—Tevet 14:1
1516—Kislev 3:2; Iyar 8:2
1517—Kislev 27:4
1518—Av 16:1
1519—Tevet 1:6; Tammuz 8:3
1521—Kislev 20:3
1523—Shevat 20:2; Sivan 14:4; Tammuz 13:3
1524—Tevet 17:1; Adar 28:5
1525—Adar 24:4; Sivan 22:1
1526—Kislev 4:2
1528—Nisan 28:2
1529—Sivan 13:2
1530—Tevet 2:2
1531—Tevet 8:2
1532—Kislev 8:1
1533—Av 27:1
1534—Iyar 28:3
1535—Sivan 24:2; Tammuz 27:3; Elul 15:1
1536—Sivan 17:3
1537—Nisan 16:11
1539—Adar 1:6
1540—Tishri 19:2; Sivan 6:8
1541—Ḥeshvan 4:3; Sivan 23:3; Av 15:9
1542—Tishri 27:1; Elul 11:2
1544—Nisan 10:5
1546—Shevat 10:2; Nisan 30:2
1548—Av 5:2
1549—Shevat 6:3; Tammuz 21:2
1550—Nisan 16:12
1551—Kislev 18:2; Elul 11:3
1552—Iyar 29:5
1553—Tishri 1:17; Ḥeshvan 13:2; Elul 2:3; 23:2
1555—Tishri 22:4; Ḥeshvan 19:1; Tammuz 23:3; Av 10:8; Elul 2:4
1556—Iyar 3:3; Tammuz 24:3; Elul 19:1
1557—Ḥeshvan 23:2; Iyar 1:6; Tammuz 22:1

1558—Ḥeshvan 1:4; Kislev 1:4; Av 20:2
1559—Tevet 25:2; Tammuz 17:11; Elul 19:2
1560—Adar 22:2; Nisan 14:8; Iyar 2:3
1563—Adar 20:3; Iyar 7:6; Elul 11:4
1564—Nisan 11:3
1565—Shevat 24:3; Adar 15:3
1566—Kislev 16:1
1567—Tammuz 8:4; 21:3
1569—Shevat 29:1; Adar 9:2
1570—Tishri 27:2; Shevat 3:4; Adar 11:4; Tammuz 22:2
1571—Ḥeshvan 21:1; Kislev 19:1; Av 9:13
1572—Iyar 18:3; Av 5:3
1573—Kislev 12:1; Shevat 24:4; Iyar 2:4
1575—Adar 18:1; Nisan 13:5; Tammuz 8:5
1576—Elul 4:3
1577—Iyar 1:7; 7:7; Sivan 5:7
1578—Kislev 13:2; Elul 1:9
1579—Av 10:9
1580—Nisan 2:4
1581—Kislev 3:3; Sivan 30:1
1582—Elul 16:1
1583—Shevat 27:1
1585—Kislev 22:3; Nisan 23:3
1588—Iyar 6:5; Sivan 7:5; 14:5
1589—Ḥeshvan 2:2; Adar 15:2
1590—Sivan 9:3; Elul 20:3
1591—Shevat 3:6
1592—Elul 9:5; 24:5
1593—Ḥeshvan 18:1; 28:1; Nisan 20:4; Iyar 29:6
1596—Tishri 10:17; Kislev 17:3; Shevat 21:2
1597—Tishri 1:18; Nisan 6:1
1598—Shevat 1:4
1599—Nisan 21:8; Av 25:3
1600—Tishri 5:3
1601—Adar 9:3
1605—Iyar 14:1
1606—Nisan 24:2
1608—Elul 13:1
1609—Elul 18:4
1610—Tevet 10:7; Nisan 4:1; Av 21:1; 23:1
1611—Kislev 1:5
1612—Adar 3:2; Tammuz 29:2

1613—Elul 8:4; 18:5
1614—Nisan 19:4; Av 8:3; Elul 27:2
1615—Kislev 11:2; Nisan 24:3; Iyar 27:2
1616—Ḥeshvan 15:3; 22:2; Adar 20:4; 29:1; Iyar 16:5
1617—Tishri 18:3
1618—Shevat 27:2; Tammuz 29:3
1619—Ḥeshvan 14:1; Tevet 5:2; Adar 7:8; Elul 5:1
1620—Nisan 30:3; Av 4:3
1621—Kislev 6:1
1622—Tishri 15:6; Kislev 22:4; Tevet 22:1
1624—Iyar 16:6; Sivan 12:2
1625—Tishri 21:5; Shevat 23:4; Elul 11:5
1626—Kislev 12:2; Av 9:14
1627—Tevet 13:1
1629—Tishri 26:2; Sivan 15:5; Tammuz 5:4
1630—Tishri 21:6; Nisan 11:4
1631—Kislev 5:2; Nisan 10:6
1632—Tevet 9:8; Nisan 29:1; Tammuz 15:2; 28:3
1633—Tishri 28:4; Av 13:2
1634—Tevet 5:3; Iyar 4:5
1636—Nisan 8:2; Iyar 8:3
1637—Tishri 4:2; Nisan 9:4; Iyar 20:3; 29:7; Tammuz 21:4
1638—Tevet 19:1
1639—Shevat 18:2; Tammuz 14:6; 26:1
1640—Shevat 13:1; Adar 20:5; 24:5; Tammuz 8:6
1641—Adar 5:1; Tammuz 1:6
1643—Ḥeshvan 21:2; Kislev 8:2; Adar 1:7; Elul 14:1
1644—Nisan 7:3; Tammuz 21:5
1645—Tishri 1:19; Nisan 11:5
1646—Tammuz 9:4
1647—Adar 1:8
1648—Tishri 5:4; 15:7; Ḥeshvan 17:4; Tevet 12:3; 19:3; 27:1; Adar 8:1; 27:5;
      Sivan 4:5; 20:3; 22:2; Tammuz 4:6; Av 3:1; 9:15; 28:3
1649—Kislev 19:2; Shevat 1:5
1651—Sivan 18:2
1652—Tevet 1:7; Adar 12:5
1654—Tishri 1:20; Tevet 29:3; Iyar 9:1; Tammuz 23:4; Elul 6:2; 9:6; 25:3
1655—Tishri 3:4; 14:6; 15:8; Ḥeshvan 5:2; Nisan 19:5
1656—Ḥeshvan 22:3; Shevat 10:3; 27:3; Adar 16:4; Sivan 22:3; Tammuz 3:4
1657—Kislev 20:4; Shevat 21:3; Iyar 7:8; 8:4
1658—Adar 20:6; 28:6

1659—Tishri 2:5; Tevet 2:3; Nisan 30:4
1660—Heshvan 10:3; Nisan 28:3
1661—Shevat 2:2; Tammuz 27:4
1662—Adar 1:9
1663—Elul 8:5
1664—Tevet 28:3; Iyar 10:6; Sivan 15:6
1665—Adar 16:5
1666—Nisan 27:2
1667—Shevat 26:1; 30:1; Iyar 8:4; Av 21:2
1668—Tishri 18:4; Kislev 21:2
1669—Nisan 15:17
1670—Adar 7:9; Nisan 29:2; Av 8:4; 9:16
1671—Tishri 6:2; Sivan 11:1; 12:3
1672—Sivan 9:4
1673—Adar 17:2; Nisan 17:2; Elul 19:3
1674—Shevat 24:5; Adar 8:2
1675—Av 24:3; Elul 15:2
1676—Tishri 10:18; Tevet 17:2; Tammuz 19:3
1677—Heshvan 24:1; Adar 19:1; 26:2
1678—Shevat 1:6; 13:2; Nisan 10:7; Sivan 13:3
1679—Tevet 12:4; Iyar 11:6; Sivan 7:6
1680—Iyar 9:2
1681—Nisan 15:18; Iyar 6:6
1682—Adar 2:3
1683—Tishri 4:3; Heshvan 4:4; Tammuz 20:1
1684—Tevet 9:9; Shevat 17:3; Elul 10:2
1685—Heshvan 8:4; Kislev 6:2; Adar 10:3; Elul 15:3
1686—Heshvan 28:2; Av 15:10
1687—Heshvan 12:4; Kislev 2:2; 5:3
1688—Kislev 4:3; Adar 23:5; Tammuz 12:4
1689—Shevat 21:4; Sivan 15:7; Tammuz 20:2
1690—Tevet 20:3; 21:3; Iyar 18:4; Av 1:9; 2:4
1692—Nisan 9:5; Iyar 5:1
1693—Nisan 24:4; Sivan 5:8
1694—Heshvan 28:3; Elul 2:5
1695—Tishri 3:5; Kislev 29:3; Elul 13:2
1696—Sivan 23:4
1697—Tishri 16:6; Sivan 6:9
1698—Iyar 4:6
1699—Adar 3:3; Sivan 27:6
1700—Heshvan 1:5; 4:5
1701—Nisan 19:6
1702—Kislev 3:4; Tevet 1:8

1703—Ḥeshvan 30:1; Iyar 17:5
1704—Kislev 24:6; Shevat 18:3
1705—Sivan 13:4
1706—Ḥeshvan 17:5; 24:2; Shevat 3:6
1707—Ḥeshvan 12:5
1708—Sivan 4:6
1709—Kislev 7:5
1710—Iyar 25:5; Elul 26:4
1711—Ḥeshvan 29:2; Tevet 23:1
1712—Kislev 10:1; Nisan 8:3; Iyar 3:4; Elul 16:2
1713—Tishri 4:4; Adar 14:5; Iyar 6:7
1714—Tevet 14:2; Nisan 7:4; 13:6
1715—Ḥeshvan 30:2; Elul 7:6
1716—Sivan 16:3; Tammuz 28:4; Av 5:4
1717—Nisan 30:5
1718—Tishri 19:3; Adar 1:10; 2:4; Iyar 1:8; Tammuz 22:4; Av 25:4
1719—Tevet 26:2; Nisan 9:6; 21:8; Tammuz 18:4; Av 10:10
1720—Ḥeshvan 8:5; 10:4; Nisan 15:19; Tammuz 10:4
1721—Nisan 8:4
1722—Nisan 9:7
1723—Sivan 5:9
1725—Tevet 17:3
1726—Iyar 13:3
1727—Kislev 2:3; Nisan 22:5; Iyar 15:6; Sivan 21:3
1728—Tevet 17:4; 28:4; Iyar 1:9; Sivan 5:10
1729—Shevat 4:1; Adar 22:3; Sivan 13:5; Elul 14:2
1730—Nisan 21:10; Sivan 3:6; Tammuz 24:4; 25:2
1731—Adar 10:4; Iyar 22:3
1732—Tevet 10:8; Av 18:2; Elul 12:2
1733—Iyar 22:4; Tammuz 28:5
1734—Tammuz 6:4; 15:3
1735—Ḥeshvan 3:4; Nisan 26:3
1736—Tishri 7:4; Kislev 3:5; 13:3; Elul 29:2
1737—Kislev 27:5; Elul 27:3
1738—Kislev 27:6; Shevat 14:1; Tammuz 27:5
1739—Tishri 17:2; Adar 20:7
1740—Tevet 23:2; Shevat 5:1; 22:2; Nisan 15:20; Sivan 10:6; Tammuz 16:3; Elul
    11:6
1742—Kislev 4:4; 4:5; Shevat 22:3
1743—Adar 28:8; Tammuz 15:4
1744—Kislev 21:3; Tevet 13:2; Nisan 16:13; Sivan 27:7
1745—Tevet 24:1; Adar 27:7

1746—Sivan 26:1
1747—Tishri 3:6; 12:3; Adar 18:2; Iyar 26:3
1748—Nisan 4:2; 19:7; Av 11:3
1749—Sivan 7:7; Tammuz 4:7; 5:5; 23:6
1750—Nisan 11:6; Elul 4:4
1751—Tevet 8:3; Sivan 11:2
1752—Shevat 6:4
1753—Heshvan 3:5; Elul 16:3
1754—Tevet 17:5
1756—Heshvan 23:3; Shevat 14:2; Tammuz 6:5
1757—Kislev 1:6; Sivan 7:8
1758—Heshvan 19:2; Kislev 25:6; Elul 15:4
1759—Heshvan 9:4
1760—Tishri 1:21; 1:22; Heshvan 13:3; Shevat 16:1; Sivan 7:9; Elul 27:4
1761—Kislev 1:7; 13:4; Shevat 21:5; 29:2; Sivan 14:6
1762—Kislev 11:3; 11:4; Adar 23:6; Sivan 8:1; 25:5; Av 28:4
1763—Kislev 26:5
1764—Nisan 1:13; Iyar 9:3; 26:4; Elul 21:5
1765—Shevat 24:6; Nisan 26:4; Sivan 21:4
1767—Kislev 29:6
1768—Tishri 11:5; Kislev 13:5; Tammuz 5:6
1769—Iyar 13:4
1770—Kislev 21:4; Nisan 7:5
1771—Kislev 19:3; 29:4
1772—Nisan 8:5; 17:3; Iyar 22:5
1773—Sivan 6:10; Tammuz 19:4
1774—Nisan 2:5; Tammuz 10:5; 11:1
1775—Tishri 4:5; Shevat 21:6; Adar 25:5; Iyar 28:4
1776—Tishri 2:7; 12:4; Shevat 24:7; Nisan 30:6; Tammuz 14:7; 17:12; Av 20:3
1777—Heshvan 23:4; Nisan 13:7; 28:4
1778—Iyar 12:4
1779—Shevat 24:8
1780—Tishri 16:7; Elul 27:5
1781—Heshvan 2:3; 14:2; Kislev 25:7; Tevet 12:5; 26:3; Tammuz 27:6; Av 22:4;
       Elul 17:5
1782—Tevet 7:2; 16:1; Shevat 10:4; 20:3; Nisan 17:4; Av 16:2
1783—Tishri 21:7; Heshvan 30:3; Shevat 1:7; Adar 1:12
1784—Heshvan 13:4; Kislev 29:5; Iyar 26:5; Sivan 5:11; Av 11:4
1785—Tishri 25:2; Kislev 28:2; Tevet 24:2; Sivan 7:10; Tammuz 25:3
1786—Tishri 12:5; Heshvan 6:3; 22:4; Kislev 8:3; Shevat 5:2; Iyar 19:2; Elul 22:1
1787—Adar 21:2; Tammuz 21:6; Av 8:5; Elul 3:2
1788—Tevet 21:4; Iyar 2:5
1789—Shevat 1:8; Adar 8:3; Iyar 10:7; 11:7; Av 5:5; 9:18

1790—Kislev 23:4; Shevat 13:3; Adar 6:7; 15:5; Iyar 10:8; Sivan 3:7; 27:8; Tammuz 7:1
1791—Tevet 5:4
1792—Kislev 23:5; Shevat 28:3; Iyar 4:7; 26:6; Tammuz 22:5
1793—Tishri 25:3; Kislev 18:3; Tevet 29:4; Iyar 14:2; 17:6
1794—Heshvan 23:5; Kislev 27:7; Adar 18:3; Nisan 6:2; Iyar 18:5; Sivan 25:6; Tammuz 6:6; 24:5; Elul 22:2
1795—Sivan 11:3; Tammuz 21:7
1796—Tishri 15:9; Nisan 18:5; Av 11:5; 17:3; 29:2; Elul 2:6
1797—Tishri 19:4; Heshvan 11:5; 23:6; Tevet 3:2; 11:4; Nisan 1:14: Tammuz 17:13; Av 9:19; 11:6
1798—Kislev 19:4; Tevet 13:3; 22:2; Adar 4:6; Sivan 11:4; 23:5
1799—Kislev 25:8; Shevat 5:3; Adar 24:6; 29:2; Nisan 15:21; Iyar 5:2; 8:5; Sivan 26:2; Av 25:5
1800—Kislev 5:4; 18:4; 29:7; Shevat 2:3; Iyar 5:3; 17:7; 20:4; 20:5; Elul 27:6
1801—Heshvan 15:4; Adar 18:4; Nisan 25:5
1802—Tishri 7:5; 13:3; 14:7; 16:8; Tevet 29:5; Adar 3:4; 20:8; Nisan 30:7; Elul 24:6
1803—Tishri 21:8; Heshvan 26:2; Adar 25:6
1804—Kislev 6:3; 15:3; 17:4; Tevet 7:3; 14:3; 17:6; Av 17:4
1805—Adar 29:3; Tammuz 4:8
1806—Tishri 21:9; Tevet 13:4; Adar 11:5; Nisan 1:15; 21:11; 27:3; Tammuz 15:5; Av 2:5
1807—Heshvan 9:5; Shevat 4:2; 25:1; Adar 1:13; Iyar 8:6; Av 5:6; 25:6
1808—Tishri 1:23; 26:3; Kislev 25:9; Tevet 1:9; 6:2; 27:2; 29:6; Shevat 25:2; Adar 18:5; Nisan 3:3; Sivan 1:7; Tammuz 25:4
1809—Tishri 25:4; Heshvan 22:5; Kislev 22:5; Nisan 20:5; Iyar 19:3; 19:4; Av 26:1
1810—Tishri 6:3; Shevat 30:2; Iyar 6:9; Sivan 6:11; Tammuz 15:6; Av 6:2
1811—Tishri 18:5; Adar 16:6; Sivan 22:4
1812—Tishri 19:5; 27:3; Kislev 23:6; Tevet 24:3; 26:4; Shevat 28:4; Adar 27:8
1813—Kislev 9:2; 25:10; Adar 1:14; 18:6; Sivan 28:2
1814—Shevat 1:9; Sivan 2:3
1815—Tishri 14:8; Kislev 4:6; Av 9:20
1816—Shevat 4:3; Adar 6:8; Nisan 11:7; Tammuz 6:7
1817—Tishri 18:6; Shevat 13:4; Adar 20:9; Nisan 8:6
1818—Tishri 18:7; Heshvan 22:6; Nisan 11:8; Sivan 26:3
1819—Heshvan 1:6; 23:7; Kislev 29:8; Av 30:2
1820—Tishri 4:6; Tevet 20:4; Shevat 3:7; Elul 6:3
1821—Tishri 26:4; Adar 27:9; Sivan 14:7
1822—Adar 11:6; 14:6
1823—Tevet 2:4; 7:4; Adar 18:7
1824—Tevet 2:5; Shevat 18:4

1825—Tishri 3:7; Ḥeshvan 27:2; Kislev 9:3; Shevat 27:4; Adar 8:4; Nisan 5:2; 9:8; Elul 18:6
1826—Tevet 26:5; Adar 17:3; 19:2; Nisan 19:9; Iyar 22:6; Sivan 17:4; Tammuz 21:8
1827—Kislev 9:4; Adar 1:15; 28:10; Tammuz 1:7; 2:2; 4:9; Av 11:7; Elul 15:5
1828—Tishri 6:4; Nisan 10:8; Av 24:4
1829—Ḥeshvan 24:3; Tevet 27:3; Adar 25:7; Av 13:3
1831—Shevat 25:3; Nisan 28:5; Tammuz 29:5; Elul 6:4
1832—Ḥeshvan 22:7; Tevet 29:7; Adar 19:3; Iyar 25:6; Sivan 7:11; Av 1:10
1833—Shevat 24:9; Adar 14:7; Iyar 3:5; Av 6:3
1834—Ḥeshvan 4:6; Kislev 23:7; Sivan 8:2; Tammuz 8:7
1835—Tammuz 28:6; Av 26:2
1836—Tishri 1:24; Kislev 13:6; 26:6; Tevet 23:4; Av 13:4
1837—Tishri 13:4; Kislev 20:5; Tevet 24:4; 25:3; Iyar 13:6
1838—Tishri 2:8; Adar 7:10; Iyar 11:8; Tammuz 15:7
1839—Tishri 25:5; Nisan 12:4; Sivan 1:8
1840—Ḥeshvan 10:5; Kislev 28:4; Adar 1:16; 14:8; Tammuz 14:8; Av 1:11; 29:3
1841—Tishri 9:6; Ḥeshvan 28:4; Tevet 18:3; Shevat 9:2; Tammuz 25:5
1842—Ḥeshvan 6:4; 19:3; 26:3; Kislev 30:2; Shevat 23:6
1843—Tishri 19:6; Ḥeshvan 19:4; Sivan 26:4; Tammuz 6:8; Av 20:4
1844—Kislev 3:6; 6:4; 14:3; Tevet 9:11; Elul 9:7
1845—Tishri 11:7; Ḥeshvan 5:3; Tevet 25:4; Adar 1:17; Nisan 20:6; Tammuz 10:6
1846—Nisan 25:6; 29:3; Sivan 30:2
1847—Tishri 6:5; Ḥeshvan 19:5; 24:4; Kislev 24:7; Shevat 27:5; Sivan 29:2; Av 10:11
1848—Ḥeshvan 27:3; Kislev 17:5; Adar 16:7; Nisan 3:4; 14:9; 16:14; 22:6; Iyar 23:5; Tammuz 15:8; 18:5; Av 21:3; Elul 7:7
1849—Ḥeshvan 20:3; Shevat 15:3; Adar 9:4; 10:5; Sivan 15:8; 26:5; Av 9:21; Elul 28:4
1850—Ḥeshvan 3:6; Kislev 16:2
1851—Adar 3:5; 18:8
1852—Tevet 1:10; 24:5; Shevat 27:6; Sivan 17:5; Tammuz 22:6; Elul 19:5
1853—Iyar 3:6; Elul 29:4
1854—Kislev 21:5; Tevet 7:5; 19:3; Tammuz 19:5; Av 16:3
1855—Tishri 30:2; Ḥeshvan 27:4; 28:5; Shevat 28:5; Sivan 19:1; Tammuz 16:4; Elul 15:6; 27:7
1856—Ḥeshvan 12:6; 27:5; Tevet 4:3; Adar 12:5; 24:7; Sivan 1:9
1857—Shevat 8:4; Iyar 3:7
1858—Nisan 14:10; Tammuz 12:5; Av 15:11
1859—Kislev 7:6; Shevat 22:4; Adar 10:6; Sivan 10:7

1860—Tishri 3:8; 25:6; Heshvan 10:6; 21:3; 26:4; Kislev 6:5; Shevat 8:5; 20:4; Iyar 5:4; 10:9; 25:7; Tammuz 6:9; Elul 4:5

1861—Kislev 11:5; 30:3; Tevet 11:5; 22:4; Adar 17:4

1862—Tishri 10:19; Heshvan 5:3; 16:2; Kislev 25:11; Shevat 7:2; Adar 10:7; 20:10; 22:4; Tammuz 3:5; Elul 23:3

1863—Tevet 10:9; 16:2; Adar 1:18; Nisan 21:12; Iyar 3:8; Tammuz 13:4; 15:9; 20:3; 27:7

1864—Tishri 10:20; Heshvan 8:6; Kislev 5:5; 5:6; Nisan 5:3; 27:4; Iyar 10:10; Elul 28:5

1865—Tishri 10:21; 14:9; Heshvan 3:7; Shevat 9:3; Nisan 4:3; Iyar 22:7

1866—Tishri 11:6; Tevet 28:6; Shevat 4:4; Adar 23:7; 29:4; Nisan 13:8; Sivan 5:12

1867—Tishri 4:7; 10:22; 19:7; 26:5; Kislev 24:8; 26:7; Shevat 30:3; Elul 9:8

1868—Tishri 17:3; Kislev 17:6; 19:5; 30:4; Tevet 13:5; Shevat 8:6; 17:4; Tammuz 13:5; Av 27:2; Elul 3:3

1869—Heshvan 5:4; 11:6; 29:4; Kislev 10:2; Shevat 5:4; Iyar 5:5; 24:1; Tammuz 1:8; 24:6; 24:7

1870—Tishri 18:8; 29:4; Tevet 5:5; Adar 14:9; 14:10; 15:6; Tammuz 15:10; Av 4:5; Elul 19:6

1871—Kislev 25:12; Tevet 19:4; Nisan 19:10; 25:7; Iyar 28:5; Sivan 22:5; Tammuz 3:6; 13:6

1872—Adar 11:7; Nisan 14:11; Sivan 17:6; Tammuz 16:5; Elul 27:8

1873—Heshvan 1:7; Tevet 4:4; 10:10; Sivan 29:3; Tammuz 13:7; 23:7

1874—Heshvan 5:5; 12:7; 29:5; Kislev 18:5; Nisan 4:4; Iyar 3:9; 16:7

1875—Tishri 4:8; Adar 8:5; 27:10; Nisan 1:16; Elul 5:2; 25:5

1876—Kislev 20:6; Nisan 25:8; Iyar 23:6; Elul 13:3

1877—Tishri 27:4; Nisan 19:11; 26:5; Sivan 5:13

1878—Tishri 16:9; Heshvan 7:1; Nisan 23:4; Iyar 5:6; 29:8; Tammuz 12:6; 29:6; Av 1:12; 3:2; 9:22

1879—Tishri 1:25; Kislev 6:6; Shevat 1:10; 16:3; Sivan 11:5

1880—Tishri 13:5; Shevat 27:7; Sivan 23:6; Tammuz 22:7

1881—Tishri 9:7; 21:10; Tevet 3:3; Adar 14:11; 22:5; Nisan 2:6; 26:6; 28:6; Iyar 6:10; 10:11; 11:9; 16:8; Sivan 21:5; 25:7; Tammuz 1:9; Av 3:3; Elul 8:6

1882—Tishri 15:10; 24:2; Kislev 14:4; 21:6; 25:13; Tevet 2:6; 13:6; Shevat 5:5; 19:2; Adar 24:8; Nisan 12:5; Iyar 21:1; 26:7; Sivan 6:12; 7:13; 13:6; Tammuz 19:7; Av 9:23; Elul 26:5

1883—Shevat 13:5; 25:4; Adar 16:8; 27:11; Iyar 3:10; 15:7; Tammuz 29:7; Av 5:7; 7:3; 20:5; 25:7; Elul 6:5

1884—Heshvan 5:6; 12:8; 18:2; Kislev 26:8; Shevat 16:4; Iyar 11:10; Sivan 29:4

1885—Heshvan 10:7; Tevet 5:6; Shevat 16:5; Nisan 4:5; Av 13:5

1886—Tishri 11:7; 17:4; Adar 7:11; 8:6; 11:8; 24:9; 26:4; Iyar 16:9; Tammuz 26:2

1887—Kislev 3:7; Shevat 19:3; Adar 4:7; 27:12; Tammuz 10:7

1888—Ḥeshvan 14:4; Kislev 24:9; Tevet 19:5; 27:4; Adar 27:13; 27:14; Iyar 18:6; Sivan 24:3; Tammuz 5:7

1889—Kislev 6:7; 18:6; Adar 7:12; Nisan 19:11; Iyar 19:5; Tammuz 10:8; Av 17:5; Elul 16:4

1890—Ḥeshvan 20:4; Tevet 13:7; 25:5; 29:8; Adar 7:13; 29:5; Nisan 13:9; Av 20:6

1891—Ḥeshvan 25:3; Kislev 20:7; Shevat 2:4; Adar 1:19; 18:9; 25:8; Nisan 15:22; Iyar 10:12; Sivan 3:8; Av 9:24; 24:5; Elul 4:6; 7:8

1892—Ḥeshvan 28:6; Kislev 16:3; 20:8; Shevat 5:6; Iyar 4:8; Sivan 12:4; Elul 24:7

1893—Tevet 20:5; Shevat 5:7; 7:4; Adar 8:7; Nisan 5:4; 6:3; 9:9; Sivan 12:5; Tammuz 27:8; Av 28:5; Elul 8:7

1894—Tishri 15:11; Shevat 28:6; Adar 29:6; Iyar 19:6

1895—Tishri 20:2; Tevet 9:12; Elul 13:4

1896—Tevet 1:11; 24:6; Shevat 30:4; Iyar 6:11; 8:7; Sivan 1:10; 7:14; Av 2:6

1897—Ḥeshvan 17:6; Kislev 17:7; Shevat 30:5; Adar 16:9; Nisan 20:7; Iyar 16:10; Sivan 4:7; 17:7; 29:5; Elul 1:10

1898—Tishri 15:12; Ḥeshvan 10:8; 17:7; Kislev 6:8; Tevet 19:6; 29:9; Iyar 17:8; Sivan 18:3; 19:2; 27:10; Tammuz 14:9; Av 17:6; Elul 10:3

1899—Tishri 5:5; 16:10; Tevet 8:4; 20:6; 25:6; 28:7; Shevat 23:7; Nisan 5:5; 9:10; 20:8; 21:13; Iyar 2:6; 17:9; Sivan 7:15; 19:3; Av 5:8; Elul 9:9; 18:7

1900—Ḥeshvan 22:9; Shevat 23:8; Adar 7:14; 8:8; 10:8; 13:7; 25:9; Av 18:3; Elul 9:10; 10:4

1901—Tevet 16:3; 19:7; Shevat 12:1; Adar 18:10; Iyar 28:6; Tammuz 2:3; 15:11; 17:14; Elul 28:6

1902—Tishri 17:5; Kislev 15:4; 21:7; 25:14; Adar 12:6; 13:8; 15:7; 17:5; 25:10; Sivan 22:6; Tammuz 5:8; 24:8; 24:9; 25:6; 26:3

1903—Tishri 22:5; 25:7; Shevat 28:7; Nisan 6:4; 16:15; 18:6; 22:7; Sivan 29:6; Tammuz 8:8; Av 30:3; Elul 1:11; 16:5; 22:3

1904—Kislev 25:15; Adar 14:12; Iyar 14:3; Sivan 1:11; 9:5; 10:8; Tammuz 20:4

1905—Tishri 23:7; Ḥeshvan 2:4; 26:5; Shevat 5:8; 6:5; Adar 3:6; 12:7; Nisan 16:16; 19:13; Iyar 21:2; 24:2; 27:4; Sivan 6:13; Tammuz 5:9; 24:10; 27:9; Av 10:12; 23:2

1906—Tevet 11:6; Shevat 20:5; Adar 11:9; Nisan 1:17; Iyar 18:7; Sivan 8:3; Tammuz 13:8; 19:8; 29:8; Elul 17:6

1907—Tishri 22:6; 22:7; Shevat 9:4; Sivan 7:16; Av 11:8; 21:4; Elul 4:7

1908—Shevat 6:6; Adar 5:3; 7:15; 8:9; 22:6; Nisan 18:7; Sivan 8:4; Elul 18:8

1909—Tishri 23:8; Kislev 18:7; Tevet 14:5; 27:5; Nisan 20:9; 21:14; Iyar 12:5; 16:11; Sivan 10:9; 21:6; Tammuz 29:9; Av 10:13; 29:4

1910—Kislev 5:7; Shevat 15:4; Adar 2:5; 4:8; Iyar 12:6

1911—Ḥeshvan 1:8; Tevet 24:7; Shevat 16:6; Adar 25:11; Av 15:12; 25:8

1912—Tishri 19:9; Tevet 18:4; Nisan 24:5; 28:7; Sivan 12:6

1913—Kislev 13:7; Tevet 21:6; 23:5; 27:6; Shevat 14:3; Adar 6:9; 16:10; Tammuz 18:7; Av 30:4; Elul 20:4

1914—Tishri 16:11; Ḥeshvan 14:5; 16:5; Kislev 9:5; 29:9; Tevet 4:5; Adar 18:11; Iyar 5:7; 20:6; Av 9:25; 19:2; Elul 24:8

1915—Tishri 1:26; Kislev 12:3; Tevet 14:6; 26:6; Adar 16:11; Nisan 6:5; 8:7; Elul 5:3; 10:5

1916—Adar 21:4; Iyar 10:13; 18:8; 23:7; 23:8

1917—Ḥeshvan 14:6; 15:5; 17:8; 22:10; Kislev 1:8; 23:8; 24:10; Tevet 1:12; 18:5; Shevat 24:10; Adar 22:7; Nisan 5:6; 12:6; 17:5; 22:8; Iyar 12:7; 28:7; Sivan 4:8; Elul 5:4

1918—Ḥeshvan 20:5; Kislev 7:7; 18:8; Tevet 12:6; Shevat 8:7; 23:9; Adar 11:10; 24:10; 29:7; Nisan 6:6; 14:12; Iyar 7:9; 20:7; Tammuz 17:15; Av 7:4; 12:3; 15:13; 21:5

1919—Ḥeshvan 8:7; Adar 7:16; 21:5; 23:8; Nisan 5:7; 16:17; 19:14; 25:9; Iyar 22:8; Tammuz 7:2; Elul 5:5

1920—Tishri 13:6; 15:13; 25:8; Ḥeshvan 5:7; Kislev 17:8; 25:16; Shevat 29:3; Adar 11:11; 22:8; Nisan 13:10; 16:18; Iyar 2:7; 6:12; 6:13; Sivan 5:14; Tammuz 15:12; 19:9; Av 7:5; 26:3; Elul 25:6

1921—Tishri 30:3; Ḥeshvan 17:9; Adar 1:20; Nisan 15:23; 23:5; 27:5; 29:4; Iyar 3:11; Av 28:6; Elul 29:5

1922—Tishri 9:8; Ḥeshvan 11:7; 20:6; Kislev 17:9; 26:9; Shevat 24:11; Nisan 18:8; Tammuz 28:7; Av 10:14; Elul 28:7

1923—Tishri 1:27; 19:10; Shevat 5:9; Tammuz 8:9; Av 24:6

1924—Ḥeshvan 15:6; 26:6; Kislev 25:17; Shevat 7:5; 18:6; Nisan 26:7; Sivan 11:6; Tammuz 19:10; Av 12:4; 27:3; Elul 7:9

1925—Tishri 18:9; Kislev 27:8; Shevat 15:5; 28:8; 30:6; Nisan 6:7; 7:6; Iyar 26:8; Sivan 17:8; Av 28:7

1926—Kislev 22:6; Shevat 13:6; Nisan 16:19; Iyar 19:7; Sivan 13:7; Av 21:6; Elul 4:8

1927—Tishri 18:10; 27:5; Kislev 20:9; Tevet 28:8; Shevat 7:6; 29:4; Adar 10:9; Sivan 30:3; Tammuz 2:4; Elul 2:7

1928—Tishri 9:9; Nisan 6:8; Iyar 24:3; Sivan 15:9; Tammuz 21:9

1929—Ḥeshvan 6:5; Iyar 11:11; Sivan 23:7; Tammuz 20:5; Av 8:6; 17:7; Elul 6:7

1930—Ḥeshvan 8:8; Kislev 3:8; 6:9; Shevat 7:7; Sivan 28:3; Elul 15:7

1931—Tishri 1:28; Ḥeshvan 19:6; Tevet 23:6; Shevat 15:6; Adar 5:4; Nisan 29:5; Tammuz 15:13

1932—Tishri 30:4; Kislev 13:8; 22:7; Shevat 17:5; Adar 3:7; 20:11; Iyar 27:5; Av 19:3; 29:5

1933—Ḥeshvan 7:2; 18:3; Kislev 2:4; 4:7; Shevat 3:8; 3:9; Adar 7:17; 25:12;

Nisan 1:18; 5:8; 11:9; 25:10; 28:8; 30:8; Iyar 14:4; Sivan 4:9; 22:7; 27:11;
Tammuz 27:10; Av 29:6; Elul 24:9; 29:6

1934—Heshvan 24:5; Shevat 25:5; Adar 4:9; Iyar 16:12; 22:9; Tammuz
21:10; 24:11; 26:4; Av 21:7; 22:5

1935—Sivan 8:5; Tammuz 11:2; 14:10; Av 9:26; 21:8; Elul 3:4; 17:7; 17:8

1936—Heshvan 5:8; Kislev 22:8; Tevet 12:7; 23:7; Shevat 19:4; Adar 11:12;
Nisan 27:6; 28:9; Iyar 25:8; Sivan 26:6

1937—Heshvan 15:7; Kislev 1:9; Tevet 1:13; Nisan 9:11; 22:9; Sivan 7:17;
Tammuz 23:8; Av 26:4

1938—Tishri 12:6; 12:7; 15:14; 19:11; Heshvan 1:9; 3:8; 5:9; 11:8; 15:8; 18:4;
21:4; 23:10; 26:7; Adar 9:5; 20:12; Nisan 4:6; 25:11; 28:10; Iyar 9:4; 27:6;
Sivan 9:6; 12:7; 14:8; Tammuz 7:3; 16:6; Av 21:9; 24:7; 26:5; 29:7; Elul
5:6; 9:11; 21:6

1939—Tishri 6:6; 16:12; 23:9; 25:9; 29:5; Heshvan 2:5; 6:6; 9:6; 11:9; 13:5;
13:6; 15:9; 22:11; 30:4; Kislev 3:9; 4:8; 10:3; 11:6; 12:4; 16:4; Tevet 4:6;
10:11; Shevat 4:5; 10:5; Adar 24:11; 29:8; Iyar 1:10; 6:14; 20:8; 28:8;
Tammuz 17:16; Elul 1:12; 14:3; 16:6; 17:9; 19:8; 20:5; 21:7; 22:4; 23:4; 29:7

1940—Tishri 2:9; 14:10; 20:3; 25:10; 29:6; Heshvan 15:10; 24:6; Kislev 2:5;
9:6; Tevet 20:7; 20:8; Shevat 15:7; 29:5; Adar 19:5; 26:5; 29:9; Nisan 1:19;
22:10; Iyar 2:8; Sivan 8:6; Tammuz 1:10; 29:10; Av 5:9; Elul 6:8; 14:4;
16:7

1941—Tishri 1:29; 2:10; 5:6; 7:6; 9:10; 9:11; 11:8; 12:8; 13:7; 14:11; 14:12;
21:11; 24:3; 24:4; 25:11; 29:7; Heshvan 2:6; 2:7; 3:9; 4:7; 7:3; 7:4; 8:9; 16:6;
16:7; 19:7; Kislev 3:10; 4:9; 6:10; 10:4; 14:7; 18:9; 22:9; 25:18; Tevet 2:7;
10:12; 10:13; 10:14; 20:9; 23:8; Shevat 12:2; 22:5; 23:10; 23:11; 25:6;
Nisan 9:12; 9:13; 11:10; Iyar 17:10; Sivan 6:14; 9:7; 16:4; 27:12; 28:4; 28:5;
29:7; 29:8; 30:4; Tammuz 1:12; 2:5; 2:6; 3:7; 3:8; 4:10; 6:10; 6:11; 6:12; 7:5;
12:7; 12:8; 13:9; 16:7; 17:17; 19:11; 19:12; 20:6; 20:7; 23:9; 26:5; 28:8;
29:11; Av 2:7; 4:6; 4:7; 7:6; 9:27; 14:6; 19:4; 22:6; 25:9; Elul 4:9; 9:12; 9:13;
9:14; 9:15; 13:5; 14:5; 14:6; 16:8; 19:9; 22:5; 23:5; 23:6; 26:6; 27:9; 27:10

1942—Tishri 24:5; Heshvan 14:7; 18:5; 26:8; Kislev 2:6; 5:8; 11:7; 12:5; Tevet
14:7; Shevat 2:5; 27:8; Adar 2:6; 7:18; 12:8; 13:9; 23:9; 27:15; Nisan 5:9;
10:9; 12:7; 23:6; 29:6; Iyar 20:9; Sivan 13:8; 15:10; 18:4; 20:4; 26:7;
Tammuz 5:10; 7:6; 13:10; 21:11; 28:9; Av 2:8; 2:9; 8:7; 14:7; 15:14; 18:4;
21:10; 26:6; Elul 1:13; 3:5; 5:7; 13:6; 13:7; 20:6; 24:10; 27:11; 29:8; 29:9

1943—Tishri 3:9; 15:15; 15:16; 17:6; 21:12; 27:6; Heshvan 4:8; 5:10; 6:7; 7:5;
Tevet 26:7; 29:10; Shevat 12:3; 27:9; 28:9; Adar 2:7; 2:8; 6:10; 8:10; 17:6;
22:9; Nisan 14:13; 14:14; 19:15; 26:8; Iyar 3:12; 7:10; 10:14; 11:12; 11:13;
14:5; Sivan 8:7; 18:5; 18:6; Tammuz 22:8; Av 1:13; 3:4; 15:15; 18:5; Elul
11:7; 23:7

1944—Tishri 20:4; Heshvan 13:7; 13:8; 20:7; 22:12; Kislev 10:5; 17:10; Tevet
15:3; 16:4; Shevat 12:4; 16:7; 22:6; Adar 12:9; 21:6; 24:12; Nisan 3:6; 4:7;

7:7; 21:15; 21:16; Iyar 4:9; 5:8; 10:15; 11:14; 22:10; Sivan 6:15; 9:8; 14:9;
Tammuz 5:11; 17:18; 18:8; 20:8; 22:9; Av 4:9; 12:5; 13:6; 22:7; 24:8; 25:10;
Elul 15:8; 17:10; 29:11

1945—Heshvan 11:10; 17:10; Kislev 11:8; Shevat 12:5; 29:6; Adar 6:11;
18:12; 27:16; Nisan 13:11; 17:6; 29:7; Iyar 2:9; 15:8; 16:14; 17:11; 19:8;
24:4; 24:5; 27:7; Sivan 11:7; Elul 16:9; 22:6; 29:12

1946—Tishri 21:13; 25:12; Kislev 16:5; Shevat 12:6; Adar 28:11; Iyar 21:3;
Sivan 2:4; 30:5; Tammuz 5:12; Av 16:4; Elul 9:16

1947—Tishri 12:9; Kislev 17:11; 17:12; 23:9; Tevet 1:14; 2:8; 16:5; 18:6; Adar
16:12; Iyar 4:10; Tammuz 29:12; Av 1:14

1948—Tishri 6:7; 7:7; 11:9; 13:8; 15:17; 18:11; 19:12; 22:8; 24:6; 26:6; 27:7;
Heshvan 3:10; 6:8; 7:6; 26:9; Kislev 3:11; 5:9; 5:10; 7:8; 10:6; 14:8; 18:10;
23:10; 24:11; 25:19; 26:10; 27:9; Tevet 28:9; Shevat 5:10; 21:7; Adar 7:19;
12:10; 17:7;21:7; 26:6; 30:2; Nisan 1:20; 4:8; 6:9; 10:10; 13:12; 23:7; 26:9;
Iyar 1:11; 2:10; 2:11; 3:13; 4:11; 5:9; 5:10; 5:11; 5:12; 5:13; 6:15; 6:17; 7:11;
7:12; 7:13; 8:8; 8:9; 9:5; 9:6; 9:7; 10:16; 10:17; 11:15; 11:16; 11:17; 13:7;
14:6; 14:7; 14:8; 14:9; 15:9; 18:9; 18:10; 19:9; 19:10; 19:11; 20:10; 23:9;
23:10; 24:6; 24:7; 27:8; 28:9; 29:9; Sivan 3:9; 3:10; 3:11; 4:10; 6:16; 6:17;
12:8; 13:9; 14:10; 23:8; 23:9; Tammuz 2:7; 3:9; 4:11; 4:12; 4:13; 4:14; 6:13;
7:7; 10:9; 11:3; 12:9; Av 4:9; 7:7; 11:9; 11:10; 12:6; Elul 10:6; 13:8

1949—Tishri 20:5; Heshvan 16:9; 28:7; Kislev 18:11; 22:10; Tevet 1:15; 1:16;
2:9; 6:4; 12:8; 18:7; 23:9; 24:8; 25:7; 27:7; Shevat 15:8; 18:7; 25:7; Adar
3:8; 3:9; 6:14; 9:6; 19:6; 26:7; Nisan 4:9; 19:16; 23:8; Iyar 12:8; 16:15;
Tammuz 23:10; Av 3:5; Elul 14:7; 18:9

1950—Tishri 13:9; Shevat 2:6; 10:6; Iyar 28:10; Sivan 3:12; Tammuz 20:9; Av
10:15; 13:7; Elul 11:8

1951—Kislev 7:9; Adar 27:17; Nisan 27:7; Sivan 4:11; 13:10; 15:11; Av 9:28;
11:11; 12:7; 29:8; Elul 7:10

1952—Heshvan 21:5; Kislev 2:7; 22:11; Tevet 8:5; 15:4; Shevat 8:8; Nisan
24:6; Iyar 18:11; 20:11; Av 21:11; 30:5; Elul 18:10

1953—Tishri 8:4; 25:13; Heshvan 7:7; 15:11; Kislev 4:10; 10:7; Tevet 20:10;
26:8; Shevat 26:2; Adar 18:13; 27:18; Nisan 9:14; 14:15; Sivan 27:14; Elul
24:11

1954—Tishri 10:23; Heshvan 21:6; Adar 25:13; Nisan 3:7; 3:8; 24:7; Sivan
12:9; 24:4

1955—Tevet 9:13; 23:10; Nisan 19:17; Tammuz 29:13; Av 8:8; 19:5

1956—Heshvan 24:7; 25:4; 26:10; 26:11; 27:6; 28:8; 29:6; 30:5; Kislev 1:10;
9:7; 14:9; Tevet 6:5; Shevat 24:12; Adar 18:14; Nisan 17:7; Sivan 19:4

1957—Tishri 16:13; Heshvan 4:9; Kislev 5:11; 16:6; Shevat 4:6; 20:6; 25:8;
Adar 1:21; 5:5; 29:10; Nisan 5:10; Sivan 7:18; 19:5; Tammuz 11:4; 21:12;
Elul 17:11

1958—Tishri 25:14; 28:6; 30:5; Ḥeshvan 13:9; Kislev 6:11; Shevat 13:7; Iyar 27:9; Av 17:8

1959—Kislev 24:12; Shevat 25:9; 26:3; Adar 12:11; Nisan 1:21; Tammuz 9:5; 19:13

1960—Kislev 1:11; Tevet 6:6; Adar 2:9; 15:8; Nisan 14:16; Iyar 14:10; 26:9; Tammuz 10:10

1961—Kislev 13:9; 26:11; 26:12; Tevet 8:6; Nisan 25:12; Tammuz 23:11; Av 18:6

1962—Kislev 2:8; 26:13; Adar 9:7; Iyar 28:11; Sivan 23:10; 23:11; 29:9; Tammuz 9:6

1963—Tishri 12:10; Kislev 12:6; 19:6; Tevet 15:5; Nisan 29:8; Tammuz 18:9; 21:13

1964—Ḥeshvan 8:10; 23:11; Tevet 20:11

1965—Tishri 7:8; 18:12; Ḥeshvan 2:8; 26:12; Shevat 17:6; Adar 17:8; 21:8; Iyar 11:18; Tammuz 7:8; 20:10

1966—Tishri 8:5; Kislev 27:10; Tevet 1:17; 7:6; 10:16; 17:8; Elul 14:8

1967—Ḥeshvan 2:9; Adar 17:9; Iyar 12:9; 26:10; 27:10; 27:11; 28:12; 28:13; 29:10; Sivan 1:12; 1:13; 2:5; 3:13; 4:12; 18:7; 20:5

1968—Kislev 25:20; 25:21 29:10; Shevat 9:5

1969—Shevat 8:9; 10:7; Adar 3:10; 8:11; Iyar 4:12; 13:8; Tammuz 21:14; Elul 20:7; 20:8

1970—Kislev 24:13; 26:14; Shevat 25:10; Adar 2:10; 11:13; 11:14; Iyar 6:18; Tammuz 17:19; 26:6; Av 5:10

1971—Kislev 1:12; Tevet 14:8; Adar 10:10

1973—Tishri 10:24; 10:25; 13:10; 17:7; 20:6; 26:7; 27:8; 30:6; Ḥeshvan 11:11; 16:10; Kislev 6:12; 26:15; Iyar 11:19; Elul 25:7

1974—Ḥeshvan 20:8; Kislev 27:11; Tevet 24:9; Shevat 29:7; Adar 10:11; Sivan 8:8; 13:12

1975—Ḥeshvan 5:11; 12:9; Kislev 6:13; Nisan 29:9; Tammuz 22:10

1976-Tammuz 6:14

1977—Kislev 10:8; Tevet 4:7; 15:6

1978—Elul 15:9

1979—Kislev 5:12; Adar 27:19; Nisan 2:7; 28:11; Iyar 2:12

1980—Ḥeshvan 16:11; Shevat 8:10; 9:6; 18:8; Adar 1:22; 10:12

1981—Sivan 5:15

1982—Iyar 2:13

Bibliography

American Jewry and the Civil War, by Bertram W. Korn. Philadelphia, 1951.
American Overtures, by Avram V. Goodman. New York, 1936.
Ancient Aliyot, by Cecil Roth. New York, 1942.
Anguish of the Jews, by Edward H. Flannery. New York, 1965.
Anziklopedia le-Toladot Gedolei Yisrael. Tel Aviv, 1947.
Anziklopedia shel ha-Ziyonut ha-Datit, Jerusalem, 1958.
Apocrypha, edited by Manuel Komroff. New York, 1936.
    Book of Jubilees
    Esdras
Bible
Century of Jewish Life, by Ismar Elbogen. Philadelphia, 1946.
Black Book of Polish Jewry, edited by Jacob Apenszlak, 1943.
Court Jew, by Selma Stern. Philadelphia, 1950.
Devar Yom be-Yomo, by Hayyim Knaller. Brooklyn, 1945.
Documentary History of the Jews in the U.S., by Morris U. Schappes. New York, 1971.
Dor Dor ve-Dorshav, by Lowenstein. Tel Aviv, 1948.
Encyclopaedia Judaica. Jerusalem, 1972.
Essays in American Jewish History, by Jacob Marcus.
Europe and the Jews, by Malcolm Hay. Boston, 1960.
Exiled and the Redeemed, by Itzhak Ben-Zvi. Philadelphia, 1957.
Falasha Anthology, edited by W. Leslau.
Germany's Step Children, by Solomon Liptzin. Philadelphia, 1944.
Great Sanhedrin, by Sidney B. Hoenig. Philadelphia, 1953.
Hakhmei Yisrael, by David Halahmi. Tel Aviv, 1957.
Harvest of Hate, by Leon Poliakov. Philadelphia, 1954.
Historia shel ha-Bayit ha-Sheni, by Joseph Klausner. Jerusalem, 1951.
History of the Jews, by Heinrich Graetz. Philadelphia, 1895.
History of the Jews of Italy, by Cecil Roth. Philadelphia, 1946.
History of the Jews in Russia and Poland, by Simon Dubnow. Philadelphia, 1920.

History of the Marranos, by Cecil Roth. Philadelphia, 1947.
House of Nasi, by Cecil Roth. Philadelphia, 1948.
Hurban Litte, by Ephraim Oshri. New York, 1951.
Jew in the Medieval World, by Jacob Marcus. New York, 192.
Jewish Encyclopedia, Funk and Wagnalls. New York, 1902.
Jewish Life in the Middle Ages, by Israel Abrahams. London, 1932.
Jews: Their History, Culture and Religion. Edited by Louis Finkelstein.
    Philadelphia, 1960.
Kolbo, New York, 1945.
Legends of the Jews, by Louis Ginzberg, Philadelphia, 1947.
Megillat Taanit, Warsaw, 1874.
Midrashim
    *Akedat Yizhak, Ele Ezkerah, Maasei Asarah Harugei Malkhut. Ozar Mi-
        drashim,* edited by J.D. Eisenstein. New York, 1928.
    Bereshit Rabba, New York, 1925.
    Eichah Rabba, New York, 1925.
    Pirkei de-Rabbi Eliezer, edited by D. Luria, Warsaw, 1852.
    Tanhuma (Midrash Yelamdenu), New York, 1925.
    Yalkut Shimoni, New York, 1944.
Mishneh Torah, by Moses Maimonides. Berlin, 1926.
Ozar Yisrael, edited by J.D. Eisenstein.
Periodicals
    The American Sefardi, New York.
    Publications of the American Jewish Historical Society, Philadelphia.
    The Jewish Frontier, New York.
Personalities and Events in Jewish History, by Cecil Roth. Philadelphia, 1953.
Pilgrims in a New Land, by Lee M. Friedman. Philadelphia, 1953.
Rashi (commentary on the Pentateuch).
Return to the Soil, by Alex Bein. Jerusalem, 1952.
Seder ha-Dorot, by Jehiel Heilperin, Warsaw, 1905.
Seder Olam Rabba, New York, 1952.
Seder ha-Moadim, edited by Yom Tov Levinsky. Tel Aviv, 1955.
Sifrut ha-Historia ha-Yisraelit, by Abraham Kahana. Warsaw, 1922.
Talmud (Babylonian and Palestinian).
Toledot ha-Posekim, by S.M. Hones. New York, 1945.
Toledot ha-Zionut, by Ben-Yehuda. Tel Aviv, 1954.
Treasury of Jewish Letters, edited by Franz Kobler. London, 1952.
Universal Jewish Encyclopedia. New York, 1939.
Warrant for Genocide, by Norman Cohn, London, 1967.
Wars of the Jews, by Flavius Josephus. Translated by Havercamp.
Yahadut Latvia. Tel Aviv, 1953.
Zikhronot Yemot Olam, Ozar he-Tefilot, New York, 1945.
Zohar, Cremona, 1560.

Index

315

Algazi, Yom Tov, Adar 20:8
Algeria, Tishri 29:6; Iyar 16:10
Aliyah, Shevat 7:7; Av 26:2
Alliance, Iyar 21:1
Alliance, Israelite, Iyar 25:7
Alma Oilfields, Kislev 5:12
Alnakawa, Ephraim, Shevat 21:1
Alsace, Kislev 18:3; 22:2; 23:1; 27:3;
    Shevat 23:5; Adar 28:9; Sivan 9:2;
    Tammuz 24:5
Altaras, David, Nisan 13:6
Altari, Samuel, Iyar 19:5
Alter, Abraham, Sivan 6:17
Alter, Isaac, Adar 23:7
Alter, Judah, Shevat 5:8
Alvarez, Isabel, Tammuz 15:2
Amalek, Elul 18:1
America, Tishri 4:3; 19:3; 24:7; 30:3;
    Heshvan 1:6; 13:3; 19:2; Adar 25:9;
    27:6; 28:7; Nisan 4:5; 7:6
American Jewish Conf., Tevet 29:10
American Jewish Cong., Tevet 12:6;
    Adar 21:4
American Jewish Hist. Soc., Sivan 12:4
American Jewish Joint, Kislev 9:5; Tevet
    14:6; Nisan 5:7; Tammuz 19:10
American Red Magen David, Adar 29:7
American War of Independence,
    Tammuz 14:7; 17:12
Amiel, Moses, Nisan 13:11
Amman, Nisan 19:12; Iyar 23:9
Amnon, Tishri 1:15
Amsterdam, Tishri 1:18; 10:17; Kislev
    22:4; Nisan 20:4; Av 6:1
Ancona, Adar 9:2; Iyar 3:3; Sivan 26:4;
    Tammuz 27:3
Anglo-Jewish Ass., Tammuz 13:6
Anielewicz, Mordecai, Iyar 3:12
Aniksht, Av 4:6
Anne, Czarina Tammuz 16:3
Anti-Nazi League, Kislev 4:7
Antiochus V, Adar 28:1
Antiochus IX, Sivan 15:3
Anti-Semitism, Tishri 28:6; Heshvan
    16:2; Tevet 26:8; Sivan 4:9; Tammuz
    29:6; Av 7:3; Elul 5:3; 19:9; 26:5
Antoine, Nicolas, Nisan 29:1
Antokolski, Mark, Tammuz 5:8
Antwerp, Adar 16:5
Aragon, Tishri 14:3
Ararat, Tishri 3:7; Sivan 17:1
Arbues, Pedro de, Tishri 6:1
Argentina, Heshvan 26:4; Av 17:5
Arlosoroff, Hayyim, Sivan 22:7
Arnhem, Tishri 25
Aron, Arnaud, Nisan 13:9
Aronson, Moses, Elul 25:5

Aryeh Leib Sarah's, Adar 4:5
Aryeh Leib of Shpola, Tishri 6:3
Asch, Sholem, Tammuz 11:4
Ascher, Benjamin, Adar 8:7
Asefat haNivharim, Tishri 25:8
Ashdod, Heshvan 26:12; Iyar 24:7
Asher, Shevat 20:1
Asher Anshel, Nisan 10:6
Asher b. Jehiel, Heshvan 9:2
Asher b. Shlomo, Av 17:3
Asher of Tiktim, Shevat 4:4
Ashkenazi, Abraham, Kislev 19:2
Ashkenazi, David, Tammuz 15:3
Ashkenazi, Elhanan, Elul 27:5
Ashkenazi, Eliezer, Kislev 22:3
Ashkenazi, Gershom, Sivan 5:8
Ashkenazi, Isaac, Nisan 27:3
Ashkenazi, Israel, Sivan 1:8
Ashkenazi, Raphael, Heshvan 27:2
Ashkenazi, Saul, Sivan 14:4
Ashkenazi, Zevi, Iyar 1:8
Ashknazi, Isaac, Kislev 21:7
Athens, Nisan 21:15
Atlanta, Tishri 28:6
Auerbach, Benjamin, Elul 27:8
Auerbach, Berthold, Shevat 19:2
Auerbach, Meir, Iyar 5:6
Auerbach, Menahem, Tammuz 20:2
Auschwitz, Tishri 2:10; Heshvan 13:7;
    13:8; 14:7; 16:8; Kislev 10:5; Shevat
    12:5; Nisan 10:9; Sivan 8:6; Tammuz
    5:10; Av 21:10
Austerer, Samuel, Tevet 27:3
Austria, Heshvan 4:6; 20:2; Tevet 21:5;
    Adar 1:11; 9:5; 10:5; 27:4; 29:5; Nisan
    22:6; 25:11; Iyar 3:7; Sivan 10:3;
    Tammuz 23:2; Av 21:9; Elul 29:4
Auto-da-fé, Tishri 19:2; Kislev 3:3; 17:3;
    Adar 7:7; 24:6; Iyar 15:5; Sivan 14:5;
    Tammuz 28:3; Av 2:5; 22:3
Avtalyon b. Solomon, Heshvan 15:3
Axis, Heshvan 5:8
Ayash, Judah, Tishri 1:22
Ayllon, Solomon, Iyar 1:9
Azulai, Abraham, Heshvan 21:2
Azulai, Hayyim, Adar 11:5

Baal Shem, Elijah, Tammuz 21:4
Baal Shem Tov, Israel, Sivan 7:9
Babad, Joseph, Elul 25:4
Babi Yar, Tishri 9:11
Babylonia, Tishri 16:3; 23:5; Heshvan
    3:1; Tevet 7:1; 18:1; Adar 25:1; 27:1;
    27:2; Nisan 1:9
Bacharach, Abraham, Iyar 27:2
Bacharach, Jacob, Tevet 24:6
Bacharach, Jair, Tevet 1:8

Erfurt, Nisan 1:11; 14:7; Sivan 25:4
Ergas, Joseph, Sivan 3:6
Esau, Tishri 15:3; 15:4; Nisan 15:5
Eshkol, Levi, Adar 8:11
Eskeles, Gabriel, Adar 1:10
Estella, Adar 23:4
Esther, Tevet 1:4; Nisan 13:2
Ethical Culture, Nisan 28:8
Ettingen, Iyar 18:4
Ettinger, Isaac, Shevat 7:3
Ettinger, Mordecai, Tammuz 13:4
Ettinger, Solomon, Tevet 4:3
Ettlinger, Jacob, Kislev 25:12
Eugenius IV, Adar 11:1
Eve, Tishri 1:2; 1:3; Iyar 7:1
Evian Conference, Tammuz 7:3
Excommunication, Tishri 25:2
Expulsions, Tishri 4:3; 10:15; 15:12; 16:5;
    29:2; Heshvan 3:2; 8:5; 24:3; Kislev 4:2;
    4:5; 5:1; 9:1; 25:11; 27:3; 27:6; 29:2;
    29:9; Tevet 11:2; 13:2; 14:1; 16:2;
    Shevat 1:4; 3:3; 11:1; 21:6; Adar 1:6;
    1:11; 3:3; 6:8; 7:9; 18:9; 25:4; 27:7; 28:3;
    28:4; Nisan 2:3; 5:6; 7:4; 15:16; 15:22;
    16:12; Iyar 3:2; 6:4; 9:1; 13:2; 15:6;
    Sivan 5:6; 5:11; 10:3; 10:4; 27:5;
    Tammuz 1:5; 4:5; 8:4; 16:3; 21:2; 27:2;
    28:4; Av 8:4; 9:9; 9:12; 9:16; 9:27; 10:4;
    11:2; 11:3; 19:2; 25:1; 28:2; Elul 11:4;
    20:1; 26:2; 27:2
Eybeschuetz, Jonathan, Heshvan 3:5;
    Elul 21:5
Ezekiel, Tishri 10:11; Tevet 5:1; 12:1;
    Sivan 6:6; Tammuz 5:1
Ezekiel, Jacob, Sivan 7:15
Ezekiel b. Wolf, Shevat 24:9
Ezra, Tishri 1:14; 24:1; Kislev 20:1; Tevet
    1:5; 9:2; Nisan 1:9; 1:10; Av 1:5
Ezra HaNavi, Tevet 9:5

Fair Sabbath Law, Tishri 12:10; Sivan
    7:15; Tammuz 20:10
Falasha, Tishri 1:6; Sivan 12:1; Av 17:2;
    Elul 18:3
Falk, Aryeh Leib, Adar 8:3
Falk, Jacob, Shevat 14:2
Falk, Joshua, Nisan 19:4
Fano, Menahem, Av 4:3
Farhi, Hayyim, Av 30:2
Farhi, Isaac, Iyar 3:6
Fascism, Tishri 12:7; Heshvan 23:10;
    Adar 21:5; Nisan 29:9; Tammuz 16:6;
    Elul 9:11
Fast Days, Tishri 3:1; 10:1; Kislev 2:1;
    3:4; 5:3; 7:1; Tevet 8:1; 9:1; 10:1; Shevat
    3:1; 8:1; 22:3; Adar 9:1; 13:1; Nisan
    14:3; 23:2; 25:3; Iyar 8:4; Sivan 20:2;

20:3; 23:1; 23:5; 25:4; 27:13; Tammuz
    5:4; 10:2; 10:4; 10:5; 17:1; 21:7; 29:4; Av
    9:1; Elul 15:2
Federation of Am. Zionists, Tammuz
    14:9
Federation of Hungarian Jews in
    America, Heshvan 8:7
Federation of Jewish Farmers of Am.,
    Tevet 27:5
Federation of Rumanian Jews of Am.,
    Adar 5:3
Ferrara, Adar 11:4; 16:7; Iyar 2:4; Sivan
    4:3
Fettmilch, Vincent, Adar 29:1
Fichman, Jacob, Iyar 27:9
Figo, Azariah, Adar 1:8
Filipowski, Zevi Hirsch, Tammuz 16:5
Filorintin, Samuel, Av 10:10
Fin, Samuel, Shevat 2:4
Fine, Israel, Kislev 3:8
Finkel, Nathan, Shevat 29:4
Finland, Nisan 14:10; Sivan 6:16
Finzi, Isaac, Tishri 19:5
Fischer, Ludwig, Adar 16:12
Flavius Claudius Julianus, Kislev 1:3
Fleckeles, Eliezer, Sivan 17:4
Fleischman, Akiva, Iyar 11:11
Flood, Heshvan 17:1; Kislev 27:2; Iyar
    17:2; Sivan 1:1; Av 1:1
Florence, Heshvan 6:7; Sivan 27:8
Florida, Tishri 11:6; Heshvan 20:8
Fraenkel, David, Iyar 22:7
France, Tishri 4:3; 22:4; Kislev 2:6; Adar
    7:6; 25:2; Nisan 21:6; 24:3; Iyar 6:14;
    Sivan 4:2; Av 25:2
Frances, Immanuel, Tammuz 29:3
Francis I, Av 11:6
Frank, Anne, Heshvan 13:7; Av 25:10
Frank, Karl, Iyar 21:3
Frankel, Jacob, Elul 23:3
Frankel, Zacharias, Adar 8:5
Frankfort, Tishri 14:5; Adar 14:5; 20:4;
    Iyar 11:5; 26:4; Sivan 14:2; Tammuz
    10:4; 10:6; Av 8:2; Elul 17:4; 27:2
Frankfurter, Simon, Kislev 10:1
Franks, David, Shevat 1:8
Franks, Isaac, Adar 11:6
Frederick the Great, Nisan 11:6
Freedman, Aaron, Tishri 19:9
Freedom of Religion, Nisan 13:7; 22:6;
    Iyar 13:6
Freund, Samuel, Sivan 21:5
Friedenthal, Markus, Kislev 7:6
Friedlander, David, Kislev 23:7
Friedlander, Israel, Tammuz 19:9
Friedman, Aaron, Iyar 23:6
Frischman, David, Av 10:14

322   DAY BY DAY IN JEWISH HISTORY

Fuld, Aaron, Kislev 24:7
Furstenthal, Jacob, Shevat 28:5

Gabirol, Solomon, Iyar 4:1
Gad, Heshvan 10:1
Galante, Moses, Shevat 21:4
Galatz, Tishri 4:7; 17:3
Galicia, Heshvan 16:6; Shevat 20:3; Adar
  3:6; 16:8; Nisan 30:4
Galin, Rivka, Av 9:26
Gallego, Joseph, Kislev 14:2
Gamala, Tishri 23:4; Elul 24:3
Gamaliel, Tishri 28:1
Gans, David, Elul 8:4
Ganzfried, Solomon, Tammuz 26:2
Gaza, Heshvan 22:10; Kislev 9:7; Iyar
  7:14; 27:10
Gedaliah, Tishri 3:1
Gedaliah b. Isaac, Kislev 29:5
Gedaliah Ibn Yahya, Tishri 3:3
Gedera, Kislev 26:8; Elul 28:6
Geiger, Abraham, Heshvan 12:7
Geiger, Solomon, Elul 5:2
Genizah, Sivan 1:10
Genoa, Nisan 16:12
Genocide, Kislev 7:8; Shevat 5:11
George III, Iyar 20:4
Georgia, Tishri 28:6
Germanus, Moses, Nisan 19:6
Germany, Tishri 6:2; Heshvan 3:9; Nisan
  26:6; Tammuz 17:18
Geron, Abraham, Sivan 11:2
Gershon of Minsk, Adar 14:11
Gershoni, Zevi, Sivan 17:7
Gesevius, Heinrich, Heshvan 19:3
Geulim, Iyar 19:11
Geviha b. Pesisa, Sivan 25:1
Gevulot, Iyar 7:10
Ghetto, Tishri 1:29; 2:11; 5:6; 14:11;
  14:13; 18:8; 19:11; 24:4; 27:6; 29:6;
  Heshvan 4:8; 7:4; 7:5; 15:10; 22:11;
  26:8; Kislev 4:9; 5:8; Tevet 22:3; 23:1;
  Shevat 12:3; 15:7; 24:7; 29:5; Adar 2:6;
  2:7; 6:10; 13:10; 16:7; Nisan 3:6; 9:13;
  11:10; 14:9; 21:9; 22:10; Iyar 4:9; 8:2;
  20:9; Sivan 8:7; 18:6; 26:4; Tammuz
  21:11; Av 15:14; 15:15; 18:5; 22:6; Elul
  9:13; 13:7; 17:10; 19:6; 23:7
Gideon, Nisan 16:5
Giladi, Israel, Heshvan 20:5
Ginzberg, Asher, Tevet 28:8
Ginzberg, Louis, Kislev 4:10
Ginzburg, Simon, Tevet 15:3
Gisser, Moses, Nisan 24:6
Glanz-Leyeles, Aaron, Tevet 17:8
Glatstein, Jacob, Kislev 1:12
Goebbels, Josef, Iyar 19:8

Goering, Hermann, Tishri 19:11;
  Heshvan 18:4; Av 7:6
Golden Calf, Tishri 7:3
Goldfaden, Abraham, Shevat 6:6
Goldstein, David, Kislev 14:6
Goode, Alexander, Shevat 28:9
Gordon, Aharon, Shevat 24:11
Gordon, David, Iyar 16:9
Gordon, Eliezer, Adar 4:8
Gordon, George, Tevet 8:3
Gordon, Judah, Elul 24:7
Gordon, Mikhel, Tevet 13:7
Gottheil, Gustav, Nisan 18:6
Gottlober, Abraham, Iyar 2:6
Graetz, Heinrich, Elul 4:6
Granada, Kislev 23:3
Grand Island, Tishri 3:7
Grant, Ulysses, Heshvan 16:2
Gratz, Bernard, Heshvan 19:2
Gratz College, Tammuz 5:9
Greece, Nisan 21:16
Greenberg, Hayyim, Adar 27:18
Greenwald, Jekuthiel, Nisan 19:18
Grodno, Heshvan 9:6
Grodzensky, Abraham, Tammuz 22:9
Grodzienski, Hayyim, Av 5:9
Grosshaber, Isaac, Kislev 9:3
Grusenberg, Oscar, Iyar 28:10
Guetta, Isaac, Shevat 8:4
Gunzberg, Aryeh, Tammuz 25:3
Gur, Judah, Shevat 2:6
Gutmann, Simha, Iyar 27:5

Haan, Joseph, Nisan 9:4
Haas, Jacob de, Nisan 9:11
Hadassah, Adar 14:13
Hadrian, Tishri 9:3
Haganah, Tevet 1:14; Shevat 5:10; Adar
  22:8; 26:6; Nisan 1:20; 13:12; 23:7; Iyar
  2:10; 2:11; 3:13
Haggai, Tishri 21:3; Kislev 24:2; Elul 1:2
Hai Gaon, Nisan 20:3
Haifa, Heshvan 24:6; Nisan 13:12; Iyar
  2:11; Sivan 23:9; Tammuz 27:10; Av
  17:8
Halberstam, Hayyim, Nisan 25:8
HaLevi, Isaac, Iyar 20:6
Halperin, Abraham, Tevet 19:2
Halpern, Joel, Tishri 4:4
Halpern, Moshe, Av 29:5
Haman, Adar 13:2; Nisan 13:1; 16:8
Hamburg, Tishri 18:6
Hamishah Asar BiShevat, Shevat 15:1
Hanina Segan HaKohanim, Sivan 25:3
Hanina b. Teradyon, Sivan 27:3
Hanlish, Judah, Shevat 21:2
Hannah, Tishri 1:7

19:10; 28:9; 28:12; 29:2; Sivan 5:4; 9:1;
14:1; 15:4; 20:5; Tammuz 1:3; 3:2; 4:14;
5:2; 6:1; 9:1; 9:2; 23:1; 24:1; Av 4:1;
10:15 Elul 7:2; 19:4; 25:2
Jethro, Tishri 11:1
Jew Badge-See Badge of Shame
Jewish Agency, Av 8:6
Jewish Agricultural Soc., Adar 13:8
Jewish Battalion, Shevat 23:9; Tammuz
17:15; Elul 5:4
Jewish Brigade, Tammuz 7:6
Jewish Colonial Trust, Nisan 9:10
Jewish Colonization Ass., Elul 7:8
Jewish Congress Organization Comm.
Nisan 6:5
Jewish Court of Arbitration, Shevat 29:3
Jewish Infantry Brigade, Adar 18:12;
Tammuz 7:6
Jewish Institute of Religion, Tishri 9:8
Jewish National Fund, Tevet 19:7
Jewish National Women's Alliance,
Tevet 27:6
Jewish Pub. Soc. of America, Sivan 24:3
Jewish Sea Service, Adar 6:13
Jewish Theological Seminary, Tevet 6:3;
Adar 13:9
Jewish Theological Seminary of Breslau,
Av 16:3
Jewish Welfare Board, Nisan 17:5
Jew's College, Heshvan 12:6; 28:5
Job, Tishri 1:2; Nisan 15:10
Jochebed, Elul 7:1
Johanan Gush-Halav, Elul 8:1
John I, Heshvan 13:1
John Hyrcanus, Sivan 15:3
Jonah b. Abraham, Heshvan 8:3
Jonas, Joseph, Adar 20:9; Iyar 24:1
Jonathan b. Mordecai, Kislev 6:8
Jones, Thomas, Sivan 7:13
Joram, Nisan 1:5
Jordan, Nisan 4:9; Iyar 5:12; 6:16; 28:13
Joselewicz, Berek, Iyar 19:4; Elul 22:2
Joseph, Tishri 1:8; 22:2
Joseph II, Heshvan 2:3; Tevet 16:1; Iyar
26:4; 26:5
Joseph, Jacob, Tammuz 24:8; 25:6
Joseph b. Joshua, Tevet 15:2
Joseph of Salonika, Kislev 3:5
Joseph Samuel of Frankfort, Heshvan
30:1
Josephus, Adar 17:1
Joshua, Nisan 5:1; 10:3; 22:3; Tammuz
3:1
Joshua Hoeschel b. Joseph, Av 28:3
Jotapata, Iyar 7:3; Tammuz 1:2
Juan I, Tishri 14:3

Judah, Sivan 15:1
Judah b. Asher, Tammuz 17:8
Judah b. Dama, Sivan 5:3
Judah b. David, Kislev 7:5
Judah b. Eliezer, Adar 23:6
Judah HaNasi, Tishri 9:2
Judah Hasid, Heshvan 1:5; 4:5
Judah heHasid, Adar 13:4
Judah Leib of Lublin, Nisan 4:2
Judah Loew b. Bezalel, Elul 18:4
Judah Maccabee, Kislev 25:5; Adar 13:3
Judah b. Zeev, Adar 16:6
Judeo-Roman War, Sivan 25:2; 27:2;
Tammuz 1:2; 1:3; Av 2:1; 8:1; 17:1;
20:1; Elul 6:1; 8:1; 17:2; 24:3
Julius III, Elul 2:3
Justinian, Adar 2:1

Kagen, Israel, Elul 24:9
Kahal, Tevet 9:11
Kahana, Jacob, Adar 19:2
Kahanaman, Joseph S., Elul 20:7
Kalihari, Israel, Shevat 13:1
Kalischer, Zevi, Heshvan 5:5
Kallir, Eleazar, Heshvan 15:4
Kalman of Worms, Iyar 2:3
Kalmankes, Elijah, Nisan 8:2
Kalmansk, Abraham, Nisan 15:18
Kamenets-Podolski, Elul 9:12
Kantor, Judah, Iyar 23:7
Kaplan, Abraham, Shevat 30:5
Kaplan, Wolf, Tammuz 5:7
Kara, Avigdor, Nisan 25:2
Karelitz, Avraham, Heshvan 15:11
Karlin, Nisan 19:8
Karmiel, Heshvan 23:11
Karni, Yehudah, Tevet 2:9
Karo, Isaac, Heshvan 1:4
Kasovsky, Joshua, Iyar 26:9
Kassov, Baruch, Heshvan 14:2
Katcherginsky, Shmerke, Nisan 24:7
Katz, Benzion, Shevat 13:7
Katz, Jacob, Tevet 23:2
Katz, Joseph, Shevat 3:5
Katz, Joshua, Nisan 19:4
Katz, Naphtali, Tevet 26:2
Katz, Reuben, Nisan 17:2
Katz, Zevi, Iyar 10:6
Katzenellenbogen, Aaron, Heshvan 23:4
Katzenellenbogen, Ezekiel, Tammuz
23:6
Katzenellenbogen, Samuel, Nisan 6:1
Katzenelson, Benjamin, Kislev 6:9
Katzenelson, Berl, Av 24:8
Katzenelson, Isaac, Iyar 5:8; 10:15
Katzenelson, Judah, Tevet 26:6

Lipschutz, Israel, Tishri 3:8
Lipshitz, Noah, Tevet 29:7
Lisbon, Tishri 19:2; Iyar 16:6 Sivan 9:5
Lisitzky, Ephraim, Sivan 23:11
Lithuania, Tishri 5:6; Adar 1:5; 24:3;
 Sivan 27:13; 28:4; 29:7; Tammuz 1:11;
 7:5; 25:1; Av 27:1; Elul 2:2
Lodz, Tishri 2:11; 25:15; 29:7; Heshvan
 30:4; Nisan 22:10; Iyar 4:11; Sivan 6:13;
 Elul 17:10; 23:4
London, Tammuz 23:7; 28:5; Av 18:3
Longfellow, Henry, Tammuz 22:6
Lorberbaum, Jacob, Iyar 25:6
Louis IX, Heshvan 1:3
Louis XIII, Nisan 24:3
Lovers of Zion, Sivan 29:5
Lowenstein, Joseph, Nisan 26:7
Lubavich, Kislev 9:4; Nisan 13:8
Lubeck, Adar 3:3; 4:1; 6:8
Lublin, Nisan 5:9; Iyar 16:5; Av 4:8
Lucerne, Av 21:8
Lumbrozo, Jacob, Shevat 10:3; Adar
 20:6, Elul 8:5
Luria, Isaac, Av 5:3
Luria, Solomon, Kislev 12:1
Luzatto, Moses, Iyar 26:3
Luzatto, Samuel, Tishri 10:21
Lydda, Tammuz 3:9; 4:11; 17:19
Lynch-law, Av 27:2; Elul 5:3

Maccabean Anniversary, Elul 1:8
Maccabiad, Adar 20:11
Madagascar, Heshvan 18:4
Madrid, Tevet 1:16; Tammuz 15:2; 28:3
Magdiel, Av 12:4
Magic Carpet, Tishri 13:9; Heshvan 16:9;
 Kislev 14:8; Elul 11:8
Magnes, Judah, Kislev 24:11
Maimon, Abraham, Kislev 18:1
Maimon, Judah, Tammuz 9:6
Maimon, Solomon, Kislev 5:4
Maimonides, Moses, Tishri 8:3;
 Heshvan 4:1; 9:1; Tevet 20:1; Nisan
 14:6; Iyar 4:2; 10:5; 28:1; Sivan 3:5
Maimonides College, Tishri 26:5
Maisels, Uziel, Kislev 28:2
Maisels, Zevi, Kislev 22:7
Majorca, Shevat 6:1; Elul 1:6
Malach, Leib, Sivan 26:6
Malachai, Tevet 10:5
Malaga, Iyar 4:1
Malbim, Meir, Tishri 1:25
Malta, Iyar 20:5
Manasseh, Tammuz 17:4
Manasseh b. Israel, Kislev 20:4 Tammuz
 3:4

Mandelkern, Solomon, Adar 15:7
Mandelstamm, Leon, Elul 16:4
Manger, Itzik, Adar 3:10
Manhattan, Tishri 1:20
Mani Leib, Tishri 25:13
Manna, Adar 7:5
Mantua, Adar 22:2; Iyar 7:6
Manuel, Joel, Heshvan 20:4
Mapu, Abraham, Tishri 10:22
Marah, Nisan 24:1
Marcus, David, Sivan 3:11
Margintu, Shalom, Kislev 22:5
Margoliot, Ephraim, Av 24:4
Margoliot, Isaac, Adar 24:4
Margoliot, Judah, Sivan 22:4
Margoliot, Moses, Tevet 12:5
Margolis, Alexander, Tevet 29:5
Margolis, Meir, Iyar 10:8
Margolis, Moses, Kislev 11:2
Maria Theresa, Av. 11:3
Marijampole, Elul 9:14
Marks, David, Iyar 12:5
Marshall Louis, Sivan 30:3; Elul 6:7
Martin V, Tevet 18:2
Maryland, Adar 8:4; 28:6; Elul 8:5
Marx, Alexander, Tevet 20:10
Masada, Nisan 15:13, Tammuz 21:14
Maskielson, Abraham, Tammuz 18:5
Massachusetts, Sivan 16:3
Massena, N.Y., Tishri 9:9
Mattathias, Heshvan 15:1
Matzah, Iyar 15:2
Mauthausen, Iyar 24:4; Elul 22:6
Mayence, Sivan 3:4; Elul 7:5
Maximilian, Tishri 14:5
Mecklenburg, Heshvan 3:3; Adar 18:6
Medina, Samuel di, Heshvan 2:2
Medini, Hayyim, Kislev 25:15
Mefizei Haskalah, Tevet 10:9
Meir, Golda, Tishri 13:8
Meir Baal HaNes, Iyar 15:4
Meir of Emdin, Tevet 6:2
Meir b. Gedaliah, Iyar 16:5
Meir b. Isaac, Tammuz 17:7
Meir of Rothenburg, Tishri 10:14; Adar
 4:3; Iyar 4:3; 19:1; Tammuz 4:3
Meir Simhah haKohen, Elul 4:8
Meir b. Simon, Heshvan 8:2
Meiri, Menahem, Elul 3:1
Meisel, Frumet, Shevat 23:4
Meisel, Mordecai, Adar 9:3
Meisels, Dov Ber, Adar 14:10
Meisels, Moses, Kislev 18:4
Meldola, Raphael, Nisan 19:7
Meltzer, Isser, Kislev 10:7
Memel, Heshvan 1:9; Adar 29:8

Naphtali, Tishri 5:1
Naphtali HaKohen, Tishri 5:4
Naples, Iyar 22:2; Tammuz 8:2
Napoleon, Tishri 21:9; Adar 1:13; 18:5; 29:2; Nisan 15:21; Iyar 5:2; Tammuz 25:4
Narbonne, Heshvan 8:2; Adar 21:1
Narol, Heshvan 17:4
Nasi, Joseph, Av 10:9
Nathan b. Jehiel, Kislev 15:2
Nathanson, Joseph, Adar 27:10
Nat. Fed. of Temple Sisterhoods, Shevat 14:3
Navon, Ephraim, Nisan 26:3
Navon, Isaac, Kislev 8:3
Navon, Jonah, Shevat 16:1
Navon, Judah, Shevat 21:5
Navon Yizhak, Heshvan 16:11
Nazareth, Tammuz 10:9
Nazis, Tishri 1:28; 1:29; 3:9; 5:6; 6:6; 13:7; 14:11; 20:3; 21:11; 21:13; 25:9; 27:6; Heshvan 2:7; 4:8; 13:6; 21:4; Kislev 14:7; 16:4; Tevet 4:6; 10:12; 20:7; Shevat 12:3; 22:5; 23:10; 25:6; Adar 7:17; 26:5; Nisan 5:8; 11:9; 13:10; Iyar 4:9; 16:12; 17:10; 20:9; Tammuz 14:10; 17:16; Av 29:7; Elul 3:5; 14:4; 16:7; 17:8
Nebuchadnezzar, Adar 25:1
Negbah, Heshvan 7:6
Nehemiah, Tishri 24:1; Tevet 9:3; Iyar 7:2; Av 4:1; Elul 25:2
Nehemiah of Dubrovno, Shevat 15:3
Netanyah, Tishri 27:5
Netel, Yom Tov, Shevat 13:4
Netter, Carl, Tishri 19:8
New Amsterdam, Heshvan 10:3; Shevat 27:3; Adar 16:4; Nisan 19:5; Iyar 7:8; Sivan 22:3; Tammuz 22:3; Elul 25:3; 26:3
New England, Nisan 9:7
New Orleans, Nisan 10:8
New York, Tishri 2:7; Heshvan 4:4; 30:3; Tevet 5:5; Adar 1:14; Nisan 28:5; Sivan 23:10; Av 11:5; Elul 13:2; 15:3; 27:3
New Zealand, Av 13:7
Newark, Av 21:3
Newport, Tammuz 22:6
Nicholas I (Czar) Kislev 14:3
Nicholas II (Czar), Av 7:4
Nicholas III (Pope), Av 14:3
Nicholas V (Pope), Adar 24:2
Niemirow, Sivan 20:3
Nieto, David, Tevet 28:4
Nikolayev, Heshvan 24:3; Nisan 5:5
Nirim, Iyar 7:13
Nizhni Novogorod, Sivan 29:4

Noah, Tishri 1:5; Heshvan 27:1; Iyar 11:2; Sivan 17:1; Elul 10:1; 17:1; 23:1
Noah, Mordecai M., Shevat 3:7; Elul 18:6
Nobel Prize, Kislev 27:10
Nordau, Max, Shevat 5:9
Norway, Heshvan 14:7; Nisan 1:19
Novomisky, Moshe, Kislev 10:3
Nuremberg, Tishri 21:13; Heshvan 11:10; Iyar 16:13; Tammuz 1:5
Nuremberg Laws, Elul 17:8; 23:17

Obadiah of Bertinoro, Nisan 13:4
Odessa, Tishri 25:11; Heshvan 2:5; 4:7; Nisan 19:9
Ohio Valley, Adar 20:9
Ohole Shem Ass., Tishri 20:2
Oil, Shevat 25:10; Av 17:8
Oliphant, Laurence, Tevet 19:5
Olmo, Jacob, Sivan 7:8
Omer, Nisan 16:4
Opatoshu, Joseph, Tishri 10:23
Oppenheim, David, Tishri 7:4
Oppenheim, David, Iyar 5:1
Orleans, Jacob, Elul 21:2
Orobio de Castro, Isaac, Kislev 2:2
Otto II, Tammuz 19:2
Ottolengo, Samuel, Av 25:4
Ozer, Benjamin, Iyar 25:5

Paderborn, Adar 2:4
Padua, Elul 10:2; 15:6
Padua, Jacob, Kislev 21:5
Palestine, Tishri 13:2; 16:11; 19:10; 25:8; 28:5; Heshvan 1:2; 5:7; Kislev 1:1; 17:11; 17:12; Tevet 18:5; 28:9; Shevat 25:5; Adar 1:15; 6:12; 19:5; 24:9; 25:8; Nisan 13:12; 26:8; 29:4; Iyar 6:12; Sivan 30:5; Tammuz 28:7; Av 9:23; 14:1; 15:4; 16:4; 26:3; Elul 1:11; 28:6; 28:7; 29:11
Palestine Philharmonic Soc., Elul 29:6
Panama, Sivan 12:8
Panet, Ezekiel, Nisan 20:6
Panet, Hayyim, Nisan 19:10
Papers and Periodicals, Tishri 25:6; 30:3; Heshvan 1:8; 10:7; 28:4; Kislev 6:6; Tevet 2:4; Adar 1:18; 7:11; 9:4; 18:7; Nisan 1:17; 20:7; Iyar 3:9; 26:8; Sivan 1:9; 4:7; 5:13; 22:5; 22:6; Tammuz 2:3; 6:9; 15:5; 15:11; 19:5; 22:7; 29:9; Av 4:5; 12:3; Elul 6:6
Papiers, Jacob, Shevat 22:2
Paran, Sivan 28:1
Pardo, David, Nisan 9:6
Paris, Tishri 10:15; 11:8; Kislev 25:18; Nisan 10:9; Av 2:9

Yom Kippur War (1973), Tishri 10:24;
10:25; 17:7; 20:6; 26:7; 27:8; Heshvan
5:11; 16:10; Kislev 26:15; Tevet 24:9;
Shevat 8:10; 29:7; Adar 10:12; Sivan
8:8
York, Nisan 7:1
Yosefovich, Michael, Adar 1:5
Yosenofsky, Pinhas, Sivan 24:4
Young Israel, Tevet 18:4
Young Men's Hebrew Ass., Nisan 4:4;
Iyar 16:7
Youth Aliyah, Shevat 3:9; Adar 4:9
Yugoslavia, Nisan 9:12
Yulee, David, Tishri 11:7
Yuspi, Shammash, Shevat 13:2

Zabludowsky, Yechiel, Kislev 10:2
Zacuto, Moses, Tishri, 16:6
Zagaer, Tishri, 9:10
Zamenhof, Ludwik, Nisan 22:8
Zamosc, Israel, Nisan 17:3
Zangville, Israel, Av 21:6
Zarfati, Ben Zion, Nisan 4:1
Zebulun, Tishri, 7:1
Zechariah, Tishri 10:10
Zechariah b. Berachiah, Kislev 4:1; Tevet
10:4; Shevat 24:1
Zechariah of Kiev, Tevet 9:7
Zedekiah, Adar 27:2; Tammuz 10:1
Zeitelis, Baruch, Kislev 25:10
Zeitlin, Hillel, Elul 29:8
Zelig of Zalkova, Elul 11:6
Zelikovitch, Getzl, Kislev 22:6
Zemba, Menahem, Nisan 19:15
Zerubbabel, Tishri 1:13; 21:3; Elul 1:2;
24:2

Zev Wolf, Heshvan 28:2
Zevi of Vilna, Iyar 22:4
Zhitlowsky, Chaim, Iyar 11:13
Zhitomir, Tishri 26:4; Nisan 19:13; Av
23:2
Zikhron Yaakov, Kislev 25:13; Nisan 3:7
Zimra, David, Heshvan 21:1
Zin, Nisan 1:4
Zion, Menahem, Iyar 11:6
Zion Mule Corps, Adar 16:11; Nisan 8:7;
Iyar 23:8
Zionism, Tishri 24:2; Heshvan 12:9; 18:2;
25:3; Adar 6:9; 7:12; 11:9; 27:18; Nisan
1:17; 9:10; 18:8; 23:6; 25:9; Iyar 5:7;
10:9; 14:3; 16:9; 17:8; 25:8; Sivan 4:7;
29:5; 29:6; Tammuz 2:3; 14.9; 15:13;
20:4; 20:5; 29:10; Av 10:9; 15:12; 18:3;
21:8; 24:6; 28:6; 28:7; 30:3; Elul 1:10;
2:7; 4:7; 7:9; 9:9; 10:3; 24:8
Zionist Congress, Kislev 16:5; Tevet
14:5; 16:3; Tammuz 15:13; 20:5; 24:10;
Av 12:7; 15:12; 18:3; 21:8; 24:6; 26:4;
28:6; 28:7; 29:6; 30:3; 30:4; Elul 1:10;
1:12; 2:7; 4:7; 9:9; 10:3
Ziprish, Moses, Elul 13:1
Zlatopolsky, Hillel, Kislev 13:8
Zohar, Av 20:2; Elul 19:2
Zola, Emile, Tevet 19:6
Zror, Raphael, Kislev 27:5
Zuenz, Aryeh, Iyar 3:5
Zundel the Preacher, Shevat 27:8
Zunser, Eliakum, Elul 20:4
Zunz, Leopold, Adar 11:8
Zurich, Elul 26:2